THE ARMIES OF PHILIP IV OF SPAIN 1621–1665

The Fight for European Supremacy

Pierre A. Picouet

'This is the Century of the Soldier', Fulvio Testi, Poet, 1641

Helion & Company

The Series Editor would like to acknowledge the help and advice given by Michał Paradowski with regards to contemporary illustrations for this project.

Helion & Company Limited
Unit 8 Amherst Business Centre
Budbrooke Road
Warwick
CV34 5WE
England
Tel. 01926 499 619
Fax 0121 711 4075
Email: info@helion.co.uk
Website: www.helion.co.uk
Twitter: @helionbooks
Visit our blog at http://blog.helion.co.uk/

Published by Helion & Company 2019
Designed and typeset by Serena Jones
Cover designed by Paul Hewitt, Battlefield Design (www.battlefield-design.co.uk)
Printed by Henry Ling Limited, Dorchester, Dorset

Text, maps and colour flags © Pierre A. Picouet 2019
Colour artwork by Sergey Shamenkov © Helion & Company 2019
Front cover: Spanish musketeer ready to follow Ambrogio Spinola for the campaign against Breda in 1624–1625. Rear cover: Spanish captain of the army of Flanders from the beginning of Philip IV's reign. Both illustrations by Sergey Shamenkov © Helion & Company 2019.

Every reasonable effort has been made to trace copyright holders and to obtain their permission for the use of copyright material. The author and publisher apologise for any errors or omissions in this work, and would be grateful if notified of any corrections that should be incorporated in future reprints or editions of this book.

ISBN 978-1-911628-61-3

British Library Cataloguing-in-Publication Data.
A catalogue record for this book is available from the British Library.

All rights reserved. No part of this publication may be reproduced, stored in a retrieval system, or transmitted, in any form, or by any means, electronic, mechanical, photocopying, recording or otherwise, without the express written consent of Helion & Company Limited.

For details of other military history titles published by Helion & Company
Limited, contact the above address, or visit our website: http://www.helion.co.uk

We always welcome receiving book proposals from prospective authors.

To my wife Susana

There is no instance of a country having benefited from prolonged war

Sun Tzu's *Art of War*, Chapter 2.7

Contents

List of Illustrations & Maps	8
1. The World of Philip IV of Spain	11
1.1 The Spanish Empire of Philip IV	11
1.2 A Time of Glory and Successes: 1621 to 1626	15
1.3 A Time of Disillusionment in Northern Italy and Flanders: 1627 to 1630	32
1.4 Spain and the Swedish Phase of the Thirty Years' War: 1631–1634	40
1.5 Crucial Years Towards a Total War: 1635 to 1639	48
1.6 On the Edge of Collapse: 1640–1646	68
1.7 A Time of Recovery: 1647–1656	90
1.8 Final Collapse, the Treaty of the Pyrenees and Beyond: 1657–1665	111
2. The Structure of the Spanish Army	121
2.1 General Considerations	121
2.2 The Armies of the King	125
2.2.1 Introduction	125
2.2.2 The Army of Flanders	128
2.2.3 The Army of Lombardy	132
2.2.4 The Army of Catalonia	134
2.2.5 The Army of Extremadura and Galicia	137
2.3 The Infantry of the Spanish Army	138
2.3.1 The Spanish Tercios	139
2.3.2 The Provincial Tercios	145
2.3.3 The Tercios of the Armada	150
2.3.4 Tercios from Nations	151
2.3.5 Mercenaries, Germans, Irish and Swiss	153
2.3.6 The Auxiliary Armies of the Spanish Crown	155
2.4 The Cavalry of the Spanish Army	159
2.4.1 Cavalry Troops 1621–1640	159
2.4.2 Tercios and Trozos of Cavalry 1640–1665	161
2.5 The Artillery of the Spanish Army	166
2.6 Weapons and Equipment	168
2.6.1 Pikeman, Harquebusier and Musketeer	168
2.6.2 Harquebus and Musket	171
2.6.3 Cavalry Equipment	174

- 2.7 Tactics — 175
  - 2.7.1 Weapons Distribution Between Soldiers — 175
  - 2.7.2 Tactical Squadron Formation in Use in the Spanish Army — 176
  - 2.7.3 Firing Tactics — 178
  - 2.7.4 Tactics of the Cavalry — 180
  - 2.7.5 Tactics During a Siege — 180
- 3. Men, Logistics, and Finance — 183
  - 3.1 High Command — 183
  - 3.2 Erosion and Recruitment — 186
    - 3.2.1 Erosion of the Spanish Army — 186
    - 3.2.2 Recruitment — 188
    - 3.2.3 Movement of Troops — 191
  - 3.3 Clothing and Logistics — 193
    - 3.3.1 Clothing — 193
    - 3.3.2 Logistics — 194
  - 3.4 Discipline and Life in the Tercio — 197
    - 3.4.1 Honour and Reputation — 197
    - 3.4.2 Military Privilege — 198
  - 3.5 The Life of the Spanish Soldier in the Seventeenth Century — 199
    - 3.5.1 Soldiers in Garrison — 199
    - 3.5.2 Soldiers on Campaign and the Wandering City — 205
  - 3.6 War and the Finances of the Spanish Army — 209
- 4. Campaigns of the Spanish Armies — 213
  - 4.1 The Low Countries — 213
    - 4.1.1 The Campaign of 1622: The Battle of Fleurus, 29 August — 213
    - 4.1.2 The Campaign of 1642: The Battle of Honnecourt, 26 May — 218
    - 4.1.3 The Campaign of 1648: The Battle of Lens, 20 August — 221
    - 4.1.4 The Campaign of 1656: The Battle of Valenciennes, 16 July — 226
  - 4.2 Northern Italy and Germany — 231
    - 4.2.1 The Campaign of 1634: The Battle of Nördlingen, 6 September — 231
    - 4.2.2 The Campaign of 1636: The Battle of Tornavento, 22 June — 244
    - 4.2.3. The Campaign of 1653: The Battle of Rochetta Tanaro, 23 September — 250
  - 4.3 Campaigns in the Iberian Peninsula — 253
    - 4.3.1 The Campaign of 1644: The Battle of Montijo, 26 May — 253
    - 4.3.2 The Campaign of 1644: The 2nd Battle of Lérida, 15 May — 257
    - 4.3.3 The Campaign of 1651–1652: Siege of Barcelona, August 1651 to 1652 — 262
    - 4.3.4 The Campaign of 1663: The Battle of Ameixial, 8 June — 268
- 5. Conclusion — 273

Appendix I: The Main Fronts and their Duration During the Reign of Philip IV of Spain — 275
Appendix II: Summary of Troops of the Four Main Armies of King Philip IV — 276
Appendix III: Estimate of the Effectives of the Spanish Army of Flanders Between 1621 and 1660 — 278

CONTENTS

Appendix IV: Estimate of the Effectives of the Spanish Army of Lombardy Between 1621 and 1665 — 280
Appendix V: Estimate of the Effectives of the Spanish Army in Catalonia and Aragon Between 1635 and 1663 — 282
Appendix VI: Estimate of the Effectives of the Spanish Army of Extremadura Between 1641 and 1665 — 284
Appendix VII: Musters of Spanish Tercios Deployed in Flanders and Lombardy Between 1622 and 1647 — 286
Appendix VIII: Musters of some Provincial Tercios During the 1640–1667 Period — 288
Appendix IX: Musters from the Italian and Walloon Tercios in the Spanish Armies between 1622 and 1662 — 299
Appendix X: Musters of Irish Tercios and German Regiments in the Spanish Armies Between 1631 and 1665 — 292
Appendix XI: List of the Captains General of the Army of Flanders and the Army of Lombardy — 294
Appendix XII: List of the Viceroys of Catalonia and Captains General of the Army of Extremadura — 296
Appendix XIII: List of the *Maestros de Campo* of the Main Spanish Tercios Serving in the Army of Flanders From 1621 to 1665 — 298
Appendix XIV: List of the *Maestros de Campo* of the Main Spanish Tercios Serving in the Army of Lombardy From 1621 to 1665 — 301

Colour Plate Commentaries — 303
Bibliography — 306

List of Illustrations & Maps

Illustrations

1.1 King Philip IV in cuirassier armour, assisted by court dwarf Gaspar de Crayer (1584–1669). (Michał Paradowski's archive) — 16

1.2 Mounted portrait of King Philip IV. Hessel Gerritsz, 1591–1632. (Rijksmuseum) — 17

1.3 Prince Baltasar Carlos, Philip IV's son. The 11-year-old is presented here in cuirassier armour. Portrait attributed to Juan Bautista Martinez del Mazo, 1639–1645. (Rijksmuseum) — 18

1.4 Spanish siege of Breda in 1624. Anonymous, 1624–1625. (Rijksmuseum) — 23

1.5 Spanish siege of Grave in 1624. Anonymous, 1624–1625. (Rijksmuseum) — 23

1.6 Ambrogio Spinola, portait from 1609. Michiel Jansz van Mierevelt. (Rijksmuseum) — 25

1.7 Ambrogio Spinola at the siege of Jülich in 1622. Mattheus Melijn, 1636. (Rijksmuseum) — 25

1.8 Isabella Clara Eugenia, Infanta of Spain and Portugal, sovereign and governor of the Spanish Netherlands until 1633. Renold Elstrack, 1616–1621. (Rijksmuseum) — 26

1.9 Albert VII, Archduke of Austria, with his wife Isabella Clara Eugenia, sovereign of the Spanish Netherlands until his death in 1621. Workshop of Frans Pourbus, c.1600. (Rijksmuseum) — 26

1.10 Mounted portrait of Albert VII and Isabella. Hessel Gerritsz, 1591–1632. (Rijksmuseum) — 27

1.11 Gaspar de Guzmán y Pimentel, 1st Duke of Sanlúcar, 3rd Count of Olivares. Paulus Pontius, 1616–1657. (Rijksmuseum) — 38

1.12 Cardinal Infante Fernando of Austria. Antony van der Does, 1634–1680. (Rijksmuseum) — 43

1.13 Cardinal Infante Fernando of Austria and Archduke Ferdinand in 1634. Pieter de Jode, 1675–1685. (Rijksmuseum) — 44

1.14 Diego Mexía Felipez de Guzmán y Dávila, 1st Marquise of Leganés. Portrait from the collection of Fürstlich Waldecksche Hofbibliothek, Band 1. (Heidelberg University Library) — 58

1.15 Ratification of Spanish–Dutch Peace of Münster, 15 May 1648. Copy after Gerhard ter Borch, 1648–1670. (Rijksmuseum) — 90

LIST OF ILLUSTRATIONS & MAPS

2.1 Lancers from Spinola's bodyguard at the siege of Jülich in 1622. Mattheus Melijn, 1636. (Rijksmuseum) — 129

2.2 Spanish infantry at the siege of Jülich in 1622. Mattheus Melijn, 1636. (Rijksmuseum) — 140

2.3 Spanish infantry during the relief of Brisach in 1633. Jusepe Leonardo, 1633–1652. (Michał Paradowski's archive) — 140

2.4 Spanish harquebusiers, during the siege of Jülich in 1621/1622. Pieter Snayers, 1622–1650. (Rijksmuseum) — 143

2.5 Spanish infantry and camp followers, siege of Ostend (1601–1604). Sebastiaen Vrancx. (Michał Paradowski's archive) — 145

2.6 Spanish infantry, early 17th century. Adam Willaerts, 1617. (Rijksmuseum) — 157

2.7 Spanish cavalry, early 17th century. Adam Willaerts, 1617. (Rijksmuseum) — 157

2.8 Trumpeters of Spanish cavalry at the siege of Jülich in 1622. Mattheus Melijn, 1636. (Rijksmuseum) — 161

2.9 Spanish lancers, siege of Jülich in 1621/1622. Pieter Snayers, 1622–1650. (Rijksmuseum) — 162

2.10 Spanish cuirassier from first half of the 17th century. Paulus (Pauwels) van Hillegaert. (Rijksmuseum) — 162

2.11 Spanish cuirassier, siege of Ostend (1601–1604). Sebastiaen Vrancx. (Michał Paradowski's archive) — 163

2.12 Spanish harquebusier and lancer, siege of Ostend (1601–1604). SebastiaenVrancx. (Michał Paradowski's archive) — 164

2.13 Artillery of Spanish garrison leaving Maastricht in 1632. Jan van de Velde (II), after Jan Martszen the Younger, 1632. (Rijksmuseum) — 167

2.14 Spanish garrison leaving Maastricht in 1632. Jan van de Velde (II), after Jan Martszen the Younger, 1632. (Rijksmuseum) — 167

2.15 Details of polearms of Spanish troops. Diego Velázquez's surrender of Breda in 1625. (Michał Paradowski's archive) — 169

3.1 The harsh reality of military discipline. Jacques Callot, 1628. (Rijksmuseum) — 198

3.2 Spanish camp followers during the siege of Jülich in 1621/1622. Pieter Snayers, 1622–1650. (Rijksmuseum) — 201

3.3 A scene from the Spanish military camp, siege of Breda 1624–1625. Jacques Callot, 1628. (Rijksmuseum) — 202

3.4 Spanish field fortifications during the siege of Jülich in 1621/1622. Pieter Snayers, 1622–1650. (Rijksmuseum) — 204

3.5 Spanish garrison leaving Maastricht in 1632. Jan van de Velde (II), after Jan Martszen the Younger, 1632. (Rijksmuseum) — 207

3.6 A war veteran begging for support. Jacques Callot, 1628.] (Rijksmuseum) — 212

4.1 Spanish infantry at the Battle of Fleurus 1622 (painting often attributed as the Battle of Wimpfen, which seems to be incorrect). Pieter Snayers, 1615–1650 (Rijksmuseum) — 216

4.2 Map of the Battle of Lens in 1648 — 225

4.3 Maps of the Battle of Nördlingen in 1634. (Riksarkivet, Stockholm)   234
4.4 Spanish and Imperial forces at the battle of Nördlingen in
    1634. Pieter Snayers (Nationalmuseum, Stockholm)   239

Maps

1.1 The Spanish Low Countries in the seventeenth century   12
1.2 The Spanish territories in northern Italy in the seventeenth century   20
1.3 Map of the viceroyalty of Catalonia in the seventeenth century   65
1.4 Map of Portugal and the Spanish border where most of the
    military operations took place during the War of Restoration
    (1640–1665)   65
4.1 Battle of Fleurus fought 29 August 1622   214
4.2 Battle of Honnecourt fought 26 May 1642   220
4.3 Battle of Lens fought 20 August 1648   224
4.4 Battle of Valenciennes fought 16 July 1656   228
4.5 Battle of Nördlingen fought 6 September 1634   232
4.6 Battle of Tornavento fought 22 June 1636   246
4.7 Battle of Rocchetta Tanaro fought 23 September 1653   252
4.8: Battle of Montijo fought 26 May 1644   254
4.9: Battle of Lerida fought 11 May 1644   260
4.10: Siege of Barcelona 1651–1652   265
4.11: Battle of Ameixial fought 8 June 1663   270

1

The World of Philip IV of Spain

1.1. The Spanish Empire of Philip IV

On 31 March 1621, a young *Felipe Domingo Víctor de la Cruz,* Prince of Asturias, son[1] of Philip III of Spain and Margarita of Austria was crowned at 16 years old as Philip IV of Spain,[2] initiating one of the longest reigns in Spanish history, 44 years and 170 days. But let us focus on the Spanish empire of this period. In 1621, the Spanish Empire was a powerful and diverse political entity with:

    a. The three crowns of the Iberian Peninsula, namely, the Crown of Castile, the Crown of Aragón (including Kingdom of Aragón, Principality of Catalonia, Kingdom of Mallorca and Kingdom of Valencia) and the Crown of Portugal. To them, we must add the *presidios* or fortresses in North Africa connected with Castile[3] and Portugal.[4]

    b. The Italian territories, belonging to the Crown of Aragón, the kingdom of the two Sicilies (Naples and Sicily) and the *presidios*

---

[1] The surviving children of the couple were: Ana Maria of Austria (1601–1666) Queen Consort of France and mother of Louis XIV; Philip IV of Spain (1604–1665); Maria Ana de Austria (1606–1646), Empress Consort of the Holy Roman Empire; Carlos of Austria (1607–1632); Cardinal Infante Fernando of Austria (1609–1641).

[2] The full title was, King of Castile, of León, of Aragon, of the two Sicilies (Naples and Sicily), of Jerusalem, of Portugal, of Navarra, of Granada, of Toledo, of Valencia, of Galicia, of Mallorca, of Seville, of Sardinia, of Cordoba, of Corcega, of Murcia, of Jaén, of Algarbes, of Algeciras, of Gibraltar, of Canary Islands, of the Oriental and Occidental Indias and Islas y Tierra firme del Mar Oceano, Archduke of Autria, Duke of Burgundy, of Brabant, of Milan and Lerma, Count of Hapsburg, of Flanders, of Tyrol and Barcelona, Lord of Biscaya and Molina.

[3] Spanish presidios were, Oran (Algeria), Mazalquivir (or Mers el Kébir, Algeria), Melilla, Peñon de Velez de la Gomera, Larache (Morocco), La Mamora (actually Mehdia, Morocco) and the Alhucemas islands and Ceuta in 1640. Melilla, Peñon de Velez de la Gomera, Ceuta and Alhucemas islands are part of the Spanish Kingdom in 2018.

[4] Ceuta, Mazagão (El Jadida), Casabranca (Casablanca) and Tangiers were fortresses and cities belonging to the Portuguese Crown. In 1640 at the beginning of the war of restoration between Portugal and Spain, the garrison and inhabitants of Ceuta decided to remain loyal to the Crown of Castile. Tangiers was given to the English in 1661, Mazagão and Casabranca were lost in the eighteenth century.

THE ARMIES OF PHILIP IV OF SPAIN 1621–1665

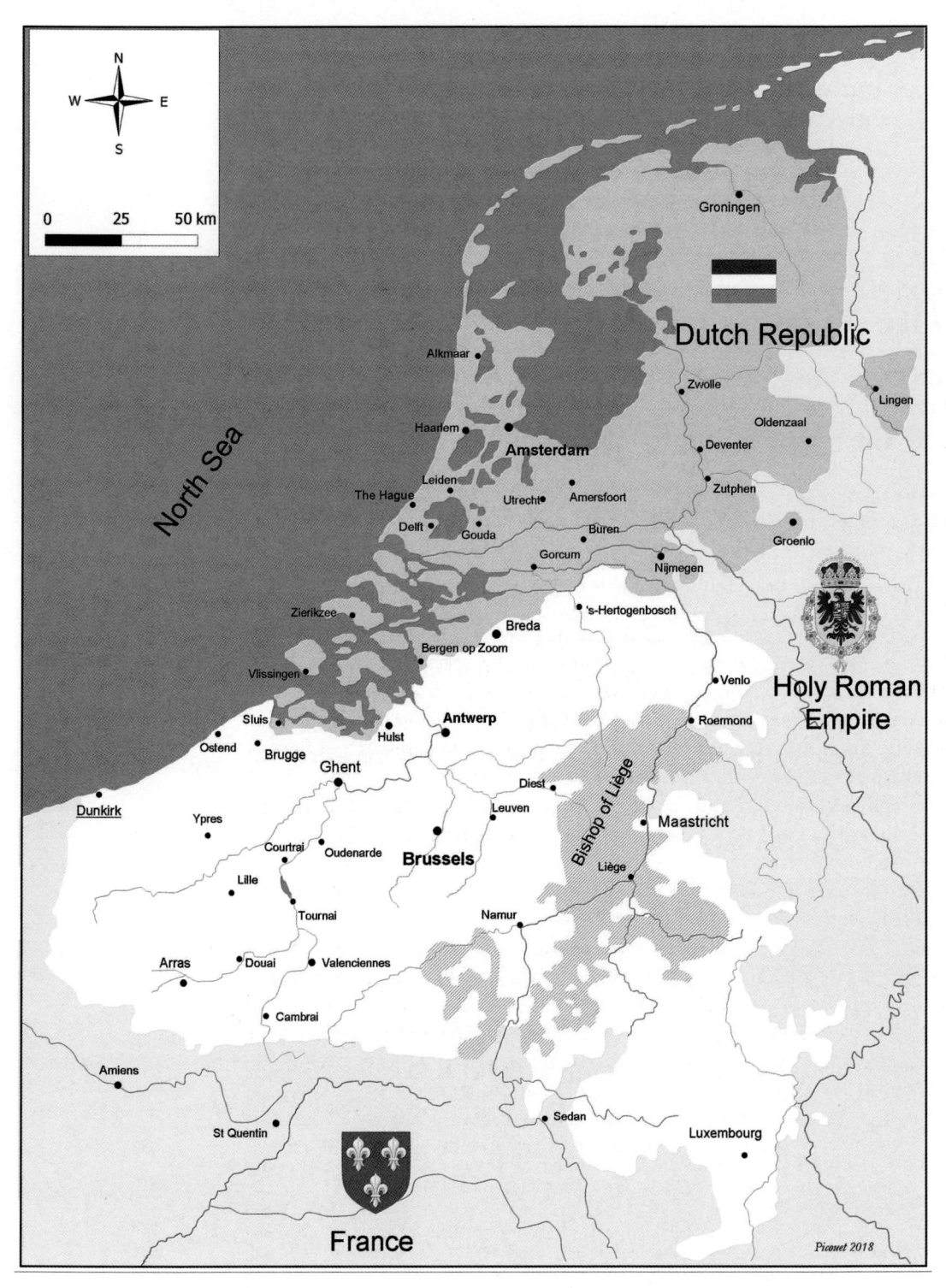

Map 1.1 The Spanish Low Countries in the seventeenth century. The Army of Flanders was the main military force stationed there and had to fight against the Dutch during the second part of the Eighty Years War (1621–1648), and the French (1635–1659).

of Tuscany[5] and the Kingdom of Cerdeña.

c. The Italian territories belonging directly to the Spanish King, the Duchy of Milan and the Marquis of Finale. The Burgundian heritage[6] with the 10 provinces of the Low Countries (Artois, Flanders, Namur, Hainaut, Brabant, Limburg, Luxembourg, Cambray, Tournay and Cambresis) loyal to Spain and the Franche-Comté.

To all that we must add the territories of the *Ultramar* empire, (the Spanish seaborne Empire), the Virreinato (Viceroyalty) de Peru and the Virreinato de Nueva España in America and the Spanish Oriental Indies (Philippine, Marianas, and Carolinas Islands). At last the Portuguese colonies, *Estado do Brasil* and the *Estado do Maranhão in America,* Angola and Mozanbique in Africa the *Estado do Índia* and numerous outposts were part of the Spanish Empire until 1640–1641.

If we focus only on the territories in Europe, the total population at the beginning of the seventeenth century (Table 1.1.) was 5.6 million inhabitants for the territories belonging to the Crown of Castile, 1.2 million inhabitants for the territories belonging to the Crown of Aragón, 1.1 million for Portugal, some 5.3 million for Italian territories and up to 1.7 million for the Low Countries and the Franche-Comté. To summarise we will have up to 14.8 million inhabitants.

Unfortunately for the Spanish, the numbers given before were the highest for the seventeenth century. In the middle of the seventeenth century the population of the Crown of Castile was down to 4.2–4.5 million inhabitants, a reduction of up to 20 percent. In Castile the reduction was mostly due to a reduction of the economic activities, the plague, the expulsion of the last Moorish population[7] and a general increase of mortality. In Italy, losses were also significant due to the war and the plague. In 1630–1632, probably 30 percent of the population of Lombardy died from the plague. In 1647 to 1652, the plague was also significant in the Crown of Aragon and in Naples. A rough estimate will give a total population of 12.4 to 12.7 million inhabitants in 1650.

The decentralised nature of the Spanish crown made the governance of the empire a difficult task. As stated (McKay, 2007) the fragmentation was not only geographical but also linguistic, cultural and above all jurisdictional. The central administration had not the authority to impose its laws. Numerous conflicts related with military, fiscal, judicial, ecclesiastic or municipal issues took place with local administration during the reign of Philip IV. Roughly, each territory had its organisation, privileges and duties[8] and was administered by a direct representative of the king. The

---

5 Presidios of Tuscany called also *Estado de los reales presidios* were the cities of Orbetello, Porto Ercole, Porto Ercole, Porto San Stefano, Talamone, Ansedonia, Piombino on the Tyrrhénian coast and Porto Longone (actually called Porto Azurro) on the Elbe Island.
6 The seven provinces were Groningen, Friesland, Overrijssel, Gueldres, Utrech, Holland and Zeeland.
7 It has been estimated that 270,000 Moors were expelled from Spain in 1609–1610 (Hugon, 2000).
8 The king's authority and temporal powers were unquestionable and all legislative, administrative and jurisdictional acts and all privileges and status were granted by him. So in most territories,

Table 1.1: Population of the different territories of Europe of the Spanish Kingdom in 1600*

Castile		Aragón		Nations	
Andalucia	1,070	Aragón	310	Portugal	1,100
Asturias	130	Catalonia	360	Sicily	~ 1,000
Castilla y León	1,890	Valencia	360	Naples	~ 3,000
Castilla la Nueva	1,150	Mallorca	160	Milan	~ 1,200
Extremadura	450			Flanders†	1,300
Galicia	500			Franche-Comté‡	400
Murcia	110				
Guipúzcoa§ & Navarre	300				
TOTAL (x1000)	5,600		1,190		~ 8,000

* J. Nadal, *La población española (siglos XVI y XVII)* (Barcelona: Ariel, 1984), and B. Bennassar and B. Vincent, *Le temps de l'Espagne XVI–XVII* (Paris: Pluriel, Hachette Littérature, 1999)

† An estimate of population of Flanders loyal to the Spanish Kingdom.

‡ The number given is from the year 1614.

§ In the seventeenth century most of the Basque country was called Guipúzcoa even if it consisted of the Lordship of Vizcaya, the Province of Guipúzcoa and the province of Alava.

representatives of the king, governors or viceroys, were controlled by the administration in place in Madrid, where the king was at the head of the administration and was supported by basically three types of council. Among the supra-territorial councils, the most important one was the Council of the State (*Consejo del Estado*) followed by the council of war (*Consejo de Guerra*) and the territorial councils (*Consejos Territoriales*).[9] The monarchy had also other administrative and specialised councils, such as the Council of the Public Finance (*Consejo de Hacienda*), Council of the Crusade, Council of the Inquisition and Council of the Orders. In theory the monarch was the president of most of them, but the burden was heavy and already in the time of Philip III, the king could be helped by a figure called the *valido*[10] or favourite, a sort of first minister. During his reign Philip IV had three *validos*: the best known was Gaspar de Guzmán, Count-Duke of Olivares (1622–1643), the others were Luis Menendez de Haro (1643–1661) and the Duke of Medina de la Torre (1661–1665). The structure of the administration was complemented by specific temporal commissions called *Juntas* to deal and

---

representatives of the king had to find a constant equilibrium between the status and privilege of the territory and the king's wishes and demands (MacKay, 2007).

9 Council of Castile, Council of the Indies, Council of Aragon, Council of Italy, Council of Portugal and Council of Flanders and Burgundy.

10 A *valido* was not a first minister but much more a person trusted or friend of the king in which he could leave the affairs of government. In some case the valido would have almost all the real power.

administrate specific domains such as the Junta of the Artillery or the Junta of the Armada.

1.2 A Time of Glory and Successes: 1621 to 1626

For the new King Philip IV of Spain and his *valido* the Count-Duke of Olivares, the main strategic objective at that time was, to keep all the territories of the monarchy, to support the Hapsburg cause against Protestants, to mitigate or reduce the activities of the Dutch East Indies Company (*Verenigde Oostindische Compagnie* or *VOC*) in Asia and of the new Dutch West India Company (*Geoctroyeerde Westindische Compagnie*) in America. For Madrid, the key of the Spanish power was the stronghold position in the Low Countries and its army, where Spain could control the affairs of Europe. Another important position was the link between Madrid and Brussels, namely the Duchy of Milan or State of Milan, as well as the control of Alpine passes (particularly the Valtellina valley) and of the Rhine valley, that made possible the Spanish Road or *Camino Español*.[11] So in the mind of the Spanish authorities, the war with the United Provinces was an attitude of self-defence to preserve the different provinces of their kingdom against more "aggressive" neighbours, the United Provinces, the Protestant princes in Germany and the French Monarchy.

1621

In April 1621, the main concern of the new Spanish government was the end of the 12-year truce with the United Provinces. It is not our concern to present all discussions that took place in Madrid and Amsterdam, but basically both belligerents thought that they had enough arguments to go to war again and we can add that in 1621 more hardline governments were in power in both capitals.[12] For the Spanish government, the truce has been considered as ruinous to the Spanish economy (Elliott, 1990) and had not stopped the numerous clashes between the Dutch, Spanish, and Portuguese in the European colonies in Asia. As foreign policy advisor at the time of Philip III, the Count-Duke of Olivares had recommended restarting hostilities with the United Provinces to have a better deal in future peace negotiations. On the other side, the growing influence of the supporters of Maurice of Nassau against the peace party and the will of the Dutch West India Company to bring war to America made the renewal of hostilities mostly inevitable. At last, the death of the Archduke Albert, sovereign of the Habsburg Low Countries, in July 1621, partisan of a moderate attitude towards the Dutch, reduced the possibilities to avoid war. We can also take into consideration the fact that at the beginning of the Thirty Years'

---

11 In 1621–1630, the full Spanish Road was to disembark troops in Genoa or Finale on the Italian coast, and later march through Milan, the lago di Como, the Valtellina valley, Lindau, the Rhine valley (Alsace, North Rhine-Westphalia) and the Low Countries.

12 Since 1619 with the execution of Johan Van Oldenbarnet, Maurice of Nassau and the supporters of the hardliners against the Spanish had full power over the destiny of the Dutch Republic.

THE ARMIES OF PHILIP IV OF SPAIN 1621–1665

War, Maurice of Nassau was supporting the Protestant cause of Frederick V Elector of the Palatinate. On the other side the Spanish were supporting the Hapsburgs in Vienna, firstly sending troops[13] and money for the Imperial army and occupying most of the fortresses of the Palatinate in 1620. For the Spanish the use of the Army of Flanders, coupled with naval[14] and economic warfare, was the solution to bring the Dutch to negotiate on favourable terms. This means that most of the money went to the Army of Flanders to undertake offensive actions, occupying positions on the main rivers (Lower Rhine and River Meuse[15] areas) of the United Provinces and with the Armada of Flanders to disrupt Dutch trading.[16] From 1621 to 1622, the Commander of the army of Flanders Ambrogio Spinola, laid siege to the city of Jullïch 5 September 1621 and on 3 February 1622, the town surrendered with honourable terms. At the same time a Spanish force of 10,000 men started an operation against the city of Sluis by the occupation of the Island of Cadzand[17] and the blocking of the estuary of the River Escaut. The occupation and construction of the fort on the island was successfully conducted but the lack of supplies and the poor living conditions took a heavy toll on the troops and in spring 1622, most of the troops have been withdrawn to a safer position.

1.1 King Philip IV in cuirassier armour, assisted by court dwarf. Gaspar de Crayer (1584–1669) (Michał Paradowski's archive)

1622

The government of Madrid asked the Archduchess Isabel to continue the military operation and with the army of Ambrioglio Spinola, the Spanish still

---

13 Tercio of Carlo Spinelli, Tercio of the Count of Bucquoy and Tercio of Guillermo Verdugo (Chalines, 1999).
14 One of the first actions of the war took place near Gibraltar, in August 1621, when a convoy of 50 Dutch ships was intercepted by six galleons and three patches from the Armada del Mar Oceano. Although outnumbered, the Spanish managed to sink five enemy ships and capture two more (Fernández Duro, volume IV, 1895).
15 The main Rivers in the Low Countries are the Rhine, the Meuse or Maas in Dutch, the Escaut or Scheldt in Dutch and the Overijsselse Vecht. The river network is rather complex and some of the main rivers such as the Rhine had different branches for example the Waal, Nederijn and the Ijssel.
16 The Spanish trade embargo, the action of Spanish privateers, coupled with the need to increase the army and to finance the Protestant cause in Germany had drastic consequences for the Dutch economy (Swart, 2015).
17 Troops involved were the Tercio of Iñigo Borja (Spanish), the Tercio of Paolo Baglioni (Italian), the Tercio of Count de la Fontaine (Walloon), two German regiments(?), Walloon companies of Artois, and six companies of Irish (Tercio of the Count of Tyrone) (Domingo Toral y Valdés, *Relación de la vida del capitán Domingo de Toral y Valdés, escrita por el mismo capitán*, CODOIN vol. 71, 1879, pp. 485–547).

had a striking force of up to 20,600 men.[18] The first operation was the capture of Steenbergen in North Brabant at the beginning of July followed by the siege to the stronghold of Bergen op Zoom 18 July. The city was the key for the control of Zeeland because it was close to the island of Tholen, but unfortunately for the Spanish it was also open to the sea and surrounded by marshes and floodable polders. The siege was a failure because the Spanish were not able to sever the communications of the city and supplies and fresh troops were regularly brought into the besieged town. By contrast the Spanish supply lines was constantly disrupted and when in September 1622 Maurice of Nassau was reinforced by a contingent of Protestant troops from the Count of Mansfeld, the Spanish, under the command of Luis de Velasco, had to lift the siege 3 October 1622. The high cost in men (up to 8,000 to 13,000[19]) and money was heavily criticised in Madrid.

Meantime in Germany the other part of the army of Flanders, under the command of Gonzalo de Cordoba, fought alongside Tilly´s Catholic league army at the Battle of Wimpfen on 6 May and the siege of Heidelberg from 23 July to 19 September 1622. In August 1622, Gonzalo de Cordoba was in the south of the Low Countries to counter the movement of the Protestant army commanded by Ernst von Mansfeld and the Duke of Brunswick-Lüneburg from the city of Sedan. The battle took place near Fleurus[20] on 29 August when the small Spanish army of 6,000 infantry and 2,200–2,400 cavalry confronted the Protestant force estimated at 6,000 infantry and 5,000 cavalry.[21] The relation of the battle it is somewhat confused and both parties claim victory, the reality is that the Spanish remained masters of the battlefield and the next morning most of

1.2 Mounted portrait of King Philip IV. Hessel Gerritsz, 1591–1632 (Rijksmuseum)

---

18 The infantry consisted of 21 tercios and regiments divided in the three old Spanish tercios of Flanders (Iñigo Borja, Simón Antúnez and Diego Mejia de Guzman), the Spanish–Portuguese tercio of Diogo Oliveira, two Italian tercios (Marcelo Judice and Paolo Baglioni), five Walloon tercios (Prince of Brabançon, Count of Henin, Count de la Fontaine, Thomas Wyngaarde and François de Merode), two tercios from Burgundy (Baron of Beauvois and Jean de Maisières), three Tercios from the British Isles (Count of Tyrone, Irish; Count of Argyll, Scottish, and Edward Vaux, English) and finally five German regiments (Philippe-Charles de Ligne, Prince of Chimay, Duke of Neoburg, Otto Fugger and Marquis of Brandenburg). The cavalry was commanded by Luis de Velasco.
19 From a letter to the King of Luis de Casuso Maeda (Archivo General de Simancacs E2313/3–4) paymaster of the Army of Flanders dated 22 October 1622, losses were 7,800 men between dead, wounded and deserters. The Dutch give 11,000 dead and wounded and 2,000 deserters.
20 A description of the battle is presented in Chapter 4, pp. 252–256.
21 1,500 to 2,000 horsemen mutinied before the battle and did not participate in the fighting.

the Protestant infantry was destroyed,[22] even if a large portion of the Protestant troops (probably 2,000 infantry and 4,000 cavalry) managed to reach Breda to join the Dutch army. The abandonment of the siege of Bergen op Zoom marked the end of the campaign and all the troops went into winter quarters.

In northern Italy and particularly in the Valtellina valley, the Catholic population[23] rose up against their Protestant masters from the Grison League.[24] The valley was a strategic crossing point across the Alps from northern Italy to the Tyrol and Bavaria and it was important for the Spanish and Imperials to keep it open for the movement of their forces. The Grison League received some help from Swiss mercenaries from Protestant cantons, but in a series of small fights,[25] the Spanish and the Imperials managed to retake control of the valley in August 1620. Between 1621 and 1622, small fighting was still taking place, but by the Treaty of Lindau, the Grison League accepted the loss of the control of the valley, occupied by 8,000 Spanish and Imperial troops.

1.3 Prince Baltasar Carlos, Philip IV's son. The 11-year-old is presented here in cuirassier armour. Portrait attributed to Juan Bautista Martinez del Mazo, 1639–1645 (Rijksmuseum).

1623

In the Low Countries, the heavy losses of the Cadzand and Bergen op Zoom operations meant that the Spanish army was not prepared to go on the offensive in 1623. At the same time there were some discrepancies between Brussels and Madrid over the best strategy against the Dutch. In fact, it was the Dutch who in February 1623 launched a surprise attack to take Antwerp. Thankfully for the Spanish, sentries were on alert and the frost blocked some of the raiding party and the audacious raid failed completely.

As usual, things were not simple in Italy and in February 1623, by the treaty of Paris, an alliance between France, Savoy, and Venice was signed against the hegemony of the Spanish in the area in order to support the Grison League in their aim to retake control of the Valtellina valley. The new alliance surprised

---

22 Total losses are always difficult to ascertain but between the battle and the pursuit of the next day a minimum of 5,000 Protestants were lost. On the Spanish side losses were probably between 800 and 1,000 men.
23 The Valtellina valley was a Catholic area extending from the Chiavenna, Morbegno, Sondrio, Tirano and Bormio. In the seventeenth century its population was estimated at 80,000 inhabitants (Martinez Canales, 2017).
24 The Grison League or the Grey League (*Graubünden* in German) was a mutual defence league covering a region known as West Tyrol, independent from the Swiss Canton. The inhabitants of the West Tyrol were mostly Protestant, but only in the Valtellina valley were Catholics in the majority.
25 For the Spanish we can cite the small battle of Tirano, when a small Spanish army of 1,300 infantrymen and 300 cavalry under the command of Jerónimo Pimentel defeated a force of some 5,000 men (3,000 Swiss and 2,000 Grison League troops) commanded by Niklaus von Mülinen (Martinez Canales, 2017).

the Count-Duke of Olivares, his last wish was to undertake a war against the French and a compromise was found around the future of the valley. The Grison League retook official control of the valley, Spanish garrison were evacuated and replaced by troops paid by the papal state. For the Spanish, the Catholic population was now under the protection of the Pope and the valley was secure to move troops to Flanders by the *Camino Español*.

1624

At the beginning of 1624, the Spanish embargoes and the action of the Dunkirk privateers had significant consequences on the economy of the Dutch Republic. With the victories of the Catholic league and Imperial armies combined with the action of the army of Flanders, the Dutch territory was also surrounded by a ring of Catholic garrisons from Bruges to Linken[26] (Germany). The Dutch economy was also under stress to support the Protestant cause in Germany and to pay a decent army of 48,000 men or more to face the Spanish.

On the other side, even if some discrepancy existed on the strategies between Brussels and Madrid, the Archduchess Isabel[27] and Ambrogio Spinola agreed to carry out a major operation to force the Dutch to negotiate a new truce. The Army of Flanders was reinforced by troops from Milan and was prepared to initiate a campaign against the symbolic city of Breda. Breda was chosen because it was an important town, south of the River Maas and a base for Dutch raiding parties in Brabant and because it was a personal property of the Stadtholder Prince Maurice of Nassau and the garrison was commanded by Justin of Nassau, a relative. Spinola was sure that the Dutch would defend the city at all costs and a victory against them would undermine their morale and will to continue the fighting. The siege of Breda would be the climax of the army of Flanders, but let us have a look at the force defending the city. The Dutch knew that Breda could be an objective of the Spanish offensive and the garrison was reinforced to reach 5,200 regular soldiers[28] and 1,800 town militia.

With an army of 18,000–24,000 men[29], Spinola surrounded the city of Breda from 27 August to 1 September 1624 while a small diversion force of

---

26 On the Dutch/German border north of the Rhine valley, the cities of Groenlo (Netherlands), Bredevoort (Netherlands), Oldenzaal (Netherlands), and Linken (Germany) provided a series of strongholds to blockade or to attack the Dutch Republic from the east.

27 Archduchess Isabel was deeply concerned about the restriction of her authority from Madrid. She did not necessarily share the view of Philip IV and the Count-Duke Olivares concerning the strategy in the Low Countries. She had to report to the Council of State on matters of martial strategy and for the siege of Breda she deliberately engaged the army of Flanders, probably without the approval of Madrid. The success was also her success against Olivares. See Alexandra Libby, 2015, "The Solomonic Ambitions of Isabel Clara Eugenia" in Ruben's "The Triumph of the Eucharist Tapestry series", *Journal of Historians of Netherlandish Art*, 7:2.

28 J.P.M. Rooze; C.W.A.M. Eimermann (2005), *De belegering van Breda door Spinola 1624–1625* Alphen aan den Rijn, Canaletto/Repro-Holland. ISBN 906469820

29 18,000 men (198 infantry companies in 15 tercios/regiments and 39 companies of cavalry) is given by Herman Hugo (*Sitio de Breda: Rendida a las armas del Rey Don Phelipe IV...* Antwerp 1627*)*, Pier Francesco Pieri (*Noue guerre di Fiandra dalli 21 luglio 1624 sino alli 25 d'Agosto 1625...* Firenze 1627) gives 20,000 infantry and 60 companies of cavalry.

THE ARMIES OF PHILIP IV OF SPAIN 1621–1665

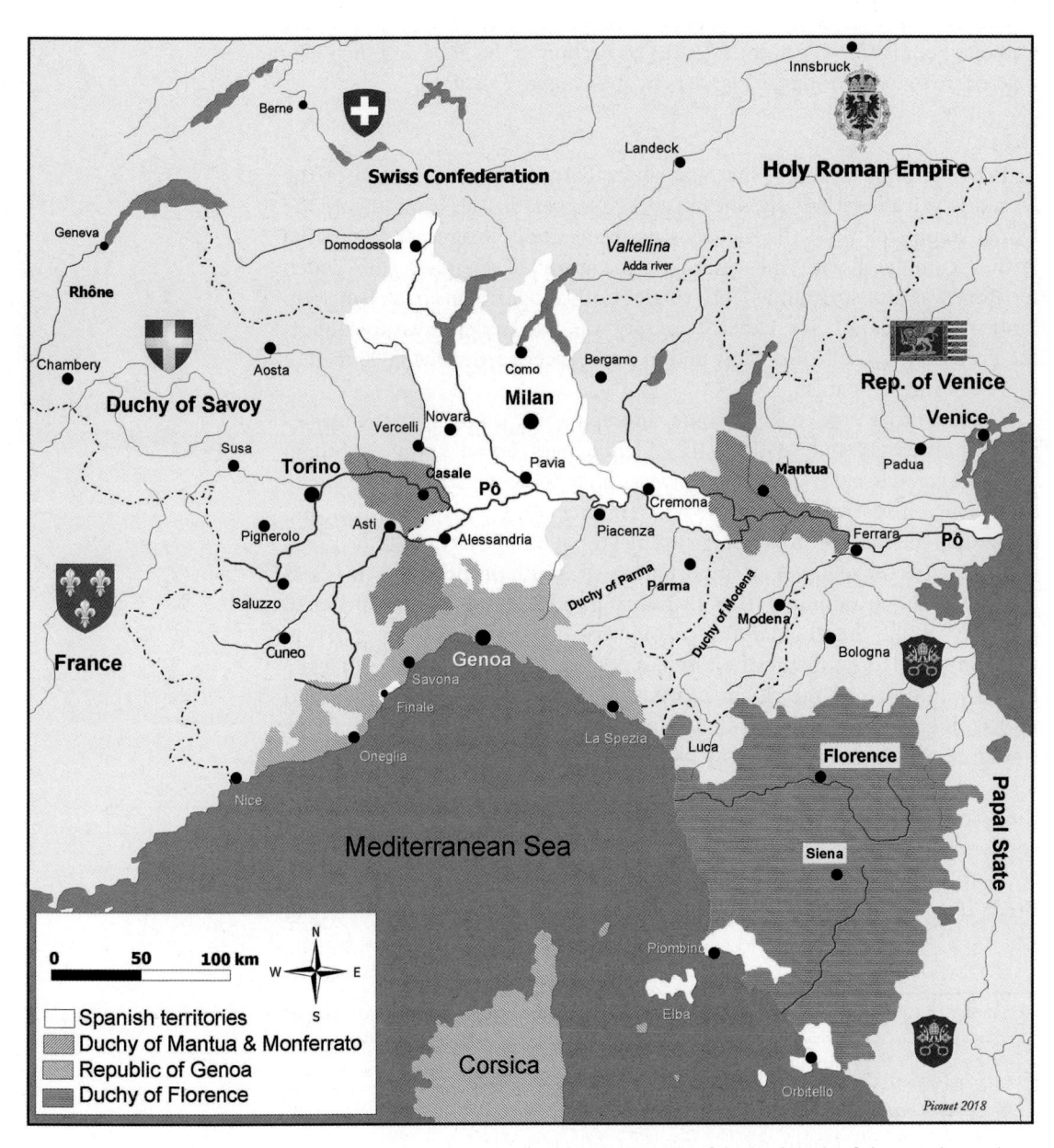

Map 1.2 The Spanish territories in northern Italy in the seventeenth century. The army of Lombardy had to fight several wars: the war of Valentina valley (1624–1626), war of Genoa (1625), war of Mantua (1628–1632), and war against France, Savoy and minor Italian princes (1635–1659).

5,000 men commanded by the Count Hendrik van den Bergh was sent to the Rhine valley. In Breda, Spinola decided to conduct a strategic siege and to blockade the city and to force it to surrender by hunger and exhaustion. The choice of such a tactic was dictated by the modern fortification of Breda,[30] a well-defended city surrounded by polders and fields easy to inundate. For such task the army of Flanders was divided intp four sections with three fortified camps[31] and a main base located at Ginneken[32] (commanded in practice by Francisco de Medina). Between the fortified camps, the Spanish erected lines of contravallation and circumvallation, the former 22 km long and the latter 27 km, which were constructed in less than three weeks. Depending of the terrain, the lines had every 400–500 m sconces or redoubts; their objective was not to hold enemy assault but to sound the alert in time to bring reinforcement to subdue the attackers. As the siege continued, reinforcements arrived[33] to improve the blockade and a new line was constructed to partially replace the old ones. The new line of circumvallation had two new sectors (called Anholt and Beauvois) to reinforce the north, now measuring 39 km and the new line of contravallation was shortened and closer to the city in the sector of Ginneken and Hage. Quickly local supplies from villages around Breda were eaten or removed by the Dutch and most of the supplies had to be brought from the south, Antwerp, Lierre, or Herentals. At first the main supply convoys followed a route of 51 km from Antwerp to Ginneken via Loenhout and Zundert, but it was too vulnerable to the Dutch raiding parties from Roosendaal. Later the main supply routes were the ones of 56 km Lierre, Rijkevorsel, Hoogstraten, Meersel-Dreef and Ginneken or the variant of 57 km Herentals, Turmhout, Meersel-Dreef and Ginneken. From the other side, cavalry detachments were sent to try to disrupt the Spanish supply lines and from the city, Justin of Nassau sent regularly detachments of the garrison to test the Spanish defence and to disturb their spadework. Beginning of October 1624, Maurice of Nassau organised a relief force of 21,000 men and dug in near Made, north of Breda. There he ordered

---

30 Breda had up to 15,000 inhabitants, and the city was defended by a modern wall with 15 bastions surrounded by a ditch of 55 to 117 metres wide, filled by the water of the River Mark. The defence was enhanced by five hornworks numerous ravelins and half-moon fortification in the ditch and had an artillery of 43 guns (Herman Hugo, *Obsidio Bredana*, Antwerp, 1626).

31 For the three fortified camps we have the first (commanded by Baron of Balançon) on the east near Teteringen (Burgundian Tercio of Balançon, German regiment of Issenburg and Imperial regiment of Anholt); the second (commanded by commanded by Paolo Baglione) in the north between Hartelbergen and Terhijden (Italian tercios of Baglione and Campolataro and the Scottish Tercio of Argyll); the third (commanded by Count of Isenburg) at Hage on the west (German Regiment of Issenburg and the Walloon tercio of the Count of Henin).

32 The camp at Ginneken contain the army staff, the main artillery park and the main supply base as well as a large force of infantry with four Spanish tercios (Tercio of Francisco de Medina, Tercio of Juan Niño de Tavora, Tercio of Juan Claros de Guzmán and the Tercio of Diogo Luis de Oliveira), two Italian Tercios (Tercio of Marcelo Justice and Tercio of Francesco Adda), two Walloon tercios (Tercio of the Count of Grobbendonck and Tercio of the Prince of Barbaçon), three German regiments (regiment of Otto Fugger, regiment of Nassau and regiment of Brandenburg), the Burgundian Tercio of the Baron of Beauvois, the Irish Tercio of Tyrone and the English Tercio of Edward Parham. The majority of the cavalry commanded by Salazar and Silva were also stationed near Ginneken (Swart, 2016).

33 For example the Imperial regiments of Ramboldo Collalto and those of Johann of Nassau.

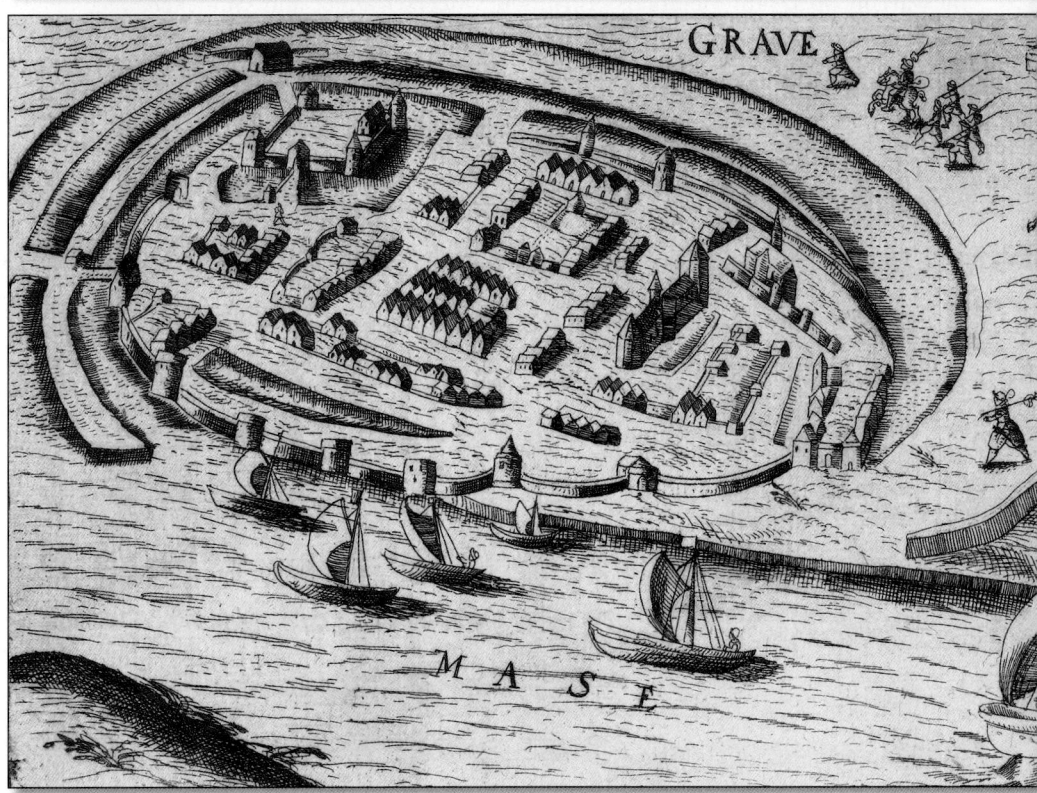

THE ARMIES OF PHILIP IV OF SPAIN 1621–1665

THE WORLD OF PHILIP IV OF SPAIN

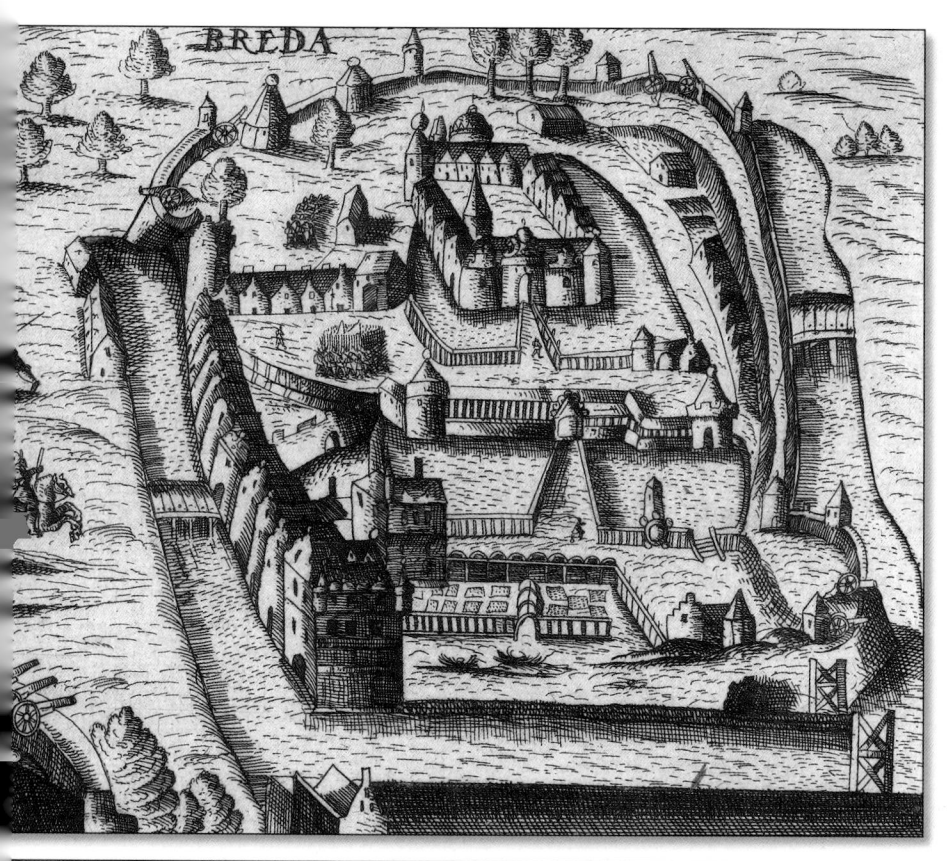

1.4 (top) Spanish siege of Breda in 1624. Anonymous, 1624–1625 (Rijksmuseum)

1.5 (below) Spanish siege of Grave in 1624. Anonymous, 1624–1625 (Rijksmuseum)

different constructions (especially a dyke on the River Mark) to inundate the Spanish fortifications, but all of them failed and at the end of the year Breda was still besieged by the Spanish.

In northern Italy, the French alliance of the previous year enhanced the Grison League demanded and when a French force of 3,000 men[34] under the command of François d'Estrées arrived in the Egandine region in summer, 4,500 Swiss and troops from the Grison League joined them. From September to November 1624, the combined force retook most of the Valtellina with little or no resistance from the papal troops,[35] but when they arrived in the west of the Valtellina, they were blocked by a small Spanish force under the command of Giovanni Serbelloni. With winter coming and the news of the invasion of Genoa, the military operation stopped, the French had fulfilled their goal to cut Spanish communication with Germany and did not want to alter too much their relation with the new Pope.

We have seen that with the end of the 12-year truce, the strategy of the Dutch had been to gain a foothold in America. In 1623, the Dutch West Indies Company was preparing an expedition to attack the weakest element of the Luso-Spanish Empire in America, the Portuguese colony of Brazil. On 23 December 1623 a powerful fleet of 32 ships commanded by Jacob Willeken with 1,400 sailors and 3,000 soldiers, commanded by Jean van Dort, sailed from Texel in Holland with the objective to take São Salvador da Bahia. On 9 May 1624, the Dutch fleet appeared at the entrance of the Bahia de Todos os Santos and the next day they managed to subdue the fort (Fort San António) protecting the entrance to the bay and to disembark 1,500 men. The Portuguese soldiers, made of raw recruits from the city,[36] were easily dispersed[37] and van Dort captured the governor of the city Diogo de Mendonça Furtado. Willeken left a garrison of 2,000 soldiers and 10 ships, sent six ships to Holland with a rich bounty of tropical wood, sugar, gingerbread and tobacco and left the rest to attack Spanish and Portuguese ships in the Atlantic. The news of the losses of the colony reached Madrid at the end of July 1624 and the Count-Duke of Olivares announced quickly the preparation of an expedition to retake the city and the reinforcement of the others colonies in America. The preparation of the expedition was a joint effort by the Spanish and Portuguese to defend their colonies. The

---

34   François d'Estrée had 10 companies from the regiment of Normandie and Vaubecourt and six companies of the regiment d'Estrées.

35   Since August 1623 a new pope, Urban VIII, was elected. Urban had a more anti-Hapsburg policy than his predecessor; his goal was not necessary to support the French monarchy but to expend the papal territory and for that Spain was more a threat than an ally.

36   In the beginning of the seventeenth century, the city of Salvador da Bahia had 1,400 houses (6,000 to 7,000 inhabitants). *L'Art de Vérifier les Dates depuis l'année 1770 jusqu'à nos jours, volume treizième* (Paris: Denain, 1832, available at the University of Michigan, Ann Arbor, USA).

37   The original attack was badly countered by the Portuguese, but already by the end of May the bishop of the city, Marcos Texeira, organised the resistance. Rapidly guerrilla warfare started in the neighbourhood of Salvador da Bahia. In 15 June 1624 Johan van Dort was killed in a small skirmish against the Portuguese. Furthermore, Marcos Texeira was able to control most of the countryside but the city was out of his reach.

THE WORLD OF PHILIP IV OF SPAIN

1.6 (above) Ambrogio Spinola, portait from 1609. Michiel Jansz van Mierevelt (Rijksmuseum).

1.7 (right) Ambrogio Spinola at the siege of Jülich in 1622. Mattheus Melijn, 1636 (Rijksmuseum).

THE ARMIES OF PHILIP IV OF SPAIN 1621–1665

1.8 Isabella Clara Eugenia, Infanta of Spain and Portugal, sovereign and governor of Spanish Netherlands until 1633. Renold Elstrack, 1616–1621 (Rijksmuseum).

1.9 Albert VII, Archduke of Austria, with his wife Isabella Clara Eugenia sovereign of Spanish Netherlands until his death in 1621. Workshop of Frans Pourbus, *c.*1600 (Rijksmuseum).

main tool was the Armada del Mar Oceano,[38] with soldiers from two Spanish tercios and one Italian tercio organised in Cadiz and the Portuguese fleet[39] with soldiers from two Portuguese tercios organised in Lisbon. On 30 November 1624, the Portuguese fleet sailed from Lisbon and on 6 December it was the turn of the Spanish fleet to sail from Cadiz.

1625

The siege of Breda was the main operation of the Spanish army in the Low Countries and all the efforts of Madrid and Brussels were dedicated to it. On the other side, the Dutch leader Maurice of Nassau, already a sick man, died 23 April 1625 and was succeeded by Frederick Hendricks of Nassau. The new statholder decided to concentrate 46,000 men (Swart, 2016) in Geertruidenberg in order to force the Spanish position and relieve Breda. On 15 May a probing force of 6,000 men[40] was sent to attack the Spanish fortification in the sector of Baglione. The attack was led by 1,000 Englishmen and managed to occupy a portion of the Terheidjen fortification, but was repulsed by a counter-attack lead by Paolo Baglione, that was to be the last major action of the siege. On 2 June Justin of Nassau was authorised to negotiate the capitulation of Breda and 5 June the garrison left the city on honourable terms. Victory was for the Spanish army of Flanders, but the terrible efforts of the last 11 months had been too much for the Spanish treasury and for the rest of 1625 the army remained mostly inactive. From a strategic point of view the defeat did not bring the Dutch to accept negotiation on a new truce as was expected by Spinola and the Archduchess.

Further to the south, the French minister, Cardinal Richelieu, wanted to select a weak point in the Spanish hegemony in northern Italy and decided to support the claim of Charles Manuel I, Duke of Savoy, to take the Marquisate of Zuccarello, a territory under Genoese control. Already, in November 1624,

1.10 Mounted portrait of Albert VII and Isabella. Hessel Gerritsz, 1591–1632 (Rijksmuseum)

---

38   The Armada had 20 galleons, seven hulks, two patches, one frigate, four pinnaces and two tartanes divided into five squadrons for a total of 2,558 sailors and 801 guns. The soldiers of the three tercios numbered 5,824 men in 72 companies (J. Valencia y Guzman, *Compendio Historial de la jornada del Brasil y sucesos de ella*, in CODOIN vol. 55, 1870, pp. 45–200).

39   The Portuguese fleet had four galleons, 14 naos and four hulks with 829 sailors, and 384 guns. The soldiers of the two Portuguese tercios numbered 3,538 men in 25 companies (CODOIN vol. 55, op. cit.).

40   The English were commanded by Colonel Vere and consisted of 800 musketeers and 200 pikemen, they were followed by French and German regiments and some artillery (Herman Hugo op. cit.).

a secret treaty was signed with Savoy to prepare the conquest and partition of the Republic of Genoa (Parrot, 2001). The French expedition force,[41] commanded by the Duke of Lesdiguières,[42] arrived in February 1625 after crossing the Alps by the Mont Cenis pass. At the beginning of March, the Allies had assembled a field army of 23,000 men[43] (8,000 for the French and 15,000 for Savoy) and had probably another 10,000 men defending Torino and the Piedmont region or to act against the territory of Genoa on the Liguria coast. Facing them, Genoa had probably a total of 13,000 men to garrison the different fortresses of the republic and to form a small mobile army. Soon the Genoese received a small reinforcement of 2,200 men from the Duke of Feria, governor of the State of Milan. For the invasion, two routes were followed, on the first the French took the city of Novi Ligure to secure the left flank against the Spanish and later moved to lay a siege against the fortress of Gavi defended by a strong contingent of 1,500–2,000 men. For the second, the Duke of Savoy took relatively easily Acqui Terme, Ovada and Rossiglione and turned back to join the French at the siege of Gavi. Here, the Genoese defended the city since 25 March but on 8 April the field army of Genoa[44] was dispersed by the Savoyards and Gavi had to capitulate on 22 of April. At the end of April, the Allies had only to cross the della Bochetta pass and captured Sanpierdarena to besiege Genoa. In fact, the French commander refused to advance, arguing that the lack of supplies, the numerous desertion and the delays to move the artillery, were factors against an attack of a big and populous city like Genoa. Meantime, the Spanish were reacting and while the Duke of Feria was organising a field army in Pavia, the Marquis of Santa Cruz arrived in Genoa with a first reinforcement of Spanish troops[45] from Naples and Sicily. These crack troops boosted the morale of the Genoese and enhanced drastically the possibility of defending their city. Therefore, the Duke of Savoy, Carlos Manuel I, decided to send a portion of his army to take some cities on the Liguria coast.[46] On the other hand, at the end of May, the Duke of Feria had enough troops[47] to move to Alessandria in order to threaten Piedmont and the communication of the Duke of Savoy. The Duke of Lesdiguière and the Duke of Savoy decided to retreat quickly to the city of Acqui Terme where a strong garrison of 2,000 men was left on 12 June and the retreat continued to Bistagno. The Spanish were quickly in front of Acqui Terme and after a poor resistance the city surrendered, obliging the Alliea to

---

41 Numbers of the expedition are not clear, we have probably a force 11,000 infantry and 1,000 to 1,500 cavalry to a maximum of 15,000 men (*Histoire abrégée de la vie de François de Bonne, duc de Lesdiguières, pair et dernier connétable de France*; J.-C. Martin de Grenoble, 1802).

42 François de Bonne, Duke of Lesdiguières, was 82 years old but was still a good commander

43 Following Saluces (1818) in Asti we have an army of 12,000 infantry and 2,500 cavalry for Savoy and 6,000 infantry and 500 to 1,000 horse for the French, a total of 21,500 men.

44 Up to 6,000 men (including the 2,200 men from the Army of Lombardy) commanded by Tommaso Caracciolo (Luca Assarini, *Delle Guerre e Successi d'Italia volume prim*, Torino 1665).

45 For the number of troops, sources diverge: the lowest we have is 2,700 Spaniards, at the highest we have 4,000 men (Spaniards and Neapolitans).

46 In 11 days (6 to 17 May), Ventimiglia, San Remo, Albenga and Port Maurice and other villages were taken by the troops of Savoy and only the city of Savona was still in Genoese hands.

47 Some 22,000 infantry and 4,000–5,000 men (Luca Assarini, *Delle Guerre e Successi d'Italia* volume 1, Torino 1665).

retreat to Asti followed by the Spanish force. Meantime an army of 8,000 to 9,000 men made of Spanish and Genoese troops went on campaign to retake the lost positions. The first objective was Novi Ligure, poorly defended by the French and after Gavi defended in theory by 1,800 men, while another column retook Rossiglione and Ovada. Isolated and in the middle of a hostile country the garrison of Gavi made a poor defence and capitulated quickly. In front of a strong position in Asti, the Duke of Feria decided to come back to Monferrato and moved north to Occianno between Casale Monferrato and Alessandria. For the Spanish the idea was to attack a position in Piedmont to force a negotiation, the new objective was the fortress of Verrua and Crescentino on the River Pô. On 5 August the Spanish army was near Verrua, but the Duke of Savoy had anticipated the movement and the fortress had a strong garrison of 4,300 men. During three months the Spanish, the French and the Savoyards fought for Verrua, but in November 1625, in the face of significant losses, bad weather, French reinforcements and the coming of winter, the Duke of Feria withdrew to Lombardy. In the south, the Genoese and Spanish forces launched an attack and retook Ventimiglia, San Remo, Albenga and Port Maurice as well as Oneglia and Ormea in Piedmont. At the end of the year France and Spain opened negotiations and on 5 March 1626 the treaty of Monzón was signed. The treaty restored the pre-1618 situation in the Valtellina, the Grison League had to recognise the autonomy of the valley and some doubts were introduced as to who could decide on transit through the valley. At the same time the treaty stopped the war between Genoa and Savoy. The intervention of the Spanish troops had saved the republic of Genoa and stopped the action of Savoy, with the uprising of French Protestants in 1625 and the war in Flanders, neither France or Spain wished to fight a war.

In the Atlantic, besides some incidents due to navigation in the seventeenth century, the combined fleets, under the command of Fabrique de Toledo, met in the Capo Verde Archipelago on 6 February 1625. Five days later, they sailed towards their objective and on 29 March they were at the entrance of the Bahia de Todos os Santos. In the meantime, the Dutch had time to reinforce the garrison of the city and in March they had 3,000 infantrymen, and a dozen of small ships with 157 guns. The first landing of the Spanish force was to occupy successfully the Fort San António defending the entrance of the bay and on 2 April, the Portuguese and Spanish Fleet anchored in the bay at few kilometres from the city of São Salvador da Bahia. The Spanish and Portuguese troops disembarked with their guns and after few days they were able to set up six batteries of three to six guns (25 guns in total). For three weeks the Dutch garrison would resist, but with no hope of receiving reinforcement[48] the Dutch governor capitulated on 28 April with 1,919 survivors. A strong garrison was left in the city and with the rest of the fleet; Fabrique de Toledo sailed to Recife. A vanguard of six galleons sailed to Cadiz, followed later by the Portuguese fleet and the rest of the Spanish one.

---

48 The irony was that on 25 May a Dutch squadron arrived in front of the Bahia da Todos los Santos with reinforcements for the garrison. Seeing the Spanish fleet and knowing that the city had fallen, the Dutch fleet returned to Europe.

The Spanish had to face not only the Dutch fleet but also an English one in the Atlantic. In March 1624, the Kingdom of England had declared war to Spain to support the Dutch war effort and the claims of the Electorate of the Palatinate. The Spanish did not want a war with England, and it came as some surprise to them to see strong English troops supporting the Dutch to lift the siege of Breda.

At the beginning of 1625, the Duke of Buckingham convinced King Charles I to attack the Spanish mainland and the treasure fleet in order to avenge the capture of territories in the Rhine valley of the Elector Frederick of Bohemia. It took several months to organise a decent English fleet to carry out the amphibious attack on Iberian ports, but on 5 October an armada of 91 ships[49] and an amphibious force of 10,000 soldiers[50] was ready to sail. Sir Edward Cecil was put in command of the expedition with the Earl of Sussex as second in command, for various reasons the Lord Admiral did not participate in the adventure. A Dutch squadron of 15 ships under the command of Wilhelm of Nassau arrived in Plymouth to participate in the expedition. The combined fleet sailed from England on 8 October and Buckingham had given to the commander-in-chief the choice to attack Sanlucar, Lisbon, Cadiz or Sevilla. During the trip to southern Spain, strong Atlantic storms were encountered, scattering the ships and alerting the Spanish. In a council of war it was decided to attack Cadiz[51] and on Saturday 1 November[52] the Dutch–English fleet appeared near the entrance of the bay. At first the Spanish were surprised, but most of the merchant ships cut their cables and escaped, while the galleys and galleons[53] took refuge in the Channel of La Carraca.[54] In another council of war, the first decision of the English was to attack Fort el Puntal defended by 120 men and eight guns to find a better anchorage in the bay than in front of Cadiz. The same night of the 1st/2nd of November, galleys and small boats carried reinforcements[55] to the city and in 13 hours up to 2,818 men had joined the garrison of

---

49 Following Magnussen (1964), the fleet had 13 Royal Navy ships, 65 converted merchant ships, 11 supply ships and six ketches for a total of 5,440 seamen and an estimated 1,400 guns.

50 The landing force was 9,978 men divided into 10 regiments with 109 companies (*The voyage to Cadiz in 1625; being a journal written by John Glanville, never before printed, from Sir John Eliot's Mss. at Port Eliot*. Sir John Glanville (1586–1661), 1883).

51 Cadiz had a regular garrison of 280 men and could be supported by 900 militiamen; all the troops were under the command of Fernando Girón y Ponce de León. The walls of the city had been updated and reinforced at the beginning of the seventeenth century. In 1625 it was the fourth time that an English fleet had attacked the city.

52 In an English source (*The voyage to Cadiz in 1625*; op. cit.) the arrival date was 22 October; I decided to take the Spanish point of view because it matches with our actual calendar.

53 The Spanish fleet had 10 galleys of the Escuadra de España commanded by the Duke of Fernandina and 14 galleons under the command of the Marquis of Crópani and the Admiral Roque Centeno.

54 It is a channel between the island of Trocadero and mainland.

55 The reinforcements were 400 infantry and 50 cavalry from Chiclana de la Frontera 401 infantry and 80 cavalry from Medina, 700 infantry and 120 cavalry from Jerez de la Frontera. Another 762 regular soldiers and 50 artillerymen were sent by the ships and galleys of the Armada (*Verdad de lo sucedido con ocasion de la venida de la armada inglesa del enemigo sobre Cadiz en primero de Nouiembre de mil y seyscientos y veinte y cinco*, University of Seville).

Cadiz. Bombardment[56] of Fort el Puntal started during the night but the fort surrendered only after 26 hours (4 o'clock in the afternoon of 2 November) of bombardment and when a landing party of 800–1,000 men disembarked to take the position. Later in the day and during the night, the English landed their troops (7,000 to 8,000 men) on the Island of León. Soon, Sir Edward Cecil discovered that the he did not have enough supplies for his troops, that the city of Cadiz was well defended, that the Island of León was unsuitable to feed his men, that his troops were undisciplined and that the Spanish were assembling troops[57] in Jerez de la Frontera. With sickness spreading in the fleet and in the troops ashore, the English took the decision to re-embark and to chase the treasure fleet. Depending on the source, the continuous skirmish and the final combat cost the English forces 1,000 to 2,000 men.[58] On 8 November the expeditionary fleet sailed from the bay of Cadiz and stayed some 17 days near Cap St Vincent but failed totally to intercept the treasure fleet and had to return to England. Winter gales and storms took a toll on the fleet during the return and in March 1626, the English could make a reckoning[59] of the fiasco of the expedition.

1626

The previous year had been a wonderful year for the Spanish monarchy and the Count-Duke of Olivares could talk of an *Annus Mirabilis* and the prestige of King Philip IV of Spain was at his climax. But the Spanish strategy had some drawbacks, in the Low Countries; the army of Flanders was reduced to a defensive strategy due to the lack of funds. The costly siege of Breda did not bring the Dutch to renegotiate a new truce, so the strategy was to continue the blockade of the Republic and to continue the attack on Dutch trade by privateers. The new hope of the Count-Duke of Olivares was the revival of the famous northern maritime plan. Thanks to the Catholic victories at Dessau Bridge[60] and Lutter[61] (Lutter am Barenberge in Lower Saxony) in 1626, the possibility of establishing a Catholic base on the Baltic Sea seemed possible. For the Spanish the objective of a "great project" aimed to disrupt Dutch trade in the Baltic and to undermine the Dutch fleet and economy. A longer term objective was to establish interconnected companies between the Spanish and Imperials to undertake trade with northern Europe and to

---

56 For the bombardment five Dutch ships, three Royal Navy ships and 20 Collier-brig ships were used. In the process two Dutch ships were damaged by the Spanish (Magnussen, 1964).
57 The Duke of Medinia Sidonia, governor of the Coast of Andalucia, sent a force of 2,800 men to reinforce the harbours of Rota, Puerto Real, Puerto Santa Maria and Sanlucar. Around Jerez de la Frontera he also manage to concentrate up to 8,300 men with 11 guns in a few days.
58 Spanish sources (op. cit.) indicate that the garrison of Cadiz made a sally to attack the English force near the El Puntal, killing a lot of them in the process.
59 Probably half of the men died from sickness, hunger, poor living conditions, drowning or fighting. Between 50 and 62 ships (including the Dutch ones) were lost in the adventure.
60 At the Battle of Dessau Bridge the Imperial army of 20,000 men under the command of Albrecht Wallenstein defeated a Danish–Protestant force of 12,000 men commanded by Ernst von Mansfeld on 25 April 1626 (Guthrie, 2002).
61 The Battle of Lutter was fought 27 August 1626. The battle was a crushing defeat for the Protestant army of King Christian IV (troops from the Lower Saxon Circle and Denmark) at the hands of the Imperial/Catholic army of the Count of Tilly (Parker, 2002).

connect it with America and Asia.[62] Fortunately for the Dutch,[63] the great plan was too ambitious, the financial problem of Spain in 1627 and the failure of Wallenstein to take the city-harbour of Stralsund in 1628 reduced the plan to bittersweet dreams.

The first clouds came from the Low Countries where the master plan was to control the rivers going to the Dutch Republic and avoid another siege like the one at Breda. The Spanish inactivity gave the opportunity to the Stadtholder Frederick Hendricks of Nassau, to successfully conduct an operation to take the fortress depot of Oldenzaal in 1626.[64] With a small army of only 8,000 to 9,000 men the Dutch had more than enough troops to subdue the garrison of Guillermo Verdugo of 700 men after a siege of just eight days, from 25 July to 1 August.

1.3 A Time of Disillusionment in Northern Italy and Flanders: 1627 to 1630

From a military and political point of view the situation of the Hapsburg and the Catholic League at the beginning of 1627 was pretty good. In northern Italy, the Duke of Savoy was not happy with the alliance with France and had switched to close ties with Spain and the new governor of the State of Milan, Gonzalo Fernández de Cordoba. In Germany, the army of the Catholic League had crushed the Danish army and more than ever the Dutch Republic had to deal with a serious threat on the Frisian border.

In fact in 1627, the biggest event in Spanish policy was the bankruptcy,[65] such a major financial event prevented Spain doing anything in the Low Countries. This was not the case for the cousin of Vienna and even with the failure of the siege of Stralsund, the last Danish-Protestant army was destroyed on 2 September 1628 at the battle of Wolgast. The peace of Lübeck was signed in July 1629, ending the Danish phase of the Thirty Years' War. The war could have ended this year, but unfortunately in March 1629 the Emperor Ferdinand II published the edict of restitution[66] (Bonney, 2002).

---

62 See Michal Wanner (2008). Albrecht Wallenstein as General of the Ocean and Baltic Seas and the northern maritime plan, *Forum Navale*, 64 pp. 8–33.
63 At the same time the Dutch could still have the financial support of France established in a new treaty signed in November 1624 and the support of England until 1630.
64 C. Duty, *Siege Warfare: The Fortress in the Early Modern World 1494–1660* (London: Routledge, 1971).
65 Since 1557, the merchant bankers of Genoa had the experience to handle capital and credit and to control most of the transactions and payments in Europe. Such skills were put in good effect by the Spanish to maintain their Empire using most of the time the gold and silver from America. The continuous wars and need for money led to a constant deficit of the Spanish budget, in 1625 and 1626 the debts reached high levels and the only solution was the bankruptcy of 1627. The bankruptcy was a major shock but did not bring down the great bankers of Genoa. The Spanish had to find other bankers, such as the converse of Lisbon to finance their war effort, meantime the Spanish armies and fleets were constrained to paralysis or to a reduction of their actions.
66 The edict of restitution wanted to restore the religious and territorial situation defined by the Peace of Augsburg in 1555, implying that the secularisation of land after 1552 was illegal. In other words, Lutherans had their place in the German Empire but Calvinism did not.

The edict was a show of authority of the Empire and the reaction against electors was to reduce the power and strength of the Imperial army to 40,000 men (excluding the contingent sent to Italy) and that of the Catholic league to 20,000 men. The timing could not be worst for the Catholics, because the Protestants had found a new champion for their cause, the king of Sweden, Gustavus Adolphus.

1627

The lack of funds combined with a crisis in the Army of Flanders' high command gave an opportunity for Frederick Hendricks of Nassau to take the initiative and to restore the prestige and pride of the Dutch Republic. In July 1627, the objective was the fortified city of Groenlo on the Republic's eastern border. Using the River Rhine to transport men, supplies and artillery, Frederick Hendricks assembled an army of 190 companies of infantry and 55 companies of cavalry, roughly 19,000–20,000 men with 75 guns (van Nimwegen, 2010). The army was unloaded at Emmerich am Rhein and surrounded Groenlo on 20 July. Immediately the Dutch started to build fortified camps and lines of circumvallation. At the same time a new supply route was established between the army and the cities of Deventer and Zutphen. Groenlo was well defended by a garrison of 1,200 infantry and 100 riders under the command of Matthijs Dulken. After 10 days, the fortified lines were complete and the Dutch installed batteries to bombard the city. The Spanish field army with some 16,000 infantry and 5,000 cavalry was now under the command of Hendrik van den Bergh and received the order to relieve the city. The lack of funds and supply delayed the arrival of the army and a first action to try to cut the Dutch supply line failed mainly due to the indiscipline of the *maestro de campo* of the Spanish and Italian tercios.[67] For the next action den Bergh decided to break the circumvallation line by a surprise attack the night of 15/16 August by 1,500 men. After an initial success, the Spanish troops were driven back by a counter-attack and were forced to retire. Seeing the impossibility of breaking the enemy line Hendrik van den Bergh withdrew to Brabant and Groenlo capitulated on 19 August. This was the first major victory of the Dutch Republic and was encouraging for the future. The Spanish and the Dutch remained inactive for the rest of the year, the first one looking at what was happening in northern Italy for the succession of Mantua and the second because strong Catholic armies were in the north and east of Frisia.

In 1627, northern Italy was not on the agenda of the Count-Duke of Olivares, peace has been restored the previous year but dynastic problems would soon arise. The Duchy of Mantua was made by two territories, the Duchy of Monferrato and the Duchy of Mantua separated by land under the jurisdiction of the State of Milan, with Mantua on the east and Monferrato on the west. Both of them were feudal territories of the Roman Holy Emperor. The Duke

---

[67] The dispute between Alonso Ladrón and the Marquis of Campolataro had an impact on the conduct of the military operation and de Berg was unable to impose his authority (A. Esteban Estringana, *Madrid y Bruselas: relaciones de gobierno en la etapa postarchiducal 1621–1634* (Leuven: Leuven University Press, 2005)).

of Mantua Vicenzo II of Gonzaga died 26 December 1627 with no natural heir. Different claimants arose to take over the Duchy of Mantua: Charles III of Nevers–Gonzague,[68] supported by Richelieu, Ferrante II, Duke of Guastalla a distant Gonzaga cousin supported by the wife[69] of Emperor Ferdinand II, and the ambitious Charles Emmanuel I, Duke of Savoy who based his claim on a portion of the Gonzaga real, the Duchy of Monferrato. For different reasons, the Duke of Savoy and the Spanish governor of Milan, Gonzalo of Cordoba, agreed on the partition of the Duchy of Monferrato and to support the claim of the Duke of Guastalla with the approval of the Emperor.

1628

The Count-Duke of Olivares was fully aware of the importance of the Mantuan succession and he decided to "forget" the war against the Dutch Republic, so the Army of Flanders remained inactive all the year as well as their Dutch counterpart. In fact the main event occurred when a Dutch fleet managed to capture the Spanish treasure fleet at the battle of the bay of Mantanzas.[70]

In Italy, Charles of Nevers–Gonzague, the French candidate, won the first round when he appeared with a small escort in front of the gates of Mantua in January 1628. In a matter of days he managed to control the city and therefore sent some troops to occupy the main position of the duchy, including Casale Monferrato, a well-fortified town and capital of the Duchy of Monferrato. The Duke of Nevers had played his cards well but to secure his duchy he needed the approval of Ferdinand II and the Emperor was reluctant to give it. France, Venice and the Papacy recognised immediately the new dukes but the Spanish argued that a French candidate could not be nominated Duke of Mantua so the Count-Duke of Olivares gave the order to the governor of Milan to occupy the Duchy of Monferrato with the support of Duke of Savoy (Martinez Canales, 2017). One of the problems for Spaniards and Savoyards was that Ferdinand II did not give any authorisation for such a military expedition and the other ones, due to the lack of funds, the Spanish Army of Lombardy had few soldiers for the operation. The campaign started 29 March 1628, when in a coordinated movement Gonzalo of Cordoba, with 8,000 infantry and fewer than 1,500 cavalry[71] moved to take Pontesturra, Nizza de la Paglia (actually Nizza Monferrato) and later to besiege Casale Monferrato, while the Savoyard army advanced in the territory capturing Trino, San Damiano di Asti, Moncalvo

---

68 Charles III was Duke of Nevers and a son of a younger brother of Vincenzo II's grandfather.
69 Eleanor of Mantua was the sister of Vincenzo II of Mantua; she wanted to re-attach the Duchy of Mantua to the Holy Roman Empire.
70 The fleet of New Spain (commanded by Juan de Benavides) sailed from Veracruz 21 July 1628; it consisted of four galleons and 11 naos armed with 223 guns. Unfortunately for the Spanish, the Dutch Fleet of 29 ships and 623 guns (Pieter de Heyn) was sailing in the West Indies with the goal to disrupt Spanish trade or even to capture the treasure fleet. With the correct information the Dutch Admiral found the Spanish fleet near Cuba, and outgunned, the Spanish decided to enter the Bay of Las Matanzas to disembark the silver from the galleon. The operation was not conducted correctly and the Dutch managed to enter the bay and capture and destroy the Spanish fleet. The booty (silver, goods, ships and artillery) was important and can be estimated from 3.6 to 4.6 million escudos (Dominguez Ortiz 1998).
71 Gonzalo of Cordoba was expecting more troops: 3,000–4,000 men paid by Genoa and a contingent of 900–1,000 Neapolitans.

and Alba. Casale Monferrato was normally defended just by 200 men, but since January Charles of Nevers had managed to send some reinforcements[72] and as we said before the city had modern fortifications.[73] Rapidly, Gonzalo of Cordoba discovered that with just 9,000 men it was impossible to storm the defences of the city and started a more conventional siege. Engulfed by the Protestant uprising,[74] Richelieu could not spare a man to support the Duke of Nevers but he authorised the French nobleman to raise an army in his realm. In August 1628, a small French force appeared in Briançon to cross the Alps, but the expedition was badly prepared and due to the lack of supplies, in a matter of weeks this army disappeared through numerous desertions. At the end of the summer, Gonzalo of Cordoba had probably 12,000 to 13,500 men but it was mostly impossible to recruit more men in Germany or Switzerland due to the lack of money. The blockade was imperfect and some supplies could still enter the city.

1629

The Mantuan succession war had become a priority for Madrid, and in the Low Countries the court of the Archduchess, in Brussels, was in disarray. The war in Italy drained most of the Spanish financial resources and the bankruptcy of 1627 meant that money was difficult to borrow on the market of Antwerp. The army of Flanders was in no condition to take on an offensive movement and could only defend its position. The Dutch council of war saw the opportunity to take the offensive launching an operation against 's-Hertogenbosch. As stated by van Nimwegen (2010), the siege of the city was the beginning of the great Dutch period of 1629–1632. At the end of April 1629, Frederick Hendricks of Nassau arrived suddenly in front of 's-Hertogenbosch,[75] a Brabantian town located five kilometres south of the River Meuse at the junction of the rivers Aa and Dommel. The Dutch, with an army of 20,000 infantry, 4,000 cavalry and 4,000 militia constructed an initial siege line in few days and later reinforced it with six entrenched camps, nine bastioned forts and 12 hornworks.[76] The defence of the circumvallation line was strengthened by the distribution of 116 guns. To attack the city a huge effort was done to drain the water from the river and the surrounding plain, using dykes and mills powered by horses. When this important structural work was complete, the Dutch were able to prepare four separate approaches. As soon as the news reached the Spanish high command, a relief army of

---

72 It is not clear how Charles of Nevers managed to reinforce the garrison of Casale Monferrato. One hypothesis is that he managed to recruit some companies of French mercenaries disbanded by the Duke of Savoy (Martinez Canales, 2017).
73 The defences of the city Casale Monferrato had been modified in the beginning of the seventeenth century, with bastions and hornworks covering the medieval wall and above all the construction modern star citadel with six bastions.
74 On 10 September 1627 the French royal army began the siege of La Rochelle, a French Protestant stronghold. After a siege of 13 months the city capitulated on 28 October 1628.
75 The city of 9,000 to 10,000 inhabitants was well defended with modern fortifications and a regular garrison of 2,500 men, and by the fact that the marshes and polders by 's-Hertogenbosch were a terrain in theory unsuitable for a siege operation (van Nimwegen, 2010).
76 C. Duty (op. cit.)

25,000 men[77] was prepared under the command of Henri van den Bergh. By middle of June, when the Spanish finally arrived near 's-Hertogenbosch, the defence of the Dutch was so strong that van den Bergh decided to withdraw and to mount a diversionary attack directly on the Dutch Republic with the help of Imperial troops.[78]

The Spanish army moved to the east, crossed the River Maas at Mook and the River Rhine at Wesel. The Dutch answer was to reinforce[79] as quickly as possible all the main towns of the region (Arnhem, Doeburg, Zutphen, Deventer and Zwol). On 23 July a small Spanish vanguard[80] managed to cross the River Ijssel at Westervoort and to take a small fortification near Ijsseloord. Frederick Hendricks of Nassau was obliged to send a small force of 5,000 men,[81] under the command of the Count of Stirum, to deal with the threat. The attack of the Spanish position was unsuccessful due to the poor coordination of the Dutch attacks and the fact that the Spanish vanguard had been reinforced. Members of the Dutch State Council asked Frederick Hendricks, unsuccessfully, to abandon the siege of 's-Hertogenbosch to deal with the threat at the heart of the Dutch province. On 28 July, the Spanish army and the Imperial troops crossed the River Ijssel and continued to the west, the Imperial army stopped in the Veluwe forest,[82] but the Spanish managed to take Amersfoort on 14 August. Unfortunately for the Spanish, by a surprise attack, the depot-fortress of Wesel on the River Rhine was taken by a Dutch contingent 19 August, cutting the supply line of the Army of Flanders in Amersfoort. In the middle of a hostile country and with little supply, Henri van den Bergh had to order a retreat below the River Rhine. In 's-Hertogenbosch the siege did not stop: on 18 and 19 July two significant defence works, Fort Isabel and Fort St Antoine, fell to the Dutch. On 11 September a great mine exploded near the Vught gate and three days later the governor of the town, Antoine Schetz, Baron of Grobbendonk, was obliged to capitulate with honourable terms. The loss of 's-Hertogenbosch was a terrible blow to Spanish prestige, but for the Dutch the victory had failed to break significantly the military stalemate that prevailed in the Low Countries (van Nimwegen, 2010).

In northern Italy, the strategic situation changed radically with the end of the siege of La Rochelle against French Protestant rebels. Cardinal Richelieu knew that the army of Flanders was on the defensive and could not undertake any action against north of France, so he convinced Louis XIII

---

77 A Dutch source (van Nimwegen, 2010) gives 30,000 infantry and 7,000 cavalry for the Spanish.
78 10,000 to 14,000 men under the command of the Count of Montecuculli (*Histoire general des pays-bas*).
79 For the operation of 's-Hertogenbosch, the Dutch made a huge effort, raising more than 100,000 men to support the army and defend the heart of the Republic.
80 Initially the vanguard had 400 Croats, five companies of mounted harquebusiers and 800 Spanish musketeers. Rapidly it was reinforced by 1,000 men and two small guns (*Relacion verdadera de la feliz entrada del Exercito Catolico en la Velua, Pays de Holandeses, y destroço que hizo en la gente enemiga, con muerte de mas de dos mil hombres della, intenta[n]do diuertir la del sitio de Volduque*. Cuenca: Julián de la Iglesia, 1629).
81 The Dutch had initially 19 companies of infantry, later reinforced by 13 companies, 10 companies of cavalry and six guns. Dutch Losses were between 200 and 2,000 men.
82 The forest was a good location to attack and plunder the surrounding villages and small town.

to organise a strong army to relieve the siege of Casale Monferrato. Soon the elite of the French army was on the move and 18 February 1629, up to 23,000 infantry and 3,000 cavalry were in the Alps near Briançon. On 28 February the French vanguards[83] crossed the pass of Montgenèvres and 4 March they were at Oulx. The main defensive position of the Savoyard army (3,000 Savoyards and 1,200 Spanish[84]) was a series of barricades in front of the village of Chiomonte. On 6 March at dawn, 1,300 men attacked frontally the first barricades, while 500 men conducted a flanking movement through the mountain. After a poor resistance, the raw recruits of Colonel Bellone abandoned their position, and the French pressed their attack using a second wave of 1,000 men. The Savoyards tried, unsuccessfully, to counterattack with a cavalry charge led by the Marquis of Ville but after some time they were forced to withdraw. The rest of the Savoyard and Spanish troops[85] were unable to keep their ground and retreated, skirmishing with the advancing French infantry. On 7 March the Duke of Savoy was near Rivoli, and the 300 to 400 men left in Susa surrendered the town two days later. Meantime negotiation between French diplomats and the Duke of Savoy were taking place, and by the treaty of Susa a truce was signed on 11 March 1629.[86] Learning of the events at Susa, Gonzalo of Cordoba decided that his main priority was now to defend Lombardy and he withdrew from Casale on 17 March. In fact the French army had serious logistical problems and combined with another uprising of French Protestants, this time in Languedoc, Richelieu was much pleased to end the affair of Mantua as soon as possible. In Spain when Olivares learned the details of treaty of Susa and the retreat of Casale, he could not believe it, a heavy blow had been delivered to the prestige of the Spanish crown. With the approval of the Spanish and the king, he immediately took some measures to reinforce the garrisons in the Pyrenean border, the Spanish tercio of Luis Ponce de Leon was raised in different provinces of Spain and money was found to contract 7,000 German mercenaries. At the same time, diplomatic effort was concentrated to gain the support of Ferdinand II, including the sending of an Imperial army. At last, Gonzalo de Cordoba was also recalled in Madrid to explain his conduct and Ambrogio Spinola was sent to Milan to become governor of the province and to take the situation in hand. In October 1629 a German army of 27,000

---

83   The French vanguard had 47 companies of infantry (Gardes Françaisess, Gardes Suisses, Regiment of Navarre, Regiment of Sault and volunteers) and 800 cavalry, for a total of 6,800–7,000 men with three guns (Périni 1893 ; Martinez Canales, 2017).
84   The ad hoc squadron of 1,200 men comprised of Spanish and Germans was commanded by Jeronimo Agustin y Agustin, *maestro de campo* of the Tercio of Lombardia (Letter of the Duke of Saboya to Gonzáles de Cordoba, Avigliana 7 March 1629, and *Copia de la relacion sobre la escaramuza que se cita en la carta anteriora*, in CODOIN vol. 54, 1869, pp. 420–425).
85   It is not clear what really happened in Susa in March 1629. Due to the fact that the King Louis XIII was with the army, the importance of the "battle" of the Susa pass is somewhat glorified in the French text. Spanish troops were in the reargard and they barely fought during this day.
86   By the treaty of Susa, the Duke of Savoy had to adopt a neutral attitude and to accept French troops in Susa. For such a price the capture of the city of Trino was confirmed and the French agreed to send him an annual funding of 12,000 escudos (Martinez Canales, 2017).

THE ARMIES OF PHILIP IV OF SPAIN 1621–1665

men[87] assembled in Lindau (Germany), crossed the Alps by the Valtellina valley and at the end of November the Imperials were in front of Mantua, and a formal attack was conducted between 22 and 24 December 1629. The defence of Mantua held and with winter coming and logistical problems, the Imperials were forced to withdraw.

1630

For the Count-Duke of Olivares the war of Mantua was still on the agenda, and the disaster in Flanders the previous year indicated that the Italian diversion had to come to an end as quickly as possible. But the war in Italy was not the only problem of the army of Flanders, the Spanish knew that a strong military leadership was needed to restore the efficiency of the army, but it is the contrary that arrived. Brussels was immersed in a deep political and moral crisis:[88] at 63 years old the Archduchess Isabella, with no heir, decide to give back the full control of the Low Countries to Philip IV, to the disgust of some Flemish and Walloon noblemen. Henri van den Bergh was accused of having contact with the Dutch leader and in 1630 he was replaced by the Marquis of Santa Cruz. One light in the sky was the signature of the Anglo-Spanish peace treaty of Madrid in November 1630. The new cordial Anglo-Spanish relationships allowed the Spanish to keep the balance with France and the Low Countries.[89] The possibility of negotiating a truce was on the agenda, but with the development of the war in Italy and the new expedition to Brazil and the conquest of Recife,[90] the

1.11 Gaspar de Guzmán y Pimentel, 1st Duke of Sanlúcar, 3d Count of Olivares. Paulus Pontius, 1616–1657 (Rijksmuseum)

---

87 The Imperial army, commanded by Rambaldo di Collalto, supported by Matthias Gallas and Johann von Aldringen, had 24,000 infantry and 3,000 cavalry but when they arrived in front of Mantua they had only 16,000 infantry and 2,500 cavalry, the rest was left to garrison the Valtellina or had deserted. The defenders of Mantua had 7,000 men and 800 cavalry and were commanded by the Duke of Mantua (Amadei 1955; Martinez Canales 2017).

88 The truce negotiations were well supported by Brussels and some members of the State Council in Madrid, but the Count-Duke of Olivares was less favourable because he wanted to negotiate with the Dutch from a position of strength and in 1630 it was not the case.

89 P. Sanz-Camañes (2009). "La diplomacia beligerante. Felipe IV y el Tratado Anglo-Español de 1630", *Cuad. hist. Esp.* v.83.

90 In 1629, the Dutch launched another expedition against the Brazilian captaincy of Permanbuco and on 14 February 1630 a naval force of 67 ships led by Hendrick Loncq with 3,780 sailors and 3,500 soldiers appeared in front of Olinda. The city was captured after a small fight and in March Recife, the capital of the Permanbuco Captaincy, and António Vaz, were taken with little effort even if the Portuguese sugar fleet manage to escape to Lisbon. The Dutch tried to expand their control, but stiff resistance from the Portuguese frustrated their attempts. The reaction in Madrid and Lisbon was to create a new relief force to reinforce the garrison of Salvador do Bahia and Paraibà. The Spanish–Portuguese fleet of 53 ships (Armada del mar Oceano 13 galleons

truce negotiation was made undesirable and useless. On the Dutch side little was achieved after the campaign of 's-Hertogenbosch, Frederick Hendricks of Nassau launched small attacks to secure the eastern border but the main actions were taking place on the sea. Using their fleet of privateers, the Spanish had some success[91] against Dutch trading and sometime bitter fighting occurred against the Dutch fleet blocking the Flemish coast.

In northern Europe, the main event of 1630 was the landing of an army 14,000 men of the Swedish King Gustavus Adolphus on the coast of Pommeria. At first the Swedish King was more concerned to recruit more soldiers[92] than to fight the Catholic force.

In north Italy, unsuccessful negotiation by the papacy was conducted to end the war during the winter, but by the end of February 1630 Ambrogio Spinola and Rambaldo di Collalto had the green light to resume the military operations against Casale Monferrato and Mantua. With a force estimated at 20,000 men, Spinola entered into a campaign and his vanguard rapidly took with ease some positions, such as Nizza de Monferrato, Pontestura or Rosignano Monferrato. On 23 May, the besiegers had surrounded Casale defended by 2,000 infantry and 300 cavalry, commanded by the Lord of Toiras. While the core of the Spanish force was besieging Casale their ally, the Duke of Savoy, supported by a small contingent of Spanish troops, had to face a new French invasion of his duchy. On 17 May Chambery was occupied by the French army directly commanded by King Louis XIII,[93] and the Tarentaise valley was conquered during the next six weeks. On 7 July another French force, commanded by Duke Henry of Montmorency, crossed the Alps at the Mont Cenis pass with 10,000 men and rejoined the French garrison of Susa. On 10 July, the French inflicted a severe defeat on the Savoyard army at Avigliana, and rapidly the Marquisat of Saluce was occupied. On 28 July the old Duke of Savoy died aged 68 years and the new duke, Victor Amadeus of Savoy, had a more pro-French attitude than his father and quickly opened negotiations with the French. In the east, the Imperial vanguard of 9,000 men defeated a Venetian force of 6,000 men on 25 May near Valeggio sul Mincio and continued south to besiege Mantua. By July 1630, the defence

---

and three patches with 324 guns and 3,586 men; Squadron of Portugal five galleons with 103 guns and 982 men, 12–18 transport ships with 3,000 soldiers and supply and 17 caravels with 700 men) sailed on 5 May 1631 to Brazil and 68 days later manage to safely disembark the reinforcements. On 12 September a naval battle took place against a Dutch fleet of 16 ships; three major Dutch ships were sunk for the price of two Spanish galleons and one Portuguese (Fernández Duro volume IV, 1895).

91 Only the privateers of Dunkirk had some success with the capture of 244 ships 1629 and 278 in 1632 (Starling 1992).

92 Sweden and France signed the treaty of Bärwalde the 23 of January 1631. By this treaty France agreed to pay subsidy of 375,000 escudos/year (400,000 reichsthalers/year) for five years. With the French money Gustavus Adolphus was able to recruit and train an army of 30,000 infantry and 6,000 cavalry in Germany. Since 1624, France had a subsidy arrangement with the Dutch; it was renewed in 1630 and 1634 (Parker 2003).

93 The army had 20,000 men, mostly infantry, and the Marshals Créqui, Châtillon and Bassompierre had the real command. Facing them we find Thomas of Savoy with 9,000 infantry (3,000 regulars, 3,000 militia and 3,000 mercenaries) and 1,000 cavalry (Périni volume III, 1893).

of Mantua was weak, mainly due to the plague[94] and on 18 July the Imperial forces[95] managed to take the main bridge of the city and to enter the centre. While the duke escaped to a neighbouring fortress, the city was sacked for three days by the Imperial force.

Meantime, in Casale, the progress of the Spanish army was slow, the lines of circumvallation and contravallation were erected and three approaches were dug to attack the city. The poor living conditions and the bubonic plague had reduced the army and constant reinforcement was needed to maintain the siege. By the end of August the city had fallen into Spanish hands, but the citadel still held out with a garrison of 1,500 men and a French vanguard had managed to cross the River Pô at Carignano. Spinola[96] was depressed and sick and he was replaced by the Marquis of Santa Cruz.[97] On 8 September a truce of five weeks was signed between the Spanish and the French, Madrid had sent orders to negotiate an armistice as soon as possible. At the end diplomacy prevailed, the plague was killing thousands of people across northern Italy, the Imperial forces were needed to the north, due to the Swedish invasion (see below), Paris had reached its most important objective and Madrid had nothing to win but to end the struggle. The peace of Cherasco signed on 19 June 1631 confirmed the inheritance of Charles di Gonzaga Duke of Nevers and Duke of Mantua, the Duke of Savoy recovered his duchy, France kept, by a secret agreement, the control of Pignerolo and the Spanish returned to Lombardy with nothing. The Mantua succession war was probably one the main failures of Olivares (Elliot, 1990).

1.4 Spain and the Swedish Phase of the Thirty Years' War: 1631–1634

Due to the presence of a Swedish army on the Baltic coast, the so-called "Thirty Years' War" would take a different path than expected for the monarchs from the Hapsburg dynasty in Vienna but also in Madrid.

---

94 The plague appeared in northern Italy in 1629. In Mantua the first case was reported in November 1629, 1,152 deaths in January, 1,088 in February, 1,100 in March, 2,243 in April, 3,978 in May, so 9,600 deaths in four months total population, with refugees doubling the city population to 60,000. It spread rapidly to the major cities of the region killing thousands of people; the origin was in the north/east of France and Germany (Amadei 1955).

95 The Imperial army was reduced to 12,400 infantry and 1,700 cavalry (Amadei 1955). Parker (2003) gives a number of 12,000 soldiers for 1631.

96 Ambrogio Spinola was removed from his command by an order of Madrid. The Count-Duke of Olivares had always distrusted the old soldier. Spinola retired to Castelnuovo di Scrivia to die on 25 September 1630; one of the great Spanish commanders died alone only with his honour.

97 Álvaro de Bazán y Benavides, second Marquis of Santa Cruz (1571–1646), from 1612 to 1630 he was commander of the Ecuadra de Galeras de Napoles, from 1630 to 1631, Governor of Lombardy and in 1632 General Governor of the Army of Flanders.

1631

The negotiation to implement the peace in Italy meant that Madrid could support the army of Flanders again with money and troops.[98] On the other side, the action of the Spanish privateers against the Dutch shipping and fishing activities, gave new targets for the Dutch commander and for this year the campaign had to be conducted to neutralise the harbours on the Flemish coast. The Dutch plan was known by the Spanish commander and when the Dutch army landed on 30 May 1631 near IJzendijke, the Spanish had already reinforced the garrison of the city of Bruges and the surrounding area. The Dutch turned back and it was at this moment the Spanish decided to launch a surprise attack on Willenstad in Holland. Again the strict secrecy of the operation was broken and when the Spanish fleet of troop-ships put to sea it was mostly destroyed at the battle of the Slaak[99] on 12 September 1631.

More to the east, in northern Germany, Swedish king Gustavus Adolphus had spent most of the previous year recruiting troops, and in spring 1631, he was ready to move to the south in an attempt to relieve the city of Magdeburg besieged by the Count of Tilly. On 20 May the city fell and immediately was sacked by the Catholic forces. The sack of Magdeburg, with the death of up to 20,000 inhabitants, was one of the most horrible incidents of the Thirty Years' War, and outraged all of Protestant Europe. In the summer, the Protestant leader had an army of 42,000 men[100] in hand and when he met the main Catholic army of 32,000 men at the battle of Breitenfeld, on 17 September 1631, he won one of the most famous victories of the Thirty Years' War. The destruction[101] of the army of the Count of Tilly was a major blow for Habsburg interests. With victory in hand, Gustavus Adolphus turned to the west through the region of Franconia, Thuringia and finally to the Rhine valley, taking Würzburg and Marienburg in October, Frankfurt in November and later Mainz[102] on 19 December 1631, where he took his winter quarters. The appearance of the Swedish troops in the west caused panic in the Catholic electorates of Mainz and Koln and gave a unique opportunity to the French. Richelieu was not very happy about the winter quarters of the Swedish army in Mainz, but by careful diplomatic effort combined with the occupation of the Duchy of Lorraine he managed to present himself as a defender of the Catholic faith. On the other side of the hill, Madrid and Brussels had no troops available to stop the Swedish advance and could not pretend to be anymore the protector of the Catholic state of the west. One must remember that from a Spanish point of view, the link with the Hapsburgs in Vienna was

---

98 In March 5, 500 infantry were sent and in July and August other 8,890 infantry (nine tercios) and 1,530 cavalry (33 companies) went to the north through the Valtellina and Rhine valleys (Ribot Garcia 1991).
99 Following van Nimwegen (2010), 83 troop-ships and 4,000 men were lost (dead, wounded, and prisoners).
100 Swedish forces 14,840 infantry and 8,060 cavalry, Saxon forces 13,000 infantry and 5,220 cavalry for a total of 27,840 infantry and 13,280 cavalry; for the Protestants 21,400 infantry, and 10,000 cavalry for the Catholics (Bonney 2002).
101 Catholic losses were appalling with 10,000–12,000 dead and 6,000 prisoners.
102 The fortress of Mainz was defended by a Spanish garrison. The strange thought was that officially Madrid and Stockholm were at peace (Negredo del Cerro, 2016).

important and that peace in Germany was crucial to face on one hand the Dutch republic and the growing interference of France in Europe affairs. For the Spanish, French money and diplomatic support was one of the motors of the anti- Hapsburg action in Europe. The Swedish advance towards the Rhine valley gave to the French the pretext to establish a French garrison in Germany, for example in the city of Trier on the banks of the River Moselle. In fact, for the Count-Duke of Olivares the irruption of the French in the German affair was even worse than the Swedish invasion. But in 1631, France was still not prepared to fight[103] the Spanish directly so all the politic action of Richelieu was to fight the Hapsburgs by proxy.

1632

With the reinforcements sent in 1631, and the signature of a new treaty with the Imperials on 14 February 1632, Olivares decided to recover the initiative in the Low Countries and in Germany. The idea of the *valido* was to organise three armies, one in the Palatinate under the command of Gonzalo de Cordoba, one in Alsace to secure the Rhine valley under the command of the Prince Gaston of Orleans[104] and the last in Catalonia under the command of the Cardinal Infante Fernando of Austria. In the mind of the Spanish authorities, the brother of Philip IV was to be sent to Lombardy and later to the Low Countries in order to have a prince of royal blood at the head of Spanish Flanders. All the nice strategy of Olivares went down when the Dutch commander Frederick Hendricks of Nassau launched his proper attack. The disaffection of some Flemish and Walloon nobles, such as Hendrik van den Bergh, towards the Spanish crown, gave opportunity for the Dutch to play a master card, the conquest of Maastricht followed by the invasion of Brabant. At the end of May 1632, an army of 28,000 men moved to the east and took without effort the towns of the Upper Gelderland (Geldern, Stralen, Venlo and Roermond). On 10 June the Dutch vanguard was below the wall of Maastricht, the Spanish were taken completely by surprise. While, Frederick Hendricks of Nassau was leaving 5,000 men to secure his line of communication in Upper Guelders in order to communicate with Nijmegen, he started immediately the construction of long and powerful lines of circumvallation and contravallation to surround the city. When trench approaches were made to attack the city, a Spanish relief force of 23,000 men commanded by the Marquis of Santa Cruz arrived in the area on 27 June. Seeing the strong position, the Marquis established a fortified camp in Lanaken, a village north of Maastricht and waited for reinforcement from the Palatinate and from the Imperial army of the Count of Pappenheim. In August, Spanish and Imperial forces had arrived in the vicinity as well as reinforcements for the Dutch army. The divided command on the Spanish side

---

103 In fact the foreign policy of Richelieu against the main Catholic power had to face strong domestic opposition and even conspiracy such as the "Day of the Dupes" on 10 November 1630, organised by a faction led by the Queen Mother Marie of Medicis and encouraged by Spain. After the "Day of the Dupes" the Queen Mother had to escape to Brussels (Parker, 2003).

104 Gaston of Orleans was the brother of the King of France Louis XIII and with his mother Maria of Medicis they regularly threatened the position of Richelieu. At the end of 1631, the prince was in Brussels to receive 234,000 escudos.

1.12 Cardinal Infante Fernando of Austria. Antony van der Does, 1634–1680 (Rijksmuseum)

made it mostly impossible to coordinate correctly an attack on the Dutch line. On 17 August, Pappenheim lost patience and without the full cooperation of the other commanders he ordered an assault on the Dutch line. The attack was a failure and the Imperial troops lost up to 1,500 men. The result was disappointment for the Spanish, the garrison of Maastricht was forced to capitulate on 22 August due to the lack of powder, Pappenheim was recalled to the east in early September and the Marquis of Santa Cruz withdrew to Brabant. On 8 September the Dutch troops occupied Limburg and on 16 November they took Orsoy on the River Rhine. The Dutch successes could have been followed by a movement towards Brussels, but the supply line of the Dutch army was overstretched, the revolt of the Flemish or Walloons against the Spanish did not occur and Frederick Hendricks of Nassau was a good commander to fight among fortresses, dykes, rivers and marshes, common in the Dutch republic although was less confident to fight the Spanish in the open field in Brabant. On the Spanish side, the Marquis of Santa Cruz was replaced

THE ARMIES OF PHILIP IV OF SPAIN 1621–1665

1.13 Cardinal Infante Fernando of Austria and Archduke Ferdinand in 1634. Pieter de Jode, 1675–1685 (Rijksmuseum)

by the Marquis of Aytona.[105]

More to the east the Swedish army of Gustavus Aldolphus started the new campaign in spring 1632 with the goal of crippling Bavaria, one of the main supporters of the Catholic League. The main combat took place on 15 April, at the battle of the River Lech between the main Catholic army of the Count of Tilly and the Swedish army. Gustavus Adolphus' infantry stormed the River Lech under the cover of his artillery and managed to repulse the opposing forces. In the combat, Count Tilly was mortally wounded and the Duke of Bavaria had to order a retreat. Bavaria now lay open to invasion and on 17 May a defenceless Munich was taken by the Swedish. In Vienna, Emperor Ferdinand II had no choice but to recall Albrecht Wallenstein to rebuild the Imperial army. In a matter of weeks, the "condottiere" had managed to create a sizeable Imperial force using his prodigious resources and the surviving Imperial regiments. By the end of May, he was able to recapture Prague[106] from the Saxons and was moving west to check the Swedish and besieged the city of Nuremberg. The Swedish king's army had deliberately sacked Bavaria, and when he learnt of the Catholic movement he stopped his campaign and moved north to confront Wallenstein. In July, Swedish reinforcements arrived and the Swedish king had more than 40,000 men in hand but the "condottiere" was well installed in his main fortified camps at Alta Veste and refused to fight a pitched battle. During more than six weeks the two armies faced each other and in the hot summer, disease, malnutrition and hunger took the lives of thousands of men. On 3 September Gustavus Adolphus misunderstood the movement of the Imperial army and launched a disastrous attack on the Alta Veste camp. Leaving 6,000 infantry and 300 cavalry in the city, the depleted Swedish broke camp and left the area to the south-west on 18 September. On the other side, Wallenstein was happy to have inflicted losses on the Swedish and few days later he was moving to the north-east, towards the city of Bamberg. For the next two months, the Swedish were in Swabia and Bavaria and the Imperials[107] were

---

105 Francisco de Moncada i Moncada, third Marquis of Aytona (1586–1635). He served the Spanish crown as ambassador to the Imperial court in Vienna from 1624 to 1629. In 1630 he was called in Flanders to take the command of the Dunkirk squadron, in 1632 he was appointed Governor General of the Army of Flanders and became Governor of Flanders by interim in 1634.
106 Prague had submitted to the Saxon army the previous year in a campaign following the battle of Breitenfeld.
107 The army of Pappenheim was recalled from to the west to participate in the campaign against Saxony.

concentrating all their forces to deal with Saxony. Gustavus Adolphus saw an opportunity to finally oblige Wallenstein to fight a pitched battle. After different manoeuvres and mistakes in both camps, the two armies met south of Leipzig. The battle of Lützen[108] was fought on 16 November 1632 and after more than five hours of heavy fighting the artillery position of Wallenstein was taken. During the night the Imperial force retreated to Leipzig and two days later to Bohemia. The Swedish had won a pyrrhic battle, losses had been heavy, particularly that of the king himself, probably shot at midday after a cavalry engagement on the Swedish right. The main consequence of the battle was that the Protestant cause had lost its leader and most of what had been done for the last two years was at risk, but for the Spanish authorities there was an opportunity to recover position.

1633

For the Spanish the previous campaign had been a disaster and Brussels thought that again it was possible to re-open negotiations for a truce or ceasefire. Discussions took place for five months but by mid June it was clear that the Dutch demands were unacceptable for the Spanish monarchy and negotiations were suspended. On the contrary, for the Dutch, the previous campaign had fulfilled all expectations and the new objective was the control of the River Rhine and the town of Rheinberg defended by 1,700 men. In 22 days, the Dutch force subdued the defence of the city and with no relief army on the horizon, the garrison capitulated on 2 June 1633. Then the Dutch Stadtholder moved to Nijmegen and waited for the result of the discussion with the French ambassador. Before going deeper into Spanish territories, Frederick Hendricks of Nassau wanted to have the guarantee that France would support the Dutch Republic not only sending money but also with troops. In September he finally moved to threaten the Brabant from the east but each time he was met by the Spanish army in front of him. For the Spanish, other actions were taking place in Madrid and northern Italy. The new plan was to re-establish the Spanish control of the Rhine valley and to support the efforts of Vienna and Bavaria against the Swedish. To do so, a mobile force of 24,000 men[109] commanded by the Duke of Feria[110] should be assembled in Lombardy and sent to the Upper Rhine and another smaller force of 10,000 men should escort the Cardinal Infante Fernando of Austria to take his governorship in the Low Countries. For the Governor of Lombardy, the organisation of an army of 24,000 men was a nightmare: in May 1633, the Army of Lombardy had only 13,840 men (Ribot Garcia, 1990). On 1 August 1633, after five months of intensive preparation to join all the components of his army, the Duke of Feria had only 19,140

---

108 A description of the battle is available in R. Brzezinski, *Lützen 1632* (Oxford: Osprey Campaign Series 68, 2001).
109 The plan made in Madrid gives infantry: 1,500 Spanish (all veterans), 6,000 Lombards and Neapolitans (4,000 veterans), 4,000 Burgundians and up to 8,500 Germans. Cavalry, 1,500 Italians and 2,500 Germans (de la Bocha et al., 2010).
110 Gómez Suarez de Figueroa y Cordoba, 3rd Duke of Feria (1587–1634).

men available. On 22 August, the Duke left Milan with 11,590 men[111] and on 12 September the Spanish commander with a small vanguard was in Innsbruck where he found another 2,300 German soldiers. In September 1633, the situation of the war in Germany was as follows: after the death of Gustavus Adolphus, the Swedish councillor Axel Oxenstierna had managed to regularise relations between the German Protestant princes[112] and the Swedes by the signature of the League of Heilbronn in April 1633. On paper, the Protestants had up to 100,000 men divided in different armies[113] and garrisons. Under the command of the Rhinegrave and Gustav Horn, they had conquered most of the cities of the Upper Rhine and further to the north won, on 8 July, the battle of Oldentorf in Westphalia. In September 1633, Horn was besieging Konstanz and the first goal of the Duke of Feria was to save the city. At first he managed to send a reinforcement of 2,100 men and later organised a powerful relief force of 12,000 Spanish and 10,000 Bavarians.[114] Outnumbered, the Swedish commander Gustav Horn decided to retire to the north losing 2,000 men in the process. The Catholic armies followed the Rhine valley and in a matter of days, the cities of Waldshut, Laufenburg, Sackingen and Rheinfelden were retaken and on 19 October the Swedish had to abandon the siege of Brisach, the first strategic objective of Feria was achieved. But while Feria and Aldringen were clearing Alsace of the Swedish/Protestant garrison and the Imperial army was doing the same in Silesia, after the victory of Steinau,[115] the Protestant commander Bernhard of Saxe-Weimar captured Regensburg on 13 November threatening again Bavaria. The slow reaction of Albrecht Wallenstein and above all his refusal to undertake a campaign to recover Regensburg obliged the Duke of Bavaria to recall the army of Aldringen. At the same time, in the west a French army had invaded again the Duchy of Lorraine threatening the Catholic forces in Alsace. Therefore the Duke of Feria was alone in a devastated country, with a small army, slightly reinforced by small contingents. Feria decided to answer the call of the Bavarians and the Spanish army turned back to the east, in order to support the Bavarians, to have his winter quarters in the Tyrol and to wait for the army of the Cardinal Infante in 1634. In difficult weather conditions and pressed by the army of Gustav Horn, the Spanish crossed the

---

111 Infantry: 2,560 men Tercio of Juan Diaz de Zamorano (Spanish), 1,590 men from the Tercio of Juan Bautista Paniguerola (Lombards), 2,181 men from the Tercio of the Marquis of Torrecusa (Neapolitans), 2,300 men from the regiment of Schamburg (German) and 1,610 men from the regiment of the Count of Solms (German). Cavalry: five companies from the Cavalry of the State of Milan with 350 men and 20 companies of cavalry from Naples with 1,000 men. Total 10,240 infantry and 1,350 cavalry (de la Bocha et al., 2010).
112 For different reasons, the Protestant electors of Brandenburg and Johann-Georg of Saxony refused to join the League. See Parker (2003) for more information.
113 In September 1633 the main Protestant-Swedish armies had some 7,000 men near Breisach in Alsace (Otto Ludwig, the Rhinegrave), 10,000 men besieging Konstanz (Gustav Horn), 6,000 men in Württemberg, 10,000 men in Donauwörth (Bernhard of Saxe-Weimar), 13,000 men in Westphalia (Baron Knyphausen) and 8,000 men in Saxony (Thurn) (de la Rocha et al., 2010).
114 The Duke of Bavaria had been convinced by the Spanish ambassador to let his field army of 6,000 infantry, 4,000 cavalry and 24 guns under the command of Johann Aldringen participate in the action in the Rhine valley.
115 The Battle of Steinau was fought 8 November 1633. See Guthrie (2002) for a detailed account.

Black Forest and arrived safely at their destination by the end of November. Unfortunately for Olivares, the harsh campaign in southern Germany and an epidemic of typhus had taken a heavy toll[116] on the Spanish forces and one of the major losses was the death of the Duke of Feria 2 January 1634.

1634

The next year, on 15 April 1634, France and the Dutch Republic concluded an "offensive" alliance against the Spanish. In the treaty France would increase the subsidies to the Dutch army and the Dutch would conduct on land and sea with all their force, but he was no question of France declaring war on Spain, although that happening was just a question of time. In Madrid, the "voyage" of the Cardinal Infante Fernando of Austria was the main objective to restore the balance in the Low Countries and Germany.

In Flanders, the first to move was the Duke of Aytona, taking a 30,000 men[117] strong field army he moved towards Maastricht in July to the surprise of the Dutch commander. The idea of Aytona was to follow the movement of a French army mobilised near Luxembourg's border and to evaluate the possibility of retaking Maastricht. The Dutch reaction was to mobilise a strong army of 18,000 men and to move to Breda. Therefore, Aytona divided his army into two corps and with the strongest one he came back to Brabant to save Breda. The Dutch did not want to confront the Spanish and with his objective to save Maastricht achieved he withdrew to 's-Hertogenbosch. The rest of the campaign did not bring any relevant military actions. In Germany, the main news was the assassination[118] of Wallenstein 25 February at Eger. The Imperial army was now at the direct command of the Emperor Ferdinand II through his son Ferdinand of Hungary. On the Protestant side, the death of Wallenstein gave the opportunity to Axel Oxenstierna to try to reinforce the league of Heilbronn, but again Brandenburg and Saxony accepted to be allied to the Swedes but they did not sign the league treaty. This year the military operation started late, with the Saxons advancing through Silesia and Bohemia, while the main Swedish armies under Gustav Horn and Bernhard of Saxe-Weimar were advancing towards the south-east, taking Landshut on 25 July. The Imperials did not remain inactive and Regensburg and Donauwörth were retaken respectively in July and on 13 August.

On the side of the Alps, the army[119] assembled by the Cardinal Infante, started its journey to rejoin the rest of the army of the Duke of Feria now commanded by the Count of Serbelloni in Bavaria. The Cardinal Infante left Milan 30 June and one month later most of the troops were resting from the passage of the Alps in the Tirol province. On 25 August the two Spanish corps were assembled in Munich and the Cardinal Infante was preparing his army to support the campaign of

---

116 Following de la Bocha et al. (2010) 26 percent of the Spanish infantry was lost as well as 57 percent of the Italian infantry and 25 percent of the German.
117 Infantry was made by four Spanish tercios, three Italian tercios, seven Walloon tercios, six German regiments, one English tercio and two Irish. The cavalry comprised 68 companies and five German regiments (Albi de la Cuesta 2015).
118 More about the German Condottiere see G. Mortimer, *Wallenstein: The Enigma of the Thirty Years' War* (Basingstoke: Palgrave Macmillan, 2010).
119 12,480 Infantry and 2,170 cavalry (Ribot Garcia, 1990).

the Imperial commander Ferdinand of Hungary. After some successes retaking Regensburg on 27 July and Donauwörth 16 August, the Catholic armies were besieging Nördlingen since 18 August. Therefore the Spanish moved towards the north and arrived in Nördlingen on 3 September. On the Protestant side, the two commanders decided to join their two armies and to march south to face their enemies. On 4 September they decided to attack the Catholic position by the south, and on 5 September after bitter fighting they had managed to take the Ländle Hill and the Heselberg wood but the key position of the Albuch hill was in Catholic hands. During the night the Catholic commanders established a strong position on the Albuch hill, with troops from the Spanish and Imperial armies. Next day, the battle of Nördlingen[120] was fought between two of the best troops available in Europe and on 7 September the magnitude of the Catholic victory could be seen. The main Protestant field armies have been mostly destroyed and the survivors, led by Bernhard of Saxe–Weimar, were fleeing to the west, towards the city of Frankfurt-am-Main. On 8 September the garrison of Nördlingen surrendered with honourable terms. The Spanish army had largely contributed to this extraordinary victory but now the main goal of the Cardinal Infante was to arrive in the Low Countries before winter. On 10 September 1634, the Spanish army left the battlefield with the core of the Imperial army. The Spanish force crossed the south-west of Germany in September and October, retaking cities and fortresses from the Swedish and on 4 November the Cardinal Infante made a triumphal entrance into Brussels.

1.5 Crucial Years Towards a Total War: 1635 to 1639

The consequence of the battle of Nördlingen was not only the re-conquest of most of the south and central Germany or the displacement of the war in Silesia, Saxony where the last Swedish army of Banérs could be found, but had also serious political consequences (Negredo del Cero 2017). The main Catholic powers, the Holy Roman Empire, the Spanish Monarchy and the Catholic princes redefined their relationship by the treaty of Ebersdorf.[121] In order to survive, the Protestant league of Heilbronn had also to redefine its alliance, Sweden was out of the scene but the French monarchy was most keen to take its place. In fact France had to rethink its alliance system to face the victorious Habsburgs and more importantly, France would have to directly engage its armies as Sweden, the Dutch Republic and the German Protestant princes could not fight alone any more. For Spain the victory had a positive impact but the Count-Duke of Olivares knew perfectly that the intervention of the French monarchy was just a question of months and the prospect of

---

120 A description of the battle is presented in Chapter 4, pp. 271–282.
121 The secret treaty of Ebersdorf signed on 31 October 1634 was supposed to revive the programme of the old Catholic League and to establish the Holy Roman Empire as a whole (including the circle of Burgundy) should assist the Spanish king (as Duke of Burgundy) in his struggle against the insurgence of the Dutch Republic, but there was nothing concerning a war against France. The future would show that the Spanish and Germans had a different interpretation of the treaty (Negredo del Cero, 2016).

fighting on two fronts in the Low Countries was not so positive. At last for the Dutch Republic the possibility of facing the Spanish and Imperial armies led to an increase of the army and a tightening of the alliance with France. In Germany, the results of the battle resurrected the possibility of concluding a peace treaty between the Lutheran prince of Saxony and the Elector of Brandenburg with the Emperor.

1635

The first significant event in 1635 was the new French–Dutch treaty signed 8 February in Paris. In the treaty the articles of previous agreements were confirmed but as noted by Negredo del Cero (2017) in the new articles the sharing of the Spanish Low Country territories was now written.[122] On the military side, the two allies would have to coordinate their attack with two respective armies of 25,000 men. On 26 March 1635, a Spanish force of 1,500 men, from Luxembourg, took Trier by surprise killing most of the French garrison.[123] For the Spanish, the action was a defensive one, because it deprived the French of a strong position on the River Rhine but for most of the German princes (including Catholic princes) the action was out of proportion and was condemned. For the French it was the *casus belli* they were expecting and on 16 May a formal declaration of war was sent to Brussels. The declaration of war surprised the Spanish authorities and while the Army of Flanders was fully mobilised, the Army of Lombardy[124] had only 13,250 men in May 1635 and most of them had not enough training due to the departure of so many veterans in 1633 and 1634. Further to the south the military structure of the Iberian Peninsula was not prepared to raise, organise, feed and maintain sizeable field armies. At last troops had to be sent in Brazil to reinforce the Portuguese force against the Dutch colony in Permanbuco.[125]

Coming back to Europe, in March 1635, Richelieu had already anticipated his move and a small French army under the command of the Duke of Rohan with the support of Protestant Swiss cantons, crossed the Alps to take control of the Valtellina valley. With his small army and the cooperation of Grison's troops, Rohan conducted a brilliant campaign,[126] defeating the Imperial

---

122 The Duchy of Luxembourg, County of Namur, County of Hainaut, County of Artois and County of Flanders for the French and the Duchy of Brabant, Duchy of Limburg, Lordship of Malines (Mechelen in Dutch) and Duchy of Gelders for the Dutch (Negredo del Cero, 2016).
123 We have to remember that the French garrison was present to protect the city against the Swedes. The French had also a garrison in Philippsburg but this one was taken by the Imperial force. At last Heidelberg and Spire were taken by the French.
124 Also the new governor of Lombardy don Diego Mexía Felipez de Guzmán y Dávila (1580–1655), first *Marquis of Leganés*, was still in Spain and was temporarily replaced by the Cardinal Albornoz and Carlos Colonna.
125 From 1633 to 1635, the Dutch had taken the Island of Itamaracá in 1633, Paraibà in October 1634 and Arraial in June 1635. Reinforcements were sent to take the offensive, but on 18 January 1636 the Spanish–Portuguese forces of 1,400 men commended by Luis de Rojas were defeated at the battle of Mata Redonda by an equivalent Dutch force commanded by Colonel Arciszevski.
126 The campaign of the Valtellina of 1635 is described in the Memoire of the Duke of Rohan (*Mémoires sur la Guerre de la Valteline*, Par Henri I duc de Rohan).

forces in different encounters[127] and the small Spanish corps[128] of the Count of Serbelloni on 9 November at the Battle of Morbegno.

In Flanders, the treaty between France and the Dutch Republic was put into practice. The 13 of May, the combined French army of 26,500–29,000 men[129] of the Field Marshal of Chatillon and Field Marshal of Brézé started their campaign in Sedan to rejoin the Dutch army of 20,000 men of Frederick Hendricks of Nassau. On 16 May the small Spanish garrison of Marche-en-Famenne surrendered to the French and three days later they were at Tinlot where detachments of Spanish cavalry were found. On the other side, the Cardinal Infante had 30,000 men in hand, divided in a small army of 8,000–9,000 men[130] under the command of Prince Thomas of Savoy watching the French and with the main force he was supervising the Dutch movement. The Spanish strategy was to not engage the enemies and remain on the defensive, but for some reason the Prince Thomas of Savoy-Carignano deployed his small army in Avein (probably between Tinlot and Huy) to ambush the French. Badly outnumber by the French force, the Spanish and Italian Tercios fought bravely[131] during the battle of Avein, on 20 May, but at the end numbers prevailed and the Spanish were mostly destroyed. The victorious French continued their advance and met the Dutch army of 20,000 men[132] coming from Maastrich near Tirlemont. The governor of the small city, Martin de Los Arcos tried to defend the place, but after three days his position was hopeless and he decided to surrender. On 10 June, while negotiation was taking place to agree on the articles of the capitulation, Dutch or French troops scaled the walls and stormed the city. Tirlemont was completely sacked and burned by the soldiers of the two nations. The horrible event had a negative effect for the French and Dutch, firstly, all the food supplies of the city were lost, secondly for the inhabitants

---

127 Battle of Livigno on 27 June, Battle of Mazzo 29 of June and Battle of Val Fraele on 31 October.
128 Infantry 4,000 men from Spanish companies from the Tercio of Lombardia and the Tercio of Saboya, the Italian Tercio of Trivulzi reinforced by companies of the Italian Tercio of Aragona and the German regiment of Ludovico Guasco. Cavalry 400 men from five companies (San Secondo, Layzaldi, Bandi, Morone and Montery) (U. Martinelli, *Le Guerre per la Valtellina nel secolo XVII*, Varese: Istituto Editoriale Cisalpino, 1935).
129 The army had 19 infantry regiments with 22,000–24,000 infantry and 5,130 cavalry (53 companies). G. Lasconjarias, Avein, 20 MAI 1635: "La France entre dans la guerre de Trente Ans", *Revue Internationale d'Histoire militaire* 82, 2002.
130 The army was made of 1,500 cavalry under the command of the Count of Bucquoy, an artillery with 12 guns and an infantry with 5,270 men coming from the Spanish Tercio of Ladrón de Guevara, Italian Tercio of Segismondo Sfrondato, Walloon Tercio of the Count of Frezin, the Lorraine regiment of François de Brun and the German regiment of the Count of Hoogstraten. To such units we should add the Tercio of Thomas Preston (Irish) and the Tercio of Ribaucourt (Walloon). Following J.L. Sanchez (2000) the last two were not present the day of the battle and de Mesa (2014) indicates that both of them were in Louvain.
131 As always it is difficult to estimate losses. For the Spanish Albi de la Cuesta (2015) gives a number of 1,500 dead and 800 prisoners, others like Parrot (2001) give Spanish losses at 4,800 men, what is sure is that all the artillery was lost. For the French losses it is even more complicated: the numbers go from only 260 men to 1,500 men. Lasconjarias (op. cit.) gives a number of 20,000 infantry and 4,000 cavalry after the battle, but most of the French losses were due to desertion.
132 A small force of 8,000 men (95 infantry companies and seven cavalry companies) under the command of the Count of Siegen-Nassau was to defend the eastern border between the rivers Rhine, Meuse, Moselle and Ijssel (van Nimwegen, 2010).

of Brabant it was not possible to see the Dutch and French as liberators of the Spanish oppression, in reality for them they were much more considered as brutal invaders. Meantime, the Cardinal Infante was joining all available force behind the River Dyle (or Dijle in Dutch) and by mid June he had some 20,000 infantry and 7,000 cavalry (Albi de la Cuesta 2015). At the same time he was sending letters to the Emperor Ferdinand II requesting the help of an Imperial army operating in western Germany. On 30 May, the Emperor had signed the treaty of Prague that ended the hostilities with the Lutheran German prince (Elector of Saxony and Elector of Brandenburg), the principle of *cuius region, eius religio* was firmly re-established in the empire. The Thirty Years' War was not over because German French allies such as Hesse-Kassel, Bernhard of Saxe-Weimar[133] in the west or the Swedish in Pomerania were still at war. Nonetheless, Ferdinand II could answer to the Spanish request and a force of 12,000 men under the command of Ottavio Piccolomini was moving for the Low Countries. For Frederick Hendricks of Nassau, no time was to be lost and a swift advance towards Louvain was carried out in order to outflank the Spanish army. The main Spanish army[134] withdrew to the city of Vilvoorde leaving a strong garrison of 4,000–4,500 regular soldiers to defend the city. On 24 June the combined French-Dutch army was besieging it but soon they discovered that Louvain would be a hard nut to crack and no easy surrender should be expected. In order to speed up the allies had serious logistical and finance problems, desertion, combat losses[135] and starving, which had taken a heavy toll on the French troops. On 4 July, the French force had fewer than 17,000 men and Frederick Hendricks of Nassau received the feared news that Piccolomini had crossed the Rhine and was close to the River Meuse.[136] Therefore the allied council of war took the decision to raise the siege and to withdraw to Aarchot. After the departure of the enemy from Louvain, the Cardinal Infante reorganised his force in three corps, the first with 21,000 men,[137] a second with probably 5,500 men (five tercios and eight companies of horse) and a third with 5,000–6,000 men (five tercios and eight companies of horse). Rapidly joined by the Imperial cavalry, the Cardinal Infante had enough men to counter-attack, blocking first the eastern approach to Brabant, and later recovering Diest on

---

133 At this stage of the war Bernhard of Saxe-Weimar was typical "condottiere". We have seen that after the defeat of Nördlingen he went to the west of Germany with the rest of the army. By October 1634, the Protestant prince refused to continue to finance his army and the Swedish were more concerned to save their position on the Pommeria and would not sent their force to western Germany. Richelieu saw the opportunity to station an army under French command on the west bank of the Rhine, and offered a particular treaty to Saxe-Weimar in November 1635. For subsidies of 375,000 escudos a year, the landgrave of Alsace and bailiwick of Hagenau, he would finance an army of 12,000 infantry and 6,000 cavalry for the French crown.
134 For infantry three Spanish tercios (Francisco Zapata, Marquis of Celada and Count of Fuenclara), four Italian tercios, one Walloon tercio, two Irish tercios, eight German regiments and for cavalry 70 companies of horse.
135 On 29 June, the Irish of Preston repulsed two French assaults inflicting 700 losses to the attackers (de Mesa 2014).
136 In fact the Imperial general had crossed the River Rhine on 18 June with a vanguard of 4,000 cavalry, including the feared Croats, while the rest of the army was still behind.
137 Albi de la Cuesta (2015).

16 July. The French-Dutch retreat was continuously harassed by the Imperial cavalry, especially the Croats, the peasants and militia of Brabant. Meantime, further to the east, on 28 July a Spanish detachment of 500 men (in fact German troops) stormed by surprise the fortress of Schenkenshans located between the rivers Rhine and Meuse, threatening the Dutch heartland. The Cardinal Infante crossed the River Meuse on 30 July near Stevensweert, taking Erkelenz and Straelen and later most of the Duchy of Cleves, (Götz, Kranenburg, Cleves and Gennep) where they were joined by the rest of the Imperial army. In October, Limburg was taken and the Cardinal Infante sent his troops to winter quarters.

In northern Italy, the French diplomacy had managed to federate Italian princes (the Duke of Savoy, the Duke of Parma, the Duke of Mantua and the Duke of Modena) against the Spanish domination, by the treaty of Rivoli [138] in July 1635. With the operation in the Valtellina, the Spanish governor, the Cardinal Albornoz, had not enough troops to face the coming invasion and decided to withdraw close to Milan and to observe the movement of the enemies. The main corps was made of French troops (12,000–13 500 men) commanded by the Field Marshal of Créqui, which crossed the Alps in July and advanced towards Lombardy in August. On 15 August, the core of the French force was in Casale Monferrato, while the rest was taking the small castle of Villata. The army of Créqui followed its route to rejoin the army of the Duke of Parma, defeating in the process a strong Spanish cavalry detachment of 24 companies commanded by Gaspar de Acevedo, on 25 September. Meantime the Duke of Parma with 6,000 men was advancing to the west from Piacenza to Pontecurone. He crossed the River Tanaro near Castelnuevo di Scrivia and finally met the French force in Sale on 3 September. The decision was taken to besiege Valenza di Pô and on 10 September the combined army was surrounding the city, and four days later the army of the Duke of Savoy Victorio Amadeo I joined the siege with 8,000 to 9,000 men.[139] Despite their best efforts, the siege was not going so well for the combined army. Valenza di Pô was well defended by the governor Martin Galiano and from time to time the Spanish commander Carlos Colonna managed to send reinforcements and supplies to the city. In fact, time was playing with the Spanish; the army of Colonna was receiving reinforcements every week while the combined army was losing more and more men. Finally on 27 October the Spanish stormed a portion of the circumvallation line defended by troops from Savoy and sent a strong reinforcement of 1,200 men. The futility of continuing the siege was acknowledged in a council of war and on 29 September the combined army withdrew to winter quarters through Monferrato, leaving their artillery siege. For the Spanish, the only bad news of the campaign was the construction of a French fortress in Breme on the north bank of the River Pô a few kilometres from Sartirana Lomellina in Lombardy. The last event of the 1635 campaign,

---

138 By the treaty of Rivoli, the four duchies and France agreed to maintain a force of 25,000 infantry and 3,500 cavalry to invade the State of Milan.

139 The total combined army is often estimated at 25,000 men in total, so if we have 10,000–11,000 men for the French, and 6,000 men for the Duke of Parma, we will have 8,000 to 9,000 for the Duke of Savoy.

in September, was the occupation of the islands of Lerins (Island of Sainte-Marguerite and Islands of Saint Honorat) on the Provence Coast facing Cannes by a Spanish naval expedition.[140]

1636

For the Count-Duke of Olivares, the success of the Spanish armies was encouraging and for the next campaign order was sent to Flanders to continue the offensive against the Dutch Republic in order to gain new territories, in order to force them to sign a treaty favourable to Spanish interests. As always reality was much different, and by the end of October 1635 the Dutch had reorganised their force to retake at all costs the fortress of Schenkenshans. The fortress was besieged for six months but despite the sending of reinforcements the Spanish garrison capitulated on 29 of April with honourable terms. Olivares was upset at this setback, partially compensated by the heavy losses of the Dutch army during the operation and by the fact that at last Vienna had declared war against France in March 1636.[141] With the loss of Schenkenshans a direct attack on the Dutch Republic was difficult to undertake and when the Cardinal Infante received news that the French were attacking the Spanish territory of Franche-Comté[142] with 20,000 men, he decided to change his plan. In effect, on 28 May the army of Condé was besieging the city of Dôle. The city was defended by a garrison of 3,800 men (720 regulars and the rest militia) commanded by the Archbishop of Besançon and outside the city the Marquis of Conflans was joining a small force to defend some castles of the province and to harass French supplies. At the end of July, a first reinforcement of 2,200 light Imperial cavalry arrived in the province to enhance the small attacks on French convoys. On 7 August, Condé received the order to abandon the siege and to move with his army in Picardy. At the same time Charles IV Duke of Lorraine, at the service of Spain, arrived in the city of Gray with some 5,000 men and rejoined the small army of the Marquis of Conflans. Charles IV had enough men and decided to move to relieve the city of Dôle, but Condé did not wait for the Imperials and withdrew on 14 August. More to the north, the Cardinal Infante was building a new offensive plan; the basic idea was to invade north of France to attract all French reserves in order to support the Spanish armies fighting in Franche-Comté and northern Italy. Following diverse authors (Albi de la Cuesta, 2015, Negredo de Cera 2016 and Parker 2003), the famous Spanish invasion was more a diversion operation than a full scale invasion with the objective to take Amiens or even Paris. The Spanish governor left a small army to observe the troops of the Dutch Republic and he gave command of

---

140 A fleet of 22 galleys and five supply ships under the command of the Marquis of Santa Cruz with (Montglat, volume I, 1825).
141 Following the agreement, for a Spanish subsidy, Imperial troops on the Rhine should conduct offensive actions against France and their German allies.
142 At that time Franche-Comté was defended by 5,000 militia supported by 250 cavalry from the local nobility and by the Tercio of Louis de La Verne with 1,280 men (see Gérard Louis, *La Guerre de Dix Ans*, Presse Universitaire de Franche-Comté, 1998).

the main army of 18,000 men[143] to Thomas of Savoy-Carignano supported by an Imperial detachment of 11,000 men[144] under Piccolomini and a league army of 8,000 men commanded by Johann von Werth, in total 37,000 men (Albi de la Cuesta, 2015). The campaign started on 28 June, with the first objective being the fortress of La Capelle defended by 700 men. After a poor defence, La Capelle surrendered on 9 July and on 25 July Le Châtellet (defended by 600 men) capitulated after a siege of three days. With only 14,000 to 15,000 men[145] the French commander, the Duke of Soissons, could do nothing to save the French position and decided to withdraw behind the River Somme. For the Spanish point of view, the French border was poorly defended so they decided to continue to advance across Picardy. On 4 August the main Spanish force was on the river and managed to force the crossing of the River Somme[146] despite a decent fight from the French force. Soissons had no choice but to set back crossing the River Oise to retire to the area of Compiegne some 80 km of Paris. The Spanish force now had enough space and cavalry parties were sent to sack and plunder the rich countryside of Picardy. The city of Roye was taken on 5 August and three days later the army of the Cardinal Infante surrounded the city of Corbie. It seemed that the idea of the Spanish was to consolidate the control of the north bank of the River Somme and when Corbie, poorly defended by 1,700 men, surrendered on 15 August most of the initial objectives of the Spanish had been met. In Paris, on the contrary, the city was in panic and from the 4th to the 12th of August it seemed that the French authorities were losing control of the situation. Richelieu had sent an urgent message to Condé and Saxe-Weimar to stop their operation and to send some of their best troops to Paris, and he organised the raising of 35,000 infantry and 15,000 cavalry to reinforce the army of Picardy. The French fears were that the Spanish and their allies could subdue the main positions of Picardy (Abbeville, Amiens, Doullens and Peronne) and push forward into Champagne and even to Paris. The threat did not materialise for different reasons: firstly, the initial goal of the operation seemed to be a diversionary operation in Picardy and for the Spanish, to be able to winter quarter some of their troops north of the Somme, was already a great success. Secondly the supply line of the Army

---

143 Thomas of Savoy was Governor of the Arms, with Johann of Nassau-Siegen as general of the Cavalry and the Baron of Balançon as general of the artillery. The infantry had probably 13,000 men and consisted of two Spanish tercios (Count of Fuensaldaña and Francisco Zapata), two Italian tercios (Cantelmo and Guasco), three Walloon tercios (Count of Fresin, Count of Villerual and Baron of Vesmal), three German regiments (Count of Hoochstrate, Spinola and Cherfontaine) and the Irish tercio of O'Neil. The cavalry some 5,000 men divided in 40 companies of the ordinary cavalry and four German regiments (4x 10 companies).

144 Imperial force estimates are 5,000 infantry (seven regiments) and 6,000 cavalry and dragoons (nine cavalry regiments and one regiment of dragoons) and 600 dragoons. League Army estimates are 4,000 infantry (five regiments) and 4,000 cavalry and dragoons (five cavalry regiments and one regiment of dragoons)

145 The 8,000 survivors of the army of 1635 were sent back to France between May and June 1636.

146 The crossing of the River Somme in the face of hostile forces took place to the west of the city of Bray. In the action the Spanish infantry (companies from the tercios of Fuensaldaña and Zapata) managed to occupy some islands and to dislodge the French infantry, particularly the regiment of Piedmont (Vincart, *Relacion de campaña de 1636*, CODOIN vol. 59, 1877).

of Flanders was overstretched and the Cardinal Infante did not want to be drawn too deep into France while the Dutch Republic was still the main enemy. Thirdly, the invasion of Picardy should have been conceived as an operation in conjunction with an invasion of Burgundy by the Imperial army of Mathias Gallas. In August only a vanguard had been sent with Charles IV of Lorraine to relieve the city of Dôle. The Imperial army lost several weeks in Franche-Comté and it was only by mid October that they moved to Burgundy, and on 25 October they were besieging the city of Saint Jean de Losne on the River Saône. Although poorly fortified, the French city presented a gallant defence and with the help of regular troops and bad weather they completely stopped the Imperial army. Gallas did not want to continue further because his supplies were low, the weather was bad, winter was coming and the Emperor needed some of his troops after the defeat at Wittstock on 4 October 1636.[147] The Cardinal Infante had no choice, after Corbie he left a strong garrison in the city and ordered withdrawal to Arras. The French force composed of the troops of Soisson reinforced by troops from the army of Condé, and by the army hastily organised in Paris, moved to retake Corbie. The new siege was laid down on 30 September, the Spanish tried, without success, to storm the French line, and after a gallant resistance the Spanish garrison capitulated 14 November.

In northern Italy the orders of the Count-Duke of Olivares were first to punish the attitude of the Duke of Parma and secondly to check the Franco-Savoyard advance. The new governor of Milan, the Marquis of Leganés, split his force in two and while Martin de Aragon was observing the French and Savoyard in the west, the Marquis of Leganés conducted the punitive expedition taking the castle of Castelsangiovanni on 11 March. Fortunately for Parma, the Spanish commander received news that the French army was crossing the Alps to rejoin the Duke of Savoy and that the force of Duke of Rohan was prepared to attack the north of Lombardy, so cautiously he withdrew to Castelnuevo di Scrivia. At the end of May the combined army commanded by Victor Amadeus I, the Field Marshal du Créqui and the Duke of Parma regrouped in Monferrato while at the same time the Duke of Rohan, with 4,500 men, was prepared to strike north of Lecco. The objective of the combined army was to conduct the war in the west of Lombardy to rejoin the army of Rohan and to advance towards Milan. Leaving the troops of Parma in Monferrato, the Franco-Savoyard army advanced to the north and on 13 June they were near Oleggio and the River Ticino. The French force crossed the Ticino near Vizzola Ticino on a boat bridge and later sent cavalry parties across Lombardy to burn

---

147 Wittstock is a decisive battle of the Thirty Years' War, it was fought between the last decent Swedish army of 18,000 men (7,700 infantry, 10,300 cavalry and dragoons and 60 guns) commanded by Johan Banérs and a Saxon–Imperial force of 18,700 men (8,500 infantry, 10,100 cavalry and dragoons and 30 guns). After this bloody battle, the Swedish victory had a profound political impact. Firstly, the destruction of the last Swedish army would probably have ended the war; victory meant that they were back on track. Secondly, the effect of the peace of Prague was gone; the Saxony and Brandenburg armies would not fight the Emperor any more. Thirdly, for the Spanish the meaning of the Swedish victory was that the Emperor Ferdinand II would concentrate most of his force in the east and the remote possibility of having a joint invasion of France was gone (Negredo del Cerro, 2016).

and destroy crops and villages.[148] On the west bank of the Ticino the Savoyard army was also moving towards Borgo Ticino. The reaction of the Marquis of Leganés was to join all available force, including militia from Milan, and to move to Abbiategrasso. When he learned of the splitting of the French and Savoyard army he decided to move north in order to catch the French force alone. On 20 June, on the news of the move of the Spanish army, the French and Savoyards decided that the French should turn around and to go back to the hamlet of Tornavento. On this spot it was possible to construct a bridge on the Ticino and the position could be fortified. On 22 June, in the morning, the Spanish army[149] was deployed and ready to attack the French position. At first the French had to face the full scale of the Spanish attack for three hours, but when their positions were collapsing, the troops of the Duke of Savoy crossed the bridge laid down on the Ticino and saved the day. For a number of hours the battle was in the balance but by mid afternoon it was clear for the Spanish that with exhausted troops and with the full deployment of the Savoyards, victory was impossible. The Spanish were able to conduct an orderly during the night and to move towards Castano Primo and later Abbiategrasso. The battle was exceptional in its length, more than 11 hours fighting in a hot summer without water or food for men and horses. The Spanish withdrawal took the Allies by surprise because some commanders were expecting new attacks 23 June and the combined army stayed in the Ticino area moving only to Somma Lombardo on 7 July. During this period, the only actions were sending cavalry parties to sack the villages of the area. In reality the combined army was tired and there was a general lack of supplies, again the poor logistics of the French were unable to keep the army on the field. The Allies failed to take Varese or Angera and to rejoin the Duke of Rohan's armies blocked by a force of 4,000 men, so the Duke of Savoy decided to end the campaign at the end of July and to return to Piedmont where the Spanish cavalry was conducting destructive raids. With an army again fit to fight, Leganés diverted a detachment of 4,500 men commanded by Martin de Aragon and a thousand militia to carry out the operation against the Duchy of Parma. With his small army, the Duke of Parma returned to defend his duchy, but he was defeated on 15 August when he was besieging Rottofreno. The Duke of Parma concentrated the rest of his regular forces to the defence of Piacenza and Parma and left the rest of country to be defended by the militia. For the next five months, the Spanish occupied most of the Duchy and with a second army from Cremona they besieged Piacenza. In December 1636, the Duke of Parma finally agreed to open negotiations with the Spanish and on 2 February 1637 a peace treaty was signed.

The last event of 1636 took place in southern Europe on the Pyrenean borders. During the summer, the Marquis of Valparaison with mainly newly raised troops[150] and the militia of Guipúzcoa and Navarre invaded the

---

148 The villages and burgs of Lonate, Ferno, Samarate, Cardano San Macario, Verghera, Amate, Crenna, Gallarate were attacked by the Allies (Hamon 2016).
149 For full details of the battle see Chapter 4, as well as Hanlon, 2016.
150 One of the only regular troops was the regiment of the Count-Duke. The fact that most of the troops were militia and raw recruits means that desertion rate was high and after the siege of Socoa the Spanish were forced to turn back and withdraw to Spain.

Labourd region in the French Basque territory, capturing and sacking the small town of Cibourne, Saint Jean de Luz and the fortress of Socoa.

1637

From Madrid, the successes of the campaign of the previous year gave confidence to the State Council and the newly created Junta de Estado, that combined attacks on France positions from Flanders, Italy and Spain were possible. In the north, the Cardinal Infante was against double offensives, so after some negotiation between Brussels and Madrid it was decided to attack in spring Venlo and Roermond in Dutch hands, before the French could react, and later in the summer to concentrate all the troops in the south to face them. In Lombardy, Leganés received orders to initiate a series of operations against Piedmont and in Catalonia the recommendation was to attack the French fortress of Leucate. On paper it was a correct plan, but as always the enemies did not play the same game. In Flanders, Frederick Hendricks of Nassau had his own problems and had to show that the French alliance was a benefit to the Dutch Republic. The initial target of the Dutch was Dunkirk to destroy the main Spanish naval base and for that operation a French subsidy of 1.1 million guilders was delivered and Louis XII pledged that the French army would open the campaign as soon as possible to distract the Spanish army. The Dunkirk operation was complicated and depended strongly on the surprise effect, and when the Dutch commander spent several weeks assembling the army and the navy in Vlissingen (Flushing) the Spanish were aware of the operation. Frederick Hendricks could not risk a defeat so he decided to move his army to a new objective and to retake Breda. The French opened the campaign sending the army of Picardy[151] to besiege Landrecies on 17 June, while the Dutch with 24,000 men were heading towards Breda on 21 July. The Cardinal Infante could not wait for the Imperial reinforcements and with 16,000 to 17,000 men moved also to try to save Breda, leaving Landrecies alone. The small garrison of 300 men of Landrecies surrendered on 26 July, and the town of Maubeuge capitulated on 5 August. In fact the Spanish had few troops available to defend the province of Hainaut, but with the arrival of the Imperial contingent in Mons on 3 August they were able to stop the French advance. Using his siege skills, Frederick Hendrick built strong defensive lines around Breda, defended by a garrison of 2,600 men. The Cardinal infante had probably 20,000 men in hand in Rijsbergen but he did not want to risk his army in futile attacks against the strong Dutch position. Instead he decided to conduct a strategic movement, and by the middle of August he crossed the River Meuse and recaptured Venlo on 25 August and Roermond 3 September, stretching the communication line between Maastricht and Nijmegen. The Dutch commander did not change his objective and Breda finally capitulated on 10 October, but the capture of Venlo and Roermond meant that the Dutch

---

[151] The French had three armies operating against Flanders: the Army of Picardy commanded by the Cardinal of La Valette with 30,000 men for the main operation, the army of Champagne commanded by the Maréchal de Châtillon with 8,000 men to invade Luxembourg and the army of Oise commanded by Rambure with 8,000 men to cover the north of France (Albi de la Cuesta 2016).

could not threaten Brabant from the east and that the Cardinal Infante could concentrate all his forces on the defence of Antwerp and Flanders. More closely, after a long pause, the French army of Picardy laid siege to La Capelle on 6 September and after a defence of 17 days surrendered on the 23rd, much to the disgust of the Cardinal Infante, who was coming with a relief force and had hoped that the fortress could resist one week more. Looking for a quick revenge, the Spanish directly attacked the 7,000 French left in Maubeuge. By a series of march and countermarch the two armies moved to Maubeuge, where La Valette finally managed to extract his force. Further to the east the French army of Chatillon entered Luxembourg and spent most of the summer sacking the countryside even if only the city of Danvillier was taken. In Franche-Comté, the French army of Longueville conducted a scorched earth policy, attacking villages and small towns (Jonvelle, Jussey, Saint-Amour) but avoiding the main centre of resistance; the local troops were unable to stop them.

In Italy the Army of Lombardy have been heavily reinforced and could muster up to 33,000 men in March 1637. With most of the French troops in the north, Leganés started the campaign conducting a series of small raids in Piedmont and Monferrato. Small towns such as Acqui Terme, Nizza Monferrato, Punzone or Agliano were taken in order to reinforce the communication to Savona and Genova. The only relevant action took place on 7 August, when the Spanish defeated the Franco-Savoyard detachment besieging Rocca di Arezzo. A last event took place facing Cannes when the French navy supported by a strong infantry contingent retook the Iles du Lerins by mid May.[152] The Count-Duke of Olivares was upset by the lack of initiative of Leganés but looking forward the strategically and political situation in northern Italy was good. In the Valtellina, diplomacy and poor French logistics had prevailed against the small army of the Duke of Rohan. The French commander had to face the mutiny and desertion of his troops due to the lack of finance and on 5 of May with the help of Spanish subsidies, Georg Jenatsch the general of the Grison troops expulsed the French from the region; later on, he signed an official treaty with Spain.[153]

1.14 Diego Mexía Felipez de Guzmán y Dávila, 1st Marquise of Leganés. Portrait from the collection of Fürstlich Waldecksche Hofbibliothek, Band 1 (Heidelberg University Library)

---

[152] The French force disembarked on 24 March, and after a conventional siege the garrison of the Island of Sainte-Marguerite capitulated on 12 May, and that of Sainte Honorat on 14 May (Fernández Duro, volume IV, 1895).

[153] The treaty would definitely be signed in 1639 and would return the Valtellina to the Grison in exchange for free passage for the Catholic force. Also the Spanish would hire the Grison's troops for the Army of Lombardy. Following Maffi 2008, up to 19,550 men served in the Spanish army between 1640 and 1658.

On 24 September, the Duke of Mantua died and on 7 October it was the turn of the Duke of Savoy. In Mantua the Duchess of Mantua left the French alliance, adopting a neutral policy towards Spain. In Savoy the regency of the Duchy[154] was in the hands of the Duchess of Savoy, Mary-Christine of Bourbon, but she had to face the ambition of her brothers-in-law Thomas of Savoy-Carignano and Maurice of Savoy.

The last operation planned by the Count-Duke of Olivares was an attack against the fortress of Leucate in Languedoc. The viceroy of Catalonia, the Duke of Cardona, had to face numerous problems to prepare a decent army and it was not until 27 August that the Count of Serbelloni could enable the campaign with 12,000 infantry,[155] most of them raw recruits, and 1,300 cavalry. The 2nd of September the Spanish were facing the fortress of Leucate defended by a small garrison of 120 men. Quickly the French governor of Languedoc, Charles de Schomberg Duke of Halluin, managed to sent a reinforcement of 1,000 men by sea while the Spanish had problems transporting the artillery siege. The military operation around Leucate was advancing slowly when the Spanish commander received the news, on 22 September, that a French relief army of 17,000 men had been organised in Narbonne with some regular troops and the militia of the province. On 27 September the Duke of Halluin, with an army of 11,000 men, arrived in the area and decided to send five columns to attack the Spanish position during the night to avoid their artillery fire. When the night was falling, the French launched their assaults and beside the resistance of the Spanish troops the French managed to storm the position and to resist the counter-attack. Five hours after the first attack, the Spanish forces were running away towards Perpignan. All the artillery and baggage were lost but most of the Spanish troops managed to escape, leaving total losses of up to 1,500–2,300 men for the Spanish and 1,200 men for the French (Zudaire Huarte 1960).

1638

For Madrid, the last campaign should have brought better results, so instruction was sent to Brussels in March 1638, indicating that the Army of Flanders should launch an attack in France to attract the French armies. The Cardinal Infante was not happy with the orders because he knew that after the fall of Breda, the Dutch would conduct an operation against Flanders. The Dutch and French envoys agreed to start the campaign in April with

---

154 Victor Amadeus I of Savoy had two sons, Francis Hyacinth (1632–1638) and Charles Emmanuel (1634–1675) and three daughters, Luisa Cristina (1629–1692), Marguerite (1635–1663) and Henrietta Adelaide (1636–1676).

155 The Spanish army was probably made with troops from seven Spanish units (Régiment of the Count-Duke, Tercio of the Count of Aguilar, Tercio of Diego Zúñiga, Tercio of Juan de Arce, Tercio of Juan de Servellon, Tercio of the Marquis of Villalba, and Tercio of the Count of Oropeza) the Italian tercio of Leonardo Mole and the Walloon tercio of the Marquis of Molinghem. Of the 12,000 infantry only 3,000 ones had military experience (Count-Duke, Mole and Molinghem). For the cavalry we have companies from the *Guardias de Castillas*, other Spanish companies raised for the campaign and the German regiment of Littcher. Zudaire-Huarte (1960) and *Informe del duque de Cardona* sobre la empresa de Loecata Carpeta: Perpiñàn, A.S. Md. (A su Majestad), 1637 Archivo General de Simancas, *Registro Guerra Antigua, 1186*.

Antwerp and Saint-Omer as objectives. The Dutch army of 18,000 infantry and 4,500 cavalry was divided in two with 5,700 men (64 companies of foot and four of horse) under Willem van Nassau-Singen with the order to blockade Antwerp from the Flemish side of the River Scheldt and the rest with Frederick Hendricks of Nassau to advance from the north. On 13 June, an amphibious operation was launched and quickly the landing party established fortified positions near the village of Kallo. Unfortunately for Willem van Nassau-Singen, the Spanish had partially anticipated the movement and as soon as possible the Cardinal Infante had 8,000–9,000 men in hand.[156] The Spanish counter-attack was launched during the night of 21/22 June and after 10 hours of desperate fighting between entrenchments and dykes; the Spanish managed to take most of the Dutch positions. At this point, panic spread in the Dutch infantry and they ran away desperately to their boats followed by the Spanish infantry, swords in hand. Of the original Dutch force only 1,500 men managed to escape to Liefkenshoek, 2,000 were taken prisoners and the rest lay dead or drowned. On the other side Spanish losses were also high with 1,000 dead and wounded, but a strong enemy position have been taken as well as an artillery train of 15 guns (six demi-cannon, six 6-pdrs and three 3-pdrs). To the south the Field Marshal de Chatillon with 10,000–13,000 infantry and 3,000 cavalry laid siege to the city of Saint-Omer on 1 June. The Spanish had a small army[157] under the command of Thomas of Savoy-Carignano in the sector but he had strict order not to give battle so the Spanish force established their base near the city of Poperinge. During the night of 8/9 June a small reinforcement of 600 men managed to enter the city. On 24 June, a Spanish detachment of 1,200 men managed to take control of a small fort in Ardres in the middle of the French supply lines. The French added another force of 12,000–15,000 men (Field Marshal de La Force) in the area and with new reinforcements[158] Chatillon was convinced to surrender the city. On 6 July the 7,000–8,000 Imperials of Piccolomini arrived to reinforce the Spanish army in Poperinge. With such reinforcements, Thomas and Piccolomini organised a full-scale attack of the French on two points while the Spanish cavalry had to distract the troops of de La Force. On 8 July, the operation was launched, the first position of Momelin was partially taken by the Imperial and the second position of the Bac was taken and a strong Spanish contingent entered the city. The only drawback was the heavy losses endured by the cavalry against La Force. Meantime, the two French commanders resolved that it would be impossible to take the city and decided to abandon the siege on 12 July and to find an

---

156 The Spanish units were five companies from the Spanish tercio of the Marquis of Velada, the Spanish tercio of Fuenclara with 20 companies, an Italian tercio of Fabrizio Doria, the Walloon tercio of Ribaucourt, the German regiment of de Brion, as well as companies from the garrison of Antwerp and companies of cavalry.

157 12,000 men divided into 4,000 cavalry and 8,000 men for the infantry with two Spanish tercios (Fuensaldaña and Saavedra), companies from the tercios of Velada, two Italian tercios, one German regiment (Spinola) and two English tercios (Palafox and Mendoza 1793, and Albi de la Cuesta 2016).

158 Following Albi de la Cuesta (2016), Châtillon had up to 22,000 men around Saint-Omer and de La Force was covering the supply lines from Abbeville and Calais.

easier target. The small town of Renty was the unfortunate target and after a gallant resistance by the Spanish garrison, the town capitulated on 9 August. Louis XIII needed a better objective and with the reinforcement of 10,000 men more, the French decided to besiege le Châtellet on 24 August. The Cardinal Infante had not enough men to confront the French army and on 14 September the place was assaulted and taken. Despite the presence of the king in the area and the mobilisation of a great number of troops, the French army had accomplished little for a heavy price. Coming back to the north of Flanders, Frederick Hendricks of Nassau resolved to continue the campaign and by mid August he was besieging the city of Gelders. Unfortunately for the Dutch the Spanish had already reinforced the garrison to 3,300 men and after 10 days of operation Frederick Hendricks had to raise the siege and end the campaign. For the Spanish authorities, the victories of Kallo and Saint-Omer had proven the efficiency of the army of Flanders,[159] but in both cases the enemies had the strategic initiative and even with the reinforcement of the Imperials, the Spanish field army was most of the time outnumbered.[160]

The province of Franche-Comté was another hot-spot of the struggle between France and Spain but this time the Spanish captain, Charles of Lorraine, had the upper hand and managed to defeat the French army of Longueville at the battle of Poligny on 19 June. This victory did not serve much the affairs of the Spanish monarchy, because in the Rhine valley, the troops of Bernhard of Saxe-Weimar, supported by French contingent managed to defeat on 2 March an overconfident Imperial army commanded by Federico Savelli. Thereafter, the campaign of Alsace would be favourable for French interest and after being reinforced with new recruits and artillery, thanks to the French subsidies, Saxe-Weimar was able to besiege Breisach on 15 June. This time, the Spanish had no troops to save the city and the Bavarian-Imperial force[161] was beaten a second time at Wittenweier on 9 August. In hope of a new relief army the governor of Breisach maintained the resistance, but after a last attempt to break the siege on 19 November, and with no more supplies, the city capitulated on 12 December (Parrot 2001). For the Spanish the loss of Breisach meant that the terrestrial road from Milan to Flanders was definitively cut and that the French had a strong foothold to enter Germany.

After the strong criticism concerning his passivity, the Marquis of Leganés had to prove that the Army of Lombardy could undertake a more vigorous operation against the French and Savoyard force in Piedmont, at last it was the wish of Olivares. On 13 March 1638, the Marquis of Leganés sent the core of his army, 14,000 men,[162] against the fortress of Breme on

---

159 We can add a small operation against the garrison of Bergen op Zoom on 24/26 July by a detachment of 3,000 men commanded by Sfonderti (Albi de la Cuesta 2016).
160 In the north we have 22,000 Dutch against 15,000–18,000 Spanish and in the south at best 8,000–10,000 Imperials and 12,000 Spanish (9,000 infantry and 3,000 cavalry) against probably 30,000 to 40,000 French for the armies of Châtillon, La Force and Brézé (Estaban Ribas 2014).
161 The Bavarian force of Götz with 6,800 infantry and 5,200 cavalry, the Imperial force commanded by Savelli with 2,000 infantry and 2,000 cavalry (W.P. Guthrie, 2003).
162 Infantry from four Spanish tercios (Lombardia, Mar de Napoles, Saboya and Mortara), the Lombard tercio of Ferrante Bolognini, two Neapolitan tercios (Carlos de la Gatta and Tiberio

the River Pô defended by 2,000 Frenchmen. Despite some actions against the Spanish circumvallation line, where the Field Marshal of Créquy died, the French force failed to rescue the garrison and Breme surrendered on 27 March. The fast success and the death of a French high-ranking officer offered a favourable opportunity for the Army of Lombardy and with new reinforcements,[163] the Spanish were able to besiege Vercelli, one of the strongholds of the Duchy of Savoy, on 26 May. The strong defence of the fortress, located on the River Sessia, and the garrison of 3,300 men made the siege a difficult task. Leganés constructed an impressive circumvallation line of 17 km and was able to resist the pressure of the Franco-savoyard army of 13,000 men commanded by the Cardinal of la Valette. Due to lack of supply and ammunitions, the city capitulated on 6 July. Leganés could have continued the successful military action, but the presence of the French army of the Cardinal of La Valette and significant losses of the siege of Vercelli, due mainly to sickness, had reduced his army, so the only event was the capture of the small town of Pontestura. Another political event was the death of the young Duke of Savoy Francesco Hyacinth, on 4 October, succeeded immediately by his brother Carlos Emmanuel a sickly infant of four years old. With the support of the Spanish his uncle, Maurice of Savoy, saw the opportunity to exercise his right as regent in place of the Duchess of Savoy who had the support of Richelieu.

The French Cardinal played another card in the south-west of France, when the army of Condé, with up to 18,500 men, crossed the River Bidasoa 21 June and rapidly took Irún, Oyarzum, Lezo, Renteria and Pasajes.[164] The Spanish monarchy did not expect a direct attack to the Iberian Peninsula and few regular troops were available. On 1 July, Condé was besieging Fuenterrabia, the only modern fortification in the region and the city was defended only by 700 men. Fortunately, the Spanish authority of Guipúzcoa reacted quickly and they managed to send reinforcement by sea. The defenders of Fuenterrabia were resisting bravely and the poor hygienic condition in the French camps was taking his toll. The naval defeat of Getaria[165] on 22 August did not alter the morale and will of the defenders and on 2 September a relief army of 13,500 men arrived in the area. On 8 September the Spanish stormed successfully the French fortification on the Guadalupe hill. French soldiers fled in panic towards the French borders, leaving behind them 1,500 to 3,000 dead and drowned, 23 guns and 2,000 prisoners. For the Spanish

---

Brancaccio), two German regiments (Prince Borso and Gille de Haes) and one company of Grisons, supported by 75 companies of cavalry (2x guards, 40x State of Milan, 16x Neapolitan and 17x German) (*Planta del sitio de Breme*. Archivo General de Simancas. Secretaría de Estado, Legajos, 03346. Con carta del Marques de Leganés al secretario Pedro de Arce, Milán 27 de abril de 1638).

163 Palafox y Mendoza (1793) gives the number of 20,000 men for the Army of the Marquis of Leganés.

164 In the last three towns, the Spanish had shipyards where four galleons under construction were captured by the French as well as 60 naval guns (Fernández Duro, volume IV 1895).

165 On 22 August the French Admiral the Cardinal of Sourdis manage to block a Spanish Fleet (11 galleons, five urcas and one frigate) in the small harbour of Getaria. With a combination of naval skills and a good use of fireships, the French manage to destroy most of the Spanish fleet of Lope de Hoce (Fernández Duro, volume IV, 1895).

authorities, 1638 was a very successful year and as usual, the Count-Duke of Olivares and King Philip IV were expecting new successes for the next year.

1639

From Madrid, the strategic movements for 1639 in Flanders was to increase the attacks against the Dutch and to contain the French in the south with he help of the troops of Piccolomini. For such an ambitious objective, the Spanish would also send a powerful fleet to challenge the Dutch on the sea and to send Spanish recruits for the Army of Flanders. In Franche-Comté the idea was to raise troops in Switzerland and the Tyrol with subsidies from Milan and Brussels to improve the defences. In northern Italy, Leganés signed a treaty with Thomas of Savoy-Carignano to carry out an offensive against the French and the regency of the Duchess of Savoy. In the Iberian Peninsula, the Count-Duke wanted to organise four armies in Catalonia, Aragon, Cantabria-Navarre and Castile, to be able to counter-attack against a French invasion like the one against Fuenterrabia the previous year. Such planning had to be adapted to the principle of reality and in Flanders, with a lack of resources, the Cardinal Infante had to adopt a "wait and see" strategy. In the north, the Dutch initiated the campaign in June, concentrating troops in Bergen op Zoom. The army of Frederick Hendricks of Nassau landed in Philippine on 18 June but the arrival of the Spanish force prevented the Dutch investing the city of Hulst in Flanders. For a month and a half, the two armies stayed face to face without any serious fighting. On 31 July, the Dutch sailed back to Bergen op Zoom and continued their movement towards Rheinberg. The plan of the Dutch commander was to attract the Spanish on the Meuse and to come back to Flanders and invest Hulst before the Spanish could do the same.[166] The stratagem did not work because it took more days to reach the environs of Hulst and when the Dutch landed for a second time, a Spanish vanguard was already on the spot and the garrison of Hulst had been reinforced. The Dutch remained near Hulst and by the beginning of October Frederick Hendricks of Nassau decided to send his troops into winter quarters. While the main Spanish army was facing the Dutch, Richelieu had opportunity to avenge the poor results of the last campaign so he concentrated three armies against the Spanish, the one of Field Marshal of La Meilleraye with 27,000 men, the one of Field Marshal of La Feuquières with 12,000 men and the one of the Field Marshal of Chatillon with 18,000 men. On 26 May La Feuquières started the siege of Thionville in Luxembourg. On 7 June a combined Imperial–Spanish force under the command of Ottavio Piccolomini launched a devastating attack on the outnumbered French force.[167] The result was the total destruction of La Feuquières' army

---

166 The Dutch commander thought that in four days, using barges and the Rhine as a "motorway", he could out-speed the Spanish and be at Hulst before them (van Nimwegen 2010).
167 At the battle of Thionville, Imperial and the Spanish forces are estimated at 14,000 men for 10,600 for the French. The Spanish contingent came from troops stationed in Luxembourg or from the regiment of Jean de Beck (commanding the vanguard). For more details see *Relation de l'Attaque faite par le Maréchal de Camp de sa Majesté Impérialle le Comte Picolomini…*, in Sieur Aubery, *Mémoire pour l'Histoire du Cardinal Richelieu*, volume 4, p. 117, Cologne, 1667 (Périni volume 3, 1893), and Patrott, 2001.

with losses amounting to 6,000 dead and wounded, 3,000 prisoners and 10 artillery guns. With a great success in hand, Piccolomini tried unsuccessfully to storm the city of Mousson on 12 June and on the 24th he crossed the Meuse to rejoin the Spanish force in Artois. The objective of the main French army was the city of Hesdin in Artois, and by 19 May the city was surrounded. Hesdin was only defended by 10 companies of Walloons (800–900 men) supported by 500 militia and a horse company. Outside, the Spanish army of the Marquis of Fuentes had only 14,000–15,000 men[168] and even if they tried unsuccessfully to sent reinforcements to the city, on 30 June the garrison of Hesdin had to capitulate. The Spanish were temporarily reinforced by the Imperial contingent but with the move of Chatillon to Luxembourg, Piccolomini had to go back to the east. La Meilleraye decided to continue the campaign with 14,000 men, but the Marquis of Fuentes managed to block the French movement and the campaign stopped in September.

The main event took place at sea,[169] the Count-Duke of Olivares had organised a powerful fleet under the command of Antonio Oquendo with 67 warships.[170] The fleet sailed on 6 September and met a first time the Dutch fleet 17 September and after a short artillery duel, the Spanish were forced to anchorage on the English coast, on the Downs on the Kent, to repair and resupply their fleet. During this resting time some of the infantry was transferred to Dúnkirk but the 21st of October a reinforced Dutch fleet, 95 ships and 12 fireships, commanded by Marten Tromp took their enemy by surprise. The Spanish fleet was totally defeated, losing probably 25 to 40 ships (burnt, captured, driven ashore), 6,000 to 7,000 men and 2,000 prisoners. By comparison the Dutch losses were estimated from 500 to 1,000 men. The only satisfactory event was, that some 6,000 Spaniards were ferried to Dunkirk to reinforce the army of Flanders (Albi de la Cuesta 2016). From a naval point of view, the Spanish acted also in Brazil, sending 41 ships with new reinforcement, commanded by Fernando Mascarenhas. Joining all available forces, the new Spanish commander decided to attack Recife, but a disastrous command and the gallant defence of the Dutch commander led to the failure of the campaign.

---

168 10,000–11,000 infantry divided into two Spanish tercios (Fuensaldaña and Velada), two Italian, one Irish, three Walloon and two German regiments and probably 4,000 cavalry including two regiments of Croats. With the arrival of Piccolomini, some of the Spanish troops (three tercios and six companies of cavalry) were sent to the north to support the army of the Cardinal Infante. Later on the Imperial troops left Artois to Luxembourg and Fuentes was left with probably fewer than 10,000 men (Albi de la Cuesta 2016).

169 For a more detail account of the so-called battle of the Downs see Fernandez Duro (volume IV, 1898) or Kirsch (P. Kirsch, *Fireship: The Terror Weapon of the Age of Sail* (Annapolis: Naval Institute Press, 2009), for the use of fireships in combat in the seventeenth century.

170 There is some debate on the composition of the Spanish fleet but there is also some consensus to find 67 warships (29 galleons, 20 urcas/Navios, 12 frigate/fluyts and five pataches) and probably 15–16 transport ships with 12,000–13,000 sailors and infantry on the warships and probably 9,000–10,000 infantry in the transport ships. (Bruce and Cogar, *Encyclopedia of Naval History* (Chicago; London: Fitzroy Dearborn, 2014), p.114; J. Alcalá-Zamora, *España, Flandes y el Mar del Norte (1618–1639)* (Barcelona: Planeta, 1975).

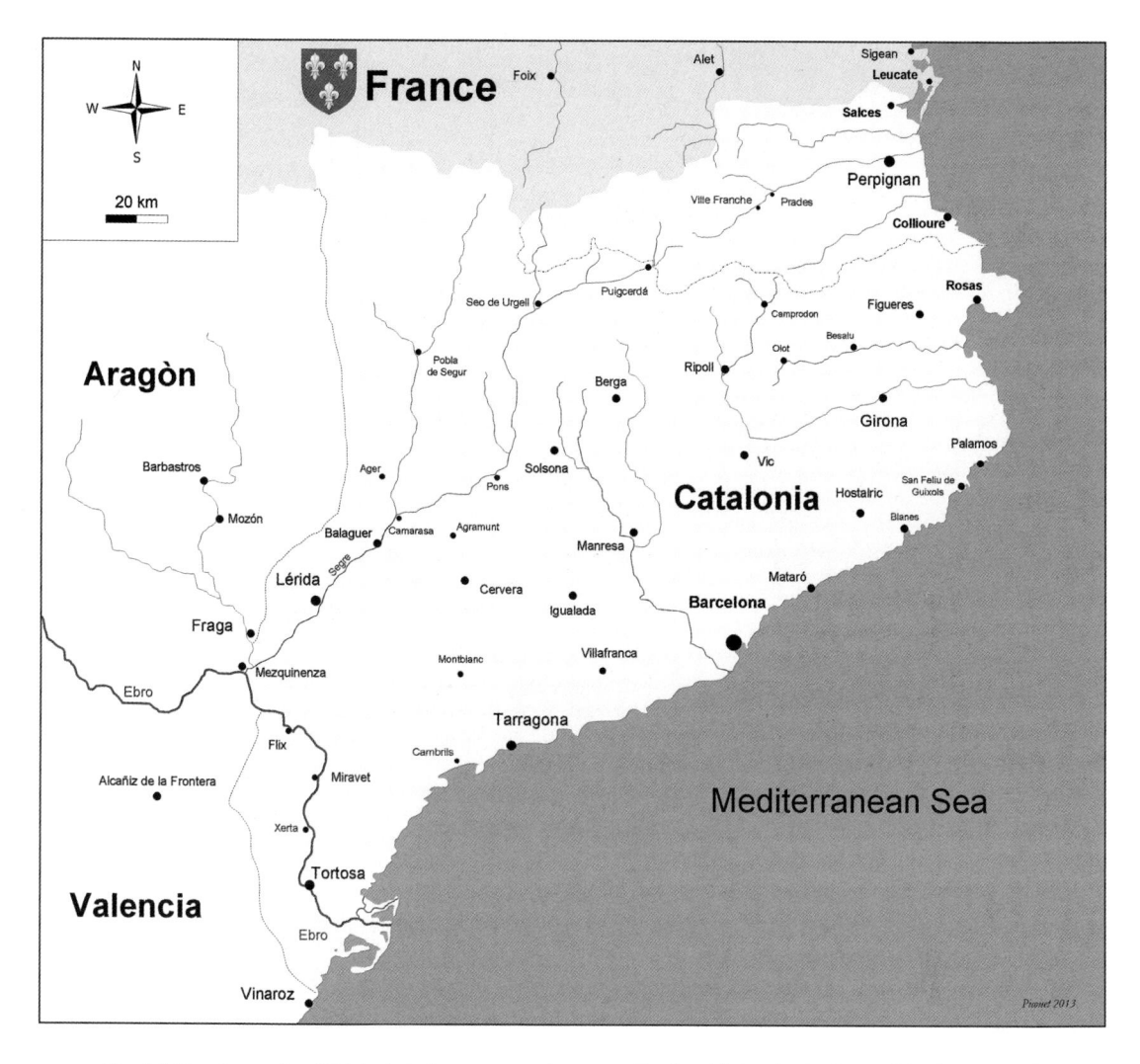

Map 1.3 The viceroyalty of Catalonia in the seventeenth century. The Spanish fought the Reapers' War (1640–1652), interconnected to the war against the French (1635–1659).

Coming back to Europe, the province of Franche-Comté was devastated by the army of Saxe-Weimar,[171] the Duke was a problem for the French with his pretention to create a duchy in Alsace, but fortunately for Richelieu, the Duke's health deteriorated rapidly in spring and on 18 July he died from fever. During summer, the Count of Guebriant managed to convince the army of Saxe-Weimar to stay in French service and by October 1639, the French were officially in control of the Armée d'Allemagne (the army of Germany) and that was not very good news for Spanish interests.

---

171 6,500 infantry (3,000 french), 5,000 cavalry (3,000 dismounted) and 300 dragoons (*Episode de la guerre de trente ans Bernard de Saxe-Weimar*, <Gallica.bnf.fr>).

THE ARMIES OF PHILIP IV OF SPAIN 1621–1665

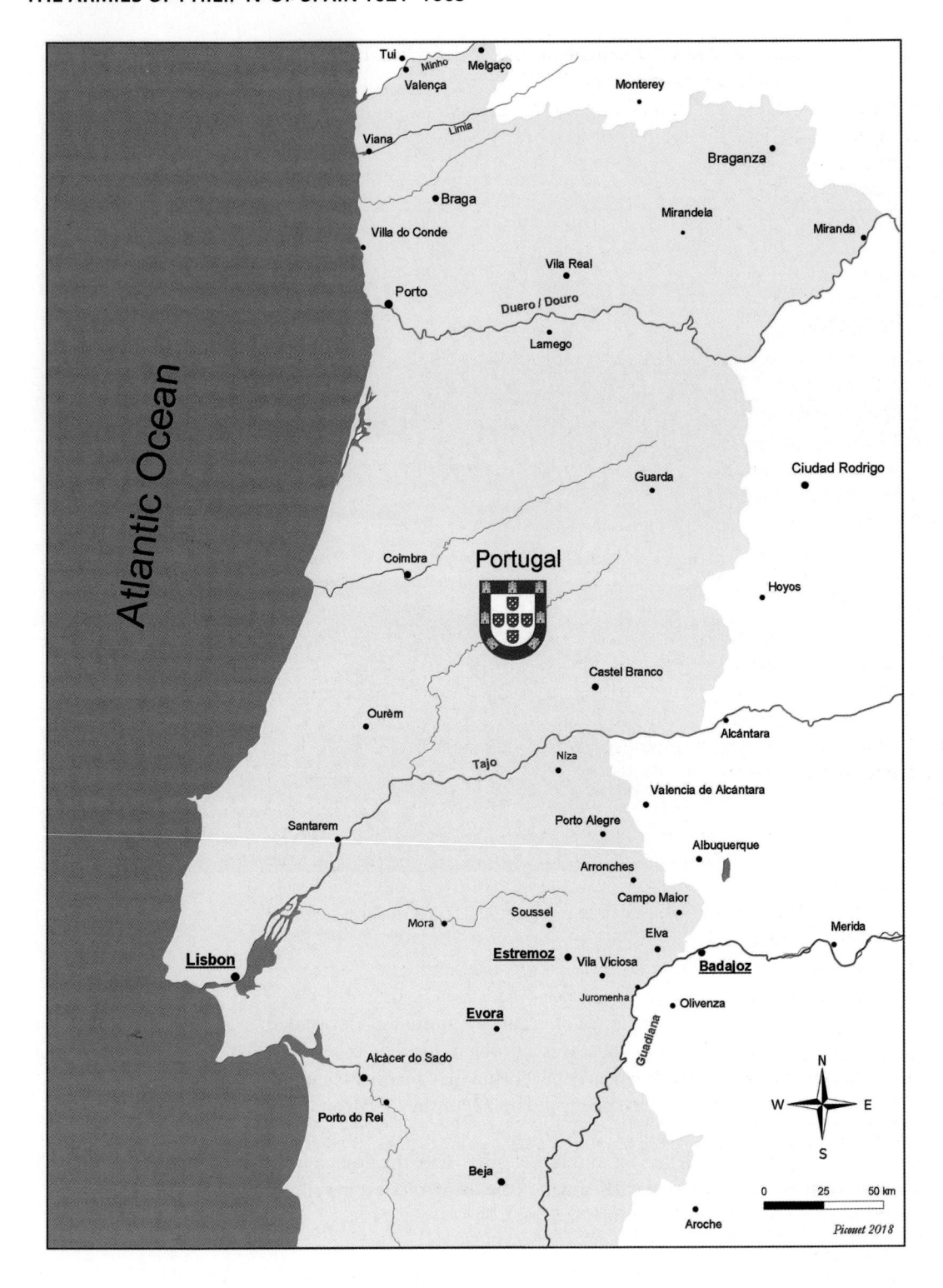

Map 1.4 Portugal and the Spanish border where most of the military operations took place during the War of Restoration (1640–1665).

In northern Italy, for the 1639 campaign, the Spanish had the support of Thomas of Savoy-Carignano and Maurice of Savoy and again their sister-in-law. Léganes started the campaign early on 19 March, sending Martin de Aragon[172] to besiege the fortress of Cengio. The French and Savoyards tried unsuccessfully to break the Spanish lines at a cost of 600 men, and on 4 April the garrison surrendered. Having secured the communication with Finale Ligure, the Spanish continued their operations and in a matter of three months, Crescentino was taken in eight days beside the garrison of 1,500 men, Asti fell on 5 May, followed by Villonava d'Asti, Trino, Chivasso, Ivrea, Verrua, Moncalvo, Trino and Santhià.[173] From his side Thomas of Savoy-Carignano easily took Cuneo, Mondivi and Ceva. On 25 July the Spanish[174] were in Torino, the city fell rapidly but the citadel of Torino was still in French hands. Leganés tried several times to take the position but was repulsed each time. On 4 August a ceasefire of 10 weeks was signed by the French and Spanish (Maffi 2014). For the French, with the losses of most of Piedmont and internal conspiracy Richelieu needed a little time to recover; for the Spanish, Léganes argued that his army was mostly depleted by the long campaign, the poor logistics, the fact that so many new positions needed a garrison and the failure to take the citadel of Torino. In Madrid, the Count-Duke of Olivares was outraged by such a ceasefire and he ordered to renew the offensive as soon as possible. On 24 October, Leganés resumed the military operation to try to catch the French army of 9,000 men of the Count of Harcourt near Chieri. The operation did not work well and the Count of Harcourt was able to escape from the trap, inflicting losses to the Spanish.

On the Iberian Peninsula, Olivares had planned to create a strong army in Catalonia, but the French mobilised before the Spanish and by 10 June the Duke of Halluin with 16,000 men was besieging the fortress of Salses defended by 600 men. By mid July the Spanish had only 8,000 regulars and 2,500 militia from Catalonia in Perpignan, not enough to attack the French lines, so despite a fiercely resistance Salses surrendered on 19 July. Meantime on the other side of the Pyrenees the French launched an invasion of Navarre with 8,000 men that was repulsed by the few regular soldiers and above all the local militia (Martinez-Ruis, 2008).

In Catalonia a general mobilisation was taking place and on 24 September the Spanish commander Enrique de Cardona had some 23,400 men[175] to

---

172 Martin of Aragón died on 23 March from a musket ball when he was inspecting the Spanish lines.
173 Most of the cities opened their doors after a short siege. The Spanish had the benefit of being helped by the supporters of Thomas and Maurice of Savoy (Novoa, CODOIN vol. 80, Madrid, 1883).
174 Infantry: five Spanish tercios (Lombardia, de la Mar de Napoles, Marquis of Tavara, Ponce de Léon and Marquis of Caracena), three Italian tercios (Bolognini, Count of Borromeo and Marquis of Serra), two German regiments (Prince Borso d'Este and Lemer) (Novoa, CODOIN 80, Madrid, 1883).
175 Regular army: 12,070 infantry (nine Spanish Tercios: Condé-Duque, Guardiola, Molina, Caballero, Guardia Su Majestad, Guzman, Armada, Provincial of Aragon and Provincial of Valencia; three Italian tercios: Montelecre, Tutavilla and Moles; Walloon Tercio of Molinghem, the regiment of the Duke of Modena and Irish Tercio of Tyrconell) and 3,060 cavalry. Catalan and Catalan militia: 8,330 infantry (10 tercios) (A 111/008 (24)). *Relacion Verdadera de Todo lo*

initiate the second siege of Salses against 2,500 French defenders. The Spanish constructed lines of circumvallation and contravallation that were tested successfully against French attacks in November. At last on 6 January the French surrendered the fortress, but afterwards (Parrot, 2001) it was more a Pyrrhic victory because the losses had been heavy, especially in the Catalan units, due mainly to epidemics.

1.6. On the Edge of Collapse: 1640–1646

Spain already had to fight on different fronts all over Europe; new trials would emerge, especially from the Iberian Peninsula. The will of the Spanish monarchy would be put to an extreme in this fight for supremacy and survival.

1640
In Madrid, the plan for 1640 was based on a powerful offensive against France using the Army of Flanders and the follow-up of the campaign in Piedmont. It was expected that the two attacks would diminish the possibility of a new French offensive in Catalonia where a small army would be based.

In the Low Countries, the Army of Flanders had in theory up to 88,000 men[176] to face Dutch and French. The Cardinal Infante divided the field army into two corps, the main one commanded Felipe de Silva and the other facing the Dutch under the command of the Count of La Fontaine. With new French subsidies,[177] the Dutch army opened the campaign in May with the objective of taking Bruges. On 21 May, a strong Dutch vanguard of 5,000 infantry and 2,000 cavalry with artillery was blocked by the Spanish and were forced to retire with losses. Between 1–3 July, the Dutch tried again to advance towards Hulst, but they were blocked by a force of five companies from the Spanish tercio of Saavedra, reinforced rapidly by others Spanish troops. The Dutch were again repulsed with losses between 400 and 2,000 men for 200 to 300 for the Spanish. As in the previous campaign Frederick Hendriks of Nassau withdrew to Bergen op Zoom and tried to carry out without success a campaign against Güeldres, as he had always a Spanish army to counter his movement.

Further to the South, the French armies[178] of La Meilleraye and Châtillon with an effective force of 31,000 men started their campaign against Arras on 6 June. Richelieu wanted a spectacular victory for this year and all the effort of the French monarchy would be dedicated to succeed it. The two French

---

Sucedido en los condado de Rosellon y Cerdaña, 24/09/1639 (University of Seville). Other sources give 12,000 men for the Catalans.
176 Up to 17,000 native Spaniards were the Army and the Cardinal Infante organised seven Spanish tercios of 20 companies. (Albi de la Cuesta 2016).
177 Estimated at 1,500,000 Guilders (675,000 escudos), with such funds 8,000 extra troops could be raised (van Nimwegen, 2010).
178 The French army of Champagne commanded by the Maérchal La Meilleraye with 10,000 infantry and 2,000 cavalry and French army of Picardy commanded by the Maréchal Châtillon and the Maréchal Chaulmes, with 15,000 infantry and 4,000 cavalry. The Maréchal du Hallier was in Lorraine with a smaller contingent of troops (Albi de la Cuesta 2016).

generals managed to confuse Felipe de Silva concerning the true objective, and when on 15 June La Meilleraye and Châtillon joined their respective armies to besiege Arras, the Spanish general could do nothing to counter the strategic manoeuvre. Arras was the capital of the County of Artois and was defended by a garrison of 1,500 infantry, four horse companies and the militia of the town. Immediately the French started the construction of a line of circumvallation as well as five fortified camps. On the Spanish side, due to the activity of the Dutch army, it took some time to join a decent force in Lille with the contingents of Felipe de Silva and of the Duke of Lorraine, and the Imperial one commanded by Lamboy. On 10 July, Mount Saint Eloi was taken but the French fortifications were too strong and full of troops. French supply convoys were harassed by the Spanish cavalry, even if on 19 July the Spanish failed to destroy a convoy of 500 wagons, 8,000 sheep and 100 cows. Between 25 and 30 July, hard hand-to-hand fighting took place in the external fortifications of Arras. Supply of such an army was always difficult and by the beginning of August the French forces were again short of supply. Richelieu decided to recall the army of du Hallier[179] in Doullens, 36 km south-west of Arras, to protect a large convoy of 5,000 wagons. In this critical situation, La Meilleraye took 12,000 men from the besieging army to increase the protection of the vital convoys for the last kilometre. However the information arrived late, it was the opportunity the Cardinal Infante was waiting for, and he decided to attack the French lines with three attacking columns.[180] After heavy fighting, the Spanish managed to open a breach in the French line, unfortunately the disorganisation and the indiscipline of the Spanish force could not prevent the success of the French counter-attack led by La Meilleraye supported by du Halliers. With the failure of the succour, the garrison of Arras had no hope to be rescued and capitulated with honours on 10 August. Although French losses during the siege had been heavy, 20,000 men (following Chavagnac),[181] Richelieu had at last his great victory after six years of campaigning. For the Spanish, the loss of the capital of the county of Artois was a terrible blow even if the defensive system of Flanders was mostly intact.

In northern Italy, the military situation was positive for the Spanish; most of Piedmont was in Spanish hands or belonged to its allies Thomas of Savoy-Carignano and Maurice of Savoy. The main drawbacks were that some key strongholds of the province (Citadel of Torino, Casale Monferato and Pignorolo) were in French hands. Contrary to orders from Madrid, the Marquis of Leganés decided to attack first Casale Monferrato with 16,000–18,000 men[182] and not the citadel of Torino. The campaign started beginning of April, but the bad weather had delayed the construction of the line of circumvallation and Harcourt with only 7,000 infantry and 2,300 cavalry

---

179 At Doullens François du Halliers was reinforced by troops and volunteers for a total of 13,000 infantry, 5,000 cavalry and 1,200 volunteers (Albi de la Cuesta 2016).
180 The first column with the Tercio of Pedro de León, two Italian tercios and a Lorraine regiment, the second with the tercio of Salazar and a Walloon tercio and the third with two Walloon tercios (Albi de la Cuesta 2016).
181 *Mémoire de Gaspard Conte de Chavagnac 1638–1669*, original edition of 1699 corrected by Jean de Villeurs, Edition Flammarion, Paris 1900.
182 Probably 12,000–14,000 infantry, 4,000 cavalry and an artillery of 14 guns.

appeared undetected. On 28 April he launched a devastating attack on the Spanish lines. The Spanish Army of Lombardy lost 3,000 to 5,000 men (for 500 to 1,000 French), all the artillery and the baggage, they had to leave the siege and withdrew to Vercielli. This first encounter would mark the rest of the campaign, the victorious Harcourt decided to continue the campaign to succour the garrison of the citadel of Torino besieging the 8,000 men of Thomas of Savoy-Carignano located in the city of Torino. One of the strangest sieges of the seventeenth century would start on 10 May by the conquest of the suburb of Valentino. Harcourt had only 13,000 men and could not hope to storm the city so he rapidly constructed strong lines of circumvallation and contravallation. The Marquis of Leganés did not lose time and after receiving reinforcements from Tyrol he moved to Torino with probably 16,000–17,000 men, and on 31 May he was near the French lines. Seeing that the French fortifications were strong and with the previous defeat in mind, Léganes decided to besiege the French army. Like Russian matriochka dolls, there was a French garrison in the citadel of Torino, Savoyard troops allied to the Spanish in the city of Torino, the French army of Harcourt besieging the city of Torino and the Spanish Army of Lombardy surrounding the French army of Harcourt. Prince Thomas still held some positions outside the city, but by the end of July Harcourt had managed to take them all. On the other side, the Marquis of Léganes, in coordination with the army of Thomas of Savoy-Carignano, launched various attacks in order to break the French lines. The most significant took place on 14 July when a force of 4,000 men commanded by Carlos de la Gatta managed to storm the quarter of La Mothe-Houdancourt but was repulsed by a vigorous French counter-attack. Supplies were running low in the French camps but also in the city and most of the tentative to introduce them failed. During the siege, the coordination between Thomas of Savoy-Carignano and Leganés had started to degrade, and mistrust between the allies was increasing with time. At last, seeing that Léganes did not want to risk his army in a full-scale attack on the French position, and with no supply to continue to resist, Thomas of Savoy-Carignano signed a ceasefire on 16 September. Four days later he was granted honourable terms for the capitulation and on 24 September he was moving towards his stronghold at the city of Ivrea. After this bitter end, Léganes had to withdraw to Lombardy and saw the French entering the city of Torino. This promising campaign had been a total disaster for the Spanish, but worse had happened in the Iberian Peninsula.

In Catalonia, the years of misunderstanding between Olivares and the local elite, the high cost in human life of the siege of Salses, the wishes of Olivares to quarter the infantry of the royal army[183] in Catalonia and the abuses of the troops during winter had left the province in a state of pre-insurrection. On 3 May the spark of insurrection was lit up when a column of Italian soldiers from the Tercio of Moles was attacked in the burg of

---

183 The Infantry of 8,180 men divided into six Spanish tercios (Coount-Duke, Provincial of Aragon, Molina, Guardia Su Majestad, Aguilar and Caballero), two Italian tercios (Moles and Tutavilla), the Walloon tercio of Molinghem, the regiment of the Duke of Modena and the Irish Tercio of Tyrconnell (Eliot, 1965).

San Celoni (Picouet 2014). The following were typical insurrection and counter-insurrection actions with reprisals from the troops and new violent actions from Catalan peasants. On 7 June, the mobilisation of 300 of the 2,000 reapers present in Barcelona for the procession of the *Corpus Christie* degenerated rapidly and all Castilians present in the city were chased and most of them killed, including the Viceroy Santa Colona. In the absence of civil power, the Spanish commander Juan de Garay decided to regroup some 7,000 men in the Roussillon and in Rosas, while the rest fled to the north of Valencia territory or to Aragon. Richelieu would not miss an opportunity like this, he rapidly sent emissaries to negotiate with the new Catalan authorities represented by Pau Claris and his supporters that had taken the control of the *Consell de Cent*.[184] On 7 September, by the treaty of Cervet, Catalonia became a republic under the protection of the king of France.[185] On the other side the Spanish government was totally taken by surprise by the uprising and the death of the viceroy. The Marquis of Los Vélez was sent to Zaragoza to organise the new royal army and to subdue the province as soon as possible. On 25 October, Los Vélez was in Tortosa[186] with most of the army and on 6 December he could start the campaign with a force of 25,000 men.[187] On 24 December, the town of Tarragona was taken without resistance and on 23 January the Catalan militia was defeated in Martorell. When they arrived in Sants a few kilometres from Barcelona centre, the Spanish army had been reduced to 15,000 infantry and 2,000 cavalry due to desertion and garrisons left in Tarragona and Villafranca del Penedes.[188] On 26 January 1641, the Spanish attack on Barcelona[189] started by an assault on the castle of Monjuich located south of the main city on a hill at 170 m above sea level. For several hours the Spanish army tried unsuccessfully to take the position and when the French-Catalans launched a small counter-attack

---

184 The *consell de cent* was a governmental institution of the city of Barcelona. In 1640 it was led by Francesc of Tamarit i de Rifà.
185 With the treaty of Ceret the French Monarchy agreed to send 6,000 infantry and 2,000 cavalry that would be paid by the new Catalan authorities. Also the Catalans agreed to raise 5,000 infantry and 500 cavalry.
186 Some of the members of the local bourgeoisie were against the insurrection and opened the gates of the city to the Spanish.
187 The royal army had 23,000 infantry and 18 units, divided into five Spanish regiments/tercios from nobility (Duke of Medinacelli, Duke of Infantado, Gran Prior de Castilla, Marquis of Mortara and Duke of Pastrana y de Sesa, commanded most of them by their lieutenant colonel), eight Spanish tercios (Count-Duke, Marquis of los Velez, Presidios de Portugal, Martin de los Arcos, Pedro de la Saca, Fernando de Tajada, Alonso de Calatayud and Diego de Villalba) two provincial tercios (Castilla and Guipúzcoa), the Walloon tercio of the Count of Isenghien, the Portuguese tercio of Simón Mascarenhas, the Irish tercio of Tyrconnell, some Italian companies, 3,100 cavalry (Trozo of Rodrigo de Herrera, Trozo of Álvaro de Quiñones, Trozo of Filangieri, Trozo of the Duke of San Jorge and a guard company) and an artillery train of 24 guns (De Melo, Francisco Manuel, *Historia de los movimientos, separación y guerra de Cataluña* (Madrid: Castalia, 1996).
188 E. De Mesa (2001), *La batalla de Montjuic 1641*. Desperata Ferro <https://www.despertaferro-ediciones.com/pdf/La_batalla_de_Montjuic.pdf>, consulted 24 January 2018.
189 Barcelona was defended by four tercios from the Coronelia of Barcelona and four Catalan companies of cavalry, two French regiments (Sevignan and Espenan) and some companies of French cavalry (Picouet 2014).

most of the exhausted Spanish troops withdrew.[190] With a demoralised army, without proper logistics to carry out a formal siege, the Marquis of los Velez ordered a general withdrawal to Tarragona, where more troops deserted. The war of the reapers had started and was engulfed in a struggle for hegemony between France and Spain.

The last event of this disastrous year happened in the west of the kingdom of Portugal. Since 1580 Spain and Portugal had the same king but the two kingdoms remained separate with two administrations. With the outbreak of the war with the Dutch Republic, the main concern of the Portuguese was the defence of their empire in Brazil, Africa, and India while the Spanish were more interested in the war in Europe. The divergence created a split between the elite of Portugal favourable to Spain, and those not. At the same time most of the common people were against the Hapsburg dynasty and their wars (Maffi 2014). On 1 December a group of Portuguese noblemen easily took the royal palace of Lisbon, deposed the Vice Queen Margaret of Savoy and proclaimed the Duke of Bragança King of Portugal as João IV of Portugal. Spain had no troops[191] to face such a new challenge and in the following weeks most of the understrength Spanish garrisons fell to the rebels with little fighting. In January 1641, all Portugal was in the hands of the supporters of João of Bragança, only Ceuta remained loyal to Spain.[192] The *war of the restoration* had started.

1641

For the Spanish monarchy, 1640 have been an *annus horribilis* and the possibilities to adopt an offensive strategy against France and the Dutch Republic was much reduced. For the Count-Duke of Olivares, the new priority was the war in the Iberian Peninsula and particularly in Catalonia, so the best troops available in the Iberian Peninsula would be sent to the north-east and not to counter the rebellion of Portugal.[193] On the other front, Flanders and Italy should undertake actions to reduce the pressure on the Catalan front. At the same time in the south of Spain, the Duke of Medina Sidonia was playing a dangerous game with a plot to incite rebellion in the region of Andalusia[194]. In France, the Count-Duke was also supporting a

---

190 The numbers of raw recruits, the lack of trained officers had probably played a role in the failure of the attack (De Mesa, 2001).
191 The citadel of Lisbon had only a garrison of 500 men and in the rest of the country, including the Azores Archipelago, only 1,500 men were available (Maffi 2014).
192 In February 1641, the Marquis of Montalvao arrived in Salvador do Bahia to communicate to the Luso-Brazilian that a new king of Portugal had been proclaimed and that Brazil was not any more part of the Spanish Empire. From that point the future of the Portuguese colony of Brazil was not a great concern for the Spanish authorities. The last irony took place during the negotiation of Münster in 1647, when the Spanish would offer the territories of Brazil to the Dutch.
193 As stated (Maffi, 2014), in 1641 the new Portuguese regime was weak and was looking desperately for the support of the French and other European powers. At that time a strong Spanish offensive with veteran troops coupled to adequate political measures could have some chance to overcome the rebellion.
194 For an overall view of the conspiracy of the ninth Duke of Medina Sidonia, refer to L. Salas y Almela, *The Conspiracy of the Ninth Duke of Medina Sidonia (1641). An aristocrat in the crisis of the Spanish Empire* (Leiden-Boston: Brill, 2013).

conspiracy against Richelieu lead by the Count of Soissons,[195] a French noble of royal blood.

In the Low Countries, the Cardinal Infante had to send veteran Walloon units[196] to reinforce the armies in Spain and with the men available he divided his mobile force in two armies, commanded by the Count of La Fontaine in the north and Jean de Beck in the south. He had also the support of a small Imperial army of 7,000–10,000 men commanded by Lamboy and had just enough money to pay the regiments raised by the French rebels in Sedan. Although facing internal difficulties, Richelieu was able to organise two main armies in the north, the army of Champagne with 13,000 men to check the plot of the prince in Sedan and the army of La Meilleraye to continue the progress in Flanders after the victory of Arras. By mid May, the army of La Meilleraye, with 25,000 men, was concentrated in Abbeville and moved towards Aire-Sur-la-Lys, the back door of the County of Flanders. On 19 May the city was besieged by the French force, while Jean de Beck was reacting, sending cavalry parties to harass French supply convoys and infantry to reinforce the garrison of Aire-Sur-la-Lys before the line of circumvallation was finished. The garrison made a gallant resistance, but on 26 July the governor capitulated with honourable terms. Further to the southeast, the army of the "malcontents" of 4,000 men led by the Count of Soisson, reinforced by 7,000 men from the Imperials of Lamboy, defeated the army of the Field Marshal of Châtillon at La Marflées on 6 July. The French force's losses were significant, some 5,000 to 6,000 men, and the victory of army of the "malcontents" could have been an important one for Olivares if the leader of the French rebels, the Count of Soissons, had not been mysteriously shot dead after the battle.[197] To the disgust of the Spanish command, the rest of the French noblemen returned to their former allegiance and were pardoned, those nobles were too powerful and Richelieu could not punish them. North of the Low Countries, Frederick Hendricks of Nassau sent his 20,000 men strong army to besiege the city of Gennep on 1 June. The Spanish army of La Fontaine could do nothing to save the city and on 29 July the governor of the city Thomas Preston capitulated with honourable terms. After the victorious siege, the Dutch commander tried again to establish a foothold against Hulst but was prevented by the Spanish and had to send his troops to winter quarters.

Coming to the south of the Low Countries, the Cardinal Infante was camped at Boëseghem, near Aire-Sur-Lys. With the arrival of Lamboy, he had enough men to confront the French army reduced by the losses suffered

---

195 The conspiracy was clearly connected with the Queen Mother Marie of Medici, and Soissons was supported by the Duke of Bouillon (brother of the famous Viscount of Turenne), prince of the independent state of the Principality of Sedan.
196 A first unit, the Tercio of Ghislain de Bryas, Marquis of Molinghem was sent in 1639 and a second unit, the Tercio of Balthazard Philippe de Gand, Count of Isenghien was sent in 1640 (Baron Guillaume, *Histoire de l'infanterie wallone sous la maison d'Espagne (1500–1800)*, Chapter VII, Académie des Sciences de Belgique, 1876).
197 The death of the Count of Soissons remains a mystery, for some the Count was murdered after the battle by a French officer paid by Richelieu, for others he killed himself when he tried to open his helmet (Monglat vol. 2).

during the siege. La Meilleraye had only 15,000 men in hand and he decided prudently to leave a strong garrison of 5,000 men in Aire-Sur-Lys and with the rest, to withdraw to the south to meet the reformed army of Châtillon (now commanded by the Field Marshal of Brézé) much reinforced by a reserve corps. The new siege of Aire-Sur-Lys started 8 August and the objective of the Spanish was to surrender the strong French garrison from hunger. On 10 August the Cardinal Infante had to leave the army due to a sudden sickness. On 23 August, the reorganised French force of La Meilleraye in combination with the army of Brézé conducted various attacks to distract the Spanish; Lens was taken in three days and La Bassée on 29 August after a siege of five days. The combined French army continued to manoeuvre, threatening Lille and Douai and besieging Bapaume on 12 September. The Spanish garrison made a poor resistance and after a siege of one week they surrendered on 18 September. Meantime the sickness of the Cardinal Infante much worried Madrid and as soon as possible they sent Francisco de Melo to assist him. De Melo arrived in Flanders by mid September and after discussion with the Cardinal Infante and the high-ranking officers of the Army of Flanders decided to continue the siege of Aire-Sur-Lys. The French army now commanded by the Count of Guiche considered that the Spanish fortifications were too strong and by the beginning of November he sent his troops to winter quarters. On 25 November the French governor of Aire-Sur-Lys started negotiations to capitulate and after long discussion with Francisco de Melo he agreed to surrender on 7 December. On 9 November, the Cardinal Infante Fernando of Austria died at 32 years old, probably from the smallpox and the heavy burden of the war against two opponents.

This year war was still ravaging Germany, and the French army called the "Armée d'Allemagne" under the command of Guébriant conducted a successful campaign in combination with the troops of Hesse-Kasel against the territory of the Archbishop of Cologne (Münster and Dorsten). Seeing that the small army of Haztfeldt was not enough to deal with the French, by October 1641 Emperor Ferdinand III decided to recall the army of Lamboy from the Army of Flanders.

In northern Italy, after the disastrous siege of Torino, the Marquis of Léganes had been dismissed and replaced by the Count of Siruela.[198] Due to the insurrection in Spain, the new Governor received orders to send some of his best troops to Spain and with the rest, Olivares told him to resume the offensive in Piedmont. Rapidly the new governor discovered that it was impossible to carry out an offensive due to the reduction of the army's strength and the discrepancies with Prince Thomas of Savoy-Garignano. Indeed, the first to move was the French army with the capture of Moncalvo on 6 March. On 12 April the French army was besieging Ivrea, the stronghold of Thomas of Savoy-Garignano, and on 23 April a full-scale attack was repulsed by the garrison. The Spanish army managed to send reinforcements to the city and on 8 May they moved against the city of Chivasso on the

---

[198] Juan Velasco de la Cueva, eighth Count of Siruela was a creature of the Count-Duke Olivares, previously he was ambassador in Genoa and had little military experience (Maffi 2014).

River Pô just 23 km east from Torino, to force the French commander the Count of Harcourt to leave Ivrea. The manoeuvre succeeded and Harcourt had to abandon the siege of Ivrea on 14 May to succour Chivasso. When it was done the French withdrew to the west to wait for the arrival of new recruits. On 28 July a reinforced French army was besieging the city of Coni defended by a garrison of 1,400 men. A diversion against Cherasco was tried again by the Spanish and the force of Thomas of Savoy-Carignano, but this time they failed and Coni surrendered on 8 September. For Olivares, the only positive news from Italy was the fact that Moncalvo was retaken at the end of September.[199] Following the Mediterranean coast towards the west, Onorato Grimaldi, Prince of Monaco, was upset with the Governorship of Milan and seeing the weakness of the Spanish decided to change sides, expelling the small Spanish garrison; a valuable harbour had been lost.

In Catalonia, the survivors of the army of the Marquis of Le Velez were in Tarragona and they were surprised on 4 May, when Philippe de la Mothe-Houdancourt with an army of 12,000 men supported by 3,000 Catalans and the French fleet of Soudis (26 vessels, four fireships and 19 galleys) appeared to besiege their city. The Spanish garrison fought desperately to keep control of Tarragona province even if Salou was lost on 9 May, and Constanti on 13 May. Several clashes were recorded between the garrison and the French-Catalan forces but on two occasions, 4 July and 23 August the Armada of the Marquis of Villafranca managed to reinforce the garrison and bring supplies. Unable to attack the city, La Mothe-Houdancourt had to abandon the siege on 25 August and to return to protect Barcelona. Further to the north the small Spanish army of the Roussillon was under attack by the 14,000 men of the army of the Prince of Condé. Methodically, the French started to destroy the Spanish defensive system, taking Le Canet, Angelets, the Castle of Laroque (actually Laroque-des-Albères) and the fortress of Saint Elme (Montglat, volume 1, 1826). At the end of the campaign the Spanish had only garrisons in Collioures, Salses, Perpignan and Rosas and the communication between the four garrisons was mostly cut and perilous. On 31 December 1641, the French tried without success to take Collioures by surprise. The attack failed but it was a clear indication that the final conquest of the Roussillon would be on the French agenda in 1642.

In Portugal, the Spanish had few regular troops and although up to 12,000 men were deployed along the border, most of them were extracted from local militia. Small actions took place along the border, such as a cavalry skirmish on 9 June favourable to the Spanish, or the Spanish failure to take Olivenza on 16 September, and the Portuguese failure to take Valverde on 29 October.

1642

From Madrid, it was clear that for the next campaign all the French effort would be concentrated in Catalonia. Spanish armies in northern Italy and Portugal would have to adopt a defensive strategy but for the Army of

---

199 The Count of Siruela had not enough troops to correctly garrison Moncalvo, so the fortification of the small town was totally destroyed.

Flanders a more offensive attitude was expected against the French in order to divert troops from the south, Brussels was only 283 km from Paris.

For the new governor of the Low Countries Francisco de Melo, another setback had to be taken into account: the 17 January, the Imperial army of Lamboy defending the Electorate of Cologne was destroyed at the battle of Kempen.[200] The consequence of this defeat was that the region of Westphalia, the Duchy of Jülich and part of the electorate of Cologne were mostly in the hands of the French or their allies (Negredo del Cerro 2016). Francisco de Melo decided to initiate the campaign as soon as possible and on 19 April, the city of Lens surrendered after a short siege of two days. On 20 April the Spanish were besieging La Bassée, defended by up to 3,000 men. On the French side, the order was to adopt a defensive position to protect the frontier.[201] The two French commanders tried to adopt a more aggressive position to save La Bassée, but after a siege of three weeks the city surrendered on 13 May. Later on the French forces split, with Harcourt taking a defensive position between Hesdin and Abbeville and de Guiche moving towards Le Châtelet on a defensive position near the village of Honnecourt-sur-Escaut to defend the Vermandois region. The Spanish high command of the Army of Flanders saw an opportunity and rapidly they moved to follow the Count of Guiche. On 26 of May the Spanish army, with 19,000 men, arrived in battle formation facing the French position in Honnecourt-sur-Escaut. The battle[202] was rapidly engaged and after hours of fighting the French army was destroyed having lost up to 3,600 men dead and wounded, 3,400 prisoners and all the artillery. It is said that, two days after the battle, de Guiche found only 1,600 men, mostly horsemen, in Saint Quentin (Périni vol. 3, 1893). After such victory, most of the Spanish officers were expecting to undertake the siege of an important place in France or in the Low Countries but de Melo thought that he had to deal with the French force of Guébriant operating near Cologne. De Melo left a small observation corps under the command of Jean de Beck in Lille and with the rest he moved to the east. During the rest of the campaign nothing relevant was achieved, the French force of Harcourt was defending their position in the south; the Dutch army was paralysed by the lack of funds and the poor results of the previous campaign, and the Spanish army had blocked a possible advance of Québriant in the Low Countries but could not effectively remain for long in the east and supported the Catholic force in Cologne.[203] It is also notable to indicate that the main German ally of the Spanish monarchy, the Holy Roman Empire, was in a difficult position.

---

200 At the battle of Kempen the Franco-Weimarian-Hessian army of 4,000 infantry, 5,500 cavalry and 23 guns under the command of Guébriant surprised the Imperial force of Lamboy. The army of Lamboy was totally destroyed losing probably 7,000 men and all the artillery and baggage (Guthrie, 2003).

201 The Count of Harcourt was the new commander of the Army of Picardy with 15,000 men to the west and the Count of Guiche was futher to the south-east with the army of Champagne with 10,000 men (Monglat volume 1).

202 For a detailed account of the battle please see Chapter 4.

203 Guébriant's army was reinforced with troops (German, French) coming from the Dutch Republic. By mid June the French commanders had 7,000 infantry and 8,000 cavalry operating between Cologne and Juliers (Parrot 2001).

During the summer, the Swedish army of Gustav Tortensson had conducted a brilliant campaign in Brandenburg, Moravia, and Silesia and when the Imperial army had caught him near Leipzig, he managed to defeat them at the second battle of Breitenfeld on 2 November.[204] For the Spanish interest, the main consequence was that Emperor Ferdinand III was only concerned by the survival of his territories where he wanted to concentrate all his troops (Negredo del Cerro 2016).

In northern Italy, the main event occured when the princes Thomas of Savoy-Carignano and Maurice of Savoy made peace with the French and the Regency of Savoy with the treaty of Torino.[205] For the Count of Siruela the "treason" of the two brothers implemented a new scenario with very bad prospects for the Spanish affair in the area. At the beginning of August, the combined Franco-Savoyard army[206] started the campaign and in a succession of weeks they captured Crescentino on 14 August, Nizza Monferrato on 3 September, and Verrua on 17 October. Alessandria and Santhià were also attacked but managed to resist thanks to the resistance of the defenders and a prompt response by the army of Lombardy. The main military operation was conducted against Tortona on 4 October, with a combined army of 10,000 infantry and 5,000 cavalry, the Count of Siruela had only 8,000 to 9,000 men to oppose them and was unable to prevent the siege or to force the line of circumvallation. The small garrison of 1,300 men of Tortona made a gallant resistance but after eight weeks the defenders capitulated on 28 November with honourable terms. Distress took over the inhabitants of Lombardy and Olivares had to dismiss the Count of Siruela by the Marquis of Velada with the order to retake Tortona at any cost.

This year, Catalonia was the main objective of the French monarchy. King Louis XIII and the court were at Narbonnes. The French army had already blocked the Spanish garrisons in Perpignan, Collioures and Salses. In January 1642 the Spanish managed to reinforce the existing garrisons and provided supply. Being a harbour, where reinforcements could still arrive by sea, Collioure was attacked first and on 16 March the city was surrounded by a detachment of 2,000 cavalry later by the rest of the army, in total 10,000 men. Less than one month later on 13 April the Marquis of Mortara and the Spanish garrison of Collioure capitulated having lost their only water well

---

204 At the second battle of Breitenfeld, the Swedish had 10,000 cavalry, 10,000 infantry and 70 guns and the Imperials (Archduke Leopold and Ottavio Piccolomini) had some 16,000 cavalry, 10,000 infantry and 46 guns. Losses were estimated at 4,000 dead and wounded for the Swedish and 5,000 dead and wounded and 4,500 prisoners for the Imperials (Guthrie, 2003).

205 By the treaty of Torino, signed on 14 June 1642, Maurice of Savoy and Thomas of Savoy-Carignano would recognise the Duchess of Savoy as regent of the Duchy. Maurice of Savoy would keep control of the city and citadel of Nice as well as the harbour of Villefranche while Thomas of Savoy-Carignano would keep control of Ivrea and Biella. Both of them would have to expel the Spanish garrisons of their territories and at the end of the regency they would return all their fortress cities to the Duke (Montglat volume 1).

206 The combined army had 7,000 infantry and 5,000 cavalry and was commanded by Thomas of Savoy-Carignano with the support of the French commanded by the Duke of Longueville. Reinforcements were sent regularly to the combined army (Saluces, volume 4, 1818).

with the explosion of a mine.[207] A strong garrison was left in the fortress and with the rest the French commander La Meilleraye [208] went to strengthen the blockade of Perpignan. In order to send reinforcement and supply to Perpignan, the Spanish Marquis of Povar organised a mobile detachment of 3,000 men to cross Catalonia. The detachment was intercepted by the French army in Catalonia on 26 and 30 of March and totally destroyed or captured including the Marquis of Povar. Following his victory, the Count of La Mothe-Houdancourt failed to take Tortosa by surprise on 2 and 3 May, but by contrast he managed to take the town of Monzòn in the province of Aragon on 10 June. The last attempt to supply Roussillon was performed, sending a powerful fleet[209] that was intercepted by the French fleet based in Barcelona. From 30 June to 2 July, the two fleets fought bravely, but with the loss of three galleons to one French ship of the line, the Spanish admiral had to withdraw to the Baleares Islands, and the fate of Perpignan was sealed. The garrison of Perpignan held out for two more months, but on 10 September, Flores Davila had to capitulate with honourable terms with only 500 men fit for service out of an original garrison of 3,000. Salses, the last bastion of the Spanish presence in the County of Roussillon, surrendered few days later. The Count-Duke of Olivares had still an army estimated at 16,000 men in Tarragona. On 21 September the army of Catalonia moved towards Lérida, there they met another Spanish force commanded by the Marquis of Léganes. On 7 October the whole army, estimated at 15,000 infantrymen, 5,000 cavalry men and nine guns, marched towards Vilanoveta, south of Lérida, to find a Franco-Catalan army of 13,000 men deployed on a hill near the small burg. Throughout the whole day the Spanish forces attacked the French position, but poor coordination and the performance of the French cavalry frustrated the Spanish efforts. With the night coming, Léganes had to order withdrawal to Torres de Segres and Zaragoza. During the battle,[210] the Spanish had lost probably 1,500 to 2,000 men between dead, wounded and prisoners for 500 men for the French, but due to heavy rain, lack of supplies, diseases and a high desertion rate, the Spanish army ceased to exist as a fighting force.

On the Portuguese front fighting was characteristic of a secondary front where the Portuguese took some small villages and the small town of Cheles.

The popularity of the Count-Duke of Olivares was close to nil amongst the Spanish population, but above all amongst the Spanish nobility, he was obliged

---

207 Delamont, Ernest, *Siege de Perpignan. 1641–1642*, "Extrait de l'Histoire du Roussillon de 1639 jusqu'a nos jours", Perpignan, 1873.

208 Following Delamon op. cit., the French had up to 22,000 infantry and 4,000 cavalry, probably an exaggeration, 20,000 men including the volunteers seems to be more accurate.

209 Following C. de la Roncière (La Roncière 1920), the Spanish fleet was under the command of Juan Alonso Idiáquez, Marques of Ciudad Real, with 36 galleons/ships of the line, 10 galleys, three frigates, three pataches, six fireships, six tartanes and 35 long boats.

210 Pere Lacavalleria, *Relació compendiosa de tot lo que ha passat desde que lo exèrcit del rei de Castella ha partit de Tarragona y de la senyalada victòria que lo senyor mariscal de la Motte ha guianyada a la vista de la ciutat de Lleida*. [http://soltorres.udl.cat/jspui/bitstream/10459/1901/1/PLLE-1-0002.pdf]

to resign at the beginning of 1643.[211] In France, his great enemy Cardinal Richelieu just had time to savour his victory; he died 4 December 1642.

1643

For the next campaign, the authorities in Madrid sent a message to Francisco de Melo to undertake a strong diversion to attract the French army to the north and reduce the pressure in Catalonia. The objective of the Spanish governor was a small fortified town called Rocroi guarding the entrance of the valley of the River Oise. The Spanish were caught by surprise by the arrival of the French army of the Duke of Enghien in the afternoon of 18 May. The next day the two armies fought during most of the morning but the result was a tactical French victory. French losses were estimated at 4,500 men and the Spanish at fewer than 10,000 men if we take into account the capitulation of 2,500 men, a treatment usually given to a fortress garrison.[212] Rocroi was not the end of the army of Flanders, soon Jean de Beck had an army of 16,000 men to cover the south of the Low Countries while Andrea Cantelmo was in the north with 9,000–10,000 men to observe the Dutch army. For Frederick Hendricks of Nassau, the campaign was disappointing: all his advances were blocked by the forces of Cantelmo, reinforced by troops from the main army.[213] Most of the fighting was skirmishing between detachments of infantry and cavalry or cavalry alone, the Spanish won near Maastricht and the Dutch in Brabant. By the end of September the Dutch army went to winter quarters, it was clear that without good coordination with the French, the Dutch could not execute a significant advance in Flanders. Meantime French king Louis XIII died on 14 May, leaving a five-year-old son, and with a victory in hand, the regent Queen Anne of Austria and her first minister *Giulio Raimondo Mazzarino*, better known as Cardinal Mazarin, could assure their power over the French nobility. After the battle, the Duke of Enghien sent his army to the south to refresh and to receive reinforcements and on 16 June he was besieging the city of Thionville. The Spanish garrison made a strong resistance and it was only after 56 days, on 10 of August, that they agreed to capitulate.

In the east Field Marshal Guébriant with 12,000 men had conducted a campaign in southern Germany but he was unable to take the important city of Rottweil and had to withdraw to the Rhine valleys, waiting for reinforcement (Estaban Ribas 20). With the end of the siege of Thionville, the Duke of Enghien was obliged to send up to 8,000 men for the French army of Germany, Mazarin wanted a powerful force in the Rhine valley to subdue the last Imperial-Bavarian and Spanish[214] garrisons of the area. In the Low Countries, Francisco de Melo received a letter from Charles of Lorraine, the commander

---

211 The Count-Duke resigned 23 January 1643 and was exiled to Loeches and later to the town of Toro, where he died 22 July 1645.
212 After a long controversy, losses could be estimated at 1,500–2,000 dead, 3,826 prisoners and up to 2,500 men included in the capitulation. Some of these men were found in the army of Catalonia in 1644, others came back to Flanders (Picouet 2010).
213 Vincarts, *Relación de la campaña del año 1643*, CODOIN vol. 75, Madrid 1880.
214 Spanish troops had held the city of Frankenthal in the Palatinate since 1621. In fact the garrison left the city only in 1652 (Negredo del Cerro, 2016).

of the Bavarian contingent, asking him to send troops to help him to check the French. In September, there were no more activities in the south or north and Francisco de Melo took the decision to send a small force of 4,000 men. With a force of 17,000–18,000 men, Guébriant took the decision to conduct a winter campaign and by 7 November he was besieging Rottweil. The city surrendered on 19 November but Guébriant received a fatal wound and died five days later. The new French commander Josep Rantzau decided to go into winter quarter with his forces in Tuttlingen and the surrounding area. On the other side the Imperial-Bavarian army had close to 20,000 men including the detachment of 4,000 men from the army of Flanders and by a surprise attack they destroyed the French army on 25 November at Tuttlingen. French losses were close to 11,000 men[215] for 1,000 men on the Catholic side. Rottweil was retaken 19 December after a siege of three weeks.

In northern Italy the order of the governor of Lombardy was to retake Tortona at all costs. The Italian operation started 7 February when a vanguard of 3,000 men took the convent of Saint Dominique near the city. Joined by the rest of the army, the 10,000 Spanish (Saluces volume 4, 1818) started the construction of a line of circumvallation and four gun batteries to bombard Tortona. On the other side, Thomas of Savoy-Carignano with 10,000 men tried unsuccessfully to send reinforcements on 5 March. The combined army was slightly reinforced by French new recruits and with this army the prince besieged the city of Asti on 12 April. Engulfed in the siege of Tortona, the Spanish failed to reinforce Asti and the city was obliged to surrender on 5 May after a poor resistance. Tortona finally capitulated with honourable terms on 27 May, but the Spanish army was in poor state after a siege of four months and was unable to counter the movement of the Franco-Savoyard army. With close to 20,000 men the Spanish enemies were able to besiege the city of Trino on 7 August. After a gallant resistance Trino capitulated on 27 of September and on 28 October the small town of Pontestura surrendered after a siege of 14 weeks.

In Catalonia, after the disastrous previous year, the new Spanish commander the Marquis of Hinojosa, tried to take Flix and Miravet on the River Ebro during the first three months of the year. Each time the Count of La Mothe-Houdancourt was able to counter the Spanish movements, particularly at Miravet when the Spanish lost up to 1,200 men.[216] In summer, La Mothe-Houdancourt was left with few troops and had to adopt a defensive position. At the end of July the Spanish cavalry[217] conducted a successful raid against the French quarter located south of Lérida, inflicting serious losses. In September another operation against Flix failed but by 21 October

---

215 If we take into account the losses of the battles of Honnecourt, Rocroi and Tuttlingen, the French losses are close to 22,500 men, while the Spanish losses amount to 11,000 men and the Imperial-Bavarian ones to 1,000 men, but for the good fortune of the French they could recover better than their enemies from their defeats.

216 J. Sanabre, *La acción de Francia en Cataluña en la pugna por la hegemonía de Europa: 1640–1659* (Barcelona: Reial Acadèmia de Bones Lletres de Barcelona, 1956). Eva Serra (ed.).

217 The Aviso of 3 August 1643 (*Memorial Historico*, volume 33) claims that the French losses were 1,500 dead and wounded and 1,000 prisoners. These numbers are exaggerated.

Felipe da Silva, the new commander of the Spanish army[218] moved to the north to retake Monzòn. On 29 October the city was surrounded and after a resistance of more than one month, the French governor capitulated on 2 December. Meantime, La Mothe-Houdancourt stayed around Lérida with some 10,500 men, on the news of the capitulation of Monzòn all the French positions in the County of Ribagorza were evacuated and the garrison of Lérida was fortified with six infantry regiments.[219]

On the Portuguese front, few actions took place and it was only in September that a Portuguese army of up to 14,000 men commanded by the Duke of Obidos launched a surprise attack against Badajoz (Maffi 2014). The operation failed totally due to the poor preparation of the Portuguese and the defence of the city. The Portuguese conducted minor operations against Valverde de Leganés on 14 September, Alconchel on 28 September and other smaller burgs and villages (La Albuera, Almendral, La Torre de Miguel Sesmero, Alconchel, and Higuera de Vargas) in October.[220] At last in Galicia, the town of Salvatierra was lost to the Portuguese and retaken by the Spanish with the support of the militia of the province.

1644

The Spanish Council of State was preparing an important operation to shift the balance in Catalonia and for that they gave order to Francisco de Melo to carry out an operation against France. The answer of the governor of the Low Countries was clear, without more money and men such task was impossible. In reality Mazarin had already decided to transfer the main effort of the French army to Flanders and Germany. The French and Dutch objective was to attack the County of Flanders, Gravelines and Dunkirk for the French and Ghent for the Dutch. With 21,000–22,000 men the new French commander, the Duke of Orleans, surrounded Gravelines on 1 June. The Spanish army had no other option to avoid a new general confrontation against the French so they just tried to send reinforcements to the city. Most of them failed, such as the one with 400 men on 4 July (Montglat, volume 1, 1826) and on 29 July the Spanish garrison was forced to capitulate with honourable terms when a breach had been made in the walls. Further to the north, Frederick Hendricks of Nassau spent most of June in Flanders to prevent de Melo joining all his forces to relieve Gravelines (van Nimwegen, 2010). At last by the end of July he was free to undertake an offensive campaign and this time he selected the fortress of Sluis van Ghent defended by 2,300 men. On 28 July the 20,000 men strong Dutch army had surrounded the position and was constructing as fast as possible a strong line of circumvallation. The Spanish had only a mobile force of 10,000 men in the area and could do little to interfere. When Francisco de Melo managed to assemble a consistent

---

218 Spanish forces have been estimated at 8,500 infantry, 3,000 cavalry, 300 dragoons and an artillery train of 20 guns (Picouet 2014).
219 Following the *Gazette de France* of 1644, la Mothe-Houdancourt had in January 1644, 16 infantry regiments: six in Lleida, three in Balaguer, two in Flix, one in Miravel, two in the Empurdà and two in Villafranca.
220 F.D. Costa, *A Guerra da Restauração 1641–1668* (Lisbon: Livros Horizonte, 2004).

force of 20,000 men,[221] on 5 August, he found Sluis van Ghent surrounded by powerful Dutch fortifications and decided not to test them. Finally on 5 September the garrison of Sluis van Ghent capitulated after a siege of 40 days. For the new Spanish governor of Flanders, the Marquis of Castel Rodrigo, it was clear that the Army of Flanders could not properly face a double invasion with a mobile force of only 30,000 men or less.

In Germany, the Bavarian army had to withdraw after the inconclusive Battle of Freiburg and the only good news for the Spanish was the signing of a ceasefire in the province of Franche-Comté. The ceasefire was followed by the treaty of Joux (26 March 1645), the province would become neutral in exchange for subsidies to the French crown until the end of the war between Spain and France. The geographical position and the attacks on Lombardy and Flanders meant that the Spanish never had the possibility to properly defend this territory.

In northern Italy, the Marquis of Velada knew that his army had been left with little resources and he lacked both men and money to carry out offensive actions. Prince Thomas of Savoy-Carignano first conducted the Franco-Savoyard army against the fortress of Breme at the end of June, but after a formal siege of 22 days facing a strong opposition he turned his army against an easier target, Arona, on 26 July. The siege did not go well because the Spanish were able to introduce several reinforcements in the city and on 7 August he decided again to withdraw. Meantime the Marquis of Velada launched cavalry raids in Piedmont and a surprise attack to retake Asti on 28 July.[222] On the other side of the hill, Thomas of Savoy-Carignano had better luck against Santhìa, the city was besieged on 14 August and surrendered on 7 September. Later on, the Franco-Savoyards had to besiege again the citadel of Asti between 18 September and 1 October. At last a French column tried to take the harbour of Finale Ligure but was prevented by an action of the Marquis of Velada.

On 6 February His Majesty King Philip IV left Madrid and arrived on the 13th in Zaragoza. With the arrival of the king, the build-up of the army sped up and on 1 May 1644 Felipe da Silva could present to the king his field army in Berbegal, 20 km west of Monzòn. The Spanish had assembled[223] a force of 9,550 infantry, 4,340 cavalry (600 dismounted) and an artillery train of 24 guns. On 4 May the army started the campaign to retake Lérida, at first da Silva moved towards the city of Balaguer but in the face of the French reinforcement of the city, had to dismiss the operation on 11 May. Two days later most of the Spanish army was located on the Noguera River some kilometres south-east of the village of Albesa while a strong vanguard was south of Lérida. On the side and with the arrival of a contingent of troops

---

221 Losses of the French army during the siege of Gravelines had been important and they were too exhausted to continue military operations in August (van Ninwengen, 2010).
222 3,000 Spanish infantry failed to take the city but managed to take the citadel of Asti (Saluces, volume III).
223 See Chapter 4 for a description of the Second Battle of Lérida.

from France, La Mothe-Houdancourt had up to 9,000 men,[224] and on 14 May they were a few kilometres from Lérida. The Spanish commander decided to join most of his troops[225] and on 15 May he launched an attack on the French position. The battle was a full success for the Spanish, even if 2,000 French (most of them wounded) managed to rejoin the garrison of Lérida. French losses were 3,500 to 4,000 men for 500 on the Spanish side (Picouet 2014). With victory in hand, da Silva could besiege Lerida, building first a long line of circumvallation. To maintain the siege, Spanish reinforcements arrived from Aragon and Valencia while on the other side the Count of La Mothe-Houdancourt received new troops from France and was able to field again 9,000 men by the end of June. On 17 June, the Spanish captured an external fortification called the fortress of Gardeny and managed to repulse all the French attempts to send supplies to the city. At last 30 July, after a siege of 10 weeks the French garrison of Lérida capitulated with honourable terms. At the beginning of August, the situation was paradoxical, the Spanish army was exhausted after a long and difficult siege, while the French army located near Barcelona was ready for action with all the reinforcements arrived from France. La Mothe-Houdancourt sent most of his army[226] to the south to again besiege Tarragona defended by 3,000 men.[227] On 7 August the city was surrounded and for one month had to endure the bombardment and attacks of the Franco-Catalan force. On 10 September the new Spanish commander Andrea Cantelmo arrived in the area with an army of 12,000 men (9,000–10,000 infantry and 2,600 cavalry), to relieve the defenders of Tarragona. The French did not want to fight and withdrew to Barcelona having lost probably 3,000 men during the siege. The campaign did not finish there, coming back to the west; the Spanish took Balaguer on 29 September after a siege of a few days as well as Agramunt on 6 October.[228] Ager was taken on 29 October after a fierce resistance of the 500 Catalans of the garrison. At the beginning of November, Cantelmo sent the rest of the Spanish army to winter quarters.

On the west of the Iberian Peninsula, the Portuguese decided again to have a more offensive attitude and in May an army of 9,000 men commanded by Matias Albuquerque was operating north of the Spanish main base Badajoz. The Spanish commander the Marquis of Torrecuso decided to confront the

---

224 Following Miguel de Parets (*Memorial Historico* vol. 24) La Mothe-Houdancourt had only 7,000 foot and 1,500 horse. Gonzalo et al. (1997) gives 9,000 foot and 2,000 horse.
225 In this case we have 6,000 infantry 3,000 horse and four light guns. The rest were with the heavy guns and the baggage or had deserted.
226 An estimate of the French army in front of Tarragona gives 12,000 men supported by a Catalan auxiliary force of 400 horse and 1,000 Foot (Tercio of Josep Sacosta and Tercio of Alexo Semmanat).
  Infantry: the Tercio of Lisbon (Spanish), commanded by Diego de Aguilera, the Tercio of Pablo Parada (Spanish), the Tercio of Clemente Soriano (Spanish), the Tercio of the Earl of Tyrone (Irish), the Tercio of Pierre de Mande (Walloon), some German companies under the command of Captain Millane, two companies of the militia of the city and one company from Tortosa. Cavalry: 300 horses in eight companies (Picouet 2014).
227 *Campaña de 1644*, CODOIN volume 95, 1890.
228 The French tried to take back the city during the siege of Arger, but withdrew rapidly when Cantelmo sent a Spanish detachment to relieve Agramunt.

invasion with an army of 6,000–6,500 men on 26 May near Montijo.[229] The following battle was confused and both camps claim for victory, but if we consider that the Portuguese had to abandon the campaign and withdraw to Portugal, we can talk of a minor Spanish victory. After summer, military operations were normally stopped due to the intense heat, to be resumed in the autumn. Having received reinforcement, the Marquis of Torrecuso launched an operation against the Portuguese city of Elvas 18 km west of Badajoz on 10 November. But seeing the small progress of the siege and the good fortification of the city, the operation was abandoned and on 8 December the Spanish were back in Badajoz.

1645

In Flanders the previous year had been difficult and the Spanish governor of the province, the Marquis of Castel Rodrigo, was expecting the worst for 1645. Madrid was still asking for offensive actions, but the governor was well aware that the French and the Dutch were coordinating their offensive[230] to outnumber the army of Flanders. To face the threats the Spanish had the support of two auxiliary armies, the Imperial one of the Baron of Lamboy and that commanded by the Duke of Lorraine. The French opened the campaign with the objective of taking Mardyke on the Flemish coast with an army of 30,000 men commanded by the Duke of Orleans. While the French vanguard was advancing towards Watten, the Spanish forces commanded by Ottavio Piccolomini[231] were deployed between Cassel and Wormhout. On 17 June a significant detachment of the French force, reinforced by the garrison of Boulogne, managed to cross the River-canal de la Colme near Looberghe, with heavy losses.[232] The rest of the French army arrived rapidly and the outnumbered Spanish troops withdrew towards the canal of Bergues and Dunkirk. On 23 June the French army was surrounding Mardryck and on 5 July the line of circumvallation was made and on 11 July the garrison surrendered. Although some Spanish officers wanted to attack the French, Piccolomini was aware that the Spanish army was too weak and decided not to move. On 26 July, the Fort of Linck (near the actual village of Spycker) was taken after a siege of five days and on 27 July the French army was besieging Bourbourg, defended by 1,400 men.[233] The garrison of the city surrendered on 7 August after a poor resistance. The Spanish commanders were obliged to distribute most of the infantry to defend the main cities of the County

---

229 See Chapter 4 for a full description of the battle.
230 Following Vincart (*Relación de la campaña de 1645*, CODOIN vol. 67, 1877), the French and Dutch would be ready to launch their respective attacks on 4 June.
231 Ottavio Piccolomini was made Duke of Amalfi by Philip IV of Spain after his victory at the battle of Thionville of 1639. He was made governor of the arms in the Army of Flanders in 1644 until 1647 (Gonzáles de León, *Road to Rocroi*).
232 The French had to face a strong counter-attack from a detachment of Spanish cavalry commanded directly by Piccolomini and Lamboy and later by some infantry. The arrival of strong French reinforcements made the crossing possible. It said that the French losses were up to 2,000 men, but the Spanish also suffered significant losses. Vincart, *Relación de la campaña de 1645*, CODOIN 67, 1877.
233 Vincart, *Relación de la campaña de 1645*, CODOIN vol. 67, 1877.

of Flanders (Ghent, Bruges, Dunkirk and Antwerp), leaving his field army reduced to probably no more than 16,000 men.[234] During the rest of the campaign, the French were unmolested in Artois,[235] Cassels was taken rapidly, followed by Béthune on 29 August, Lillers on 1 September and Saint-Venant the next day,[236] Merville and Estaire fell in early September and Armentières on 10 September. Only Comines and Lille made a consistent resistance and were kept in Spanish hands.

In the north, the army of Frederick Hendricks of Nassau initiated some operations from Sas van Ghent to test Spanish defence of the land of Waas. In July some 30,000 men had been concentrated between Sas van Gent and Oosburg but they sank into inaction for weeks much to the displeasure of the French envoys (Van Nimwegen 2010). On 26 September the Dutch learned that more than 16,000 men commanded by Field Marshal Gassion and Field Marshal Rantzau were near Sint-Joris and after some discussion the two armies agreed to meet at Mariakerke on 28 September. Meantime the Spanish army, being greatly outnumbered, was covering Antwerp and Brussels. Moving back to the north-east, the Dutch managed to break the Spanish defence at Melle between Ghent and Denderleew and suddenly appeared in front of Hulst on 30 September, the Spanish were taken by surprise. The garrison of 1,600 men made a poor resistance and the city capitulated on 4 November. At that time the French and Dutch army went into winter quarters, but the campaign was not finished yet and by a surprise night attack the Spanish retook Fort Mardyck.

Further to the east, different events took place in 1645, from the military point of view, the Imperial army suffered heavy losses at the bloody battle of Jankau[237] on 6 March but recovered some prestige during the siege of Brno (3 May to 23 August). Further to the south-west the Bavarian army of Baron von Mercy was defeated at the battle of Nördlingen on 3 August.[238] In the diplomatic arena, Holy Roman Emperor Ferdinand III had set up a round of negotiations in December 1643 in Münster and Osnabrück. In 1645 all factions, including the major powers in Europe as well as the small German states, had delegates in one of the two towns.

---

234 38 squadrons of cavalry (some 5,500 men), the army of Lamboy (some 6,000 men), 2,000 infantry (4x tercios) and 2,000 cavalry (12–14 squadrons). Vincart, *Relación de la campaña de 1645*, CODOIN vol. 67, 1877.
235 *Mémoire de Montglat*, volume 2, 1826.
236 Following Van Ninwegen (2010), the capture of the towns was due to the weakness of the Spanish garrisons, for example Béthune had a garrison of 200 men and Saint-Venant of 400 men.
237 At Jankau, the Imperial armies commanded by the Graf von Hatzfeld and the Count von Götz had 5,000 infantry (six brigades), 10,500 cavalry (50 squadrons), 500 dragoons and 26 guns were defeated by a similar Swedish army commanded by the Field Marshal Torstensson with 6,100 infantry (eight battalions), 9,430 cavalry (47 squadrons) and 60 guns (450 gunners). Imperial losses were close to 9,500 men including some 4,500 prisoners and the Swedish some 4,000 men (Guthrie late war).
238 The Bavarians (9,600 men) had started the campaign well, destroying the French army of Turenne (9,000 men) at Mergentheim on 2 May. The French (17,000 men) sent reinforcements and at the battle of Nördlingen or Alerheim, on 3 August, they defeated the Bavarian force (15,000 men) killing Mercy in the process (*Histoire de l'armée et de tous les régiments depuis les premiers...*, vol. 2).

If we come back to Italy and despite the instruction of Madrid to carry out an action against Trino, the Marquis of Velada was paralysed by the lack of money and men. In June 1645, the army of Lombardy had some 21,500 men (Maffi 2014) but could field only 7,500–8,000 men. The campaign started late because Prince Thomas of Savoy-Carignano was waiting for French recruits[239] and on 22 August he was besieging Vigevano 36 km south-west of Milan on the River Ticino. The city fell rapidly but the castle resisted longer and was captured on 13 September. The inaction of the Marquis of Velada was criticised and the Spanish governor decided to move not only to retake Vigevano but also to fight the Franco-Savoyard army. The battle took place on 18 October along of the canal of la Mora near the village of Proh, between a Spanish army reduced to 6,300 men and a detachment of the Savoyard army with 5,000 men. After seven hours of heavy fighting, the Savoyard army withdrew from the battlefield, leaving 1,000 men behind it. The victory boosted Spanish morale and at the end of November the Marquis of Velada was in front of Vigevano. After a gallant resistance the French force capitulated on 16 December.

In Catalonia, the success of the previous year had given hope to the Spanish and for the French side there was a growing degree of dissatisfaction among the Catalans towards the viceroy. La Mothe-Houdancourt was dismissed and arrested at the end of 1644 and the new viceroy the Count of Harcourt would receive strong reinforcements to re-establish the French position; at that moment, for Mazarin, Catalonia was as crucial as Flanders. On 2 April, 8,000 men of the count of Plessis-Praslin coming from Italy started the siege of Rosas,[240] defended by 2,000–3000 men,[241] it was the last Spanish outpost in northern Catalonia. The siege was temporarily stopped by heavy rain but with the arrival of 10,000 men under the command of the Count of Harcourt, the siege resumed and on 29 May the garrison capitulated with the honour of the war. The French commander did not lose time and with a reorganised army of 12,200 men[242] he advanced towards the River Segre. On the opposite side, the Spanish commander had now 11,000 to 11,500 men[243] and decided to take defensive positions behind the upper River Segre. Between 15 and 18 June the French offensive started and by an outflanking movement, they defeated the Spanish forces (4,000 men) opposing them and took the bridge on the River Segre near Camarassa. On 22 June, the French force defeated the core of the Spanish force at the battle of Saint Lorenz.[244] Some days later,

---

239 In Spring, most of the French regiment of Italy was sent to Catalonia (*Mémoire de Montglat* volume 2).

240 For the operation the French were supported by a fleet of the Lord of Montigny with 12 ships of the line, four fireships and four boats and the galley squadron of the Baron of Baumes with 10 galleys (Picouet 2014).

241 In 1643, the garrison had 3,000 foot (we will find the Tercio of the Armada and the Tercio of Diego Cavallero) and 300 horse. In his memoir the Marques of Chouppes (*Mémoire du Marquis de Chouppes*) gives 3,000 foot and 500 horse.

242 Plessis-Besançon in his memoir gives for the infantry 800 officers, 7,500 soldiers, 2,400 horse and 1,500 Catalans (*Mémoire de Plessis-Besançon*).

243 *Memoir of Novoa* in CODOIN vol. 86, 1895.

244 In six days of intense fighting, Spanish losses could be estimated at 6,000 or 7,000 men (Picouet 2014).

on 5 July, the French were besieging the city of Balaguer. On 25 August, Cantelmo escaped from Balaguer with 2,000 men and the governor of the city, Simon of Mascareña, had to capitulate on 20 October due principally to a shortage of supplies. Meantime, the Spanish suffered another disgrace on 2 September when a small force of 400–600 cavalry and 1,500 infantry was defeated trying to capture Flix.

In Portugal the "small" war between infantry and cavalry from both parts continued along the border and the main event was the operations of the Spanish army[245] in the neighbourhood of Olivenza. There the Spanish commander was able to defeat the Portuguese in several small encounters, taking the bridge of Ayuda (called also bridge of Olivenza) and harassing the countryside but he was unable to besiege Olivenza and had to return to Badajoz.

1646

In the Low Countries the situation of the Army of Flanders was disastrous and the only strategy of the Spanish high command was to wait for the enemies actions and to hold the ground as much as possible. The General State of the Dutch republic agreed that the old objective of capturing Antwerp was possible but meantime the Dutch diplomats sent to Münster had also the task to negotiate a truce with the Spanish. In fact, after the campaign of the previous year and the French movement towards Flanders and Bruges in particular had alerted the Dutch that a powerful French kingdom could be their future neighbour. For some of the Dutch elites, particularly in the province of Holland, that was a terrific prospect. Nonetheless the military campaign started when the French armies of the Duke of Orleans and the army of the Duke of Enghien, 35,000 men in total, assembled in Templeneuve (Montglat, volume 2, 1826), moved to besiege Courtrai on 13 June. After 16 days of siege the garrison of 2,000 men surrendered while the army of Flanders[246] remained inactive due to the usual lack of funds but also to the profound division in the Spanish high command concerning the strategy to adopt. Later the French force moved to the north while the Spanish army was giving ground and withdrawing towards Bruges. A French detachment of 4,500 men was sent to support the Dutch army. On 31 July, Bergues–Saint-Winoc was taken and on 25 August, after a resistance of 21 days, Fort Mardyk surrendered. The French forces were reinforced by the army of La Férté-Seneterre and on 5 September Furnes was captured, and the investment of Dunkirk was completed on 25 September. On 11 October the garrison of Dunkirk capitulated while again most of Spanish army remained inactive or covering Antwerp.

The Dutch army conducted some operations near Antwerp but the resistance of the Spanish forces (Maffi 2014) showed that the conquest of the

---

[245] The Spanish army had some 5,000 infantry and 2,000 cavalry (Estébanez Calderón, volume 1, 1885).

[246] Montglat (*Mémoire de Montglat* volume 2), stated that the Spanish had an army of 30,000 men, it was probably the full Spanish field army, divided as always with a corps facing the Dutch and the rest against the French. The Dutch used to field a minimum of 20,000 men, so with the 35,000 men of the French armies, the Spanish were still outnumbered.

city would be a difficult task. The Dutch commander tried to outmanoeuvre the Spanish, moving to Bergen op Zoom and to launch an attack on Liers, but the Spanish army moved to Duffel to block the enemy advance. At last Frederick Hendricks of Nassau returned to the old idea of using the River Meuse and on 10 October they were besieging Venlo defended by only 400 men. The Spanish commander reacted quickly and on 16 October and 21 October they managed to send up to 1,500 men to reinforce the garrison and the siege of Venlo was raised on 29 October (van Nimwegen, 2010). In fact the Dutch Republic had mostly agreed with Spanish envoys to sign a truce for 1647, the alliance with France was losing supporters and the general state position was that if the Spanish agreed on different Dutch demands a peace treaty could be negotiated in Münster.

In Italy, the main concern of the governor of Lombardy was again to hold position and to conduct small military operations when it was possible, particularly in Monferrato. In reality the main objective of Cardinal Mazarin, was to bring the war to the Spanish position in Tuscany called the *presidios de Toscana*, and particularly Porto Ercole and Orbetello. On 9 May, the French fleet[247] commanded by Admiral of le Maille Brézé, Duke of Fronsac, disembarked the army of Thomas of Savoy-Carignano. Two days later, the French forces were besieging the city of Orbetello and Porto Ecole, defended by Pedro de la Puente for the first and by Carlo della Gatta for the second (Maffi 2014). At first the French operation went well, but the closer they were from the walls the harder was the Spanish resistance. On the news that the French fleet was in Tuscany, the Spanish authorities prepared a fleet[248] in Spain, commanded by the Count of Linares, and a relieve army in Naples. On 14 June the two fleets met near the island of Giglio, but due to the weakness of the wind, the galleons on both sides had to be assisted by the galleys. The battle took place all through the day, but the inconclusive action ended when the two fleets separated at dusk. On 23 June a detachment of the Spanish fleet managed to destroy or capture the 70 tartanes containing the supplies of the French army. The Spanish disembarked 3,300 men but failed to breach the French lines around Orbetello. On 15 July a relief Spanish army[249] organised in Naples and commanded by the Marquis of Torrecuso arrived in the Dune of Feneglia at few kilometres from the French lines. Three days later, after small skirmishes, the French high command decided to abandon the siege and to re-embark. The last events took place in October when a

---

247 French Fleet of 28 galleons (ships of the line), eight fireships, 21 galleys and 70 supply ships (called tartanes). The army had some 9,000 infantry (12 French regiments and two Piedmont regiments), 2,000 volunteers (mostly horsemen) and 600 cavalry (Ademollo, *Assedio di Orbetello*, 1883).

248 On 14 June the Spanish Fleet had 25 galleons and frigates, eight fireships, 30 galleys and five transport ships. At that time the French admiral had 25 galleons, 10 fireships, 20 galleys and four transport ships (Ademollo, *Assedio di Orbetello*, 1883).

249 The Spanish army is estimated at 7,000 infantry (including companies of the Tercio Viejo de Napoles) and 2,000 cavalry. The cost of the French failure was estimated at the loss of 6,000 men and 21 guns by the viceroy of Naples (Ademollo, *Assedio di Orbetello*, 1883).

new French expedition,[250] commanded by la Meillerayre, took Piombino on 9 October and Porto Longone two days later. Such successes at the end of campaign would convince the Duke of Modena to change sides and to give his allegiance to the French monarchy.

Catalonia was the third strike against the Spanish monarchy and the Count of Harcourt was ready to retake the city of Lérida. With a reinforced army of up to 19,000 men,[251] he launched the operation on 28 April. On 12 May, Lérida was surrounded and had a garrison of 4,400 men[252] commanded by Gregorio de Brito. Lérida had been prepared for the siege and it was expected that hard conditions would debilitate the French army and that the city could be succoured by a relieving army. On the other side, Harcourt decided to surrender the city by hunger and he constructed a significant line of circumvallation connecting redoubts and fortified camps to protect his army. For four months, continuous fighting and sickness coupled to a hot and dry summer had reduced the strength of the French army despite the arrival of reinforcements at the end of July. At the end of September, the Spanish army of the Marquis of Léganes went out of Fraga to save Lérida. On 5 October the Spanish army was near the city but the news were not very good, the French fortifications were stronger than expected and worse, the French soldiers were alerted and prepared to receive an attack. Therefore, the Marquis of Léganes decided to carry out different operations to cut Harcourt from his supply lines coming from Barcelona. By mid November, Léganes could see that his strategy had failed: the army of Harcourt had been resupplyed by three convoys and could hold five weeks more while the Spanish army in the middle of a devastated country was losing men at high rate. In a council of war the Spanish[253] decided to attack the French lines still defended by up to 13,000 men, and on 22 November, at 10:40 p.m., the position of Fort Rébé was stormed by the Spanish infantry. The Count of Harcourt decided to counter-attack immediately in the middle of the night with all his troops. For several hours the French tried unsuccessfully to retake Fort Rébé and the positions lost previously, but the Spanish held the line and early in the morning when the French commander learned that a Spanish convoy protected by 1,100

---

[250] The French expedition to the island of Elbe (Porto Longone) and Piombino on the Continent, was important with 25 ships of the line, seven Portuguese ships, 15 galleys and transport ships with 5,840 infantry (La Roncière 1920).

[251] Pradet (*Memorial Historico*, volume 24) gives 12,000 foot and 5,500 horse for the French army without the Catalans, estimated at 1,500 men.

[252] The garrison of Lérida was prepared for the siege and was made of a mix of soldiers (Spanish, Walloons and Germans) defeated in San Lorenz the previous year and new recruits with no experience. 700 men were located at Fort Gardeny, 3,000 men in Lérida and the rest were unfit for service (Picouet 2014).

[253] The Spanish army was deployed in a vanguard with seven cavalry squadrons and five battalions coming from nine Spanish tercios (Guardia del Rey, Galeones/Armada, Villamayor, Villava, provincial of Navarre, provincial of Zaragoza and three provincial tercios of Aragon), two Walloon tercios (Calonne and Van der Straeten) and the Irish tercio of Fitzgerald; a battalion of seven cavalry squadrons and five battalions coming from four Spanish tercios (Lisbon, Silva, Salgado and Garcés), three Italian tercios (Lorenzana, Pignatello and San Felices) and two German regiments (Seebach and Grosfeit). In total 5,500 infantry and 2,000 cavalry and eight light guns (Picouet 2014).

THE ARMIES OF PHILIP IV OF SPAIN 1621–1665

1.15 Ratification of Spanish–Dutch Peace of Münster, 15th May 1648. Copy after Gerhard ter Borch, 1648–1670 (Rijksmuseum).

men had managed to breach the ill-defended French lines on the north and enter the city, he knew that the battle was lost. Having lost up to 3,500 men, 36 guns and all the baggage, the French commander reinforced the garrison of Balaguer and withdrew to Barcelona.

In Extremadura and Portugal, the lack of money and men on both sides limited the military operation. Most of the actions took place around a Spanish fortification called Fort Telena or Fort Léganes[254] on the River Guadiana, when the Portuguese failed to take Valencia de Alcántara.

1.7 A Time of Recovery: 1647–1656

The 1640–1646 period had been particularly dramatic for the Spanish monarchy, with the uprising of Catalonia and Portugal combined with significant defeats of its military forces. Despite all the misfortune, the French and Dutch were unable to take Antwerp, Bruges, Ghent, Cambrai

---

254 Following an old map of 1644, Fort Telena was located where the River Gaya joined the River Guadiana at seven to eight kilometres south-west of Badajoz (Portugal 1644 No 918 BNP. National Library of Portugal).

and Brussels, the Duchy of Lombardy was holding ground and the territory of Catalonia was partially (Lérida and Tarragona) in Spanish hands.

1647

In the Low Countries, the signature of a ceasefire in 1647 followed by a peace treaty on 30 January 1648, between the Dutch Republic and the Spanish Monarchy was a major diplomatic achievement. The ceasefire of 1647 signed on 8 January confirmed the inability of Dutch and Spanish commanders to decide the 80 years of war on the battlefield in a difficult country like the Netherlands. The Spanish needed to concentrate all their efforts to face the French attacks while the Dutch did not see the purpose of continuing a useless war, especially after the death of Frederick Hendricks of Nassau on 17 March 1647.

Coming back to military affairs, the new governor of the Spanish Netherlands was the brother of Emperor Ferdinand III, Archduke Leopold Wilhelm of Austria, a prince of royal blood and an able military commander, an ideal candidate to restore order and harmony in the Spanish high commands of the Army of Flanders. The ceasefire with the Dutch Republic meant that all the Spanish field army could be concentrated against the French force and a Spanish offensive was likely to reduce the pressure on Catalonia. On 11 May, the Spanish army[255] was in front of Armentières defended by a garrison of 2,000 French. After a siege of 18 days, the garrison of Armentières capitulated while the French armies commanded by the Field Marshal of Rantzau and the Field Marshal of Gassion remained inactive. Comines was retaken 11 June after a siege of eight days, Lens was retaken in June and the Spanish could successfully send succour to Saint-Omer, besieged by the French. Faced by the division in the French command, the Archduke could continue the offensive and this time he was besieging Landrecies on 28 June. Although French reinforcements were sent to the two field marshals, they did not want to attack the Spanish line of circumvallation and the garrison capitulated on 18 July. During the siege operation, Rantzau went to the coast to undertake a diversionary attack, taking Dixmude on 13 July while Gassion moved to the east taking La Bassée on 19 July after the poor resistance of the garrison. At the beginning of August, Rantzau failed to take Fort Neuwendaam and on his way back his rearguard was badly shaken by the counter-attack on 3 August. In August the Spanish managed to frustrate the capture of Lens even if the city finally capitulated on 3 October after a new siege of nine days. Seeing that Lens could not be saved, the Archduke moved to retake Dixmude on 25 September and after a siege of 20 days the garrison capitulated on 14 October despite the efforts of Rantzau to introduce reinforcements.

---

255 An estimate gives 10,000 cavalry and 20,000 infantry (including six Spanish tercios: Tercio of Baltasar Mercader, Tercio of the Count of Garciez, Tercio of Count of Linares, Tercio of Gaspar Bonifaz, Tercio of Bernabé de Vargas Machuca, and Tercio of Gabriel de Toledo) while the French forces are estimated at 22,000–25,000 men (A. Rodríguez Villa, *Historia de la campaña de 1647 en Flanders*, Madrid 1884).

Further to the east, in September, the Viscount of Turenne was harassing the Duchy of Luxembourg with a small force of 6,000 men[256] and the Baron of Beck was sent with an army estimated at 7,500–8,000 men[257] to protect the duchy.

In November the Spanish and French forces went to winter quarters and the French army of Germany moved back to Germany.

After the fiasco of Orbetello and the new alliance with the Duke of Modena, Cardinal Mazarin had the Duchy of Lombardy as a target. To face the new threat, the Duke of Frías, the new Spanish governor since February 1646, had few men and money and carried out only some military operations in Monferrato. In September 1647, the Duke of Modena with some 8,000 men (Hanlon, 1998) and finally crossed the River Pô to attack the region of Cremona in Lombardy. He occupied the unfortified town of Casalmaggiore and started to harass the countryside. His actions were met by the militia of Lombardy and 2,000 men of the regular army and due to bad weather, lack of supply the Duke of Modena fell back to his territories.

In fact the main problem of the Spanish monarchy was more to the south in the kingdom of Naples and Sicily. Due to a high fiscal pressure, the first riot appeared in May in Palermo, capital of Sicily. The local Spanish viceroy the Marquis of Los Vélez had to face the revolt of Guiseppe d'Alessi but with the support of the local nobility loyal to King Philip IV, the uprising was mostly over by September 1647 even though incidents occurred all over the island until spring 1648. Much different was the revolt of Massaliano that started on 7 July in Naples. The cause was fiscal pressure and the continuous levies of men for the monarchy, but the viceroy of Naples, the Duke of Arcos was left with little military support[258] to face the revolt and above all the rebellion spread all over the kingdom.[259] Madrid could not tolerate the rebellion of the kingdom and as soon as possible a fleet sailed from Spain commanded by John of Austria, the bastard son of the king Philip IV. When it arrived in Naples, in October,[260] the Spanish were unable to retake the control of the populous city. Meantime the high nobility loyal to Spain managed to organise a small army of 4,500 men, was able to harass the rebels but not to enter the city. Cardinal Mazarin could not lose such opportunity and in November he sent the Duke of Guise and subsidies to support the rebellion. At first Guise with only 700 regular soldiers managed to impose a relative discipline on the Neapolitan rebels and to break the encirclement, capturing Salerno, Avellino

---

256 In theory the army of Turenne should have been higher with 3,000 men more, but when the Weimarians led by Colonel Rosen learned that the next campaign would be outside Germany they mutinied and abandoned the French army of Germany (*Mémoire de Montglat*, volume 2).

257 Jean de Beck had with him two Walloon tercios, seven German regiments of infantry and four German regiments of cavalry and five light guns (*Relación de la campaña de 1647 en Flandres…*).

258 The Spanish forces were concentrated in two fortresses in Naples, Castelnuovo overlooking the city and Castel dell'Ovo at the entrance of the Bay of Naples.

259 Large districts of the Abruzzi, Calabria and Puglia were controlled by the rebels, sometimes supported by the local nobility (Hanlon, 1998).

260 In October 1647, the Spanish fleet (Armada Mar Oceano and squadrons of galleys) had up to 31 warships and eight fireships and 22 galleys but only 4,000 soldiers with little supply (P. Giannone, *Histoire Civile du Royaume de Naples, traduit de l'italien*, volume 4, Book XXXVII, Chapter 3, 1742).

and Aversa. Guise failed to attract the high nobility to him and while he was claiming for absolute power for him he also failed to understand the fragile base of his authority (Hanlon, 1998).

In Catalonia, Mazarin had nominated the prince of Condé[261] as the new French viceroy but the prince had high political aspirations and for that he wanted a fast and rapid victory in order to be able to return to Paris with glory and as quickly as possible. On the other side, the Spanish commanded by the Marquis of Aytona were unable to organise a powerful force to match the army of Condé so they had to rely on the power of their fortresses in Lérida and Tarragona. On 23 April, the French general had 14,000 men and an artillery siege of 35 guns and on 13 May he was besieging Lérida.[262] Condé wanted a quick victory, so the plan was to take directly the main Spanish position at the citadel of Lérida using the French artillery superiority. The third siege of Lérida was an intense experience for soldiers of both sides; it looked more like a fight of the First World War with continuous bombardment and heavy hand-to-hand fighting. After seven weeks of siege, and despite the arrival of 7,500 men as reinforcements, the troops of Condé were down to 13,000–13,500 men. For the common French soldiers the siege was particularly difficult, with the numerous attacks of the garrison, a high casualty rate, the hot weather and the presence of hundreds of cadavers of their fellows visible in the trenches and on the hill. On 16 July, Condé received bad news, the Spanish relief army[263] was prepared to get out of Fraga at any time and worst at all, miners had found strong rocks, difficult to dig out, and it would take weeks to be under the wall. Condé did not want to risk a confrontation with a weak army so three days later, to the surprise of the Spanish defenders, he abandoned the siege and moved to a fortified camp 18 km east of Lérida, near the Borges Blanques, to rebuild his army. On the other side Aytona had to repair the citadel of Lérida and reinforce the garrison of the city, he sent back 1,000 men to Tarragona and followed his instructions to not risk a battle against Condé. The two armies revived in October; the French managed to retake the Castle of Ager on 10 October after a short siege of four days. On 24 October, the governor of Tarragona launched an assault on Constanti, but the quick reaction of Condé prevented the capture of the city and the Spanish had to withdraw rapidly. Both armies went into winter quarters in November and the Prince of Condé returned rapidly to Paris, for him he had nothing to do in Catalonia: his future was with the King and the army of Picardy.

On the Luso-Spanish border, once again the Portuguese conducted military operations in Extremadura, threatening Badajoz, but the prompt

---

261 Louis II of Bourbon was born 8 September 1621 in Saint Germain (France) and died 11 November 1686 in Chantilly (France). He was Duke of Enghien until 1646 and became the IV Prince of Condé on 26 December 1646, he was a *prince de sang*. Louis of Bourbon was one of the best French generals of the seventeenth century and was nicknamed *Le Grand Condé*.
262 The garrison of Lérida was still commanded by Gregorio Brito with 2,140 infantry, 500 cavalry and 700 militia (Picouet 2014).
263 The Marquis of Aytona had probably 10,000 infantry and 3,200 cavalry (Picouet 2014).

reaction of the Baron of Molinghem, the new Spanish commander, obliged the Portuguese to fall back to their base.

1648

In the Low Countries, the Spanish governor had instructions to take the offensive to distract the French from Catalonia. At the beginning of February, Archduke Leopold sent the Spanish army in a surprise attack against Courtrai but due to the awareness and strength of the French garrison the attack failed (Montglat, volume 2, 1826). The campaign started really in May when the Prince of Condé moved to besiege the city of Ypres. On 12 May he had surrounded the city and on the 19th the line of circumvallation was finished. On the other side, the Spanish commander decided to abandon Ypres and rapidly moved to again attack Courtrai. This time the French garrison (2,000 men) was totally surprised and after few days they had to surrender on 23 May. Coming back to Ypres, the Archduke tried to save the city but on 28 May the Spanish garrison capitulated. In June, the Spanish conducted some operations in Artois and even in France. On 16 June, Field Marshal Rantzau tried to raid the city of Ostend with a fleet of 50 ships and 3,000 men but the Marquis of Sfondrati was waiting for him and managed to annihilate the French force and to capture Rantzau. On 9 August the Archduke captured the city of Furnes after a siege of 10 days. On 18 August, the Spanish had retaken Lens, but two days later the army of Flanders was defeated by the Prince of Condé, losing 8,000–9,000 men.[264] On 27 August, the victorious French army was again besieging Furnes and on 10 September with no hope to be succoured, the garrison capitulated. The news from Paris was not good at all for the monarchy and the Prince of Condé was recalled to re-establish civil order. The situation in the French kingdom was not as good as it seemed. The total war imposed by Richelieu and by Mazarin had increased strongly the taxes to maintain the army. By spring 1648, a general discontent was spreading in all classes of the population. In Paris the events started on 15 January when the parliament of Paris refused to sign seven tax edicts to finance the war. During spring and most of summer and despite the effort of Mazarin, the judicial officers of the parliament not only continue to refuse to pay but also condemned all the financial schemes of the monarchy. With the victory of the Prince of Condé in hand, Mazarin decided to arrest the leaders of the parliament, but the feeling of the common people of Paris was against him and on 27 August, during "la journée des barricades" the people of Paris erupted in open rebellion. The rebellion of the parliament of Paris called *la fronde parlementaire* (1648–1649) was followed by the rebellion of the nobility (1650–1653). The *Fronde* was the last rebellion of the French nobility against the monarchy but at the end it facilitated the emergence of absolutism.[265] For the Spanish the *Fronde* was an opportunity to retake the control of what had been lost and to bring the war to France.

---

264 In a sense, the Battle of Lens was a repetition of the Battle of Rocroi, see Chapter 4 for more details.

265 For the *Fronde* events see A.L. Moote, *The revolt of the judges: the Parlement of Paris and the Fronde, 1643–1652* (Princeton, NJ: Princeton University Press, 1972).

Further to the east, on 24 October, the treaty of Westphalia[266] was signed in Münster and Osnabrück, it would end the conflict known as the Thirty Years' War but it did not end all the conflicts arising out of the last two decades, particularly the conflict between Spain and France. Already the Spanish and the Dutch Republic had signed a document on 30 January 1648, ratified in Münster on 15 May of the same year. With the treaty of Münster the French monarchy was more concerned to have an advantageous position against Spain, in order to isolate the Spanish kingdom, than to make peace (Negredo del Cerro 2016). For the Spanish authorities they had to exploit all the weakness of the French to be able to negotiate with advantages.

At the beginning of 1648, the situation of Naples was still out of control despite the presence of John of Austria. On 12 February, the Duke of Guise failed to take the main castle of Naples and in March the Count of Oñate was nominated viceroy of Naples. With the use of a mix of negotiation and force in the city of Naples and the use of the army of Neapolitan nobility supported by Spanish troops to subdue the countryside, the Spanish managed to fracture the unity of the rebels. On 5 and 6 April, the Spanish troops managed to enter the big city taking control of all the strategic points and gates of Naples. Left alone, the Duke of Guise was captured a few days later, and the rebellion of Naples was over.

In Lombardy, the Marquis of Caracena was the new governor of the province and had to deal with the forces of the Duke of Savoy in the west and the offensive of the Duke of Modena in the east. In spring, the core of the Spanish army was on a line between the River Pô and the River Oglio, facing the Franco-Modenese army located in Casalmaggiore. On 29 June, the Duke of Modena and the French commander the Field Marshal of Plessis-Praslin, managed to defeat and breach the Spanish line inflicting losses of 2,000 to 3,000 men to the army of Lombardy (Clonard, vol. 4, 1854). Reinforced by 4,000 to 5,000 men from the army of Savoy (Marquis of de Ville), the combined army of more than 16,000 men besieged Cremona on 22 July. The siege did not go so well for the Duke of Modena: resistance of the garrison was stronger than expected and progress was slow, the Spanish could still send reinforcements to the city,[267] the Spanish cavalry was harassing the French supply lines. In September, the lack of supply became an issue and heavy rain was disrupting the approach trenches. At the same time, the Spanish army was in Pizzighettone, 20 km west of Cremona, receiving reinforcements from Germany and Naples, so on 7 October Plessis-Praslin and the Duke of Modena decided to abandon the siege and to withdraw to Casalmaggiore having lost up to 8,000 men. At the end of the year the Duke of Modena had only 6,000 men in hand (Maffi 2014).

---

[266] In reality two complementary treaties both signed the same day in Münster, between the Holy Roman Empire, the Kingdom of France and their respective allies; but not the Kingdom of Spain and the one in Osnabrück involving the Holy Roman Empire, the Kingdom of Sweden and their respective allies, including the Kingdom of Spain.

[267] The Duke of Parma was more favourable to the Spanish, so during the siege the Spanish could transfer troops through his territory to reinforce Cremona or to send supply (Maffi 2014).

In the Iberian Peninsula, military operations were not a priority for Madrid or Paris. In Catalonia, the Count of Schomberg was nominated viceroy in May, and he decided to take the offensive, besieging the city of Tortosa on the River Ebro. On 10 June a portion of the army crossed the river in Flix and the rest went towards Tortosa. The blockade was reinforced by troops transported directly from Provence. The Spanish reaction was to launch an unsuccessful diversion against Flix and on 13 July after a poor resistance Tortosa capitulated (Montglat, volume 2, 1826).

1649

Following the previous campaign and above all, the disorders generated by the *Fronde* of the parliament, Madrid thought that it was time to transfer the war to France. Unfortunately for the Spanish, the finances of the monarchy were in poor state after so many years of war and most of the time the Spanish Generals would have to fight on one side against the lack of funds and the other one against the French armies. In the Low Countries Archduke Leopold started his campaign on 5 March, dividing his forces into two armies,[268] one to invade France and the other to blockade French garrisons in Flanders. He divided the invasion force into three corps, one with the army of the Duke of Lorraine,[269] one with the Count of Fuensaldaña and the last one at his own command. The Spanish found little resistance and even the Duke of Lorraine managed to arrive near Crepy, 36 km south-east of Saint Quentin, but the lack of support from the French rebels,[270] the bad weather, the fear of being cut from their logistic base, and new instructions from Madrid, made the Archduke decide to abandon the campaign. On 11 April the Spanish forces were blocking the city of Ypres[271] and after a gallant resistance the French garrison capitulated on 10 May with honourable terms (Vincart, *Campaign de 1649*). At the same time, the detachment of the Army of Flanders under the command of the Count of Fuensaldaña was besieging Saint-Venant on 20 April, and in five days he managed to capture the town.

On the French side, the Queen Regent Anne of Austria decided to retake the offensive in order to join all the French against the Spanish enemy. With all the troops available, the French commander Count of Harcourt marched towards Cambrai, one of the main fortresses of the Spanish Netherlands.

---

268 Infantry available (30 units): six Spanish tercios (Gaspar Bonifacio, Gabriel Toledo, Balthasar Mercader, Francisco de Deza, Fernando Solis and Bernabé de Vargas), three Italian tercios (Marquis of Bentivoglio, Juan de Liponti and Giuseppe Guasco), 10 Walloon tercios (Marquis of Saint-Martin, Count of Meghem, Count of Cammerage, Count de la Motterie, Count of Bruay, Lord of Hellesmes, Baron de Brucq, Count of Annapes, baron of Rieulay and Lord of Stoppelaar), 11 German regiments (Count of Nassau, Baron of Wanghe, Baron of Berlo, Colonel Oswald Pluren and Colonel Jacques Schlebusch, Count of Isenburg, Colonel Colbrant, Juan de Monrroy, Pieter-Ernest von Wolf, Baron of Rouveroy and Colonel Holdeiandt) and the Irish tercio of Murphy. Vincart, *Campagne de 1649*, 1894.

269 An estimate gives 5,000 infantry and 4,000 cavalry for a total of 32–33 weak regiments (Vincart, *Campagne de 1649*, 1894).

270 The lack of support of the rebels was probably due to the signature on 11 March 1649 of the Peace of Rueil, a compromise between the Parliament of Paris and the French monarchy (*Mémoire de Montglat*).

271 During the same campaign the fortress of Knokke was captured by the Spanish.

On 24 June the French forces were surrounding Cambrai but on 3 July the Spanish managed to reinforce the garrison with 1,500 men (Montglat, volume 2, 1826) and two days later the French were obliged to abandon the siege. During the rest of the campaign the two armies[272] were manoeuvring but the Archduke did not want to risk a battle due to the superior numbers of the French cavalry. The last of the campaign in Flanders took place on 9 October when the Count of Sfondrati captured la Mothe-aux-Bois after a siege of four days (Maffi, 2014).

In Lombardy, the Marquis of Caracena conducted a winter campaign to subdue the Duke of Modena. In the middle of February, the Army of Lombardy systematically harassed the countryside, taking the towns of Pomponesco, Gualtieri, Castelnuovo and Brescello. On 27 February the Duke was obliged to sign a peace treaty with the Marquis of Caracena. With an exhausted army, the Spanish conducted only raiding cavalry parties in Piedmont and Monferrato for the rest of the year.

In Catalonia, the poor action of the previous year and the lack of funds delayed the military operation and the Spanish commander, the Marquis of Mortara, could only start the campaign in September with an army of 15,000 men.[273] He managed to capture Montblanc on 22 September. At the beginning of October Salou, Constanti and Sitges were taken in a few days and by mid October Villafranca del Penedes. On the other side, the French conducted raids in the north of the viceroyalty of Valencia.

In Portugal, like the previous year no major operations were undertaken, the lack of veteran troops meant that all the military fighting consisted of parties of cavalry and infantry raiding the opposite villages and housing along the borders.

1650

Despite the treaty of Rueil, France was immersed in a civil war with a proportion of the nobility against the monarchy. From Madrid, this was an opportunity to recover territories and the main efforts were placed in Flanders and Catalonia. In the Low Countries, for the Spanish the question was, what could be the best attitude to stir trouble in France in order to enjoy a military superiority to regain the territories lost over four decades. The Count of Peñaranda, the political adviser of the Archduke, was in favour of carrying out an invasion of France to support the rebels, particularly the Viscount of Turenne,[274] but a significant proportion of the military high command was more in favour of besieging a city in Artois or Flanders. The Archduke took the decision to invade France: on 4 June with the core of the

---

272 In July German reinforcements of nine infantry regiments, three cavalry regiments and one dragoon regiment arrived but the Spanish did not want to risk a hazardous battle (Maffi 2014).
273 *Relación de los feliz sucesos que han tenido las armas de su majestad gobernadas por Don Juan de Garay, general del ejército de Cataluña y el número de las villas y lugares que se han rendido a la obediencia de nuestro señor. Año del 1649.*
274 Already at the end of 1649 Turenne was a supporter of the *Fronde,* and in April 1650 he signed an alliance with the Archduke to fight for Spain (Turenne, 1735).

army[275] he moved to besiege the well-defended city of Guise,[276] 26 km northeast of Saint Quentin, while a detachment of the army of Flanders moved to capture Le Câtelet. On 15 June, after a siege of three days, the fortress of Le Câtelet was captured and in Guise a line of circumvallation had been built. Unfortunately for the Spanish, a large convoy with supplies for the army in Guise was intercepted and destroyed by the French cavalry at the end of June. In Guise, the fierce resistance of the French garrison combined with the poor logistics and the destruction of the convoy induced the Spanish to abandon the siege on 11 July and move back to their base. The Spanish setback was temporary, the French only had a field army of 12,000–13,000 men,[277] and after a short pause to reorganise the army, the Spanish marched towards La Capelle on 24 July. In 13 days, the fortress of La Capelle capitulated on 3 August; after the victory, the Archduke decided to support the military operation of Turenne in Champagne with a powerful army of 30,000 men.[278] First the city of Vervins was captured followed by Marle on 13 of August, Moncornet on the 15th and Rethel the 18th of August without fighting.[279] On 26 August, a vanguard commanded by Turenne defeated a French detachment of 3,000 to 4,000 men in Fisme, only 30 km west of Reims. After a long advance in French territory, the Archduke decided to carry out peace talks with the Duke of Orleans in Paris. After some weeks, the negotiation failed[280] and the Spanish moved again, this time to besiege Chaumont-Porcien and above all Mouzon on 27 September. The garrison of Mouzon managed to resist up to 40 days and it was only on 6 November that the city capitulated. For the Spanish it was time to come back to their winter quarters, leaving behind a small Spanish force commanded by Esteban Gamara, a detachment of the army of the Duke of Lorraine and the troops of Turenne. The last event of the campaign took place in December, when Mazarin joined 16,000–20,000 men to retake Rethel. The French force surrounded Rethel on 9 December and five days later the garrison capitulated. Meantime, Turenne had managed to join 8,000 to 9,000 men[281] but on 15 December he was defeated by Field Marshal Plessis-Praslin, with 11,500 men[282] near a village

---

275 Probably some 12,000 infantry and 7,000 cavalry (Turenne, 1735).
276 Guise was city well defended by modern walls and a citadel with 2,000 soldiers and up to 1,200 militia (Vincart, *Relación de la campaña de 1650 en Flandes*, CODOIN vol. 75, 1880).
277 Vincart, *Relación de la campaña de 1650 en Flandes*, CODOIN 75, 1880.
278 Taking into account the army of Flanders, the auxiliary army of the Duke of Lorraine and the small army of Turenne the Archduke had some 16,000 infantry and 13,000 to 14,000 cavalry (Vincart, *Relación de la campaña de 1650 en Flandes*, CODOIN vol. 75, 1880).
279 Other small towns were also captured during the march of the army (Vincart, *Relación de la campaña de 1650 en Flandes*, CODOIN vol. 75, 1880).
280 See Montglat, *Mémoire de Montglat*, and Vincart, *Relación de la campaña de 1650 en Flandes*, CODOIN vol. 75, 1880.
281 Proper estimate of 3,500 infantry (seven battalions) and 5,000–5,500 cavalry (37 squadrons) divided between the Army of Flanders, Esteban Gamara, 2,200 cavalry and 1,800 infantry, the army of Lorraine (Fauges) 1,000 infantry and 2,000 cavalry and the army of Turenne 700 infantry and 1,000–1,500 cavalry. The infantry of Lorraine did not participate in the battle and was captured afterwards (Vincart, *Relación de la campaña de 1650 en Flandes*, CODOIN vol. 75, 1880; and Susane volume 8, 1853).
282 Estimate 6,000 infantry (13 infantry battalions) and 5,500 cavalry (58 cavalry squadrons) (Susane volume 8, 1853).

seven kilometres north of Rethel, losing 4,200 men in the battle.[283]

In Lombardy, the Marquis of Caracena was left with few resources, nonetheless he sent his small army to harass Piedmont around the city of Asti. After a few weeks, the Spanish army returned quietly to Lombardy, the Savoyards or the French were too weak to carry out any operations. In Italy the main military operation took place in Tuscany, when a powerful Spanish fleet of 29 warships, 22 galleys, four fireships and 80 transport ships with 10,900 men,[284] commanded by John of Austria, arrived near the Island of Elba the 24 May. The next day, the Spanish disembarked a detachment of their army to besiege Piombino, on the Continent, while the rest disembarked to besiege Porto Longo on the Island of Elba on 27 May. Spanish forces from Lombardy arrived (3,000 men) to complete the siege of Piombino and on 21 June the French garrison surrendered. The Swiss garrison of Porto Longo, in French service, presented a better resistance and acceded to capitulate only on 31 July.[285]

In Catalonia, the first actions took place in the viceroyalty of Valencia, when a French detachment started to besiege Castellon on 5 May. When the Spanish relief force arrived in the area, they obliged the French to abandon the siege on 25 May and to return back to Tortosa (Maffi 2014). At the beginning of September, the Marquis of Mortara was in charge of all the military operations in Catalonia and rapidly he sent 9,000 men against Flix. This time the weak Franco-Catalan army of 6,500 men could do nothing and Flix was captured on 25 of September, followed on 15 October by Miravet after a siege of 13 days. With reinforcements from southern Italy, Mortara reorganised his army[286] and on 19 October he was surrounding Tortosa. Despite the numerous operations to send reinforcements and supply[287] to the city, the garrison of Tortosa capitulated on 4 December.

1651

For the Spanish monarchy, the main objective of this year was Barcelona and all the other armies had to undertake military operations to support it. In the Low Countries, Archduke Leopold had two objectives: to keep alive the civil war in France and to attract the main French reserve to the north far away from the Catalan front. As usual the main problem of the Army of Flanders was the lack of funds to organise a decent field army. In 1651, the Archduke did not have enough money, in spring, to pay the so-called *pan de*

---

283 Losses of the Army of Turenne are estimated at 1,200 dead, 3,000 prisoners including the infantry of Lorraine captured after the battle, the artillery (six to eight guns) and baggage (Périni volume IV, 1893).
284 Maffi (2014), Fernández Duro, volume IV 1895.
285 *Relación de lo sucedido en las empresas de Pomblin y Longon hasta el día 22 del presente mes de junio 1650,* CODOIN vol. 13, Madrid 1848, pp. 414–420.
286 The army besieging Tortosa had up to 15,000 men, probably some 11,400 infantry (22–25 tercios and regiments) and 3,500 cavalry. Maffi 2014, and Marquis de Olías y de Mortara, *Conquista de Cataluña,* 1655.
287 The main events took place 24 November when a French fleet of four ships was defeated by six Spanish galleys trying to introduce troops and supplies by the River Ebro (Fernández Duro, volume V, 1898).

municion or ammunition bread, the artillery train and the subsidies to the French rebels. To enhance his problem, in May the Viscount of Turenne[288] changed sides again and returned to the service of the French monarchy.

In September, the Army of Flanders was ready for action and seeing no positive news from the French rebels, the Archduke sent a detachment to take Furnes. After only five days of siege the town surrendered, while the rest of the Spanish army moved towards Bergues-Saint-Winoc, captured on 4 October. The Spanish continued the campaign, capturing between 20 and 27 October Hénin, Bourbourg and Linken before going to their winter quarters (Maffi 2014). In France, on 7 September the majority of Louis XIV was proclaimed and the Prince of Condé entered into open rebellion and asked for the support of Spanish authorities.[289]

In Italy, the Marquis of Caracena was complaining once again the lack of resources to attack the Franco-Savoyard forces, despite this he maintained his army in Monferrato and by mid August he conducted his forces towards Moncalieri, harassing the entire province around Torino. After two weeks of operations and seeing that the capital was well defended, the Spanish returned to Lombardy to take their winter quarters. In fact the main event in Lombardy was the secret treaty signed between the Spanish governor and the Duke of Mantua concerning the restitution of the city of Casale Monferrato to the Duke, and the implementation of a garrison of Swiss soldiers paid by the Spanish (Maffi 2007).

This year, the main effort of the Spanish was Catalonia and particularly Barcelona. Despite the difficulties of organising an army for a military operation like the siege of Barcelona, a city of 40,000–50,000 inhabitants, the timing was favourable to the Spanish. Due to other priorities and the civil war in France, Catalonia was defended by a weak French army fewer than 5,500 men[290] supported by the Catalan militia. The plague epidemic, which had started in 1647 in Valencia and spread to most of the Spanish Mediterranean coast, had reduced the capacity of the city to resist a siege. Nonetheless, the Spanish had to face serious difficulties when the Marquis of Mortara marched out of Lérida on 5 July with only 8,000 men. In August, John of Austria took command of all the operation and the Spanish army grew to 13,500 men[291] with a fleet of 60 sails and 22 galley ships.[292] On

---

288 In May Turenne and his brother the Duke of Bouillon rallied the King. See A.M. Ramsay, *Histoire du Vicomte de Turenne, Maréchal, Général des Armées…* volume 2, Paris, 1735.

289 The Prince of Condé, the Prince of Conti and the Duke of Longueville had been imprisoned from 18 January 1650 to 16 February 1651. In April 1651 Mazarin was exiled in Cologne and Condé was dominant in the scene of Paris, but the Queen played her cards well and managed to divide the Frondeurs. At the end of August 1651 and above all after 7 September the second war of the princes began, led by Condé (1651–1653). (W. Gibson (1998), *A Tragic Farce: The Fronde (1648–1653)*, Elm Bank Modern Language Studies, 146 pages. ISBN 978-0950259581).

290 3,000 infantry and 2,500 cavalry following Marques de Olías y de Mortara, *Conquista de Cataluña*, 1655.

291 With reinforcements John of Austria had the 8,000 men of Mortora, 3,300 men from southern Italy, 1,000 men from Castile, 1,200 from Valencia and 42 guns. In December they were reinforced by up to 1,650 infantry (Meseguer and Bell, 2012), and Marques de Olías y de Mortara, *Conquista de Cataluña*, 1655.

292 17 warships, 22 galleys and other smaller ships (Meseguer and Bell, 2012).

23 August, the town of Prades was taken followed by Mongat 25 August, Sarria on 1 October, Sans on 3 October and Hospitalet 11 october, Tarrasa 7 November and finally the castle of Ciurana on 27 November. With the last operation Barcelona was totally surrounded[293] and the Spanish could install artillery to bombard the city (Maffi 2014).

1652

From Madrid, the priority was again the siege of Barcelona and like the previous year the objective of the Archduke Leopold was to maintain the *Fronde* of the princes in France and to recover positions in the Low Countries. In Lombardy, the secret treaty with the Duke of Mantua opened new perspectives and the possibility of attracting French reserves away from Catalonia.

In the Low Countries, the first main operation was carried out against Gravelines on 11 April and after a gallant resistance and with no hope to be succoured they capitulated on 18 May (Monglat Volume 2, 1826). Meanwhile, Fort Madryk was retaken on 21 April. The Spanish high command wanted to start the siege of Dunkirk, but the instruction of Madrid and the letters from the Prince of Condé requesting an invasion of France changed the objective of the campaign and Dunkirk was only blocked by a small army. By mid July the core of the Army of Flanders, commanded by the Marquis of Fuelsaldaña, conducted an invasion of France following a route from Guise, Crécy-Sur-Serre and the River Oise, threatening Noyon and laying siege to the town of Chauny, captured on 16 July[294] after a short siege of four days. On 22 July, the Spanish left Chauny to rejoin the army of the Duke of Lorraine in Fismes, there with overstretched logistics and differences with the French rebels, the Marquis of Fuelsaldaña came back to Flanders, leaving the Army of Lorraine and a contingent of the Spanish army to the command of Condé. The siege of Dunkirk was resumed on 4 September and rapidly the Spanish managed to totally blckade the city by land and by sea, and on 16 September the French garrison capitulated. The last event was a campaign in Champagne with the army of Condé, with the capture of Vervins, Chateaux-Portien, Rethel and Sainte-Menehould on 14 November.

Further to the south, in the area of Bordeaux, the *Fronde* was active and the Spanish decided to send a fleet and troops to support them. The Spanish, commanded by the Baron of Waterville, decided to fortify Talmont–en-Gironde and Bourg-Sur-Dordogne.

In Italy, with the treaty with the Duke of Mantua in hand, the Marquis of Caracena decided to take the offensive and on 4 May the city of Trino was under siege. Despite heavy rain and the Savoyards' movement to reinforce the city, the garrison of Trino was obliged to capitulate on 28 May. Without losing time, the Marquis of Caracena outmanoeuvred the Savoyard army of

---

[293] To the surprise of the Catalan the Count of Marsin escaped from the city on 5 October with 1,200–1,500 men to rejoin the Prince of Condé in Guyenne (Meseguer and Bell, 2012).

[294] At the siege the Spanish force was estimated at 10,000 infantry, 7,000–8,000 cavalry and 18 guns. The French had assembled up to 4,000 to 5,000 men in the area but during the siege 2,000 of them were prisoners or dead. *Bulletin de la société académique de Chauny*, 1888/T08. pp. 176–179.

the Count of Verua and on 25 June was surrounding Crescentino. On 3 July the city surrendered and all its fortifications were destroyed; later Caracena came back to Lombardy to prepare the siege of Casale Monferrato. With the support of a small contingent of 3,800 men[295] sent by the Duke of Mantua, the Spanish finally laid siege to Casale Monferrato on 25 September. The declaration of the Duke of Mantua to the inhabitants of the city resulted in control of the town with little resistance, but the French garrison decided to resist in the citadel and in the castle. The castle capitulated on 10 October after a heavy bombardment, and on 22 October it was the turn of the citadel (Maffi 2014). For the Spanish it was a great success, after so long the city and the citadel of Casale Monferrato were in their hands[296] after the failure of 1629, 1630 and 1642.

As we said before, the priority of the Spanish was the siege of Barcelona. During winter the Spanish army had been reduced to less than 8,000 men due to combat losses, desertion and plague epidemic. The Cardinal Mazarin had sent troops from Italy in the province of Roussillon and in January 1652, the French commander the Marquis de la Mothe-Houdancourt was concentrating a franco-catalan army of 8,600 men and 6,000 militia in Hostalric and Sant Cugat del Vallès.[297] On 27 January La Mothe moved to Barcelona, retaking Tarrasa in the process but when he faced the Spanish line of circumvallation he thought that his army was too weak to attack such entrenchment and moved to San Boi to establish a fortified camp. Finally on the night of 22/23 April the French managed to enter Barcelona with 600 infantry and some cavalry (Montglat, volume 2, 1826) and left the rest of the mobile army to the command of Saint André Montbrun. On the Spanish side, reinforcement was coming regularly and by summer the Spanish army had probably 12,000–13,000 men.[298] On 3 August a French fleet of eight ships was forced to withdraw in the face of the Spanish one. At the beginning of September a Franco-Catalan army of 7,500 men tried to breach the Spanish lines but were repulsed with heavy losses. In other parts of Catalonia, Balaguer was taken by surprise on 8 July, and in September, Mataro (16th) and Blanes (27th) were captured. Around Barcelona fighting continued, but after a siege of 14 months and with no hope of relief and a general amnesty granted by the Spanish king, the big city decided to capitulate on 11 October. On the news of the surrender of Barcelona, most of the towns of Catalonia (such as Girona, Palamos, Vic or Solsona) changed sides, only the harbour of Rosas remained with the French.

---

295 The contingent had 3,500 infantry and 300 cavalry and was commanded by the Marquis of Gonzaga. *Histoire militaire du Piemont*, volume IV.

296 In reality a garrison of 800–1,000 German and Swiss soldiers on Spanish pay went to occupy the citadel. *Histoire militaire du Piemont*, volume IV.

297 Meseguer and Bell (2012) give 7,000 infantry, 1,600 cavalry and 6,000 militia called *sometents* from all provinces of central and north Catalonia (Emporda, Vic, Rosselló, Cerdanya, Manresa, Berga, Seu d'Urgell, la Segarra).

298 12,000 men is the number given around Barcelona (by Meseguer and Bell 2012) but we must not forget that the Spanish had to maintain strong garrisons, particularly in Lérida, Tarragona and Tortosa.

1653

The previous year had been successful for the Spanish monarchy and the possibility of ending the war with favourable terms seemed reasonable. But some of the successes had been possible by the civil war in France and when Cardinal Mazarin made his entrance in Paris on 3 February it is said that the episode of the *Fronde* was mostly over. Madrid decided to continue to support the Prince of Condé and the Archduke was asked to conduct operations in France while the Spanish armies in Italy and Catalonia should remain inactive. In the Low Countries, Viscount Turenne conducted a winter campaign to retake Chateau-Porcien. After a long pause to reorganise his army, Turenne went in Champagne retaking Rethel on 9 July after a siege of six days. At the end of July, the Archduke sent the Army of Flanders[299] to invade again the north of France, in support of Condé, taking small towns such as Montdidier and Roye on 5 August. The two armies started to manoeuvre to take the best position but without risking a pitched battle. At the beginning of September, seeing that the main French towns had a good garrison, the Archduke moved towards the east to besiege Rocroi on 7 September followed by the French who went to besiege Mouzon on the 9th. The fortress of Rocroi resisted three weeks and capitulated on 30 September, while Mouzon capitulated on 26 of September (Montglat, volume 2, 1826). Due to the chronic lack of resources the Spanish had to go back in their winter quarters while the French managed to continue the campaign, capturing Sainte-Menehould on 27 November after a long siege of 35 days. Further to the south in Aquitaine Bordeaux the last strongholds of the supporters of Condé fell to the French royal army, including the Spanish positions of Talamont-sur-Gironde and Bourg-sur-Dordogne. With the capitulation of Bordeaux on 27 July, the *Fronde* was completely over, Louis XIV and Cardinal Mazarin had won against the French nobility, only the Prince of Condé and some of his supporters had taken refuge in the Low Countries to continue the combat.

In Italy, the loss of Casale Monferrato had been a heavy blow to the French and Savoyards. For the next campaign, Mazarin wanted to recover some positions and sent the Count of Quincy with 6,000 men, while the Marquis of Caracena was inactive due again to the lack of resources. In July and August the French commander moved to the region of Alessandria and Tortona and spent most of the summer harassing the countryside. On the opposite side, Caracena with some 8,000 men moved to counter the French operation. With the end of the military operations in Aquitaine, more French troops were sent as well as troops from the Duke of Savoy, and the French Field Marshal of Grancey took command of the allied forces regrouped near the village of Castillo di Annone. By mid September he decided to move towards Alessandria and the Marquis of Caracena saw an opportunity to cut the French supply line crossing the Tanaro. On 22 September the Spanish were laying a new bridge of boats when French scouts appeared on a nearby

---

[299] An estimate of the combined army gives up to 25,000 men (Quincy, 1726).

hill. On 23 September the core of the Spanish army[300] had crossed the river when the whole allied army deployed in front of them. In the following battle both sides suffered losses,[301] but the Spanish managed to kept the ground, so we can talk of a tactical victory (Maffi, 2014). The rest of the campaign proved inconclusive and both armies went into winter quarters.

In Catalonia, the Spanish army was mostly inactive and had to face an invasion conducted by 6,500 men commanded by Jacque de Plessis-Bellière. On 16 June the French crossed the Pertus pass and on 22 June they were besieging Castello d'Empuries defended by some 700 men.[302] After a siege of 13 days the Spanish commander had to capitulate due to lack of ammunition. The French commander decided to proceed with the campaign and on 12 July he was surrounding Girona, defended by 2,500 men and the militia. On 26 July the Field Marshal of Hocquincourt arrived with new reinforcements[303] and took command of all the French forces. The defenders offered a stiff resistance while the poor hygiene conditions in the French camp reduced the troops and horses. At last John of Austria managed to organise a relief army of up to 7,100 men[304] and on 21 September he was at Cassá de la Selva, 13 km south of Girona. On 24 September the Spanish successfully stormed the French position, obliging Hocquincourt to abandon the siege and withdraw to Perpignan, having lost 1,300 men.

1654

At the beginning of the new campaign, the Spanish governor of the Low Countries had to deal with the Duke of Lorraine. At the beginning of the year, the Archduke published a proclamation on abuses committed by Lorraine's troops in the Low Countries and in Liège. The poor discipline of his troops was a source of complaint but also his failure to attend the demands and commands of the Spanish High command in the previous campaigns as well as his poor relationship with the Prince of Condé. However, according to rumours the Duke had intended to betray Flanders to the French,[305] therefore on 25 February he was arrested in Brussels and his troops were

---

300 An estimate of the Spanish army would give 8,000 men in 10 infantry battalions from five Spanish tercios (Lombardia, Saboya, Mar de Napoles, Aragón and Santillana), three Italian tercios (D'Este, Ala and Brancaccio), the tercio of the militia of Milan and 15–16 cavalry squadrons (Brussoni, 1661).

301 It appears that the Franco-Savoyard losses were 800–900 men while the Spanish losses numbered probably fewer than 200 men (Galeazzo Gualdo, 1672).

302 Emilio Grahit y Papell, *El sitio de Gerona 1653*, Gerona 1892.

303 With the reinforcements the French had up to 8,000 infantry and 4,000 cavalry. *Relación verdadera de la famosa Vitoria que ha tenido el serenísimo señor Don Juan contra la armada de Francia en el sitio de Girona …por Juan Gomes de Blas, Año 1653*, University of Granada.

304 The Spanish Infantry had 5,340 men divided into the Spanish tercio of the Guardia de Castilla, two tercios from the Armada (Velasco and d'Avila), three provincial tercios of Catalonia (Margarola, Gilabert and Areny) and two Italian tercios (Baron de Amato and Visconti). The cavalry had 1,800 men (Guards, Spanish companies, Trozo de Borgoña and Trozo de Flandes). *Segunda Relación muy copiosa del socorro que el Seteníssimo Señor Juan de Austria, Principe de la Mar, dió a la Ciudad de Girona, el miércoles 24 de Septiembre deste Año de 1653*, Juan Gomes de Blas, 1653, University of Granada.

305 Ósiochrú M. (2005), "The Duke of Lorraine and the International struggle for Ireland 1649–1653", *The Historical Journal*, vol. 48, pp. 905–932.

given to his brother François de Lorraine. The lack of reinforcements, particularly for the Spanish and Italian tercios, was also a strong concern for the Archduke and coupled with lack of financial resources meant that he had to give the initiative to the French. The objective was the city and citadel of Stenay, a stronghold of Condé on the French border, and on 3 June, the vanguard of the French forces (Marquis de Farbert) was in front of the city.[306] The garrison was a mixture of Spanish and Condé's troops,[307] the Spanish guarding the city and the French the citadel. On 19 June the lines of circumvallation were mostly finished but on 23 June the Spanish managed to send convoys with supplies and a reinforcement of 200–300 men.[308] On the opposite side, the question was whether to send the army of Flanders to relieve Stenay or to carry out another operation. The Archduke took the decision to besiege the capital of the County of Artois, the town of Arras, defended by a strong garrison of 5,000 men[309] commanded by the Count of Mondejeu. On 2 July, the Spanish army of 26,000 men[310] reinforced by the Army of Lorraine (François of Lorraine) and the troops of the Prince of Condé arrived in Arras. On 14 July the line of circumvallation was done and the next day they started the approach trenches. On 19 July the French armies[311] of Field Marshals Turenne and de la Férre were constructing a fortified camp in Mouchy-Le-Preux eight kilometres east of Arras. With the capitulation of Stenay, the French forces were reinforced by the 5,000–6,000 men from the army of Field Marshal Hocquincourt. On 24 August Turenne was ready to attack, and moved the three French corps north of the Spanish line of circumvallation. The three assaults were launched at 1:00 p.m. on 25 August and managed to breach the Spanish defence on two points. Despite a vigorous counter-attack by the Prince of Condé two hours later, the French held their position and the Spanish managed to extract most of their troops thanks to a brilliant rearguard action from Condé (Aumale, vol. 6, 1892). Although all the artillery and baggage was lost, the Spanish managed to mitigate their losses during the battle, estimated at 3,000 men by Turenne (Turenne 1735), mostly infantry. After the defeat, the Army of Flanders was still a sizeable force and the French army was able only to take the town of Le Quesnoy-en-Artois on 6 September and the last fortress of Condé in France Clermont-en-Argonne on 23 November.

In Lombardy, the Spanish and French armies were weak and unable to carry out significant military actions. It was only in September that significant skirmishes took place on the River Bormida when the Franco-Savoyards tried

---

306 At the same time the French were conducting a specific propaganda tour with the coronation of Louis XIV in Reims. The ceremony took place on 7 June in the presence of all the high nobility of the kingdom, Louis was known as the master of France.
307 Spanish 810 infantry, Condé 430 infantry, 70 cavalry and 120 militia (*Le Siege de Stenay*, 1883).
308 *Le Siege de Stenay*, 1883.
309 Monglat, volume 2, gives 4,000 infantry and 1,000 cavalry, but on the first day of the siege reinforcements of 400–500 men managed to enter.
310 As always, numbers of the Spanish army varied following sources from 22,000 to 30,000 men. Our estimate gives 25,000–26,000 men, 15,000–16,000 men for the Spanish, 5,000–6,000 men for the Army of Lorraine, some 4,000 men for the army of Condé.
311 Probably some 14,000 men.

to penetrate the region of Milan without success (Maffi 2014). In reality the main action, in Italy, was a tentative but vain attempt of the Duke of Guise to retake the operation in Naples. On 5 October the expedition[312] sailed from Toulon, on 13 November after a long journey, they disembarked near Castellammare di Stabia. The small town, defended by the militia, was taken easily and fortified. On 17 November, the French advance was checked at Torre Annunziata by a first contingent of Spanish troops and Guise had to withdraw to Castellammare di Stabia. During the following days more Spanish and Italian troops arrived in the area and prudently the Duke of Guise decided to re-embark and sailed back to Provence, having lost 1,500 men.

In Catalonia, the Prince of Conti took the field with 5,500 men (Paret, tomo V, vol. 25, 1893), and moved towards Villefranche-de-Confluent on 26 June. On 6 July the garrison of the town capitulated and the Prince of Conti moved to the Pertus pass. During summer, most of the fighting took place in the High Ampurdán region between the French cavalry and their Spanish counterparts. The French managed to send supply convoys to the fortress of Rosas and to harass the countryside. On 16 of August the French army moved as far as San Celoni 50 km north of Barcelona (Paret, Tomo V, v ol. 25, 1893). Returning to Perpignan, Conti received reinforcement and by the end of September he moved again and on 8 October a French army of 10,000 men was besieging Puigcerdà defended by 2,100 men.[313] Despite a brave defence, the garrison capitulated on 21 October at the death of its governor Pedro Valenzuela.[314] In front of an impotent Spanish army, the French continued, taking La Seu d'Urgell,[315] Baga, Olot, Campropdon Ripoll and Berga. The Prince of Conti tried to blockade the city of Vich, but due to the resistance of the garrison, the lack of guns and the oncoming winter he decided to withdraw to Perpignan.

1655

French power was raising again, King Philip IV of Spain and his *valido* Luis de Haro were well aware of the precarious economic situation of the kingdom. During the winters of 1654–1655 a new round of negotiations, promoted by Mazarin, was taking place. The French pretentions had been lowered but for the Spanish court they were still contrary to their interest and influence in Europe.[316] At the same time the Spanish were worried by the deterioration

---

312 23 ships, six galleys and transport ships with 7,000 infantry and 150 cavalry (Fernández Duro volume V, 1898).
313 The French had some 6,000 infantry and 4,000 cavalry with three 40-pdr siege guns. The garrison had 1,200 regulars (Catalan tercio of Banyoles, Neapolitan tercio of Lunati, a German regiment and an Irish tercio), 50 cavalry and 900 militia from the countryside (Paret, volume 25, 1893).
314 *Mémoires*, Roger de Bussy-Rabutin, Paris, volume 1.
315 In reality in La Seu d'Urgell, the population welcomed the "invasion" and in a middle of an enthusiastic celebration opened the gates to the French (Paret, volume 25, 1893).
316 One of the main problems for the Spanish monarchy was the place of the Prince of Condé, the territory of the Duke of Lorraine and the need to establish a real peace. Mostly they were a misunderstanding between Madrid and Paris, and the Spanish were not convinced at all by the sincerity of the French when Mazarin presented a more detailed plan in July to the Spanish envoy Pedro de Baos (Israel, 1997).

of their relations with the English protectorate of Cromwell,[317] after the first Anglo-Dutch war.

In the Low Countries, the Archduke was complaining of his lack of resources to carry out the orders of Madrid and it is not a surprise when the French armies of Turenne and la Ferté with respectively 16,000 and 10,000 men started the new campaign and 18 June the city of Landrécie was surrounded. While the line of circumvallation was built in three days, Archduke Leopold Wilhelm of Austria arrived in the area with his troops.[318] Seeing the French entrenchment as too strong, he wanted to make a diversion, invading France, unfortunately the garrison of Landrécie capitulated on 14 July after a poor resistance (Maffi 2014). The Spanish army withdrew to Valenciennes and in the coming months the French army was able to capture the city of Condé on 17 August and the city of Saint-Ghislain on 25 August. To mitigate the French advance, the Spanish launched several cavalry parties to successfully disturb the French supply convoys. In November, with the heavy rains of autumn, both armies went to winter quarters, but in December 1655 Duke François of Lorraine deserted to the French with 24 weak regiments.[319]

In Italy, situation was again difficult for the Spanish; Mazarin had finally convinced the Duke of Modena[320] to join the Franco-Savoyard alliance against Spain. With the possibility of attack from the east and the west, the Marquis of Caracena initiated the campaign in March, besieging Reggio Emilia with 6,000 infantry and 2,000 cavalry.[321] Bad weather, strong resistance and above all the news of a concentration of Franco-Savoyard troops obliged the Marquis of Caracena to recall his forces. On the other side, the allied army initiated the campaign in June, crossing the river Ticino and establishing a fortified camp in Binasco to wait for the army of Modena.[322] On 21 July the allied forces of 22,000 men was completed and moved towards Pavia. Meantime the Marquis of Caracena had strength garrison of the area and Pavia was known defended by 3 600 men commanded by the count of Trozzi, the field Spanish army was left with less than 10 800 men.[323] The siege started formally on 24 July, but and despite their efforts, the allies failed to

---

317 Already in the second semester of 1654, Oliver Cromwell planned to implement his "western design", an ambitious project to conquer Spanish colonies. M.C. Harmington, *The worke wee may doe in the world. The western design and the Anglo-Spanish struggle for the Caribbean 1654–1655*, thesis, Florida Sate University, 2004.
318 An estimate gives 20,000 men (Maffi, 2014).
319 Up to 4,000 men, 1,500 infantry (six regiments) and 2,500 cavalry (18 regiments) while 700–1,000 men remained loyal to Spain. Already 300 men (two regiments) had deserted in 1654 (Calmet, Abbé de Sémone, *Histoire de Lorraine, qui comprend ce qui s'est pqssé de plus mémorable…*volume 6, Nancy 1757).
320 In this deal the niece of Mazarin Laura Martinozzi would marry the son of the Duke of Modena.
321 *Relación verdadera de la feliz Victoria que dios …vha sido seruido conceder a las armas católicas del rey D. Felipe Quarto … Contra del rey de Francia sobre el sitio de Pavia…* A 111/122(095), Gómez de Blas, Juan, University of Seville.
322 An estimateof the army of the Duke of Modena (including French units) is 3,500 infantry and 1,800 cavalry (F.M. Pirogallo. *Le Glorie di Pavia dallo stretto assedio e liberatione di essa…*Pavia 1655).
323 The garrison of Pavia had 2,600 regular infantry, 600 militia and 400 cavalry. We have some fluctuation in the Spanish army but an estimate of 7,000 infantry and 3,800 cavalry could be correct (*Relación verdadera …* 111/122(095), op. cit.).

take the city. The Spanish twice managed to reinforce the garrison, and to seriously disturb the line of communication of their enemies, and with the reinforcement of up to 5,000 men[324] from Naples, Caracena could block the allied force capturing Arena di Pô and taking position in Mortara. Having lost 8,000 to 10,000 men and having an overstreched supply line, the Allied commanders decided to abandoned the siege the night of 13/14 September. At the end of the campaign and following instructions from Madrid, the Marquis of Caracena initiated a long journey towards Brussels to replace the Count of Fuensaldaña.

John of Austria was complaining bitterly that with less than 10,000 men it was difficult to defend the principality of Catalonia. The French army of the Prince of Conti initiated the campaign, besieging Cadaqués on 22 May. Five days later the town was in French hands and Conti could move to Castellón de Ampurias on 5 June, and the town was captured 3 July after a siege of four weeks. The French army moved to different location in the region, La Bisbal d'Empordà, Besalu, while French contingents were occupying towns suh as Solsona or Organa. In September, the Spanish commander received the news that the French were moving to besiege Palamos with the support of the French fleet.[325] The siege did not go well for the small French army of 7,000 men, the garrison was stronger than expected and when they learned that a Spanish fleet[326] commanded by Luis Fernandez de Córdoba was coming, Conti decided to withdraw to Perpignan. The two fleets met finally near Barcelona, and after a full day of combat the French withdrew to Toulon, having lost two ships, and the Spanish returned to Cartagena (Espino López, 2014). In the centre of Catalonia, the Spanish managed to retake Berga on 9 October after a siege of seven days and on 17 October they defeated a French force of 3,000 men in the area.[327] The last events in Catalonia took place when the Spanish sent an expedition[328] to recapture Solsona. The city was taken on 8 December, after a siege of 17 days, and the fortifications were harassed. The problems for the Spanish monarchy did not ended there; the western design of the Lord Protector of England threatened

---

[324] 4,000 infantry (700 Spanish, 1,500 Italians, 600 Irish and 1,200 Germans) and 1,000 cavalry (F.M. Pirogallo, *Le Glorie di Pavia dallo stretto assedio e liberatione di essa…* Pavia, 1655).

[325] An estimate of the fleet gives 17 warships and five fireships commanded by the Duke of Vendôme (La Roncière, 1920).

[326] An estimated 12 galleons, four frigates, three fireships and 13 to 15 galleys (*Relación verdadera…* 111/122(095), op. cit.).

[327] On 16 October a small Spanish force of 1,100 infantry coming from Vich (troops from the Tercio of Lisbon, Tercio of Villapando, Tercio of Rossell, Tercio of Espinossa and Walloon tercio of the Baron of Clerch, and 1,400 cavalry) managed to defeat the 2,000–2,500 infantry and 800 cavalry of the French army. The battle cost up to 600 dead and 600 prisoners to the French for probably 100 to 200 men for the Spanish (Paret, volume 25, 1893).

[328] With a landing force of 2,000 infantry (Tercio de la Armada del Mar Oceano and Tercio of Fernandez Carrillo), the Spanish had probably 4,000 infantry and 2,000 cavlary. The French garrison had probably 250 to 400 men (*Relación verdadera de la famosa vitoria, que han tenido las Armas de su Magestad, governadas por el Seteníssimo Señor Don Juan de Austria, en la recuperación de la ciudad de Solsona, en el Principado de Cataluña, sucedida a 7 de diciembre, Vispera de la fiesta de la Concepción de la Virgen Santisima Nuestra Señora. Año de 1655*. Juan Gómez de Blas, Virtual Library of Andalucia).

directly their control of the Caribbean islands. On 13 and 24 April an English expeditionary force[329] tried in vain[330] to take Santo Domingo on the island of Hispaniola, and later the English commanders decided to change target and to sail to Jamaica. The English made a successful landing on 10 May and were able to take the capital Santiago de la Vega a week later although guerrilla fighting continued in the island for the next five years.[331] The main consequence of the English expedition was a declaration of war by Cromwell in October 1655. The declaration of war was followed by an Anglo-French peace treaty signed on 28 November; it was another burden for the Spanish crown, and this one would prove to be decisive.

1656

At the beginning of the year, the prospect of the year for the Spanish monarchy was complicated, it was expected that the French offensives would be mainly concentrated in Flanders and northern Italy to achieve significant successes. To improve the efficiency of the army of Flanders and relations with the Prince of Condé, Archduke Leopold resigned from office and was replaced by John of Austria. Also the Count of Fuensaldaña was sent to Lombardy and replaced by the Marquis of Caracena as *Gobernador de las Armas*. Rapidly the son of Philip IV discovered that without adequate resources and subsidies it would be difficult to prepare an army to take the offensive. Meantime he managed to achieve a diplomatic success with the signing of the treaty of Brussels on 2 April with exiled English Royalists, previously located at the French court.[332]

As in previous years, the French forces initiated the campaign in the Low Countries with two armies, that of Field Marshal Turenne with 16,500 men and that of Field Marshal la Ferté with 9,000–10,000 men. At first the target of the French armies was Tournai, and on 12 June a vanguard was sent but the Spanish reacted rapidly and when Turenne earned that 4,000 men were in the area, he decided to change objectives and to besiege Valenciennes. On 15 June, the army of Turenne was located east of River Escaut and the next day it was joined by La Ferté on the west of the river, Valenciennes, defended by 1000 men[333] was surrounded. The Spanish army[334] reacted rapidly, and on 27 June they arrived near the French lines and installed a fortified camp

---

329 The English expedition force sailed on 25 December 1654 with 18 warships and 20 transport ships with 2,500 soldiers commanded by William Penn (naval) and Robert Venables (army). More troops, some 3,000 to 4,000 men, were later embarked in Barbados to take part in the expedition (Harmington, 2004 op. cit.).
330 The English expedition was known to the Spanish governor in Santo Domingo the Count of Peñalva, and the island was reinforced by 200 regular soldiers from Cuba. The details of the combat in Hispaniola can be found in Harmington (2004, op. cit.).
331 In Jamaica the 150–200 Spanish abandoned the city and conducted guerrilla warfare against the English for the next five years (Harmington, 2004, op. cit.).
332 To assist a Royalist insurrection in England, the Spanish promised a body 6,000 men to Charles Stuart combined with an army of his own raised among the English, Irish, and Scottish present in Flanders (Firth, 1902).
333 Following the sources the garrison, commanded by the Count of Henin, had 1,000 to 2,000 regular troops and the militia of the town.
334 Probably 22,000 men, see Chapter 4 for a detailed account of the military operation.

near Trith Saint Léger. On 14 July, John of Austria and the Prince of Condé decided to attack the position of the army of La Ferté. The night of the 15/16 July a diversion force of 3,500–4,000 men moved to carry out a small attack on the fortification of Turenne, the core of the Spanish army moved to the north while a small detachment was left in the fortified camps. With the dark of the night the Spanish launched a triple attack, storming the French camps. The army of la Ferté was totally destroyed, while Turenne was obliged to undertake a retreat to Le Quesnoy. With the victory in hand, the Spanish moved towards the city of Condé-sur-l'Escaut on 20 July. The city made a gallant resistance of one month but on 18 of August it capitulated. The campaign was followed by the sending of Spanish raiding parties in France, even if Turenne managed to capture La Capelle on 27 of September after a short siege of three days.

In northern Italy, the death of Thomas of Savoy-Carignano left the Franco-Savoyard army[335] under the command of the Duke of Modena supported by the Duke of Mercoeur. This time it was decided to directly attack Lombardy and the objective was the city of Valenza del Pô, surrounded on 24 June. The siege was a difficult operation, the Spanish managed to introduce small reinforcements on two occasions but after a resistance of 82 days, the garrison of the city capitulated on 16 September with honourable terms. The victory of Fontana Santa[336] against the army of Modena, on 6 July, did not end the siege and the Principe Trivulzio (governor in interim of the State of Milan) with a weak army of 8,000 men[337] could do nothing to prevent it. Despite the heavy blow to Spanish pride and the fact that for the first time in 10 years a stronghold of Lombardy had been lost, the attack on Lombardy – a feudal territory of the Holy Roman Empire – by another feudal territory led to the sending of an Imperial army to support the Spanish.[338]

In Catalonia the new viceroy, the Marquis of Olias and Mortara, had few resources to carry out military operations against the French. On the other side the French commander was also weak in troops and both sides spent the year sending raiding parties against their enemies' lines.

The Spanish monarchy had also to face other threats; one of them was the presence of an English squadron sent to disrupt Spanish trade from Andalucía to America and Europe and to try to intercept the treasure fleet.[339]

---

335 The French and Savoyards numbered 13,000 to 14,000 men (*Relacion verdadera de la famosa Vitoria que dios nuestro señor se ha seruido conceder a las armas de su majestad en el estado de Milan …. Contra el exercito del Duque de Modena*. Juan Gómez de Blas. A 111/122(104). University of Seville).

336 In Fontana Santa, the Spanish army managed to destroy the army of Modena of 3,500–4,000 men, inflicting losses of 500 dead and 1,200 prisoners (*Relacion verdadera de la famosa Vitoria … Contra el exercito del Duque de Modena*. op. cit.).

337 One estimate gives 5,000 infantry and 3,000 cavalry (Quincy, 1726).

338 The Spanish Ambassador in Vienna managed to convince Ferdinand III to send an army to save the State of Milan. At the end of September an auxiliary Imperial army of 6,800 men (commanded by the Baron of Enkevort) arrived in Milan, unfortunately it was too late to save Valenza del Pô (Maffi, 2007).

339 In 1656 Admiral Robert Blake managed to intercept the fleet of *Tierra firme* on the Spanish coast a few kilometres from Cadiz. In the process one galleon and one urca were sunk, one galleon and one urca were captured by the English with maybe two million pesos on board and

1.8 Final Collapse, the Treaty of the Pyrenees and Beyond: 1657–1665

The previous years had been favourable to the Spanish Monarchy and the last victory in Valenciennes had prompted a round of negotiations when the French envoy Hugues de Lionnes was sent to Madrid to evaluate a possible peace between the two countries. It is not our purpose to discuss the results of a long and arduous negotiation, and at the end nothing happened. It is difficult to assess who to blame for the failure, sometimes it seems that Spain had missed an opportunity to end the war but on the other hand who knows if Mazarin was not determined to extract advantages to proclaim the supremacy of France (Israel, 1997) and he needed to buy some time to have successes on the battlefield. We have also to consider that the French were expecting significant advantages with their offensive alliance with the English when they signed the treaty of Paris the 23 March.[340] For England the alliance was a necessity to reduce the damage of the Spanish privateers from Dunkirk and Ostend to their mercantile fleet.

On the Portuguese front, the main news was the death of King Joao IV of Portugal the 6 November.

1657

In the Low Countries, victory in previous years had given hope to recover some positions in the province, but the news of the Anglo-French alliance meant that the Flemish coast would be soon a major target. Therefore, John of Austria and the Prince of Condé decided to start the campaign as soon as possible with 12,000 men (Quincy, 1726) and on 15 March the Spanish army was besieging Saint-Ghislain. The garrison presented a strong resistance for eight days but on 23 March the French governor had to capitulate. In May, the French army[341] of Field Marshal Turenne was advancing towards Flanders (Saint-Omer and Aire les Lys) while the army of Field Marshal of la Ferté was invading the Duchy of Luxembourg, the Spanish had to divide their force to counter the threats. Knowing that Cambrai had an understrength garrison, Turenne decided to change his plan and he rapidly sent his army to besiege the town. On 28 May Cambrai was surrounded, but fortunately for the Spanish side, the Prince of Condé managed to breach the French lines and to enter the city with 4,000 cavalry. Further to the east, la Ferté managed to surprise the Spanish when he moved to besiege Montmédy on 12 June. The small town had a small garrison of 700 men commanded by the Lord of

---

"one urca and one patache" ran aground on the Spanish coast. Only two ships arrived in Cadiz (M. Fernández Martínez & V. Stapells Johnson, 1992, "Escuadra de 1656: Un Cambate naval en la bahia de Cadiz", *Revista International de los Estudios Vascos*, volume XXXVII, pp. 113–165.

340 With the treaty of Paris it was agreed that the English would support the French with 6,000 infantry and their fleet to capture Gravelines, Mardyck and above all Dunkirk (D.L. Smith, "Diplomacy and the religious question: Mazarin, Cromwell and the treaties of 1655 and 1657", *E-rea* 11.2, 2014, posted online 15 July 2014, consulted 19 February 2018 <http://journals.openedition.org/erea/3745>; DOI : 10.4000/erea.3745

341 An estimate in April gives 24,000 men (L. Lemaire (1920), "Dunkerque et la politique de Mazarin'" *Revue du Nord* 21, pp. 1–21).

Malandry (Maffi 2014). The Spanish failed to introduce reinforcements and John of Austria[342] decided to conduct a diversion attacking the countryside in the River Oise valley. Despite a gallant resistance and with the death of the Spanish governor, the garrison of the citadel of Montmédy capitulated 6 August. The campaign was not over; the army of la Ferté was exhausted but Turenne had been reinforced by 6,000 men from the English army and was ready to strike. The objective was the city of Saint-Venant, surrounded 16 August. The garrison capitulated 13 days later after a poor resistance, despite the destruction of a convoy full of supplies on 21 August near Liliers and a diversion conducted against Ardres near Calais. The English were pressing to continue the campaign towards the coast, Bourbourg was taken and on 3 October Madryck was captured after a short siege of five days. With this last event both armies went to winter quarters.[343]

In northern Italy, with the support of the Imperial army, Count Fuensaldaña had conducted a blockade of the city of Valenza del Pô during winter. The situation changed on 2 April when Holy Roman Emperor Ferdinand III died. The commanders of the Imperial contingent decided to adopt a more neutral attitude, waiting for orders. At first the allied army managed to send a large convoy of supplies to the garrison of Valenza del Pô and later moved towards Alessandria to besiege the city on 17 July. Only defended by 1,300 men and the militia, the city needed reinforcements and on 5 August the core of the Spanish army[344] was in Castelazzo Bormida. The next day the Spanish tried unsuccessfully to breach the French line of circumvallation. Meantime, Fuensaldaña sent at the same time cavalry raiding parties to disrupt the supply line. On 15 August the Spanish managed to take an island on the river Bormida and to connect with the defenders. On the other side the efficient Spanish action against their supplies and the conquest of the island obliged the Duke of Modena to raise the siege on 18 August, having lost up to 6,000 men for only 500 Spanish (Saluces volume 4, 1818). In Catalonia, the Spanish were the first to enter campaign, when in April a small force of 3,000 men was sent to retake the Seu d'Urgel. The operation failed due to the arrival of French reinforcements in the area and the Spanish had to abandon the siege on 13 May. During the summer, the two weak armies conducted some minor operations in the Ampurdan, but in September the French governor of Castellfollit de la Roca gave the town to the Spanish. On 28 October a French column sent to Castellfollit de la Roca to retake was totally destroyed by the Marquis of Mortara.

This year significant military actions took place on the Portuguese frontiers. With the death of Joao IV and the regency of Luisa Medina Sidonia, the Spanish monarchy saw an opportunity to carry out successful military

---

342 At this time the Spanish had probably 15,000 men including a contingent of 2,000 men (four regiments) from the auxiliary army of Charles Stuart (Firth, 1902).

343 It is interesting to notice the English losses during the campaign, although no significant or costly military actions took place, English losses were estimated at one third of the original force (Firth, 1902).

344 Fuensaldaña made a significant effort to join up to 16,000 men to save the city, even if a small proportion of these troops were defending the borders with the Duchy of Savoy (Maffi, 2014).

actions. A powerful field army of 14,000 men[345] was organised by the Duke of San German and on 11 April the Spanish were besieging Olivenza defended by a garrison of 2,000 men. The Portuguese sent an army[346] to save the place but were stopped by the strong Spanish lines of circumvallation. The Portuguese tried a diversion with an unsuccessful surprise attack against Badajoz on 15 May and a failed siege against Valencia de Alcántara some days later. Finally Olivenza capitulated on 30 May. The campaign was followed by the captured of Mourão on 20 June after a siege of seven days. In summer the two armies were in their summer quarters, and in October the Portuguese managed to retake Mourão on 28 October.

1658

In Madrid, the decision of the Spanish minister Luis de Haro to send more money to the army of Extremadura would have consequences for the resources available for the army of Flanders and the Army of Lombardy (Maffi 2014). In the French government, Cardinal Mazarin had to give priority to the operation in Flanders to comply with the treaty with Cromwell. On the other side, John of Austria was complaining to Madrid that money had to be sent urgently because it was impossible to extract enough funds from the Low Countries to prepare the army for the next campaign. In reality the campaign started well for the Spanish: on 30 March the governor of Hesdin handed over the city[347] to John of Austria and on 14 May a French detachment was destroyed in a vain attempt to capture Ostend.[348] Despite such successes, the Anglo-French army[349] of Field Marshal Turenne was ready for action by mid May and on 25 May Dunkirk was surrounded.

Dunkirk was defended by the Marquis of Leyde with a garrison of 2,200 men and for John of Austria a relief army had to be organised as soon as possible. While the Anglo-French army was conducted the siege operation, the Spanish commander was joining all his forces in Ypres. On 3 June, the final decision was taken to save Dunkirk at all costs and soon after the Spanish army moved to the north, crossing the canal of Furnes on 10 June. Later on, the Spanish army of 14,000 men took position on the sandhills between Leffrinckoucke and Zuydcoote, waiting for the rearguard with the rest of the infantry and above all the artillery. On the other side, Turenne took the decision to attack the Spanish forces and on the night of 13/14 June he went out from his entrenchment with 15,000 men. Early in the morning the French force was deployed and started a slow march towards the Spanish position. John of Austria was caught by surprise in an unfavourable position and had to draw up his force as quickly as possible between the sea and the canal of Bruges-Fermes.[350] During the battle,

---

345 The field army had 11,140 infantry and 3,530 cavalry, the rest – some 2,000 infantry and 620 cavalry – was in garrison (Rodríguez Hernández & P. Rodríguez Rebollo, 2007).
346 The Portuguese army had some 12,000 infantry and 3,500 cavalry (Estébanez Calderón volume 1, 1885).
347 *Avisos de Jeronimo de Barrionuevo (1654–1658)*, volume 4, Madrid 1894.
348 The Marshal of Aumont had been induced by a spy to attack Ostend by sea (Maffi, 2014).
349 A rough estimate of the army gives 25,000 men.
350 The Prince of Condé urged John of Austria to extract the army from this position unsuitable for the cavalry. Unfortunately, the Spanish commanders did not follow this advice and fought a

the Anglo-French army supported by the English navy inflicted a crucial defeat to the Spanish after a fight of four hours. The Spanish army lost up to 5,000 men[351] and while most of the Spanish cavalry managed to escape, the infantry was destroyed. Despite a gallant resistance the garrison of Dunkirk capitulated 10 days later on 24 June. With the fall of Dunkirk and the disarray in the Spanish ranks, Turenne could initiate a brilliant campaign to subdue Flanders. On 28 June the French were besieging Bergues-Saint-Winoc and five days later the 800 men of the garrison capitulated (Montglat volume 3, 1826). The next objective was Furnes, captured on 4 July and Dixmude on 7 July. On 27 July the French army was reinforced and with 12,000 men Field Marshal La Ferté was moving to besiege Gravelines while Field Marshal Turenne was moving towards Dixmude and Nieuwpoort with 10,000 men.[352] After a resistance of 22 days, the garrison of Gravelines capitulated with honourable terms on 27 August. Soon after, Turenne moved quickly to east and on 7 September he was surrounding Oudenarde. A Spanish cavalry detachment was defeated trying to defend the town and on 10 September Oudenarde surrendered. French victory continued, Menin was taken some three days later and on 15 September Turenne was besieging the city of Ypres. Although an important Spanish stronghold, John of Austria decided to concentrate all his forces to protect Nieuwpoort, Ostend, Ghent, Bruges and Brussels. On 25 September the garrison of Ypres capitulated, in few months Turenne had managed to damage seriously the Spanish line of defence, for Brussels the only light was a success near Hesdin against French cavalry on 12 November, but for the Spanish governor, it was urgent to make peace.

In northern Italy the situation was also gloomy despite the success of Alessandria the previous year. During winter, the Duke of Modena had managed to convince the Duke of Mantua to change side and the governor of the State of Milan was surrounded by enemies. The Duke of Modena and the Baron of Navailles decided to conduct the campaign from the east of Lombardy and on 16 June their army was out of Casalmaggiore. On the other side, the Spanish decided to take position behind the River Adda and to reinforce the garrisons of Cremona, Sabionetta and Pizzighettone. On 9 July they were at Castelleone and on 13 July the River Adda was crossed at Cassano d'Adda and all the army regrouped near Marignano. The Spanish had been outmanoeuvred and Fuensaldaña withdrew to protect Milan, leaving troops in Lodi. Meantime in the west the army of Savoy captured by surprise the city of Trino on 22 June. After resting, the Savoyard army continued to the River Ticino while the French army of the Duke of Modena moved first to Alessandria and then to the same river harassing all the countryside of the south of Milan. The two armies met near Cascina Santa Sofia and moved to besiege the city of Mortara on 5 August.[353] Waiting from reinforcement

---

pitched battle (Montglat, volume 3, 1826).
351 Human losses were significant, but above all Spanish morale had been badly shaken, and for weeks they were unable to react to the French advance (Maffi, 2014).
352 For the force of Turenne we have 7,000 infantry and 3,000 cavalry (Quincy, 1726).
353 Around Mortara, the allied army was composed of 8,000 French and 2,000 Savoyards while the garrison had 1,200 men (Quincy, 1726).

from Naples, the Marquis of Fuensaldaña was unable to save the city and on 25 August the garrison capitulated. In September, the Spanish commander failed to retake by surprise Valenza del Pô and the only good news for the Spanish was the death of the Duke of Modena on 14 October.

In Catalonia, despite the weakness of the army, the Marquis of Mortara managed to take by surprise Camprodón on 4 May. The next day a French detachment sent to retake the city was defeated, losing 500 men.[354] In July the new French commander Saint Aubais organised a French army of 8,000 men and moved straight to retake Camprodón and on 29 July the small town was besieged. The Marquis of Mortara joined all his troops, 5,000 men,[355] and marched to relieve the city. On 15 August the French army was totally defeated losing 1,400 to 1,500 men, fortunately for the French, the Marquis of Mortara had not enough men to carry out an operation in Roussillon and the campaign ended.

In Extremadura, the initiative came from the Portuguese in an attempt to pressure the French while they were negotiating with the Spanish. The army of Portugal, with 17,000 men[356] and commanded by Joao Mendes de Vasconcellos, launched a risky offensive against Badajoz. On 16 June the Portuguese were besieging the city, defended by a strong garrison of 6,000 men[357] commanded by the Duke of San German. The strong resistance of the garrison, the difficulty to supply the large Portuguese army, the elevate temperature of the summer made the operation difficult. On 8 August, the Duke of San German breached the Portuguese line a rejoined Mérida to organise the relief army. On 11 October, faced with the prospect of having to fight a Spanish army of 15,500 men[358] with an army exhausted and diminished by a long siege, the Portuguese officers decided to abandon the operation and to go back to Elvas in Portugal. Beside the contrary advice of the Duke of San German, the Spanish *valido* Luis de Haro decided to continue the campaign and sent a reinforced army towards Elvas. On 16 October, the Spanish army was besieging the city and constructing a line of circumvallation. Elvas had a strong fortification and a garrison of up to 8,000 men,[359] but due to a plague epidemic during the siege, men fit for service were much reduced. While the siege was in progress, the Portuguese assembled a relief army of 10,900 men,[360] and on 14 January

---

354 N. Feliu de la Peña y Farell, *Anales de Cataluña y Epílogo breve de los progresos, y famosos hechos de la Nacion Catalana…desde la primera Poblacion de España … hasta el presente de 1709*, vol. III, Barcelona 1709.

355 Spanish with 2,000 infantry (Tercio of Salamanqués, Tercio of Valencia, Tercio of Navarre, tercios of the Diputacío, Tercio of Barcelona and 200 men from the armada), 600 militia, 2,000 cavalry and 400 dismounted cavalry; while the French had 4,000 infantry and 2,300 cavalry at the moment of the battle (*Felicissima Victoria que han tenido las católicas armas … sobre le Castillo de Campredon qye tenia sitiado Monsiur de Santoné*…. Juan Gómez de Blas, A 111/122(110), University of Seville.

356 An estimate gives 14,000 infantry, 3,000 cavalry, 20 guns and two mortars (L. Menezes volume III, 1759).

357 4,000 infantry and 2,000 cavalry (de Menezes volume III, 1759).

358 12,000 infantry and 3 500 cavalry under the command of Luis de Haro the *valido* of King Philip IV (Estébanez Calderón volume 1, 1885).

359 A. Duarte (2003), Linhas de Elvas, 1659, 'Prova da força', Lisbon: *Tribuna da História*.

360 8,000 infantry, 2,900 cavalry and seven to nine guns (de Menezes volume III, 1759).

1659 they successfully stormed the Spanish lines. The following battle was a crucial defeat for a Spanish army reduced to 13,000 men (due to desertion and sickness) with losses of up to 3,000 men (much more were lost by desertion) for 600 of the Portuguese.[361] At the beginning of September, the Spanish also conducted an invasion in north of Portugal with the army of Galicia[362] to harass the countryside south of the River Minho and to besiege the Castle of Monsão on 17 October. After a long siege, where the Spanish had to send reinforcements, the garrison finally capitulated on 5 February 1659.

1659

The previous year had been a critical one and the French had managed to inflict serious and significant defeats to the Spanish, especially in Flanders. The long and difficult negotiation between the two kingdoms resumed and the Spanish sent new envoys to Lyons to start to negotiate a truce. At last a suspension of hostilities was decreed on 8 May to stop a long and bloody war. On 9 June the preliminaries of a peace treaty were signed in Paris, it took month of hard talks between Luis de Haro and Mazzarin to finally sign the peace of the Pyrenees on 7 November 1659,[363] on the Island of Pheasants on the River Bidassoa. The end of the war marked a certain dominance of France, unfortunately for the Spanish people it did not mark the end in the Iberian Peninsula and by the end of the year King Philip IV could devote all the resources[364] of the kingdom to address the situation in Portugal. Philip could maybe grant the viceroyalty and other privileges to the house of Braganza but he had to stay nominally King of Portugal, conditions that the Portuguese would certainly never accept.

1660

The application of the peace of the Pyreneees was not easy and during most of the year the Spanish and French continued to negotiate to establish completely the numerous articles of the treaty. At the same time, the death of Cromwell on 3 September 1658 and the following political turmoil that favoured the return of the English monarchy of Charles II, gave the opportunity to negotiate a peace treaty signed in September 1660.

In the Iberian Peninsula, the Spanish Monarchy wanted to take the offensive on the Portuguese regime as soon as possible and all the viceroy and governors were asked to send their mercenaries veteran units[365] to

---

361 For a full description of the battle see A. Duarte (2003), op. cit.
362 2,000 regular troops and 4,500 militia and 600 cavalry commanded by the Marquis of Viana. (*Diari relacion de lo sucedido al exercito de Galicia gouernado pro el marques de Viana, desde 28 de Agosto del año pasado de 1658 que entro en el reyno de Portugal, hasta 17 de febrero de 1659*. Juan Gómez de Blas, A109/041(26). University of Seville).
363 For a full description of the negotiation and agreement of the treaty of the Pyrenees please see D. Séré, *La paix des Pyrénées: Vingt-quatre ans de négociations entre la France et l'Espagne (1635-1659)* (Paris: Honoré Champion, Collection Bibliothèque d'histoire moderne et contemporaine, 2007).
364 The problem for the Spanish, was that the resources that could be mobilised in 1660 to fight against Portugal were fewer than those available 20 years previously.
365 At the end of 1660, from Lombardy three Italian tercios and three German regiments with 3,640 men were sent as well as 2,420 new recruits from Napoles divided into a Neapolitan tercio and

Extremadura. It was particularly true for the armies of Flanders and Lombardy when Italian and German units were sent to Badajoz while the Spanish tercios were kept to garrison the two territories. Officers from the armies of Flanders and Lombardy were also sent to command and trained the troops. Philip IV of Spain ordered his son John of Austria to command the army of Extremadura while the Duke of Osuna was sent to command the army Galicia, and the smaller army of Castile was organised in Ciudad Rodrigo. From a military point of view the only events were the capture of the Castle of La Albergueria de Argañán on 7 March by the Portuguese and the arrival of 600 French mercenaries commanded by the Count of Schomberg.[366]

1661

This year Madrid started its offensive against Portugal in order to gain a favourable negotiation ground. Meantime the Portuguese managed to find a potential ally with the marriage contract between Charles II of England and Catherine of Braganza signed on 23 June. From a military point of view England would assist Portugal with 2,000 infantry and 1,000 cavalry as well as 10 warships to defend Lisbon.[367] For the Spanish it was urgent to carry out military operations inside Portugal. With an army[368] of 10,000 infantry and 5,000 cavalry John of Austria decided to take an indirect approach avoiding lengthy operations against Campo Maior or Elva and moved towards Ouguela and later Arronches on 15 June. Further to the north, The Duke of Ossuna crossed the northern border from Galicia and started to besiege Valença on 19 July. With an army made mostly of militia from Galicia, a high desertion rate from the foreign troops and the strong resistance of the Portuguese the siege failed and the Spanish had to abandon it on 19 August. In July, the small army of Castile took the fortress of Val de la Mula and recaptured the castle of La Albergueria de Argañán. The campaign did not end there, the Spanish army captured Alconchel the 2nd of December after a short siege of six days.

1662

The previous campaign had been disappointing for Madrid, even with a reinforced army, the Spanish had taken only minor positions and John of Austria was asked to be more ambitious. The young general decided this time to carry out operations against the fortress of Juromenha in order to have access to the province of Evora. The Spanish army had close to 18,000

---

a German regiment. From Flanders up to 5,500 men were sent in 1661 and 1662 (Rodríguez Hernández & P. Rodríguez Rebollo, 2007).

366 The task of the Count of Schomberg was to reorganise and train the Portuguese army, paid by new taxes implemented on the trade for sugar from Brazil and spices from Asia. Therefore Schomberg was nominated *Maestro do Campo General de l'Alemtejo* (Général Dumouriez, *Campagnes du Maréchal de Schomberg en Portugal depuis l'année 1662 jusqu'en 1668*, London 1807; and Gonzalez Lopez, 1973).

367 For the help of 3,000 men, weapons and ships, Portugal would hand over the cities of Tangiers and Bombay as well as trade rights fin Asia and Brazil and 2,000,000 cruzados (Gonzalez Lopez, 1973)

368 Général Dumouriez, op. cit.

men,[369] and started the campaign from Badajoz and after some manoeuvres to confuse the Portuguese he went directly to Vila Boim and Borba. The last city and castle were taken and the Spanish decided to move to the fortress of Juromenha defended by 2,500 men (de Menezes, volume III, 1759), on 17 May. The siege was successful and despite a Portuguese army in Extremoz, the garrison finally capitulated on 9 June after a siege of 24 days. After this success, John of Austria moved to the Alentejo region capturing several burgs (Veiros, Monforte, Alter do Chão, Capeç0 de Vide and Crato) and on 11 July the Spanish went to summer quarters. For the rest of the year, little action took place from one side or the other.

1663

From Madrid's point of view, the results of the previous campaign of John of Austria and the political instability in Lisbon,[370] gave an opportunity to be more ambitious against Portugal. The Spanish crown wanted to conduct more aggressive actions with on one hand the use of the armada and privateers against Portuguese trade and communication and on the other a strong military force operating deeper in Portugal. Due to the lack of resources, on the naval side only some Spanish privateers were operating on the Portuguese coasts while John of Austria was preparing the army of Extremadura. On 6 May, the Spanish forces started their spring campaign. After a march of eight days, the Army of Extremadura was besieging Evora on 15 May. The second town of Portugal, defended by 4,000 men and militia, was not strongly fortified and capitulated after a siege of nine days. The same day, 25 May, the army of Portugal[371] commanded by the Marquis of Vilaflor and the Count of Schomberg was located behind the River Degebe (probably near Nossa Senhora de Machede) and even if they could not prevent the fall of Evora, they managed to cut off the supply line of John of Austria from Spanish bases (Badajoz and Juromenha). In reality, despite the successful capture of Evora, the Spanish army was in a precautious situation in the middle of enemy territories, with strong enemy fortresses (Estremoz, Elvas, Campo Maior) between them and the Spanish territory and with a Portuguese army in the neighbourhood. After some rest, the Spanish commanders decided to present battle and moved near the River Degebe to attack the Portuguese camp. The Spanish failed totally to cross the river and after a fierce skirmish and some bombardments they were obliged to return to Evora. Therefore the next day, the decision was taken to leave a strong garrison of 3,800 men in Evora, with the siege guns and part of the baggage, with the rest[372] to move towards Arronches to wait for new reinforcements.

---

369 An estimated 13,000 infantry and 5,000 cavalry. At the siege of Juromenha the Spanish seem to have had 8,890 infantry and 5,370 cavalry (Estébanez Calderón volume 2, 1885).

370 In June 1662, the Queen Regent of Portugal Luisa de Guzman was removed from power and sent to a convent by her son Alfonso VI and his favourite the Count of Castello Melhor. The measure was not popular, mainly because the king was physically and mentally weak (de Menezes volume IV, 1759).

371 At that moment with probably some 11,000 infantry and 3,000 cavalry (de Menezes, volume IV, 1759).

372 The number estimated from a muster taken on 25 May gives 11,120 infantry and 6,000 cavalry (Estébanez Calderón volume 2, 1855). During the battle Spanish forces available were probably

On the night of 5/6 June, the Spanish army outmanoeuvred the Portuguese, however, two days later, the Portuguese army managed to pin down the Spanish rearguard, and on 8 June the Spanish commander was obliged to deploy his army in a defensive position on hills around Ameixial (actualy Vittoria do Ameixial), north-west of Estremoz. Late in the afternoon the Portuguese decided to attack the Spanish positions and in three hours managed to inflict a crucial defeat on their opponent. Spanish losses were heavy and two days later the Army of Extremadura managed to reach Arronches where up to 12,000 men were found.[373] The Portuguese did not follow the Spanish and went straight to retake Evora. From the 14 to 24 June, the Spanish garrison of Evora resisted the Portuguese attack but with no hope to be succoured the Spanish governor, the Count of Sartirama, capitulated. The victory of Ameixial had doomed Spanish wishes to end the war and had consolidated the position of the young King Afonso VI.

1664

The defeat of the previous year had lowered the morale of the Army of Extremadura and despite the instruction of Madrid, John of Austria was not ready to carry out any significant military operations. In fact it was the Portuguese army that initiated the campaign in 1664. At the beginning of June, it crossed the frontiers of Castile and laid siege to Valencia de Alcántara on 12 June. John was unable to assemble a coherent relief army and after a gallant resistance the garrison commanded by Juan de Avila y Mejia capitulated on 24 June. The Duke of Osuna, the new commander of the army of Castile,[374] decided to carry out an operation against the town of Castel Rodrigo. On 3 July the Spanish were besieging the city when a small Portuguese army of 3,000 men[375] commanded by Pedro Jacques de Magalhães arrived in the vicinity to succour the town. The Spanish commander could not judge their numbers well and decided to withdraw to Castile. Unfortunately, during the retreat the Spanish forces were totally routed on 6 July losing three quarters of the initial force[376] and all the guns. Further to the south the Spanish also evacuated their positions in the Alentejo region and on 26 September they dismantled the fortress of Arronches.

1665

At the end of the previous year Juan José de Austria was dismissed by his father Philip IV of Spain and replaced by the Marquis of Caracena. To carry out a military operation inside Portugal, the new commander asked for new reinforcements and thousands of men, including Swiss regiments, were

---

closer to 9,000 infantry and 5,500 cavalry (*Carta de Juan de Austria al rey*, in Estébanez Calderón volume 2, 1885).
373 A Spanish source (Estébanez Calderón volume 2, 1855) gives losses of 3,450 infantry and 1,860 cavalry, a Portuguese source (de Menezes volume IV, 1759) gives 10,000 men. The difference could be due to propaganda or different calculation, the real numbers must be between 6,000 to 7,000 men, 40 to 50 percent of the original force.
374 Probably 4,000 infantry, 700 cavalry and nine guns (de Menezes volume IV, 1759).
375 2,500 infantry, 500 cavalry and two light guns (de Menezes volume IV, 1759).
376 Losing between 2,500 to 3,300 men (Estébanez Calderón volume 2, 1885).

raised to increase the army of Extremadura. The campaign started earlier this year, when the Spanish failed to retake Valencia de Alcántara by surprise on 20 March. On 22 May, the Marquis of Caracena had a field army of 21,500 men[377] and on 1 June he marched towards the frontier of Portugal with the design to besiege Vila Viçosa. The city was defended by 1,300 men (including 190 militia) and was probably more a symbolic objective than a military one. On 9 June, the Spanish army was in front of Vila Viçosa and quickly managed to storm the suburbs and the town, but the Portuguese were still masters of the castle. On 13 June the news of the arrival of a relief army reached the Spanish headquarters and because no proper line of circumvallation had been made, the Marquis of Caracena decided to present battle when it was possible. The Portuguese army had some 20,500 men[378] while the Spanish[379] had suffered losses during the siege and had to leave troops to contain the garrison. On 17 June, the two armies were finally facing each other and after terrific and indecisive fighting, the better coordination of the infantry and cavalry gave victory to the Portuguese. The Spanish army retreated in confusion to Juromenha losing thousands of men[380] and all the artillery. The dream of subduing Portugal was gone forever on 17 September, when King Philip IV of Spain died after a long reign of 44 years of continuous war to preserve the hegemony of the Habsburg dynasty and of the Spanish monarchy. From the decision to resume the war with the Dutch republic in 1621 to the War of Restoration against Portugal, the armies of Philip IV, made of native Spaniards but also Italians from Lombardy and Naples, Walloons from the Low Countries and numerous mercenaries, fought for the king with diverse fortunes. The war with Portugal was not over but it would be the task of the regency of Maria Anna of Austria to bring an end to this useless war and to face and resist the growing power of the France of Louis XIV.

During most of Philip IV's reign Spain had maintained his rank, but the resurgence of the French kingdom and the crisis of Castile had reduced the efficiency of the monarchy. Still, the Spanish could have concluded a more favourable peace with France particularly in 1656, but at the end the Spanish government had too many enemies, fought for too many years and managed to exhaust all the resources of the multinational Spanish monarchy.

---

377 15,000 infantry, 6,500–7,000 cavalry, 14 guns and two mortars (de Menezes volume IV, 1759).
378 de Menezes, volume IV, 1759.
379 Probably 11,000 to 12,000 infantry and 6,000 cavalry. Some 2,000–2,300 infantry and cavalry were in Vila Viçosa with 1,000 sick soldiers, and 650 men (mostly cavalry) were in Borda.
380 Losses are estimated at 10,000 Spanish and 2,700 Portuguese from the battle and siege (de Menezes, volume IV, 1759).

2

The Structure of the Spanish Army

2.1 General Considerations

The structure of the Spanish army was established during the reign of Isabella the Catholic and Ferdinand of Aragon, namely the Catholic monarchs in Spanish history. At the end of the fifteenth century and beginning of the sixteenth, the Spanish authorities, unified in a single kingdom, recognised that with the end of the *reconquista*[1] episode the main war effort should focus in the wars outside the Iberian Peninsula and particularly against the Kingdom of France.[2] For that, a specific military structure was designed with an internal army based on a cavalry corps called the *Guardias de Castilla* and an external army based on specific infantry units. With the rise of the Spanish Empire of Charles V, the permanent Spanish units were renamed tercios of Spanish Infantry. The structure was mostly unaltered during the reign of Philip II and Philip III. And at the beginning of the reign of Philip IV the military structure of the Spanish monarchy was principally based on:

    a. An administration made of officials and officers in charge of payment and intendancy in the different territories of the Spanish empire connected with the government in Madrid.
    b. An internal army located in the Iberian Peninsula and the *presidios* of North Africa based on: mobile troops from the *Guardias de Castilla*;[3] a series of fortresses covering the northern border of the Iberian Peninsula, along the Pyrenean Mountains, located for example in Salses (Catalonia), Perpignan (Catalonia), Jaca (Aragon), Pamplona (Navarre) and Fuenterrabia

---

1 Officially, the *reconsquista* was a period from 722 to 1492 when the Christian kingdoms from the Iberian Peninsula fought to expel their Muslim counterparts.
2 R. Quatrefages, 1996, *La revolución militar moderna: el crisol español* (Madrid: Ministerio de Defensa, 1996).
3 The *Guardias de Castilla* was a cavalry force of 1,680 men distributed in 24 companies (Clonard chapter 4, 1851).

(Guipúzcoa); a series of fortresses protecting the main harbours and shipyards in the peninsula, Barcelona (Catalonia), La Palma de Mallorca (Mallorca), Valencia (Valencia), Alicante (Valencia), Cartagena (Murcia), Malaga (Granada), Cadiz (Andalucia), Sevilla (Andalucia), Lisbon (Portugal), Orio (Vizcaya), Bilbao (Vizcaya) and Santander (Guipúzcoa); at last, a series of Fortresses or *presidios* located along the North African coast and Morocco, in order to protect the south of Spain and Portugal from the Moors as well as the trading route to Asia.

c. An external army located in the other territories of the empire consisting of troops of professional native soldiers framed in the Spanish Tercios, supported by others professional soldiers from all the parts of the Empire (Italy, Low Countries, Burgundy) and mercenaries. In 1621, those units were mainly based in Italy, in the Low Countries and in the Palatinate (Germany). The external army was also deployed in the numerous fortresses and castles belonging to each territory, such as those of Milan, Naples in Italy; Anvers, Ghent, Courtray and Brussels in the Low Countries; or Dôle in Franche-Comté. Finally each territory had a body of militia according to its internal law, customs and rules.

As we can see the Iberian Peninsula was partially demilitarised with only a small number of infantry companies and the cavalry companies of the *Guardias de Castilla*. The defence of the realm was subdivided into nine General Captaincies or *Capitanias General* in Spanish (*Canarias, Castilla la Nueva, Castilla la Vieja, Galicia, Extremadura, Jaen, Costa de Granada, Costa de Andalucia* and *Guipúzcoa)*, four other territories called *Principato de Asturia, Reino de Sevilla, Reino de Navarra and Reino de Murcia,* the four territories of the Crown of Aragon *(*vice-royalties of *Aragon, Baleares* or *Mallorca* and *Valenci*a and the principality of *Catalonia)* and the Kingdom of Portugal.

In all of these territories we will find a representative of the king, called captain general, governor, or *viceroy*, depending on the nature of the territory. Table 2.1 presents most of the high officers in each territories and armies, representing the three branches, infantry, cavalry and artillery. Normally the governor or *viceroy* was also captain general. With some small modifications, the territories outside the Iberian Peninsula had a similar structure. The governor of a territory was supported by an administration of military affairs supervised by two main officers, the *veedor general* (general inspector) and *Superintendente de la Justicia Militar* (superintendent of military justice), entitled to report directly to the monarch (Andujar Castillo, 1999). Such administrative structure exists in all territories of the monarchy and in the field armies, but although independent they tended to depend on the goodwill of the captain general of the territory (Gonzáles de León, 2009). In this administrative structure we will have normally, the *veedors* (inspectors), *contadores* (controllers), *pagadores* (paymasters), *tenedores de*

THE STRUCTURE OF THE SPANISH ARMY

Table 2.1: General structure of Spanish armies' high command. Adapted from Parker (1990), Maffi (2007), and Gonzáles de León (2009).

Spanish (English)	Task
Capitán General (captain general)	High-ranking officer in command of all the military structures in the territory. As governor of the province he needed to have strong diplomatic and political experience and ability.
Gobernador de las Armas* (governor of the arms)	Where created and occupied the rank took some of the tasks of the *Maestro de Campo General*. Therefore the authority of the *Maestro de Campo Genera* tended to decrease.
Maestro de Campo General[†] (infantry general)	The captain general's right hand. He could take command of the army in the absence of the captain general. He needed to have a strong expertised in military affair. He was responsible for the organisation and training of the infantry.
Capitán General de la Caballería[‡] (captain general of the cavalry)	Highest rank for the cavalry branch, his duty was to organise and train the troopers.
Capitán General de la Artillería[§] (captain general of the artillery)	For this rank, in a world were sieges were the most important operations, highly technical and mathematical skills were required. This officer had also to keep a record of the artillery's guns available in fortresses and for field duty, and to prepare the artillery train.
Gobernador de Plaza Fuerte (governor of fortresses)	The *Gobernador de Plaza Fuerte* was responsible for the defence of their fortress and acted independently from field officers. He was ranked according to the importance of the fortress he had to guard.

[*] The rank of governor of arms was created in 1630 in the army of Flanders and extended to the army of Lombardy (Maffi 2007).

[†] The *Maestro de Campo General* was assisted by the *Teniente General de Maestro de Campo* (lieutenant general of the *maestro de campo*) and had a staff with a dozen or more men, a general quartermaster, normally four engineers and eight to 12 *entretenidos* serving as couriers or secretaries.

[‡] Like the *Maestro de Campo General*, the *Capitán General de la Caballería* relied on a staff with one *Teniente Capitán General de la Caballería*, *entretenidos*, and secretaries.

[§] The *Capitán General de la Artillería* relied on an important staff of engineers and *Tenientes General de Artillería*. See the paragraph on artillery.

bastimento[4] and *proveedores* (suppliers), they are important elements of the Spanish military system. All these local commands were under the order of a national administration, located in Madrid, the State Council (*Consejo de Estado*), the Supreme Council of War (*Consejo Supremo de la Guerra*), the General Treasury of Spain (*Veeduria y Contaduria General de España*).

The last branch of Philip IV's military was the navy, divided into different "armadas" or fleets to protect trading and the movement of troops in the

---

4   *Tenedores de bastimento*: officer in charge of maintaining and storing supplies before distribution.

Atlantic Ocean and in the western Mediterranean Sea. Since the sixteenth century, the Mediterranean area, the *Armada de las Galeras* (galley fleet) was one of the most organised and important for the Spanish crown with up to 146 galleys in 1574.[5] In reality the Armada was divided in different *escuadras* or squadrons, the *Escuadra de las Galeras de España*, *Escuadra de las Galeras de Napoles*, *Escuadra de las Galeras de Sicilia* and *Escuadra de las Galeras de Cerdeña*. Allied Italian states such as the Galleys of Genova or individual nobles would also provide ships for the Spanish fleet. With the translation of the main fighting area in the Atlantic and the heavy cost to maintain large numbers of galleys,[6] the *Armada de las Galeras* lost its importance in 1634; the total number of ships was 42 and only 26–27[7] in 1649.

The other part of the navy was made of round ships (mainly galleons,[8] frigates[9] and patches) able to sail in the Atlantic Ocean, the English Channel and the North Sea. With the naval ordinance of 1633, the organisation, structure and goals of the Atlantic fleets were reorganised. The most important fleet was the *Armada de la Guarda de la Carreras de las Indias*, with the task of escorting the merchant ship convoys from America to Spain and vice versa. The armada normally had eight galleons and three patches in 1620; the main Armada was the *Armada del Mar Oceano*[10] with the task of covering the Atlantic coast. It was the main fighting force of the Spanish Monarchy with a fleet of 40 galleons in 1623,[11] but in 1638–1639 the fleet lost up to 59 major ships in the battle of Getaria (11 galleons destroyed) in 1638 and the Battle of the Downs (43 ships,

---

5 I. Thompson, *War and government in the Habsburg Spain, 1560–1620* (London: University of London, 1976).
6 In the seventeenth century we find three types of galleys, the capitana, the patrona and the ordinary galleys. The first two had a command function and had more men. Typically a capitana and patrona had respectively 62 and 46 seamen (*Gente de mar*), 360 to 250 rowers (*Gente de remo*) and 144 to 106 soldiers (*Gente de guerra*). An ordinary galley had 40 seamen, 160 to 200 rowers and 83 soldiers (J.M. Marchena Giménez, *La vida y los hombres de las galeras de España: (siglos XVI–XVII)*. Thesis from the Universidad Computense de Madrid, 2011).
7 Probably 9–10 galleys for the Spanish Squadron, 10–11 galleys for the Neapolitan Squadron and two to three galleys for Cerdeña's Squadron.
8 In Spanish service in the seventeenth century, a galleon was a full warship of 350 to 870 Spanish tons (later on 1,100 tons). By the Ordinance of 1633 it was expected to have for the biggest galleons, a flagship (*Capitana*) and second in command (*Admirante*), 18 seamen and 28 soldiers for each 100 tons and for an ordinary galleon 16 seamen and 26 soldiers for each 100 tons. So an ordinary galleon of 1639 like the *San Francisco* of 490 tons, from the Armada of Flandes, should have a crew of 78 seamen (including 14 officers) and up to 127 soldiers and 34 guns (C. Hormaecha, I. Rivera and M. Derqui, *Los Galeones Españoles del siglo XVII* (Barcelona: Museum Maritim de Barcelona, 2012).
9 The frigate of the seventeenth century was an original ship design of the Low Countries. Frigates were ships of 130 to 300 tons in 1639, 300 tons later on, with 18 to 24 guns. For example, in 1639, the frigate Santa Clara from the Armada of Flandes was ship of 140 tons with 18 guns (E.G. Torralba-Perez, 2011, *Las Fragatas de Vela de la Armada española 1600 1850, Su evolución técnica*).
10 From 1633, the Armada was divided in three escuadras or squadrons, the first called *Escuadra de la Guarda del Estrecho*, covering the strait of Gibraltar and Andalucia, the second, *Escuadra de Lusitania* covering Portugal and Galicia, the third *Escuadra de las Cuatro Villas* covering Cantabria and the Basque Country.
11 In 1623 the Armada had 40 ships divided into 15 galleons for the first squadron, 13 for the second and 12 for the third (J.H. Parry, *Spanish Seaborne Empire* (Berkeley: University of California Press, 1990).

most of them galleons) in 1639. The main fleet was crippled by such losses of good ships, naval officers and sailors. Other priorities meant that funding was scarce and it was impossible to rebuild enough ships to compete against the Dutch.[12] Nonetheless the ships of the *Armada del Mar Oceano* continued to fight the French navy with some successes.[13] The *Armada del Mar Oceano* was supported by the *Armada de Flandes*,[14] fighting in the Channel and the North Sea. The *Armada de Barlovento* and the *Armada del Sur* were located respectively in the Caribbean and on the Pacific Peruvian coast. Finally there was a fleet protecting the Spanish territories of the Philippines.[15]

2.2 The Armies of the King

2.2.1 Introduction

King Philip IV ruled a vast territory of 20 million km^2, but the heart of his empire and the source of his power depended on his professional forces deployed in Europe. The 1621–1665 period was a fight for supremacy in Europe against not only the French monarchy, the colossus[16] of Western Europe, but also against other states, such as the United Provinces or the Duchy of Savoy, rebellious institutions in Catalonia and Portugal and also the North African states and Moorish tribes. The majority of the troops of the monarchy were deployed in the numerous garrisons all over the empire but the core of the Spanish offensive forces from 1621 to 1640, was structured in the Army of Flanders and the Army of Lombardy. With the uprising in Catalonia and Portugal, the Army of Catalonia-Aragon became an important force fighting against the French while the Army of Extremadura was fighting against the Portuguese. In Appendix II, musters over the 44 years of the reign of Philip IV have been compiled for the four main Spanish armies. At the beginning of his reign Philip IV's infantry consisted of 39 units divided into four Spanish tercios in the army of Flanders,[17] two Spanish

---

12 After 1648 and the signature of the Peace of Westphalia, it was the Dutch navy which supported the Spanish one.
13 In 1650 the Armada numbered 29 ships (17 directly from the *Armada del Mar Oceano*, six from the *Armada de Flandes* and six from the Armada of Ragusa, Italy), to support the siege of Tortosa (Duero, *Armada de España*, volume 4, 1898).
14 From 1621 to 1664, the armada of Flanders had six to 30 ships. In R.A. Stradling, *The Armada of Flanders: Spanish Maritime Policy and European War, 1568–1668*, Cambridge Studies in Early Modern History (Cambridge: Cambridge University Press, 1992).
15 In 1616 in the naval battle of Honda de la Playa a Spanish squadron of seven vessels and three galleys, commanded by Juan Ronquillo, defeated the Dutch squadron, commanded by Joris van Spilberge (Fernandez Duro, volume III, 1895).
16 In the seventeenth century, French population oscillated from 18 to 20 million inhabitants (Benoît Garnot, *La population française: aux XVIe, XVIIe et XVIIIe siècles* (Paris: Ophrys, 2005)).
17 *Tercio Viejo de Flanders* (MdC Simao Antunes), *Tercio Viejo de Holland* (MdC Iñigo de Borja y Velasco), *Tercio Viejo de Brabant* (MdC Marquis of Leganez) and *Tercio de Cordoba* (MdC Gonzalo Fernández de Cordoba).

tercios in the army of Lombardy,[18] two Spanish tercios in southern Italy,[19] and three tercios in the Iberian Peninsula.[20] He had also a minimum of 13 Italian tercios, 11 Walloon tercios, and two Burgundian tercios as well as an Irish tercio (Tercio of the Count of Tyrone), a Scottish one (Tercio of Count of Argyl) and probably nine German regiments (Clonard volume 4, 1851). To those numbers we must add the cavalry, companies from the Cavalry of the State of Flanders, the Cavalry of the State of Milan, the Cavalry of Naples, and the *Guardias de Castilla*, as well as guards companies for the governors of the different territories.

As reflected in Appendix II, the Army of Flanders had 37,200 infantry and 7,000 cavalry in 1620, while the Army of Lombardy had 16,560 infantry and 1,890 cavalry. In the Spanish Peninsula, the forces were integrated in the tercios of Armada, the garrison of Portugal (around 2,000 men), garrisons around the peninsula and for the cavalry the *Guardias de Castilla* (25 companies) and the *Guardias de las Costa* (four companies). For 1634 and 1639, Rodríguez Hernández (2017) gives respective garrisons in the Iberian Peninsula[21] of 6,320 and 4,460 men, far away from the theoretical number of 12,800 men. In total, we have some 8,000 to 15,000 men,[22] including some 1,500 cavalry and troops from the armada. To the troops stationed in the peninsula we must add the ones in the fortress (*presidios*) of North Africa. For example, in Oran and Mers el Kébir, the garrison was 1,200 to 1,400 men in the first half of the seventeenth century reduced to 1,000–1,100 men from 1634 to 1640 (Rodríguez Hernández, 2017). In total garrison for all *presidios* was between 2,500 to 3,500 men[23] and in the case of emergency, as when the Turks and Moors attacked Oran in 1643 or in 1655, reinforcements were sent from Seville and Malaga.

In southern Italy, in the Kingdom of Naples and the Kingdom of Sicily, the Spanish had two tercios of Spanish infantry. The *Tercio Viejo de Naples*[24] was the backbone of the defence of Naples supported by the garrisons in the 29 castles and fortresses of the kingdom, the companies in the galleys of the Armada of Naples.[25] The cavalry of the State of Naples consisted of 16 companies of men-at-arms (up to 1,000 cavalry), a contingent of six companies of light cavalry of ordinance increased to 20 in the 1640s, and four companies of Albanese horsemen (called *Startiodes*). In total for Naples, in normal circumstances, we might have at best a permanent force of 8,000 men (Ribot Garcia 1993, and Maffi 2015). In Sicily the defence of the island was the task of the *Tercio Viejo de Sicilia* and the number of troops was

---

18 *Tercio Ordinario de Lombardia* (Luis Fernández de Cordoba), and *Tercio de Saboya* (MdC Juan Cárdnas y Manrique Lara)
19 *Tercio Viejo de Naples* (MdC Pedro Sarmiento de Pastrana) and *Tercio Viejo de Sicilia* (MdC Manuel Ponce de León).
20 *Tercio of Lisboa o Portugal* (MdC Juan Chacón de Avila) consisting of Spanish in Portugal, *Tercio de la Armada del Mar Oceano* (Mdc Juan Osorio) probably in Andalucia and on board the ships, and a tercio of Portuguese, the *Tercio de la Armada de Portugal* (MdC Francisco de Almeida).
21 Garrisons for fortresses in Portugal, Galicia, Cadiz, the Basque Country, Navarre, Aragon, Catalonia and the Balearic Islands.
22 Maffi (2014), gives a total of 12,390 men in 1613 and 14,600 men in 1622.
23 In the 1630s, the theoretical number was close to 4,390 men (Rodríguez Hernández, 2017).
24 In 1654 the tercio had only 24 companies and around 2,700 men (Maffi 2014).
25 In 1637 the number of galleys in the Armada of Naples was only 12 (Ribot Garcia, 1993).

probably in the best case 4,000 to 5,000 for Sicily for most of the reign of Philip IV. Taking into account the two numbers, Naples and Sicily should have had a permanent garrison of 9,000 to 12,000 men.

That was not the only force available for the Spanish king: the Franche-Comté was also a territory of the Circle of Burgundy. The territory was lightly guarded with some garrison troops in the castle of Dôle. In 1635 with the war with France, the Spanish could not send easily reinforcements. Most of the time, the defence of the territory relied on some Spanish and Burgundian regular units,[26] regiments of mercenaries (Swiss or Germans) and the militia (some 5,000 men). In 1637, the defence had 5,950 men deployed in 1,150 men from regular units, 2,600 men from the Army of Lorraine and 2,200 Imperials.

So in 1621, if we add the different garrisons we arrive at 14,500 in the Spanish Peninsula, 11,000 men in southern Italy, 4,000 in North Africa and 500 between Sardinia and Franche-Comté, in total some 30,000 men. If we include the estimate established for the Army of Flanders and the Army of Lombardy, the total number could be close to 93,000 men. With the situation in Flanders and Italy (crisis of Mantua 1628–1631) the total number of troops of the Monarchy increased to up to 120,000 men in 1633. All through the following decades, the European situation and the arrival to power of a new ambitious minister in France,[27] meant that the Spanish authorities had to dedicate more and more money and other resources to face all the threats. In 1635, the official declaration of war by the French meant that the struggle for supremacy had entered a crucial point.[28] In 1637 the Spanish had up to 120,000 men in the Low Countries and northern Italy, 14,600 men in Catalonia and probably 10,000 to 15,000 men in the rest of the Peninsula. If we take into account a minimum of 11,000 men between Naples, Sicily and Sardinia, 3,000 in North Africa and 1,500 in Franche-Comté we arrive at a sum close to 160,000 men. The Climax for the Spanish forces arrived between 1640 and 1644, when the revolts in Catalonia and Portugal required the levying of thousands more men, particularly in the Iberian Peninsula. In 1640, just before the tempest, the number of troops was close to 180,000 men (88,300 in the Low Countries, 36,600 in Lombardy, 37,000 in the Iberian Peninsula and 17,000 in the other territories). In 1645, the forces involved in the four main armies was 140,000 men (83,500 in the Low Countries, 21,500 in Lombardy, 24,000 in Catalonia and 15,000 in Extremadura), not including the men in the Armada, garrisons in the rest of Spain, North Africa and southern Italy (maybe 20,000–25,000 men). In 1647, the same armies had 65,500 men in the Low Countries, close to 20,000 men in Lombardy, 24,600 in Catalonia and probably 9,000 in Extremadura, making up 120,000 men. In 1651/1652, we might find 80,000–85,000 men in the Low Countries and northern Italy, 20,000 men in Catalonia and 8,000–

---

26 From 1,000 to 2,000 men in the year 1636–1646 (G. Louis, *La guerre de dix ans: 1634–1644*, Besançon: PU de Franche-Comté, Dôle, 1998).

27 Armand Jean du Plessis de Richelieu, called the Cardinal de Richelieu, was also Duke of Fronsac. He was born 9 September 1585 and died 4 December 1642. He was a state man, and the main minister of King Louis XIII. The main goal of his foreign policy was to reduce the hegemony of the Hapsburg faction in Madrid or Vienna and to restore the "grandeur" of the kingdom of France.

28 Borroguero Beltrán (2006) gives 79,000 men in Germany, Italia and Catalonia and 70,000 for the Army of Flanders, so a maximum of 150,000 men for 1635.

9,000 in the Army of Extremadura, giving a total of 108,000 to 113,000 men for the four armies. If we take into account a minimum of 10,000 men in the rest of Spain, 12,000 men between Naples, Sicily and Sardinia and 3,000 in North Africa, the total might reach 132,000 to 137,000 men. In 1659, with the war with France at its end, 65,000 to 70,000 men were still fighting in the Low Countries, 20,000 in North Italy, 8,000 in Catalonia and 17,000 in the Army of Extremadura still totalling up to 110,000 men. To finish the long list, in 1665 most of the troops were fighting against Portugal. If we take into account the information available, 40,000 to 50,000 men were along the Portuguese border, no more than 25,000 men in the Low countries and Lombardy, maybe 15,000 men in the rest of Spain and North Africa and 11,000 men in the south of Italy, in total between 90,000 and 100,000 men.

2.2.2 The Army of Flanders

Since the end of the seventeenth century, the Army of Flanders was the best organised and trained, and most powerful fighting force of the Spanish Monarchy. The main goal of the troops deployed in the Low Countries was to maintain the sovereignty of the Spanish king and to deal with the rebellion of the seven provinces[29] of the Low Countries forming the Republic of the Seven United Provinces, formed by the Union of Utrecht in 1588.

In 1621, the United Provinces was an organised state able to pay and maintain an army of 51 260 men (3,970 cavalry and 47,290 infantry). From this date to the end of the war in 1648, the size of the Dutch army reached a peak at 60,030 men (6,950 cavalry and 53,080 infantry) in 1643, decreasing to 35,430 men in 1648 (4,240 cavalry and 31,190 infantry).[30] In reality the main superiority of the Dutch was a strong navy, a lot of good and modern fortresses, money to pay their army complement by subsidies from the French kingdom and the fact that they always fought near or not to far away from their logistics centres.

The other goal of the Army of Flanders was to defend the corridor of the Rhine valley, the so-called Spanish corridor *o Camino español* but above all, concerning the war with France, to have always a mobile force to threaten the heart of the French monarchy.[31] We have to be aware that the distance between Cambrai and Paris is less than 200 km and between Brussels and Paris 300 km. For the Count-Duke of Olivares, the Army of Flanders was the instrument to maintain the hegemony of the Hapsburgs in Europe.

---

29 The seven provinces were the Duchy of Guelders, the County of Holland, the County of Zeeland, the Lordship of Groningen, the Lordship of Utrecht, the Lordship of Frisia and the Lordship of OverIjssel.

30 H.L. Zwitzer, "'De militie van den staat': Studies over het leger van de Republiek der Vereinigde Nederlanden", Ph.D. thesis, University of Utrecht, 1990.

31 The frontier with France was defended already by the end of the sixteenth century by a series of 23 fortresses and cities with permanent garrisons and professional soldiers: the County of Artois, Renty, Hesdin, Avesnes, Arras, Bapaume, Saint-Omer, Béthune and Arien; Lordship of Cambray, Cambray, Bourbon and Câteau-Cambresis; County of Hainaut Landrecies, Marieburg, Tournay and Le Quesnoy; city of Namur; Duchy of Luxembourg, Malandry, Chavancy, La Frette, Monmedy, Danvillers, Luxembourg and Thionville (H. O'Donnell, 1983, *La Seguridad de los paises bajos, requisitos para la empresa de inglettera de 1588, revista de Historia Naval*, Num. 2, pp. 107–116).

THE STRUCTURE OF THE SPANISH ARMY

2.1 Lancers from Spinola's bodyguard at the siege of Jülich in 1622. Mattheus Melijn, 1636. (Rijksmuseum)

The Army of Flanders was commanded by the governor of the Low Countries and captain general,[32] supported by a *Gobernador de las Armas* and various *Maestro de Campo Generales*.[33] The following officers were the general captain of the cavalry[34] and general captain of the artillery. The increase in the number of tercios and regiments in the Army of Flanders and the correlating numbers of *maestros de campo* and colonels made the implementation of discipline more difficult than before. In 1622, the Army of Flanders had 18 tercios and regiments representing 338 infantry companies, in 1643, the total of tercios and regiments was 39, representing 489 infantry companies and in 1659 we have up to 1,104 infantry companies (Gonzáles de León, 2009). For the cavalry the number of companies was 56 in 1622 and 219 in 1659. The solution was to adopt, from the Imperial army, the rank

---

[32] Archduchess Isabel of Austria (1621–1633), Francisco de Moncada, Marquis of Aytona (1633–1634), Cardinal Infante Fernando of Austria (1634–1641), Francisco de Melo, Marquis of Villanueva (1641–1644), Manuel de Moura, Marquis of Castel Rodrigo (1644–1647), Archduke Leopold Wilhelm of Austria (1647–1656), John of Austria (1656–1660), Luis Francisco de Benavides Carrillo (1660–1664) and Francisco de Moura Corterreal, Marquis of Castel Rodrigo (1664–1668).
[33] In 1634 13 *Maestro de Campo Generale*s were appointed in the Army of Flanders, themselves aided by 10 *Tenientes de Maestro de Campo Generales* (Gonzáles de León, 2009).
[34] In the Army of Flanders, the old company of ordinance created by the Duke of Burgundy still existed with 600 to 1,000 men, commanded by a general of the heavy cavalry, although itsequipment was closer to that of cuirassiers (Gonzáles de León, 2009).

of *Sargento General de Batalla* or sergeant general. The officer was directly subordinated to the *Maestro de Campo General* and he was responsible for organising and coordinating tercios and regiments in an army corps. By late 1650 we could find a dozen *Sargento General de Batalla*. The rank of *Sargento General de Batalla de Caballería* was also created in 1648 in the Army of Flanders to coordinate the cavalry regiments and tercios. The forces fighting in the Low Countries were financed by the general military budget of the Spanish Monarchy assigned to Flanders but also by the administration of the Low Countries via the "finance" budget. In 1626 (Esteban Estringana 2004), the budget could pay 1,700 cavalry and 12,000 infantry.

The Army of Flanders was a multinational force but the Spanish tercios and soldiers of the Spanish "nation" were its heart. Since the middle of the sixteenth century, the Spanish "nation" had some prerogatives reinforced by the policy of Philip IV with appointments in the high command of the army. Such prerogatives would have consequences in the efficiency of the army deployed in Flanders, because other nations, particularly the Walloons and the Italians, would challenge such advantages.[35]

After some dissertation on the military structure, let us have a look at the fighting power (Appendix III) of the army deployed in the Low Countries. From 1621 to 1635, the main fighting force of the Army of Flanders was the infantry with an average of 60,000 men most of the time, while the cavalry was only 6,800 to 7,400 strong,[36] giving a ratio infantrymen / horsemen of 8.4. The prominence of the infantry could be explained by the fact that for the war in the Netherlands – a country full of rivers, canals, marches, polders and fortified cities – infantry and artillery were more important than the mobile cavalry and the Spanish infantry was probably one of the best in the area. The Spanish, but also the Italians, were seen as crack troops able to undertake whatever operations were necessary. Before 1639, the Spanish "nation" represented 7 to 9 percent of the total infantry (Table 2.2) organised in three to five tercios. For example in 1633, the three Spanish tercios had 3,760 in 51 companies, representing 8.4 percent of the total infantry (Saavedra, 1986).

The most numerous nationality was the Walloons, the inhabitants of the Low Countries loyal to Spain, with 40–50 percent of the infantry organised in tercios or in companies to garrison the numerous fortresses and cities of the region. They were followed by the German regiments, representing 30–40 percent of the infantry, then the Italians, four to seven percent, the Irish, two to nine percent and the Burgundians, one to three percent.

With the war with France in 1635, the Spanish needed to boost the Army of Flanders, especially with an increase of mounted arms. The fighting on the southern border was more suitable for cavalry and the Spanish had to quickly improve their cavalry. From 7,000 horsemen in 1637 (a ratio of 11.1 between infantry and cavalry), the cavalry rose to up to 21,000 men in 1657, representing 30 percent of the total of the Army of Flanders (ratio of 2.4 between infantry and cavalry). In the period 1623 to 1634, five

---

35 For more details of the relations between nations in the high command, we recommend the book written by Gonzáles de León (2009).
36 As we have seen before, the army of the United Provinces had only 5,000 to 7,000 horsemen.

Table 2.2: Distribution of the nationalities in the Army of Flanders.
Data from Parker (1991), and Maffi (2014).

Infantry	Spanish	Italians	Burgundians	Walloons	Germans	British*
1623	3,740	3,910	700	21,640	21,040	3,810
1633	5,690	3,790	2,010	33,270	21,060	1,780
1640	17,260	3,870	1,070	37,110	14,930	2,690
1643	10,440	3,350	940	31,440	16,070	1,190
1647	9,680	2,410	670	24,130	14,310	2,520
1661	5,480	1,180	450	8,180	7,470	2,320

* In fact most of them were Irish.

itineraries tercios were sent from Italy to reinforce the troops in Flanders and disbanded immediately. From 1635 to 1639, the Spanish received strong reinforcements,[37] mainly by sea, but with the wars in Catalonia and Portugal and the defeat at the Battle of the Downs in 1639, Spanish reinforcements became scarce and the total Spanish infantry started to decline. In 1640 we had a peak of 17,260 Spanish, representing 22.4 percent of the total infantry in seven tercios and free companies. From this date numbers decreased due to losses in battle, illness and desertions. In 1647, the total of Spanish infantry was just above 10,000 men, 18.4 percent of the total in six tercios and free companies. The decline continued, and at the end of the war in 1659, the six tercios had only 3,760 men. The end of the war would help to stabilise the situation but it was only with the next monarch, Charles II of Austria, that the Spanish would again send, in 1668, strong reinforcements from the Iberian Peninsula to the Army of Flanders. For the period 1640 to 1660, all reinforcements[38] arrived by sea.

The Army of Flanders was a powerful war machine, but due to the specificity of the war in the Low Countries, numerous fortresses, castles and cities needed a strong garrison[39] and even in 1622, Ambrogio Spinola the main *Maestro de Campo General* of the army had only a field army of 20,000 men, the rest were in garrison with the small army of Gonzalo de Córdoba in Germany.[40] In 1629, and during the siege of 's-Hertogenbosch the Spanish could field only an army of 24,000 men, not enough to attack the 28,500

---

37 An estimate of nine tercios sent by sea during the period especially in 1639, but it seems that five of them were disbanded rapidly.
38 For example from 1648 to 1653, 2,500 men were raised in Galicia and sent in four boat trips to Flanders (A.J. Rodríguez Hernández, "De Galicia a Flandes: reclutamiento y servicio de soldados gallegos en el ejército de Flandes (1648–1700)", *Obradoiro de historia Moderna*, N.º 16, 2007, pp. 213–251.
39 In 1623 more than 50 fortresses, castles, and citadels had a permanent garrison in the Low Countries (Esteban Estringana, 2004). In 1639 209 separate garrisons from thousands of men were maintained, from important citadels to outposts of 10 men on a dyke. In total such garrisons required a total of 33,400 men (Parker 1991).
40 Gonzalo de Cordoba had a force of up to 14,000 men, but 6,000 men had to be left in garrison in the Low Palatinate to cover the Spanish Road. At the battle of Wimpfen on 6 May 1622, his force was estimated at 6,000 men and 2,000 cavalry and at Fleurus on 29 August 1622, the Spanish had 8,000 men.

men of Frederick Hendricks. In 1635 with the war with France, the Army of Flanders had to field two main armies, one against the French, commanded by Thomas of Savoy (7,000 men) and the most important against the Dutch, commanded by the Cardinal Infante (28,000 men). For the same campaign[41] the Dutch could field 26,000 men and the French 33,000 men. In 1644, the field army against the French had 21,790 men and the one facing the Dutch 13,590 men, the rest, close to 40,000 men (53 percent) had garrison duty or did not exist. Facing them the French could deploy the same year 30,000 men and the Dutch 16,000 men. In 1647, following Maffi (2014), the Spanish field army had 33,580 men (51.8 percent) and in 1656 we still have 34,770 men. Definitely an important fighting force but most of the time, especially after 1635, the Spanish did not enjoy numerical superiority on the field.

2.2.3 The Army of Lombardy

At the beginning of the sixteenth century, the control of the State of Milan or Duchy of Milan had been the main objective of the Swiss and French monarchy, indicating the importance of controlling northern Italy. The control of such territory by the Spanish had been a long and difficult struggle with victories and defeats. In 1559, with the peace treaty of Cateau-Cambresis, the supremacy of the Spanish monarchy over the State of Milan was recognised by the French, and Milan became an important dominion for the Hapsburgs for their communication with the Low Countries and Vienna. It was also an important place from which to control the numerous Italian states, such as the Duchy of Savoy, the Republic of Genoa, the Duchy of Mantua, the Duchy of Parma, the Duchy of Modena and the Republic of Venice. The main instrument to achieve such control was the Army of Lombardy. As we said before, Milan was also the connection with the Low Countries and the departure of the numerous contingents sent to the north by the Spanish Road. Therefore, the garrison in peacetime[42] was always above 6,000 men (Maffi, 2007).

The state of Milan was governed by a governor and a captain general of the state,[43] followed by the *Gobernador de las Armas* but in the Army of Lombardy the position was only occupied from 1638 to 1642,[44] the rest of the time it remained vacant. Following the hierarchy we had the *Maestro de Campo General* of the state of Milan, a post active only in time of war in Lombardy. In the State of Milan, it followed the captain general of the cavalry of the state of Milan and after 1635, also, the captain general of the Neapolitan cavalry serving in Milan. In Milan the cavalry had also a *Teniente General* of the cavalry of Milan and the other officers were the captain general of the artillery and the *Comissario del exercito*. The next officers were the governor of the fortresses, the *Maestros de Campo* of the tercios, colonels of the regiments

---

41 Luna y Mora, *Relación de la campaña de 1635*, CODOIN vol. 75, 1880.
42 In 1560 the official garrison was set up at a Spanish tercio of 3,000 men, a fixed garrison (*presidios ordinarios*) of the numerous castles with 2,000 men a contingent of cavalry, men-at-arms and light cavalry with 1,000 horsemen.
43 In the high command, the prerogative of the Spanish "nation" was less problematic in Milan than in Flanders, because most of the positions were better distributed between Spanish and Italians.
44 By Francisco de Melo from 1638 to 1640 and by the Cardinal Teodoro Trivulzio from 1640 to 1642 (Maffi 2007).

and various *Comissarios de la caballeria* to lead the cavalry of the state. The state of Milan had up to 21[45] fortresses and castles implemented in the main cities of the state but also to defend key positions with an ordinary garrison called in Spanish *presidios ordinarios*. In 1621, the Army of Lombardy had up to 20,000 men due to the crisis of the Valtellina valley and the organisation of reinforcements for the Low Countries. Therefore, Lombardy was full of soldiers divided into 82.2 percent for the infantry, 8.4 percent for the *presidios ordinarios* and 9.4 percent for the cavalry. From 1621 to 1633, the number of troops in the Army of Lombardy oscillated strongly from 9,000 men to 30,000 men due to the different crises in northern Italy, the succour of Genoa, the operations to control the Valtellina valley and the War of the Mantuan Succession. In 1633 and 1634, the armies of the Duke of Feria and of the Cardinal Infante were assembled in Milan before they departed to Germany and the Low Countries. In 1635, the war with France meant that Milan was an offensive base against the French and the Duchy of Savoy but also a target for invasion. The Army of Lombardy received strong reinforcements, and in 1639 the army reached up to 42,000 men serving, at least on paper. That was the peak of the Army of Lombardy; later on, the wars in the Iberian Peninsula changed the priority and Lombardy became a secondary front and the size of the army was reduced accordingly. Between 1641 and 1658, the average army size was close to 23,000 men with a minimum of 19,500 men in 1646 and a maximum of 26,800 in 1644. In 1661, the Army of Lombardy was reduced to only 7,000 men, close to the ideal number established a century before by Philip II. The ratio of infantry to cavalry (without the garrison of the *presidios ordinarios*) was 8.8 infantrymen for one cavalryman in 1621, reduced to 4.9 in 1636 and 2.7 for the period 1642–1658. The increase of the cavalry observed in the Army of Flanders happened also in northern Italy. The number of men available for a campaign was lower than the number suggested in Table 2.3. In August 1636, the Marquis of Leganés could put on the field two armies with respectively 16,000 men and 4,800 men and still have 14,800 men in garrison (Maffi 2007). In 1641, the army was down to 24,450 men and the field army had only 11,500 men. In July 1651, the field army had 12,600 men and up to 8,500 men were in garrison. The numbers of Spanish soldiers (Table 2.3) suffered also strong fluctuation with a maximum in 1640 with 12,280 Spanish (41 percent of the total infantry) to only 2,380 in 1658 (18.5 percent of the total infantry), the average being 27 percent for the period. For the 1621 to 1661 period, the number of Spanish tercios also fluctuated with two in 1623 to a maximum of six in 1638. The *Tercio de Lombardia*, the *Tercio de Saboya* and from 1635 the *Tercio de la Mar de Naples*, were always present as permanent units. One of the characteristics of the Army of Lombardy was the number of soldiers coming from Swiss cantons, most of them from Catholic cantons or from the Grisons. In 1647

---

45 The garrisons of the *presidios ordinarios* were: the Castle of Milan, Alessandria, Como, Cremona, Domodossola, Finale Ligure, Fortress of Fuentes, Lecco, Lodi, Novarra, Pavia, Pizzighetone, Pontremoli, Serravalle, Sabbioneta, Tortona, Trezzo sull'Adda, Valenza di Po, Vigevano, Abbiategrasso and Arona (Maffi 2008).

Table 2.3: Distribution of the nationalities in infantry of the Army of Lombardy.
Data from Ribot Garcia 1990, and Maffi 2007.

Infantry	Spanish	Lombards	Nations*	Germans	Others†
1623	4,520	13,340	-	-	-
1638	8,500	5,060	5,770	6,850	4,860
1640	12,280	4,080	4,690	4,420	4,810
1647	3,590	2,340	1,800	1,000	2,940
1650	3,160	2,330	2,010	2,050	2,280
1656	3,560	4,630	2,960	2,500	2,660
1658	2,380	4,690	2,130	2,900	1,100

* Nations: Neapolitans, Walloons and Burgundians. In the Army of Lombardy, 60 to 94 percent of the national troops were coming from Naples.

† In 'others' we have most of the time Swiss and Grison troops with an Irish contingent of 400 and 330 men respectively in 1656 and 1658.

half of the infantry came from these two nations and most of the time they represented 15 percent of the infantry.

But the Army of Lombardy would have not been enough to maintain control of the state of Milan without the support of the elite of the province. The pragmatism and the flexibility of the Spanish monarch and his governors, particularly with the policy of rewards (*mercedes*) was attractive to the Lombard noblemen (Hanlon 2016). The maintain and the efficiency of the army could have been useless without the strong support of the notables and population of Lombardy. Even if it is not presented in our data, people and the nobility participated in the creation of professional units but also in the militia of the state,[46] and in their resilience to give shelter and supplies but also to suffer the consequences of a permanent state of war.[47]

2.2.4 The Army of Catalonia

In 1635, with the French declaration of war, Spain had to face their principal enemy in the northern border of the Iberian Peninsula along the Pyrenean chain. The possibility of conducting military operations were in the west in Navarre and Guipúzcoa or in the east using the County of Roussilon as a military base. The first idea to have an operational army was defined in 1635 when the viceroy[48] of Catalonia the Duke of Cardona was instructed to

---

46 The militia of the state of Milan could provide thousands of men (600 to 12,000) to defend the cities, but also castles and villages from foragers. They could also be used to patrol riverbanks and to delay and harass the enemy with low intensity warfare.

47 Low intensity warfare (patrol skirmishes; raiding against villages; payment of contribution and so on) took place on daily basis between two campaigns (Hanlon, 2016).

48 In the time of Philip IV the viceroys of Catalonia were: Joan Sentis, Bishop of Barcelona (1622–1626), Luis de Armendáriz, Bishop of Urgell (1626–1627), Miguel de los santos, Bishop of Solsona (1627–1629), Gómez Figueroa y Cordoba, Duke of Feria (1629–1630), Enric de Cardona y Cordoba (1630–1632 and 1634–1638), Cardinal Infante Fernando of Austria (1632–1633), Dalmau de Queralt y Codina, Count of Santa Colona (1638–1640), Pedro Fajardo de Zuñiga (1640–1641),

prepare a field army of 4,000 infantry and 1,200 cavalry. The opposition of Catalonia to hosting an offensive army implied that it was mostly impossible to have and maintain a regular army in the territory. In reality Catalonia had a military structure based only on the garrisoning of 13 fortresses and castles.[49] In 1609 the official number was 1,250 men and most of the troops were in Perpignan (665 men with a force of 53 horsemen) and Salse (118 men).[50] The defence of Catalonia was regulated by the *Princeps Namque*[51] principle and in theory the Spanish King could call upon it. But the *Princeps Namque* could not be used for an offensive against the French and when in 1637 the Duke of Cardona launched finally the offensive against Leucate, few Catalans could be found in his army of 13,200 men. In 1639, with the invasion and conquest of the Castle of Salses, thousands of Catalans served in the army of 25,000 men[52] to recover the castle from the French. In a sense, from 1635 to 1640 the Army of Catalonia was not structured and the province was not ready to maintain an army as in Lombardy or Flanders. In 1640, the burden to billet the royal army, the indiscipline of the royal troops, coupled with the antagonism with the Spanish Crown, led to an uprising in most of Catalonia with the support of the Church and some noblemen. The result was the destruction of the royal administration in Barcelona with the death of the viceroy the Count of Santa Colona. By October 1640, the Spanish army of Catalonia lost its structure and was split in different corps, one in the County of Rousillon[53] commanded by Juan de Garay, the main army in Tortosa commanded by Pedro Fajardo de Zúñiga, Marques of Le Velez and a small force to protect Aragon commanded by Nochera. The failure of Montjuich in 1641, the losses of the County of Rossellon in 1642 and the defeat of Lérida in 1642, meant that the Catalan front became a priority for the allocation of finance and human resources and that a reorganisation of the Spanish system had to be undertaken to be able to retake the initiative. From 1643 to 1652, the goal of the Spanish was to retake Barcelona and to do that the Spanish needed to maintain strong garrison in Tarragona and Tortosa supported by the Viceroyalty of Valencia, strong garrisons in Aragon[54] and

---

Federico Colona (1641–1642), Pere de Cardona y Còrdova (1642–1644), Andrea Cantelmo (1644–1645) Diego de Guzman, Marquis of Leganés (1645–1647), Guillermo de Montcada, Marquis of Aytona (1647–1648), Juan de Garay Otañez (1648–1650), Francisco de Orozco, Marquis of Mortara (1650–1652 and 1656–1663), Juan José de Austria (1653–1656), Francisco de Moura, Marquis of Castel Rodrigo (1663–1664) and Vincenzo Gonzaga (1664–1667).

49 Castle of Salses, Perpignan, Collioure, Rosas, Puigcerda, Puigvaledor, Drassanes (shipyard) of Barcelona, Bellgarde, Torre de San José, Castle of Opol, Bellgard, Talteüll (Carrió Arumí, 2008).
50 In 1639 the garrison of Salses was close to 600 men.
51 *Princeps namque* was one of the usages of the Cort of Barcelona that regulated the use of military forces by the Prince for the defence of the Principality of Catalonia. The *Princeps namque* was created in the eleventh century and was still in use in the seventeenth century. For more see "The National Defence Clause and the Emergence of the Catalan State: Princeps Namque" in D.J. Kagay and L.J. Andrew Villalon, *Crusaders, condottieri, and cannon: medieval warfare in societies around the Mediterranean* (Leiden: Brill, 2002), pp. 57–101.
52 Catalans tended to serve for two to three months, so to maintain the provincial Catalan tercios up to strength thousands of men, maybe 30,000, were sent to the army.
53 The troops were dispersed in the area's main fortresses, Salses, Perpignan, Collioure and Rosas.
54 In 1643 Aragon had to protect three main areas against the French. The first was the Pyrenean border covered by the Castle of Canfranc, the modern fortress of Jaca, with a garrison of 400

THE ARMIES OF PHILIP IV OF SPAIN 1621–1665

Table 2.4: Distribution of the nationalities in the infantry of the Army of Catalonia. Data from Elliot (1963) and Maffi (2014).

Years	Spanish	Italians	Walloons	Germans	Others*
1640	4,440	1,710	1,030	-	1,000
1647	4,190	1,030	780	1,710	740
1650	6,420	1,610	550	2,460	390

* In 'others' we have Irish troops, and for 1640 Italian mercenaries from Modena.

Lérida from 1644 and to deploy a sizeable field army in Aragon and the west of Catalonia. For example in 1643 (cf. Appendix V), the Spanish army[55] had probably 23,000 men in Catalonia and Aragon, 12,000 of which could go on campaign. The rest was divided into some 4,000 men in garrisons in the south of Catalonia[56] (Tortosa and Tarragona), 2,000–3,000 men for the fortress of Rosas and the strong garrison of Fraga and other small garrisons[57] in Aragon, probably some 4,000 men. For the rest of the period the number of men in garrison was maintained between 7,000 to 13,000 men[58] and with an average field army of 9,300 infantry and 3,200 cavalry. The ratio of infantryman to cavalrymen was between 2.2 in 1644, 3.5 in 1647 and 2.9 in 1658, implying that the mounted arm was an important component of the army. The main difference with the old Spanish Army of Flanders and Lombardy was that to have 9,550 infantry in April 1644, the Spanish had to join up to 15 different units.[59] In 1651, it was worse: at the beginning of the siege of Barcelona, the

---

men and the small fortress of Santa Elena near Biesca. The second was the County of Ribagorza and the eastern border of Aragon, protected by the Castle of Benasque, the Fortress of Ainsa (with a garrison of 60 to 100 men), the Castle of Monzón (in French hands in 1643), the city of Fraga (garrison of up to 3,000 men) and the Castle of Mequinenza (garrison of up to 500 men). The third area corresponds to the south bank of the River Ebre, protected by the fortress of Caspe and the Castle of Alcañiz. Of course, there were other medieval fortifications (city walls or castles) of little use for the war of the seventeenth century.

55 From a letter from 11 August 1643 (A. Valladares de Sotomayor, *Semanario Erudito que comprehende...* vol. 33, pp. 11–111) the Spanish expected to join 23,000 men in Aragon: 12,500 from the Royal army (Spanish, Walloons and Italians), 4,000 from Aragon, 2,000 from Valencia, 2,000 from Andalusia and 2,500 veterans of the Army of Flanders, the Squadron who capitulated at Rocroi in May 1643.

56 The *aviso* of 1 September 1643 (A. Valladares de Sotomayor, *Semanario Erudito*, vol. 33) gives a garrison of 3,500 foot and 250 horse in Tarragona and we can estimate a garrison of 500 men in Tortosa.

57 See footnote 54.

58 In 1647, the garrison of Lérida had 2,842 foot and 505 cavalry (Catalàn 1919) and in 1649, only in Fraga, Lérida and Tarrogona we can find 6,310 infantry and 850 horsemen could be found (Maffi, 2014).

59 Six Spanish tercios (Regiment of the Guardia del Rey, Regiment of the Principe, Tercio of Martin de Mujica or Muxica, Tercio of Esteban de Ascárraga, Tercio of Alsonso de Villamayor and Tercio of Francisco Freire), two Walloon tercios (Tercio of Charles Antoine de Calonne and Tercio of André Van der Sraeten), 3x Napolitan tercios (Tercio of the Baron of Amato, Tercio of Frey Tito Brancaccio and Tercio of the Duke of Laurenzana) and four German regiments (Regiments of Galaso, Regiment of Grosfeit, Regiment of Ludwig Haumel and Regiment of the Baron of Seebach). Picouet, 2014.

8,500 infantry were provided by 24 tercios and regiments.[60]

In 1652 most of Catalonia was under Spanish control, but the war with France was not over and until 1659 a series of bitter fights took place in the Pyrenean area and province of Girona. The army of Catalonia lost its priority and the Spanish resources were sent mainly to Flanders and Italy. The numbers decreased sharply to just 10,000 men or less, in 1653 the field army of John of Austria had only 5,300 infantry and 1,800 cavalry and in 1658 for the succour of Camprodon[61] the Spanish had only 3,000 infantry (six tercios and 600 light infantry) and 1,900 cavalry. It is clear that with the few resources available, the objective of the Spanish high command was to maintain a seasonable cavalry corps to have a mobile force to counter the French incursions, but not to retake the Roussillon. On the Catalan front, most of the troops were Spanish (Table 2.4) with a percentage of 50 to 60 percent of the infantry. Numbers could change radically when new recruits arrive in the army and when the muster was done. We must not forget that a high proportion of the Spanish troops were coming from provincial tercios and militia, troops that were disbanded at the end of the campaign. One interesting thing is the mobilisation of Catalan tercios after 1652 and the fall of Barcelona.

2.2.5 Armies of Extremadura and Galicia

On 1 December 1640, when the Portuguese decided to depose Philip III of Portugal (Philip IV of Spain), to throw away the Spanish administration, and to elect Joao IV as King of Portugal, the Spanish monarchy had virtually no troops to face this situation. Soon, skirmishing and small fights occurred along the 1,214 km of frontiers between Spain and Portugal. It took time for both belligerents to organise a proper army, for the Spanish the war with Portugal was at the bottom of Spanish priorities and for Portugal they had to start from scratch to organise a decent military force.[62] Very soon the Spanish decided to organise their main field army in the province of Extremadura using the city of Badajoz as main base. The choice was dictated by the geography and by the fact that the previous invasion of Portugal in 1580 was carried out following the route, Badajoz, Elvas, Estremoz, Evora, Setubal and Lisbon, the shortest way to arrive at the heart of Portugal.

For most of the period (1641–1656), the army of Extremadura was weak (Appendix VI) with an average of 9,000 men, even if thousands of men were also deployed along the borders. Another point to be considered with the

---

60 10 Spanish Tercios (Tercio of la Cueva, Tercio del Castillo, Tercio of Torres, Tercio of Cavallero, Tercio of Viedna, Tercio of Tarragona , Tercio of Estevan, Tercio of Sada, Tercio of Azlor and Tercio of Valencia), four Italian tercios (Tercio of Garaffa, Tercio of Genaro, Tercio of Rho and Tercio of Grez), three Walloon tercios (Tercio of Calonne, Tercio of Clerc and Tercio of Franque), two Irish tercios (Tercio of O'Brien and Tercio of Tyron) and five German regiments (Regiment of Laques, regiment of Kleinhans, regiment of Vilani, Regiment of Carene and regiment of Chapuis). Picouet, 2014.

61 Miquel Parets, "De los muchos sucesos dignos de memoria que han ocurrido en Barcelona y otros lugares de Cataluña, crónica escrita", in *Memorial Histórico Español*, vol. XXV (Madrid: Manuel Tello, 1893).

62 In 1643 the first ordinance for the infantry was published, creating 10 tercios of 1,500 men. Gastão de Melo de Matos (1932), *Notícias do têrço da Armada Real (1618-1707)*, separata dos *Anais do Club Militar Naval*, Lisbon, Imprensa da Armada.

Table 2.5: Distribution of the nationalities in the infantry of the Army of Extremadura. Data from Estébanez Calderón 1885, Ribot García (2004) and Rodríguez Hernández & P. Rodríguez Rebollo (2007).

Infantry	Spanish	Italians	Germans	Irish
1643	7,840	1,270	940	610
1647	5,800	1,080	680	540
1657	12,830*	-	-	260
1659	6,100	850	1,390	60
1663	17,220	2,830	1,810	630

* 5,860 men (44.7 percent) were from the militia of Extremadura and 2,700 men (20.6 percent) from the militia of Seville (Rodríguez Hernández & Rodríguez Repollo, 2007).

army of Extremadura was that most of the troops were from the militia of Extremadura, Seville, Granada and Castile, for example in 1657, two thirds of the Infantry came from the militia of Extremadura and Seville (Rodríguez Hernández & P. Rodríguez Rebollo, 2007). This fact implies that the troops would serve for a few months or weeks and it was difficult to mount offensive actions against the Portuguese.

With the end of the war with France in 1659, thousands of veterans from the armies of Flanders, Lombardy and Catalonia were sent to Badajoz. Already in 1657, the field army of Extremadura grown up to 14,460 men (divided into 11,140 infantry and 3,530 cavalry), and in 1663 we could find 23,180 men (divided into 15,090 infantry and 8,090 cavalry), a sizeable army.

One of the problems, even in 1663, was that 17.5 percent of the infantry consisted of militia from Seville (three tercios) and Granada (two tercios). In the first year of the war, the ratio of infantrymen versus horsemen was closer to 3.5, even if for a battle like the one of Montijo in 1644, the ratio was more like 2.4 (4,000 infantry and 1,700 cavalry). Later in the war the ratio was lower, between 1.8 and 3.2, indicating an increase of the cavalry force as in the other armies of the monarchy.

2.3 The Infantry of the Spanish Army

Like in all Spanish armies of this time, the infantry was a made up of a multinational troops made of native Spaniards (including the militia), national troops (Walloons, Italians and Burgundians) and mercenaries (mainly German, Swiss, Italians[63] and Irish).

---

63 Here the Italian troops were recruited in other territories of the Italian peninsula, such as Modena, Tuscany, Venetia and Papal State, than the ones belonging to the Spanish Empire.

2.3.1 The Spanish Tercios

The military unit called a tercio was created in 1536 by the ordinance of Genoa in time of the emperor Charles V. It was an innovation in the sixteenth century because the administration of Charles V wanted a permanent force of infantry to garrison the Imperial states in Italy but also shock troops to be used at any time, everywhere to defend the empire. In 1537, Charles V already had up to seven Spanish tercios in Italy and in North Africa.[64] Such a situation meant that over time the Spanish "nation" acquired some hierarchical privileges and prerogatives, the most important of these were: the vanguards and place of honour in marching and fighting formation; authority and precedence, especially in the council of war; appointment for the officers in charge of the country's major governor ship and garrison commands (Gonzáles de León, 2009). Looking forward, the organisation of the Spanish infantry between 1621 to 1665 was regulated by the royal ordinance published in 1603 and 1617, later on replaced by the ordinance of June 1632. The first ordinance of 1603 spoke of a tercio with a headquarters of 25 men and 15 to 20 companies (Table 2.6). Therefore, companies were divided in 13 companies of pikes and two companies of harquebusiers, or 17 companies of pikes and three companies of harquebusiers. It was established that the tercios for services in the peninsula had companies of 150 men and the others for Flanders and Italy companies of 100 men. The ordinance did not give any comments concerning the distribution of the men's specialties (pikemen, harquebusiers and musketeers).

The ordinance of 1617 did not modify the structure but added that the companies of pikes must be 50 percent pikemen, and all companies were supposed to have at least 10 percent musketeers, to summarise, we are talking of tercios from 1,500 to 3,000 men.

The ordinance of 1632 was published to resurrect the old idea of a tercio of 3,000 men, but in this case the distinction between companies of pikes and companies of harquebusiers was abolished to create only one type of company of 200 men in Flanders and Italy or 250 men in the tercios raised in the Iberian Peninsula. In 1636, the Governor of Flanders, the Cardinal Infante Fernando, published a new version of the ordinance of 1632, coming back to the two types of companies, with a tercio of 13 companies of pike and two companies of harquebusiers. In Table 2.6 we present the theoretical strength of a Spanish company following the different ordinances described above. In 1644, in Flanders, the Spanish tercios were set up at 18 companies each.

The tercio had a hierarchical structure with an important *prima plana* or staff. In descending order we have:

Maestro de Campo: commanded the tercio and was chosen by the crown or by representative of the crown. The *maestro de campo* had to command

---

[64] Tercio de Sicilia (MdC Álvaro de Grado y Leguizamo, Tercio del reino de Napoles (MdC Rodrigo de Arce y Beltrán), Tercio de Lombardia (MdC Sebastian de San Miguel), Tercio de Bonas (MdC Luis Perez de Vargas), Tercio de Niza o Málaga (MdC Juan de Vargas), Tercio de Florencia (MdC Francisco Sarmiento de Mendoza) and Tercio de Diego de Castilla (MdC Diego de Castilla y Chacón).

2.2 (left): Spanish infantry at the siege of Jülich in 1622. Mattheus Melijn, 1636. (Rijksmuseum)

2.3 (below): Spanish infantry during the relief of Brisach in 1633. Jusepe Leonardo, 1633–1652 (Michał Paradowski's archive)

his unit, to ensure that orders were followed but he had to be fair when he was applying military justice. He was also the captain of a company where he commanded a squad of 20–25 men (normally his squad was made of *reformados* acting as expert councillors to command the unit). Finally he had an escort guard of eight halberdiers paid by the crown. In general the tercio was known by the name of its *maestro de campo*, but some of them had a more stable name such as *Tercio Viejo de Naples*.

Sargento Mayor (Sergeant Major): the second officer of the Tercio. He was responsible for passing the orders to the different captains of the companies. He had different duties from the billeting of the soldiers (done with the support of the sergeant of each company), the organisation of the displacement of the tercio and most of all he was responsible of the deployment of the tactical squadron in battle. For the last duty he had to know the precise number of soldiers and their specialities, and he had some knowledge in arithmetic, in order to adapt the tactical squadron to the mission of the tercio. He was also chosen by the king or by his representatives and as insignia of his office he carried a short wood baton of 0.96 m (three feet). In the seventeenth century, he had two servants and had authority over the other captains of the tercio (Albi de la Cuesta, 2015).

The others officers of the staff were:

Auditor (paymaster): in charge of the finance of the tercio, he normally had three men (two sheriffs or *alguaciles* and a notary or *escribano*) to help him with such a task.

Capitán de campaña (chief of the military police): normally with four guards, he had the task of maintaining discipline in the tercio.

Tambor mayor (chief drummer): in charge of all the musicians of the tercio and responsible to transmit the orders to the companies.

The last three were the *Furrier mayor* (chief quartermaster), *Cirujano mayor* (chief surgeon) with sometimes a doctor and the *Capellán mayor* (chief cleric) with the help of two ordinary clerics. In total we can find up to seven high officers, 17 to 18 low officers or guards and three clerics.

Concerning the company, the staff were, in descending order:

The captain: in command of the company raised by him or nominated to fill a vacancy during a campaign. Like the *Maestro de Campo* for the tercio, the captain was responsible for the welfare and reputation of his men. The captain was also responsible for choosing his subordinates in order to put the most capable in the correct positions according to their physical and intellectual capabilities. His insignia was the pole weapon called *jineta* adorned with a red fringe below the head. In combat the captain was with the squadron of pike or with the detachments of harquebusiers and musketeers, in this case he would replace the *jineta* by a pike or a firearm. The captain had normally a page to assist him called *paje de Jineta,* indicating that one of the functions of this servant was to carry the *Jineta* for the captain. Following the ordinances, a captain should have a minimum of 10 years service as soldiers and *alférez* before presenting a request.

The *alférez*: the second in command of the company and the captain's main assistant. He had to be skilled in military affairs but his main responsibility was the standard or *bandera*. The iconic *bandera* represented the king's trust, and the company's honour and reputation, so the *alférez* had to defend it at the cost of his life if necessary. As a natural target for the enemy, the *alférez* was well protected for such task with a half-armour[65] and a helmet. He had one assistant, called an *abanderado*, to help him to carry the *bandera* during the march or to protect the *bandera* when it was left behind. The standard or *bandera* was the icon of the company's honour and reputation (López, 2012). In the seventeenth century the *bandera* had

---

65 Back- and breastplate, tassets, gorget, pauldrons and arms.

Table 2.6: distribution of the men according to the ordinance of 1603/1617, 1632 and 1636.

	Ordinance of 1603/1617		Ordinance of 1632		Ordinance of 1636
	Italy	Flanders	Peninsula	Flanders & Italy	Flanders
Ordinary Company of Pikes					
Staff*	11 men	11 men	11 men	11 men	11 men
Pikes	70 men	45 men	90 men	60 men	69 men
Harquebusiers	54 men	34 men	89 men	89 men	-
Musketeers	15 men	10 men	60 men	40 men	120 men
Company of Harquebusiers					
Staff*	11 men	11 men	-	-	11 men
Harquebusiers	124 men	79 men	-	-	159 men
Musketeers	15 men	10 men	-	-	30 men

*11 men divided into three officers (captain, *alférez* and sergeant), seven junior officers (an *abanderado*, a fifer, two drummers, a furrier, a barber and a cleric), and a page.

a size of 1.70 m with a red cross of Burgundy, a red saltire resembling two roughly-knotted branches.[66] The rest of the design was totally free and was chosen by the captain. For ceremonial purposes, the standard was placed on a short shaft of 30 cm, but on the field the *bandera* was placed on a longer and more practical shaft (López, 2012). Plates E, F, G, and H present different reconstructions of *banderas* of infantry companies during the reign of Philip IV.

The sergeant: the third officer of the company, he was directly responsible for the discipline of the company. The sergeant had to know precisely the number of men and weapons of the company, in order to communicate the information to the *Sargento Mayor*. He had some knowledge in arithmetic and had to be literate to allocate and billet the men. He had to ensure that the men knew their weapons and positions in the squadron, and for that he should organise regularl training sessions. His insignia was the halberd.

The others members of staff of a company were called low officers and were the three musicians of the company (two drummers and one fifer), the quartermaster (*furrier*), responsible for the billeting of the men of the company, the barber and a cleric. So in total we can say that the staffs of the company consisted of 10 men divided into three officers and seven low officers to which we have to add the page for the captain.

The 190 or 240 men of the company were not left without some organisation. At first we could find non-commissioned officers (NCOs) called *cabo de escuadra*, they were normally in charge of a group of 25 soldiers

---

66 There was no convention regarding the size and number of knots, it would depend on the wishes of the captain (López, 2012).

THE STRUCTURE OF THE SPANISH ARMY

2.4 Spanish mounted harquebusiers during the siege of Jülich in 1621/1622. Pieter Snayers, 1622–1650. (Rijksmuseum)

and were nominated by the captain. So a theoretical company had between eight and ten *capos de escuadras*. The men and the officers were normally grouped in *camaradas* of five to eight men to share food and shelter. In the companies we can find also some specific soldiers, the officer *reformado* and the *entretenidos*.[67] The *reformado* was an officer, captain, *Alférez* and sergeant, whose company had previously been disbanded due to the lack of men in their ranks or because their company was new and was disbanded to fill the ranks of the companies of the older tercios. In this case the officers were redistributed to another company or to the army headquarters for half of their former salary. It was expected that such officers could fill a vacancy if needed. For the Spanish high command, the status of *reformado* was well recognised because they were veterans, and by their example and courageous leadership they would enhance the efficiency of common soldiers. The *entretenidos* were different; normally they were attached to a noble house. Their efficiency or utility would depend strongly on the position and ability of their patron as well as their proper years of service.[68]

To summarise all the information, in 1620, a tercio in Flanders could have 20 companies, 245 officers (25 from the *prima plana*[69]) and 1,780 soldiers (765 pikemen, 815 harquebusiers and 200 musketeers) and in Italy, 15 companies, 190 officers (25 from the *prima plana*) and 2,085 soldiers (910 pikemen, 950 harquebusiers and 225 musketeers). In 1632, a tercio in Flanders and Italy should have 15 companies, 190 officers (25 from the *prima plana*) and 2,835 soldiers (600 musketeers, 1,335 harquebusiers and 900

---

67 For some campaigns, we could also find *adventureros o criados de pelea*, they had no salary and normally would fight for free. Such persons could be found when the campaign was led by the king or another important personage.
68 Some of them could be young men with no military experience, or old soldiers with years of service but unable to reach a high rank.
69 In the calculation I decided to take out the *maestro de campo* and his page because they are included in the *prima plana* of the first company commanded by the *Maestro de Campo*.

pikemen). For the tercio in the Iberian Peninsula, we had 12 companies, 157 officers (25 from the *prima plana*) and 2,868 and soldiers (720 musketeers, 1,068 harquebusiers and 1,080 pikemen). In 1636, the organisation of the tercios of Flanders were modified as follows: 13 ordinary companies of pike, two companies of harquebusiers giving 190 officers (25 coming from the tercio *prima plana*) and 2,835 soldiers divided into 1,620 musketeers, 318 harquebusiers and 897 pikemen).

The reality shown by the numerous musters of the Army of Flanders or the Army of Lombardy was somehow very different. A muster (or *muestra*) was when the *veedors* and *contadores* would muster a company to establish the number of officers and men and their specialities to give the order to the *pagadores* to pay them. A *muestra* could also be executed, by a commander of a field army to determine the number of men before entering in campaign or at the end of the campaign. For historians, they are invaluable documents to understand the structure of an army of the seventeenth century. Unfortunately, musters were plagued by errors and frauds. In effect for a captain it was useful to increase artificially the number of soldiers or to mask deserters in order to have the same amount of money or to avoid a dissolution of his company. Due to inevitable mistakes and frauds, as suggested by Ribot Garcia (1990), up to 15 to 25 percent of the soldiers of a muster could be "fake" or "useless" soldiers unfit for service.[70] For a garrison it was even worse because it would give a false sense of protection, high command would think that a particular fortress was well protected when in reality there were not enough men to man the walls (Rodriguez Hernandez, 2015). The great Spanish tercios[71] were units, created in the sixteenth century, deployed outside Spain, in the Low Countries and Italy. In Table 2.7 we present information related to the average number of companies by tercio as well as the average number of men serving in the companies for tercios deployed in this area. Tercios had a number of companies ranking from 15 to 20, even if such a number could be lower after a battle. Normally in all companies there was an average of 9 to 10 officers and low officers. Concerning the tercio *prima plana* numbers seemed to be between 12 and 25 men so most of the time below the authorised number. Concerning the number of men per company in the 1620s–1640s there were between 70 and 116 soldiers, not so far from the ordinance of 1617. For the next decade, 1641–1650, numbers went down with the number of men per company from 50 to 90. For the last decades of the war we have less information, but companies were closer to 30 to 40 men. The numbers of companies in a tercio tended to be higher in the Army of Flanders than in the Army of Lombardy, with tercios with 15 to 20 companies in comparison with 11 to 15 companies in northern Italy.

---

70 In June 1651, the Spanish army of Catalonia had 7,133 infantry (officers excluded) in 271 companies but 986 men (14 percent) were not real (*Relación diaria de todo lo que ha sucedido desde que salio … desde el 22 de junio hasta primeros días de agosto deste año 1651*, Gómez de Blas, A 110/060(22) University of Seville).

71 *Tercio fijo de los estado de Flandes* (created in 1537), *Tercio fijo de los estado de Holanda* (created in 1581), *Tercio fijo de los estado de Brabante* (created in 1591), *Tercio fijo de Lombardia* (created in 1568), *Tercio Fijo de Napoles* (created in 1548), *Tercio Fijo de Sicilia* (created in 1568) and *Tercio de los presidios de Portugal* called also *Tercio de Lisboa* (created in 1579).

Plate A

**1620s
Sergeant; *alférez***

(Illustration by Sergey Shamenkov, © Helion & Company)

See Colour Plate Commentaries for further information.

Plate B

1630s
**Spanish musketeer from the Tercio of Idiáquez, Germany 1634;
Spanish pikeman, Army of Lombardy 1636**
(Illustration by Sergey Shamenkov, © Helion & Company)
See Colour Plate Commentaries for further information.

Plate C

1640s
Spanish sergeant, Army of Lombardy 1645;
Spanish musketeer, Army of Catalonia, 1644
(Illustration by Sergey Shamenkov, © Helion & Company)
See Colour Plate Commentaries for further information.

Plate D

1650s–60s
Spanish pikeman, Portugal 1663; Spanish musketeer, Army of Flanders 1656
(Illustration by Sergey Shamenkov, © Helion & Company)
See Colour Plate Commentaries for further information.

Plate E

E.1: Reconstruction of a *bandera* from 1606 from a Spanish Tercio (P. Snayers)

E.2: Reconstruction of a *bandera* from 1625 (Velasquez)

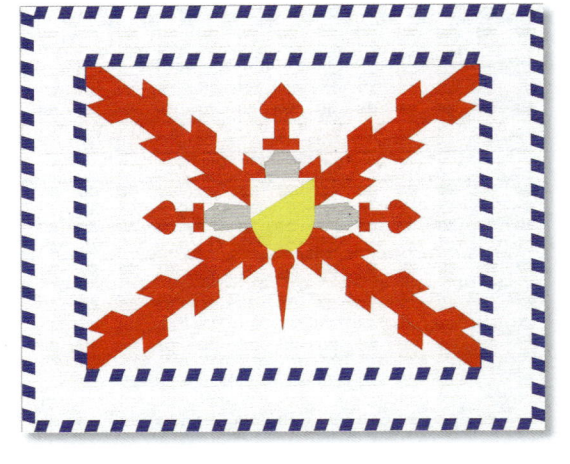

E.3 & E.4: Reconstructions of *banderas* from companies of Spanish tercios of the Army of Flanders, 1615

(Illustrations by and © Pierre A. Picouet 2019)
See Colour Plate Commentaries for further information.

Plate F

F.1: *Bandera* reconstructed from a damaged standard taken by the Swedish, probably in 1633

F.2, F.3: Modern reconstructions of models from professional tailors of *banderas de guerra*, 1618 and 1640.

(Illustrations by and © Pierre A. Picouet 2019)
See Colour Plate Commentaries for further information.

Plate G

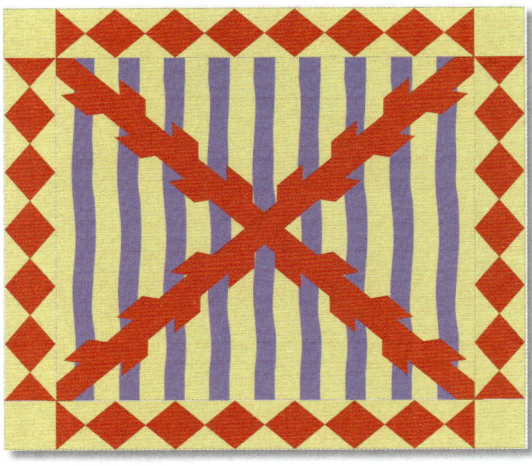

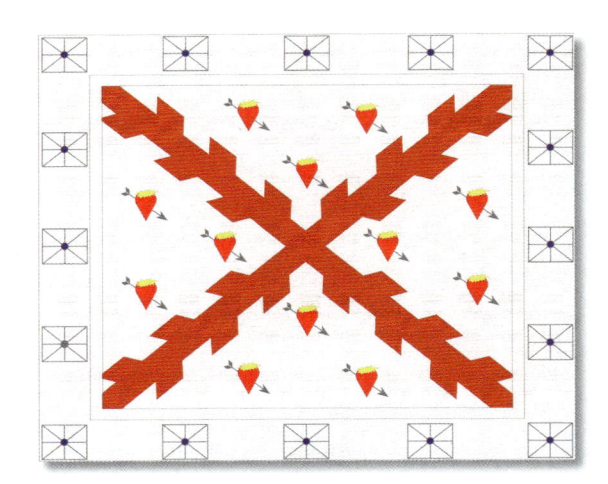

G.1, G.2, G.3: Reconstruction of three *banderas* taken between 1635 and 1643 by the French army in Flanders.

(Illustrations by and © Pierre A. Picouet 2019)
See Colour Plate Commentaries for further information.

Plate H

H.1, H.2: Reconstruction of two *banderas* of the Army of Flanders taken by the Dutch before 1648

(Illustrations by and © Pierre A. Picouet 2019)
See Colour Plate Commentaries for further information.

THE STRUCTURE OF THE SPANISH ARMY

2.5 Spanish infantry and camp followers, siege of Ostend (1601–1604). Sebastiaen Vrancx. (Michał Paradowski's archive)

After 30 years of fighting, this decrease over time is normal. For the French army, Corvisier (1992) indicates that a French infantry company in 1638 had 45 soldiers (the theoretical number was 75), 24 soldiers in 1645 (the theoretical number was 40) and 18 in 1658 (the theoretical number was 30). The decrease in some way was also favoured by the Spanish high command; a company with ratio soldiers/officers of five to six was easier to command than a company with a ratio above 10, especially if we take into account that the tactical infantry squadron of 1622 was deeper than the ones of 1652. The tendency to reduce the number of ranks implied that more men were facing the enemy and exposed to the enemy's fire. So a tighter control of the detachments of the tactical squadrons was required. In Spanish tercios such discipline was implemented by officers but also by the presence of *reformados*.

2.3.2 The Provincial Tercios

After decades of war in the Low Countries, Italy and Germany, the Spanish Kingdom had to consider seriously a new war against the French Monarchy wishing to dispute the European hegemony to the Spanish. In 1633, the question was not whether war with France could be avoided, but when it would start and how the Spanish should reinforce their position in order to meet this threat. In this case, not only Flanders, Italy or Germany would

Table 2.7: Estimate of average Spanish tercios and their companies for all periods considered. Calculations were made with data presented in appendices and completed with data from Clonard (volume 5, 1854), Estébanez-Calderón 1885, Ribot Garcia 1990, Rodríguez Hernández & Rodríguez Rebollo (2007), and Maffi 2008..

Period	Tercios	Coy.	Officers and Soldiers	Companies per Tercio	Men per tercio	Men per company
Regular Spanish Tercio						
1619–1622	4	67	5,596	17	1,400	84
1631–1634	8	142	14,197	18	1,775	100
1635–1643	5	86	7,337	17	1,645	96
1647	10	148	9,901	15	990	67
1659	6	122	2,520	20	627	31
Provincial Spanish Tercio						
1640–1642	7	100	5,153	14	736	52
1647–1657	7	92	3,572	13	510	39
1663*	15	202 ?	7,769	13 ?	518	38 ?
1667	5	92	2,962	18	592	32

* Spanish tercios in Extremadura with probably 202 companies, so we should have 13 companies/tercio and 38 men per company.

be a war zone but also the north of the Iberian Peninsula, were few regular forces were available. To share the burden of the different wars, the Spanish government had already proposed a solution in 1624 to create a mobile force to defend the monarchy, the famous *Union de Armas*.[72] With the *Union de Armas*, each of the territories had to bring a number of men for the royal armies, troops to defend their own territory and to maintain a militia. In this scheme, normally 1/7 of the men should be selected to form a field army of 20,000 infantry and 4,000 cavalry. The reform was too ambitious[73] and met strong resistance, especially in the territories from the old crown of Aragon, Valencia, Aragon and Catalonia. At the end, after years of negotiation in the Iberian Peninsula, the court of Valencia agreed to pay 1,000 men in the case of war and Aragon agreed to pay 2,000 men and Catalonia none.

In 1634 in a new attempt to have a coherent mobile force, the Count-Duke of Olivares decided to involve the Spanish nobility in the defence of the realm. The coronelia of his Majesty (*Coronolia de su Majestad*) with 21

---

72 In the Iberian Peninsula the distribution was done 44,000 men for Castile, 10,000 for Aragon, 6,000 for Valencia, 16,000 for Catalonia, 16,000 for Portugal and 6,000 for the Atlantic and Mediterranean islands. We have also 12,000 for Flanders, 8,000 for Milan and 6,000 for Sicilia (Elliott 1990).

73 In the Low Countries, local authorities were already maintaining 9,000 to 15,000 men since the beginning of the seventeenth century (Parker 1991).

THE STRUCTURE OF THE SPANISH ARMY

companies of 200 men[74] and 16 regiments of noblemen of 1,375 men[75] each were created. The experiment was not successful, and following Clonard (volume 4, 1851) the recruitment of these noblemen's regiments was not done properly and by the end of 1634, most of these units had not be raised and were not available for service. One year later, in 1635, with the French declaration of war in hand, the Spanish government created six new tercios,[76] but like the noblemen's regiments, it was difficult to find new recruits and the units did not last one year of existence and most were disbanded.

At the end of 1637, 6,055 men were extracted from the militia of Castile to form five provincial tercios[77] of 1,211 men distributed in 12 companies. Following Clonard (volume 4, 1851) such tercios had a *prima plana* of 11 men including a *maestro de campo* and a *Sargento Mayor* and for each company a staff of six men with probably three officers (captain, *Alférez*, and sergeant), low officers (two drummers and a quartermaster), four *cabos* and 90 soldiers.[78] The provincial tercio of Castile proved to be a better system, because it was financed by the militia. In other words, the villages, nobility and cities of Castile did not have to contribute only with men but in most of the cases the number of men could be changed by a sum of money to pay the existing provincial tercios.[79] The system was immediately used elsewhere, and for example at the end of 1638 to support the operation around Fuenterrabia,[80] provincial tercios were raised in Navarre, Viscaya, Alava and Guipúzcoa as well as in Castile and Aragon to support the few regular troops (Spanish, Italians and Irish) of the army of the *Admirante de Castilla* to save the city.[81] As we have seen, other territories of the Iberian

---

74 Another strong unit formed in March 1642, the regiment of Prince Balthazar Carlos (*Regimiento del principe Balthazar Carlos*). It was formed by veterans living in Madrid and was made of 18 companies of 200 men. The regiment was disbanded in 1645 at the death of the Principe.

75 The 16 regiments were raised by the high nobility o *Grandes de España*: Conde-Duque Olivares, Almirante de Castilla (Juan Alfonso Enriquez de Cabrera IX Almirante de Castilla), Condestable de Castilla, Duque of Medinaceli, Duque de Infantado, Duque de Nágera, Duque de Osuna, Condestable de Navarra, Conde de Niebla, Duque de Escalona, Duque de Medina de las Torres, Duque de Alburquerque, Duque de Sesa, Duque de Pastrana, Conde de Lemos and Conde de Oropesa (Clonard, vol. 4, 1851).

76 Following Clonard (vol. 4, 1851) the names of the *maestros de campo* were *Pedro Giron, Sebastiam Granero, Francisco de Megia, Cristobal Bocanegra*, the *Marques of Hinojosa* and *Francisco Manuel*.

77 The term "provincial" indicated that after a campaign most of the tercio was disbanded to be reformed the next year if the Cortes de Castilla could finance it. The *maestros de campo* were *Pedro de Giron, Domingo Eguia, Andres Pacheco, Diego de Caballero de Illesca* and *Francisco del Castillo*.

78 Another possibility could be tercio of 10 companies with three officers (captain, *alférez*, and sergeant), five minor officers, (two drummers, a paymaster or furrier, a cleric and a "surgeon"), four *cabo de escuadra*, 25 pikemen, 25 musketeers and 50 harquebusiers (F. Xavier Hernandez, 2003).

79 The system was also applied elsewhere: in Asturias, the province had to pay 12,000 to 14,000 escudos each year, corresponding to a ratio of 300 soldiers.

80 The siege of Fuenterrabia started in June 1638 when a French army of 21,000 men (Prince de Condé) supported by the fleet of 54 ships attacked the border city defended by a garrison of 1,300 men. Spain organised a strong army consisting of all the troops available (some 16,000 men) and managed to breach the French lines. Condé had no choice; he withdrew with the rest of his troops.

81 The army successfully attacked an exhausted French Army on 7 September 1638.

Peninsula could raise and maintain regional tercios for two to eight months to be used to defend the realm and with the authorisation of their parliament. The king could also raise troops in these territories to reinforce the regular tercios on the king's pay. In 1638, three tercios of 1,000 men of 10 companies were asked to Aragon, Catalonia and Valencia.[82] In 1640, the vice-royalty of Aragon was directly involved in the war. The collapse of Catalonia had put the French armies on the eastern border of Aragon through the large plain along the valley of the River Segre. In 1641, the Spanish monarch obtained from the *cortes* de Zaragoza (Aragon) the mobilisation of 4,800 men for six months above the normal ratio of one soldier per hundred inhabitants applied in Castile. In 1645, the demand was more reasonable and the king asked only for the service in the royal army of two tercios of 1,000 men and the payment of 500 men from the king's[83] army. Additionally, the king could call for the service in the militia for three months. Recruits of these tercios came mainly from outside the capital Zaragoza, because the city had to rise and pay its proper units for the army. Table 2.7 gives some information from provincial tercios deployed in Extremadura and Catalonia. The viceroyalty of Valencia had to defend their coast from the North African pirates and had a complex system of 96 towers and defensive posts for that purpose. In theory Valencia could recruit 10,000 militia, and in 1638 a tercio of 1,600 men was sent to Fuenterrabia. Later on, with the war in Catalonia, troops were sent to reinforce the garrisons of Tortosa and Tarragona. In 1645, Valencia and the king's council arrived at an agreement for the creation of eight tercios of infantry (*tercios del socorro de la frontera y defensa del reyno* could be translated as "tercios for the assistance of the frontier and defence of the kingdom") for services in the province of Valencia and at the frontier,[84] in total they numbered 5,000 men, 625 men/tercio (Picouet 2014). Navarre had a frontier with France and had to maintain a number of forces to garrison the fortress[85] of the province. Outside the province, Navarre contributed 4,000 men[86] to the defence of Fuenterrabia and between 1640 and 1642 Navarre raised, each year, two tercios of 1,000 men for the service in Catalonia. Later, the service for the army of Catalonia was reduced to only one tercio of 1,000 men. Extremadura had a large border with Portugal and was the host of one of the four armies of the Spanish Crown. The defence of Extremadura was mainly centred in the city of Badajoz and from 1640 to 1668, the province of Extremadura had to provide each year four provincial tercios of 1,000 men. In 1647, the four tercios were commanded by Simon de Castañizas, Juan de Zuñiga, Alvaro de Luna and Pedro de Biedma and numbered only 2,083 men (Estébanez Calderón Volume 1, 1885).

---

82 José Camón Aznar, "la situación Militar en Aragón en el Siglo XVII", Instituto Jerónimo Zurita *Cuadernos de Historia* nº8 and 9, 1955–56.
83 The new treaty established that Aragon would finance 500 horsemen for the next four years.
84 The frontier was obviously Catalonia and Valencia was supposed to support the king's army with 1,200 men (Pardo (1998), *Militaria* nº11, Universidad Computese de Madrid).
85 Pamplona was the main capital and a modern fortress with a permanent garrison of 300 men.
86 At the same time to defend Navarre, the militia was called and some 9,000 men were raised to defend Pamplona and the mountainous borders. Exceptionally, as in 1638, Navarre temporarily raised 13,000 men.

THE STRUCTURE OF THE SPANISH ARMY

Table 2.8: Estimate of the average tercios from nations (Lombards, Neapolitans, Walloons and Burgundians) or German regiments and their companies for all periods considered. Calculations were made, with data presented in appendices and completed with data from Estébanez Calderón (Volume 1&2, 1885), Ribot Garcia (1990), Rodríguez Hernández & Rodríguez Rebollo (2007), Rodríguez Hernández (2017) and Maffi (2007, 2015 and 2016).

Period	Tercios	Coy.	Officers and Soldiers	Companies per Tercio	Men per Tercio	Men per Company
Tercio of Nations						
1622[a]	2	32	2,730	16	1,365	85
1631–1633[b]	13	154	15,280	12	1,175	99
1635–1640[c]	8	128	7,745	16	1,112	69
1643	6	100	5,786	17	964	58
1647–1648	8	104	7,650	13	956	74
1647–1650[d]	8	-	3,257	-	407	-
1656–1659[e]	10	100	9,109	10	911	91
1663[f]	7	81 ?	2,828	13 ?	404	35 ?
1666[g]	3	-	1,737	-	434	-
German Regiments						
1631–1633	4	36	7,853	9	1,963	218
1640	8	120	13,837	13	1,537	115
1643	6	67	4,715	11	786	70
1647	2	20	1,695	10	848	85
1647–1650[h]	9	-	4,172	-	463	-
1663[i]	5	43 ?	1,810	9 ?	362	42 ?
Irish Tercios						
1642–1664[j]	20	165	5,481	8	274	33
1633–1659[k]	5	75	4,239	15	848	57

a. Tercio Gulsin (Walloons) and Tercio of Bralanzon (Burgundians)
b. Only Italian tercios deployed in the armies of Lombardy and Flanders
c. Tercios of nations deployed in Italy, Flanders and Catalonia
d. Italian tercios deployed in the Army of Catalonia (Maffi 2016)
e. Data only for Italian tercios deployed in the Army of Lombardy (Maffi 2007)
f. Italian tercios in the Army of Extremadura with probably an average of 12 companies per tercio and 35 men per company
g. Italian tercios in the Army of Extremadura (Maffi 2016)
h. Data available for the Army of Catalonia (Maffi 2015)
i. German regiments in the Army of Extremadura with probably an average of nine companies per regiment and 42 men per company
j. Data adapted from musters taken in the army of Extremadura
k. Data from three musters in 1633, 1653 and 1659 in the Army of Flanders (Sánchez Martin, 1999)

The provincial tercios became the workhorses of the Spanish armies in the Iberian Peninsula, they were more permanent and better trained than the militia (organised also in tercios) with *reformados* and old soldiers, even if they were not as good as the ones deployed outside Spain (the Low Countries and Italy). Most of the time a provincial tercio had 200 to 1,000 men, with a small staff of five to 13 men and five to 20 companies (companies with four to seven officers and 30 to 70 soldiers).

From 1657 to 1664, the Spanish government decided to create five permanent provincial tercios in Castile, *Tercio Provincial Fijo de Toledo*, *Tercio Provincial Fijo de Madrid*, *Tercio Provincial Fijo de Burgos*, *Tercio Provincial Fijo de Valladolid* and *Tercio Provincial Fijo de Sevilla*, in 1667 they were made of 92 companies, 636 officers and 2,454 soldiers including 332 *reformados* (Clonard, volume 5, 1854).

2.3.3 The Tercios of the Armada

There is a strong debate as to who were the Tercios of Armada in 1621. In the sixteenth century, soldiers aboard galleys,[87] galleons[88] or other ships were coming from the Tercio of Sicily, the tercios of Naples or whatever troops available at that time they were not a specific tercio of marines. It appears that the tercios of the Armada were organised probably at the beginning of the seventeenth century (Palau Cuñat 2013) to embark on board the different ships of the main armadas of the Spanish navy. All these armadas had infantry on board coming from free companies and from specific tercios, that we can call tercios of the Armada and from fixed tercios, particularly in Naples and Sicily. Considering the tercio of the Armada, between 1621 to 1668, we might find, the tercio of the *Armada del Mar Oceano*, the tercio of the *Armada de las Galeras de España* and the tercio of the *Armada de la Guarda de la Carreras de las Indias*. Such tercios were normally administrative organisations with a full *prima plana* and a variable numbers of companies. Their normal task was to provide each year companies and men to embark on the ships of the Spanish navy. For example in 1624 for the operation[89] to recover the city of San Salvador de Bahia in Brazil, the Spanish had 32 companies (2,530 men) from the tercio of the *Armada del Mar Oceano*, 26 companies (2,374 men) from a new tercio commanded by Juan de Orellana, seven companies (478 men) from the *escuadra de Viscaya* and six companies (440 men) from companies from the *escuadra de Cuatros Villas*. Troops were complemented by 16 companies (700 men) from the Italian tercio of the Marquis de Torrecuso and 25 Portuguese companies (3,538 men) from the Tercio of Francisco Almeida and the Tercio of Antonio Muniz Barreto. But the tercios and companies from the Armada could also fight with the main Spanish armies. So when the navy was not active, the Spanish used them to

---

87 Normally each active galley had a contingent of 60–70 infantrymen, called a garrison.
88 In 1665, the formulae to calculate the minimal crew of a galleon were normally one seaman per 6.3 tons and one infantryman for 2.3 tons. In 1643, the 500-ton galleon *Santiago de Portugal* had 30 guns and a crew of 300 men (30 percent seamen and 70 percent infantrymen).
89 A full story in Spanish can be found in *Compendio Historial de la Jornada del Brasil y sucesso della…* CODOIN vol. 55, p.43–200, 1870.

create temporarily ad hoc tercios of 500 to 1,000 men to fight with the field army or to garrison important fortresses such as Rosas, Lleida or Tarragona. They were known by the name of their *maestro de campo* or sometimes by the name of *Tercio de la Armada*, *Tercio de Galleon* or *Tercio de las Galeras*. For example in 1639, for the siege of Salces, the Spanish sent a powerful fleet[90] to support the operation and to mitigate the action of the French fleet. The fleet was reinforced[91] by the *Armada de la Guardia de la Carrera de las Indias*. In September the first fleet sent an ad hoc *Tercio de la Armada* commanded by Francisco de Castilla and in October, the *Tercio de Galeon*, commanded by the Marquis of Cardañosa with men extracted from the second armada. In total up to 2,500 men were sent to Salses and only 1,000 returned to the fleet in February 1640.

2.3.4 Tercios from Nations
In the territories of the Low Countries, Burgundy, Lombardy, Naples and Sicily belonging to the King of Spain, infantry troops were raised during the reign of Philip IV, were organised in tercios. For the Italian tercios, since 1591 they were organised like the Spanish tercios. Therefore, they followed the ordinance of 1603/1617 and later that of 1632 presented in paragraph 2.3.1 For the troops raised in Burgundy and in the Low Countries (Walloons), they were organised in tercios since 1603, but they had a different organisation of their companies of 200 men. In 1617 a company of Walloon had a staff of 11 men, 40 pikemen, 99 harquebusiers and 50 musketeers. In 1632, the company was organised with 11 officers, 47 pikemen and 142 musketeers (Parker, 1991). The Walloons had also another two types of free companies,[92] paid by the cities or paid directly by the finance council of Flanders, the first had nine officers and 100 soldiers and the second 10 officers, 64 pikemen and 126 musketeers. These two types of companies were normally stationed troops (Mirecki Quintero, 1993).

Of course like the Spanish, the Italians, Walloons and Burgundians never had tercios of 3,000 men, if we have a look at the data available, for example at the muster in January 1622 in the Palatinate, the tercio of Gulsin (Walloon) presented 17 companies with 159 officers (*prima plana* of 14 men) and 1,185 soldiers, giving an average company of 79 soldiers (including nine officers). For the muster of January 1631, the six tercios raised in Lombardy presented 68 companies, 670 officers and 5,566 soldiers, indicating that the average tercio had just above 1,000 men. Including data from 1633 and 1634 (Table 2.8), Italian tercios had an average of 1,175 men with 12 companies of 99 men (including 10 officers per company). For a more precise view (Appendix IX) in 1633 the Tercio Vecchio of Cantelmo of the Army of Flanders had 16 companies, 165 officers and 1,411 men. As indicated in Table 2.8, the number of men (including

---

90 In June 1639, in the harbour of Rosas, the Spanish had 36 galleons, three frigates, three patches, 10 galleys, six fireships and 41 other smaller ships called tartana and luengos (M.J. Nestares Pleguezuelo, 2000, "La Armada de la Carrera de Indias en la toma de Salces, 1639–40" (i). *Researching & Dragona* n°7, pp. 4–21).
91 The fleet left Cadiz with eight galleons and two patches with a total of 2,690 men.
92 Free companies not integrated in a tercio.

10 officers per company) per company in Italian tercios decreases slightly to an average of 69 men in the period 1635–1640. In 1643, we have data from Italian and Walloon tercios of the Army of Flanders and they presented an average tercio of 961 men divided in 17 companies of 58 men (including 10 officers per company). In detail, the Tercio Vecchio of delli Ponti (Italian) presented 15 companies, 168 officers and 737 soldiers while the Tercio of Grobbendoncq (Walloon) presented 20 companies with 219 officers and 1,021 soldiers. The same year the Tercio of Garaffa (Italian) presented 90 officers and 644 soldiers, probably in eight to nine companies. For the years 1647–1648, we have data from Italian tercios in Lombardy giving an average tercio of 1,035 men divided in 13 companies of 79 men (including 10 officers per company). In detail, the Tercio of Frey Palavesino (Italian) presented 15 companies with 175 officers (25 from the tercio *prima plana*). For the Italian tercios deployed in the Army of Catalonia, in the period 1647–1650, the situation was worse, with heavy fighting, huge losses and poor living conditions giving an average tercio down to 407 men. For the Walloons, in 1647, the tercio of the Count of Bruay had 17 companies with 179 officers and 702 men (an average company of 52 men). The same year, the Burgundian Tercio of Wateville presented eight companies with 104 officers (*prima plana* of 24 men) and 457 soldiers (average company of 70 men). For the last decades of the war against France, the average tercio of the Army of Lombardy had still 911 men divided in 10 companies of 91 men, this was probably due to the fact that the Spanish could still raise local troops for the army.

From the details presented in Appendix IX, the Walloon tercios tended to have more companies than the Italian ones deployed in the Army of Lombardy, giving average companies lower in Flanders. From 1660, effort was put into the army of Extremadura but the numbers available indicate that the average Italian tercio was still reduced, 404 men in 1663 and 434 men in 1666, with companies down to 35 men, including officers.

The effort of the Spanish dominion in Italy to support the war was important. For the Army of Lombardy from 1635 to 1659, 63 470 Lombards were recruited for the tercio of regular infantry as well as 35,000 militia (Maffi, 2008). Many more were recruited to serve in the Army of Flanders. Naples was not only financing the war but provided a significant number of troops for the monarchy. Following, Stradling (1992) 50,000 men (infantry and cavalry) were recruited and sent abroad (Flanders, Spain and Lombardy) or to the armada in just five years (1635 to 1640). At least 29,000 Neapolitans were sent to the tercios of the Army of Lombardy between 1635 and 1659. Walloons were easily recruited in the Army of Flanders and as stated in Table 2.9 they formed the core of the army; following Maffi (2014), an average 8,000 men were recruited each year with a maximum of 10,000 men at the beginning of the war with France and 5,000–6,000 men in the 1650s. In 1658, the governors of Flanders expected only 4,000 new recruits to fill the gaps. It is a huge number of men for a country of 1.5 million inhabitants that had also to support the accommodation of an army of 65,000–88,000 men. At the same time thousands of troops were sent to Spain to form regular tercios of professional troops. A rough estimate gives a total of 10,800 Walloons sent to the Iberian Peninsula from 1636 to 1654. As for the Burgundians, they were sent mainly to the Army of Flanders or the Army of Lombardy. Maffi (2007) indicates that 7,500 infantry were sent to the Army of Lombardy from 1639 to 1652 when the average number of soldiers from this territory was only 760 men each year.

The tercios of the nations, when they were sent abroad, particularly in the Iberian Peninsula, tended to be well appreciated by Spanish commanders and most of them participated in all the major actions of the Army of Catalonia and in the Army of Extremadura. For the Italian Tercio of the Army of Flanders they were regarded as good as the Spanish by some commanders.

2.3.5 Mercenaries, Germans, Irish and Swiss

Raising men from all territories of the monarchy was not enough; wars demanded always more and more men and professional soldiers, like the mercenaries who fought for money and were in great demand by all belligerents. In Spanish service, mercenaries tended to come from the Catholic states, from Germany, Ireland, Switzerland and Italy. Other nationalities were also raised during the seventeenth century. The most significant contingent was made of Germans. Normal procedure to raise a regiment was to contract, give a patent to, a nobleman[93] with the ability and finances to create and support a regiment. With the ruler's permission (for example rulers such as the Elector of Cologne, the Prince-Bishop of Münster or the Prince-Bishop of Konstanz), the new colonel would appoint the captains of his regiment with the obligation to recruit enough men in their companies in the area fixed by the ruler in his territory. The structure of the German regiment in Spanish service was very similar to the ones raised for the Bavarian Army (Spring, 2017). In theory a German regiment was made of a regimental staff[94] with at minimum a colonel, a lieutenant-colonel, a sergeant-major, a quartermaster, a legal officer and provost with his men, surgeon with his assistants, a cleric and a wagon-master and 10 combat companies. Each company had a staff or *prima plana* with a captain, a lieutenant, a second lieutenant, an ensign, a first sergeant, a quartermaster, two second sergeants, two drummers or fifers, a cleric and barber or surgeon, a captain of arms, 200 to 300 corporals (normally six), lance-corporals and soldiers. So a regiment was supposed to have between 2,000 and 3,000 men and distribution between specialities was 40 percent pikemen, 10 percent calivermen and 50 percent musketeers. Concerning the provenance of the men, the Spanish made the distinction between regiments of High Germans raised in territories of the Hapsburg house (Tyrol, Bohemia, Croatia, Silesia and Austria) and in German Catholic states (Bavaria and Swabia) and regiments of Low Germans raised in the Rhine valley (Münster, Cologne, Mainz or Trier), in central and northern

---

93 Nobleman could be of German origin or other nationalities. For example Italian nobles such as Principe Borso d'Este, the Marquis of Borgomanero or the Count of Visconti raised regiments for Spain. We find also some Walloons such as Charles de Croy or Alexandre Bournoville and Spanish Pedro de la Fuente or Ambrosio Mexia (Maffi 2015).
94 In Spanish service, depending on the colonel and the capitulation signed with Spanish authorities, the regiment's staff could have from 20 to 40 people.

Germany (Hamburg, Brandenburg, Brunswick, Hessen and so on[95]) but also in the Duchy of Lorraine and Principality of Liège (Maffi 2014). Looking at the data available for German regimental manpower we find strong variation. In 1631–1633, with newly raised regiments we arrive at an average regiment of 1,923 men with nine companies of 218 men (including up to 18 officers). In 1640, in the Army of Flanders, we have an average regiment of 1,537 men with 13 companies of 115 men (including 20 officers). In detail the regiment of the Count of Isenburg presented 17 companies with 505 officers and 1,823 soldiers while the regiments of Guilio Frangipani presented 10 companies with 167 officers and 972 soldiers. We have also data from a muster of 1643 in the Army of Flanders; in this case the average regiment had 851 men divided in 12 companies of 70 men (including 20 officers). In detail the regiment of the Count of Isenburg presented 17 companies with 502 officers and 1,075 soldiers while the regiments of Ottavio Guasco presented only six companies with 84 officers and 376 soldiers.

The Irish had strong links with the Spanish monarchy and they regularly provided levies and full tercios. In theory they were organised like the Spanish tercio following the same ordinances of 1603/1617 and 1632. For the tercios deployed in the Army of Flanders, Table 2.8 presents an average tercio of 848 men divided in 15 companies of 57 men (including 10 officers). Concerning the Irish fighting in the Iberian Peninsula, in 1638 two Irish Tercios[96] with 2,500 men disembarked in A Coruña. In 1641 and during the period of 1643–1648 more men were transferred from Ireland to Spain. In the army of Catalonia we will find always tercios[97] fighting with the field army or in garrison in Tarragona. In a muster of 1642 the Tercio of Fitzgerald presented seven companies with 64 officers (17 officers for the *prima plana*) and 347 soldiers (Appendix X).

The Swiss mercenaries were particularly important for the troops deployed in Lombardy. They followed the same system in force in the French army. The Spanish would sign a capitulation with a Swiss canton from Catholic area for a regiment or numbers of companies indicating where and against whom they should fight. In 1639 a treaty was also signed with the league of the Grisons for the use of the Valtellina valley and for the possibility to hire troops. For example (Maffi 2007) in 1642 the Spanish hired the regiment of Melchior Lussi with 1,500 men and in 1647, the Army of Lombardy (Ribot Garcia 1990) had 23 companies of Swiss with 1,791 men and 23 companies from the League of the Grisons with 1,147 men.

---

95 Already at the beginning of the seventeenth century, Spanish tended to accept German Protestant regiments fighting in the Low Countries.
96 Regarding the Tercio of Tyrone, already in service since 1624, in 1638 the *Maestro de Campo* was Shean O'Neil, 4th Count of Tyrone followed in 1641 by his son (eight years old) called Hugh Eoghan O'Neill, 5th Count of Tyrone. The other tercio was that of Tyrconnell with his *maestro de campo* Rory O'Donnell, 1st Earl of Tyrconnell.
97 Tercio of Fitzgerald (1640–1662), Tercio of Preston (1644–1646) and Tercio of O'Brien (1646–1670).

2.3.6 The Auxiliary Armies of the Spanish Crown

The Imperial Army (1624–1659)

An auxiliary army of Imperial troops was a contingent of soldiers of the German Empire, temporarily paid by the Spanish crown to fight alongside their armies in Flanders and Italy. Already in 1624–1625, during the siege of Breda, a small contingent of 4,000 men (1,000 cavalry and 3,000 infantry) under the command of the Count of Collalto was hired by the Archduchess Isabel to support the army of Spinola (Swart, 2016). In 1629, during the siege of 's-Hertogenbosch a force of 10,000 men under the command of Count Montecuccoli supported the Army of Flanders to launch a useless attack on the Dutch Republic. In 1630 and 1634, the Imperial contingents were allies of the Spanish and not auxiliaries, but with the war with France, Spain asked directly for Imperial troops that would be paid by them. In June 1635, Ottavio Piccolomini was sent to support the Army of Flanders with an army of 25,000 men.[98] In the 1636 offensive,[99] the Spanish had with them the Imperial troops of Piccolomini and the troops from the Catholic League commanded by Johann von Werth. The pressure of the Protestant armies and the policy of the Emperor to fight in the east meant that Imperial contingents, supporting the Spanish Army of Flanders, were smaller and smaller. In 1639 despite the success of the army of Piccolomini at Thionville in June, Emperor Ferdinand III had in mind the defeat of Chemnitz on 14 April and asked urgently for the return of 6,000 veterans from Flanders (Maffy 2014). In 1645, an Imperial contingent commanded by the Baron of Lamboy with 8,000 men[100] was still supporting the Army of Flanders.

After 1648 and the Peace of Westphalia, some disbanded German regiments were hired by the Spanish for the Army of Flanders, particularly to reinforce the mounted arm. In summer 1656, Ferdinand III agreed to send an Imperial contingent of 12,000 men commanded by the Baron of Enckevoort to defend the Duchy of Milan and support the Army of Lombardy. Such numbers of troops never reached Lombardy, in reality fewer than 7,000 men were sent and the Imperial contingent was closer to 5,000–6,000 men (Maffi 2008). At the same time Enckevoort had strict orders to adopt a defensive position and refused to be deployed outside the territory of the Duchy.

The Army of the Duke of Lorraine (1634–1655)

In 1633 France invaded the Duchy of Lorraine, and the Duke of Lorraine had to withdraw with his small army. In 1634 a formal alliance with Spain was signed; in theory the Duke had to raise a force of 12,000 men but in

---

98　On 18 June the Imperial army crossing the River Rhine had 12,000 infantry, 11,000 cavalry and 2,000 dragoons (Albi de la Cuesta 2015).

99　Probably for the Imperials seven infantry regiments, nine cavalry regiments and one dragoon regiment and for the Catholic League five infantry regiments, five cavalry regiments and one dragoon regiment (R. Quazza, *Tommaso di Savoia-Carignano nelle campagne di Fiandra e di Francia, 1635–1638*. Torino: Soc. ed. internaz., 1941). See also Vincart, *Campaña de 1636*, CODOIN vol. 59, 1873.

100　Probably five infantry regiments with 53 companies (3,000 men), 10 cavalry regiments with 63 troops and two regiments of dragoons (Vincart, *Campaña de 1635*, CODOIN vol. 67, 1877).

THE ARMIES OF PHILIP IV OF SPAIN 1621–1665

THE STRUCTURE OF THE SPANISH ARMY

2.6 Spanish infantry, early 17th century. Adam Willaerts, 1617. (Rijksmuseum)

2.7: Spanish cavalry, early 17th century. Adam Willaerts, 1617. (Rijksmuseum)

Table 2.9: Estimate of the cavalry troops in the Spanish Army organised in companies

Date	Location	Cavalry	Nation	Coy.	Officers	Soldiers	Total	Ref.
1633	Flanders	4x regiment of Cavalry	German	29	292	1,394	1,686	(a)
1633	Flanders	Cavalry of all Nations	All	83	732	4,982	5,714	(a)
1643	Extremadura	Italian Cavalry	Italian	9	59 (7)	328	387	(b)
1643	Extremadura	*Guardias de Castilla*	Spanish	6	16	125	141	(b)
1643	Extremadura	Ordinary Cavalry of Extremadura	Spanish	35	132 (12)	1,309	1,441	(b)
1647	Lombardy	Guards Troops	Spanish	3	18	300	318	(c)
1647	Lombardy	Cavalry of the State of Milan	Spanish	30	202 (17)	1,711	1,913	(c)
1647	Lombardy	Neapolitan Cavalry	Italian	18	127 (12)	1,112	1,239	(c)
1647	Lombardy	Regiment of Colonel Estuz	German	7	73	603	676	(c)

(a) Saavedra (op. cit.)
(b) Estébanez Calderón (volume 1, 1885)
(c) Ribot Garcia (1990)

January 1637 had only 2,700 men (five regiments of cavalry and three regiments of infantry). In 1641–1642, the Duke oscillated between France and Spain to recover his dominion, but with the second invasion of Lorraine the Duke went with Spain again. In 1644 he had a force of 5,400 men, 6,500 in December 1645 and 3,000 men in 1648. The Spanish high command had a poor opinion of the Duke's troops, they were undisciplined, had the tendency to sack friend and foe, and their value in combat was doubtful. In fact the army of the Duke was kept because the Army of Flanders needed all the men available. In 1654, the Duke was arrested, and in 1655 the army of 3,800 men was dissolved and most of its components deserted and joined regiments of the French army.

The Army of the Prince of Condé (1652–1658)

With the revolt of the *Fronde* the Prince of Condé looked for the support of the Spanish against the regime of Mazarin. At first the army of Condé was made of French units, but in 1652 mercenary troops of the Army of Flanders were also transferred to Condé. The army of Condé had 7,000 men in 1653, in 1654 he had a field army of 8,400 men. The next year he could field a sizeable force of 5,000 cavalry and 3,400 men, but only 3,500 cavalry and 2,500 infantry were troops paid directly by him, the other 2,400 men were supplied directly by the Army of Flanders. At the same time the Spanish field army of Flanders had only 3,000 cavalry and 5,000 infantry. At the battle of Valenciennes in 1656, the army of Condé had probably 2,000 infantry, 3,500 cavalry and 300 dragoons (see Chapter 4) and still in 1659, the Prince of Condé had in total 8,200 men in hand. Troops from the Army of Condé had a poor attitude towards the local population, but compared to the Army of Lorraine they fought correctly and the Prince of Condé was an outstanding commander. In reality the main problem was the deep mistrust between Condé, a prince of royal blood, and some of the Spanish officers in Brussels.

The Army of Charles II of England (1656–1660)
With the declaration of war against Spain and Cromwell's treaty with France, Charles II and his Royalist followers were expelled to the Low Countries. The Spanish acknowledged such news in order to create a diversion against England. On 2 April a treaty was signed between Charles and King Philip IV of Spain in which the Spanish promised to support an auxiliary army of 6,000 men (Firth 1902). Recruitment of the Royalist army started in the second half of 1656, and by spring 1657 they numbered between 2,000 and 3,000 men in six regiments. Recruits were Royalist English but above all Scots and Irish. The regiments were the King's own regiment, the Marquis of Livingston's regiment (Scots), the Earl Ormonde's regiment, the Duke of York's regiment, the Duke of Gloucester's regiment and Lord Bristol's or Farrel's regiment (Firth 1902). For the 1657 and 1658 campaign four and five infantry regiments were committed to the Spanish field army and in 1659 the Royalist troops numbered 4,380 men (Maffi 2014). Compared to the Cromwellian regiments, serving in Flanders and later in Portugal, the infantry under the command of the Duke of York had not the same training or motivation, and its action during the Second Battle of the Dunes in 1658 was not impressive.

2.4 The Cavalry of the Spanish Army

2.4.1 Cavalry Troops 1621–1640
At the beginning of Philip IV's reign, the cavalry did not have the same reputation and organisation as the infantry. The major unit for the cavalry was the troop or company with a differentiation for the guards troops, the troops of *caballo coraza* (cuirassiers) and the troops of *arcabucero a caballo* (horse harquebusiers). In reality for each nation a higher command existed and was commanded by a *Comissario General de la Caballeria* (general commissary of the cavalry) of the nation. So for example in the Army of Flanders we would have a the cavalry of ordinance of the country (Walloon), the Spanish cavalry of Flanders (Spanish and Italians) and the foreign cavalry, each of them commanded by a *Comissario General de la Caballeria*. In Lombardy, we would have the cavalry of the State of Milan, the Neapolitan cavalry and the foreign cavalry. The same structure would be repeated in each main army of the monarchy. In Extremadura, we would have the ordinary cavalry (Spanish), the Guardia de Castilla (Spanish) and the Italian cavalry (foreign). Besides this, in each territory we would also have two to five guards troops, some of them lancers (*caballo-lanzas*), for the high-ranking officers of the army.

THE ARMIES OF PHILIP IV OF SPAIN 1621–1665

Table 2.10: Estimate of cavalry troops in the Spanish Army organised in trozos or tercios

Date	Location	Cavalry	Nation	Coy.	Officers	Mounted	Dismounted	Total	Ref.
1644	Catalonia	5 trozos & regiments*	All	40	378	3,356	602	4,336	(a)
1649	Flanders	7 tercios of cavalry	Spanish	31	321	1,525	514	2,340	(b)
1649	Flanders	5 tercios of cavalry	Walloons	22	212	1,020	322	1,554	(b)
1649	Flanders	16 regts. of cavalry	Germans	100	998	5,022	918	6,938	(b)
1662	Extremadura	3 trozos†	Spanish	26	-	-	-	1,245	(c)
1663	Extremadure	Cavalry of Extremadura‡	All	109	598	5,556	219	6,373	(c)

* Trozo of the Cavalry of the Orders, Trozo of the Guardias de Castillas, Trozo of Roussillon, Trozo of Flanders, the Italian cavalry troops of Catalonia and the regiment of Bertho.

† The three trozos are: Trozo of the Cavalry of the Orders (eight troops), Trozo of Rossellon (eight troops) and Trozo of Milan (10 troops)

‡ 11 guards troops (two of José de Austria, two of Duke of San German, two of the captain general of the cavalry D. Correa, one of general lieutenant of the cavalry J. Mazácan, two of the general provost of the army). Trozo of Burgundy (11 troops), trozos of Guardias de Castilla (13 troops), Trozo of Milan (seven troops), Trozo of Fregenal (five troops), Trozo of the Orders (seven troops), Trozo of Flanders (10 troops), Trozo of Rousillon (11 troops), Trozo of Feria (11 troops) and Trozo of Extremadura (13 troops).

(a) Picouet 2014 and *Campaña de 1644*, CODOIN 95, 1893.

(b) J.L. Sanchez, originally at <www.tercios.org> available at <http://caballipedia.es/Plantillas_de_Felipe_IV>, consulted in May 2018, and Clonard (volume 4, 1851).

(c) Estébanez Calderón (volume 2, 1885)

In the ordinance of 1603 (Clonard, volume 4, 1851), the Peninsular troops from the *Guardias de Castilla* were set up at 60 men and in 1633 the number of troops was reduced to 19. For the rest of the territories, troops were in theory 100 men with a *prima plana* of eight men made of a captain and page, a lieutenant and a page, two trumpets, one blacksmith and a cleric, four to five *capo de escuadra* and 88 troopers. Before each campaign the different troops within a nation were deployed in cavalry squadrons, called sometimes *batallón* in old Spanish manuscripts, for the duration of the campaign. Normally, these ad hoc cavalry squadrons were disbanded at the end of the campaign. Spanish, Italian and Walloon troops had the same structure, only mercenaries were organised in regiments. The mercenaries, mostly Germans, were raised in regiments with a similar structure as provided by Spring (2017)[101] and were deployed in two or three squadrons depending of the number of horsemen available. In Table 2.9, we report an estimate of the manpower of troops of cavalry fighting in the different Spanish armies from 1633 to 1647. As we can see, in the army of Extremadura (Estébanez Calderón, olume 1, 1885) the Italian cavalry was commanded by Marcelo Flomarino, *Comissario General de la Caballeria* of the Italian cavalry of Extremadura with a staff of six men and nine troops of cavalry with 52 officers and 328 soldiers. In this case the Italians represented 20 percent of the cavalry of the army.

---

101 In 1639 Bavarian regiments of horse had six to 10 companies (troops) for 230 men for the weakest and 1,000 men for the strongest including dismounted men. An average regiment tended to have 500 men.

Following Table 2.9, if we take into account the muster of 1633, for the Spanish and Walloon cavalry, the average cavalry troop had nine officers and 60 horsemen, while the for the four German regiments they presented five to 10 troops (an average of seven cavalry troops) with an average of 73 officers and 349 horsemen per regiment. In this case each troop had an average of 10 officers and 48 riders.

Using the data for Extremadura in 1643, we have an average troop of three officers and 21 to 37 horsemen for respectively the *Guardias de Castilla* and the ordinary cavalry. The Italians presented an average troop of six officers and 37 horsemen.

In Milan, in 1647, the average cavalry troop of the state of Milan and the Neapolitan cavalry had approximately six officers and 57 to 62 horsemen, for the German regiment we had 10 officers and 86 horsemen. If we do not take into account the variation in officers, a troop in Flanders and Lombardy had more or less 50 to 70 men. In Extremadura the number of troopers and officers seemed to be lower for troops of 20 to 40 men. Guard troops tended to have more men, and in Table 2.9 we have three guards troops with an average of six officers and 100 horsemen.

2.4.2 Tercios and Trozos of Cavalry 1640–1665

The organisation of the cavalry in troops and ad hoc squadrons was not satisfactory because riders had little time to train[102] and fight together as a single unit, implying that their discipline in combat tended to be worse than a formal veteran regiment of cavalry. The low importance given to the cavalry in Flanders and in northern Italy could be explained by the pre-eminence of the infantry in the Spanish military system and by the fact that from 1622 to 1634[103] the main Spanish armies were fighting in countries[104] less suitable to cavalry operations than northern France or Germany.

2.8 Trumpeters of Spanish cavalry at the siege of Jülich in 1622. Mattheus Melijn, 1636. (Rijksmuseum)

---

102 According to Gonzáles de León (2009), in the Army of Flanders officers from cavalry companies had also the tendency to spend most of their time at the court of Brussels instead of training with their men during winter quarters.
103 During the battle of Nördlingen most of the cavalry was provided by the Imperial forces or by the Catholic league. Also after the battle, in their journey to reach the Low Countries, the Spanish army of the Cardinal Infante was "escorted" by an Imperial cavalry corps.
104 The Dutch army was organised in a similar way.

THE ARMIES OF PHILIP IV OF SPAIN 1621–1665

2.9 (above): Spanish lancers, siege of Jülich in 1621/1622. Pieter Snayers, 1622-1650, (Rijksmuseum)

2.10 (right): Spanish cuirassier from first half of 17th century. Paulus (Pauwels) van Hillegaert. (Rijksmuseum)

THE STRUCTURE OF THE SPANISH ARMY

2.11 Spanish cuirassier, siege of Ostend (1601–1604). Sebastiaen Vrancx (Michał Paradowski's archive)

THE ARMIES OF PHILIP IV OF SPAIN 1621–1665

The war against France changed the scope, now the Spanish high command needed a much better cavalry to fight on equal term with their enemies. The first modification arrived with the reorganisation of the cavalry in the Iberian Peninsula after the siege of Salses in 1639–1640. Up to 1638, the main cavalry forces in the area were the 16 troops of the *Guardias de Castilla* and the Cavalry of the Order.[105] In April 1640, the Trozo of Roussillon was formed with the cavalry troops based around Perpignan. It consisted of eight troops of 100 men and in 1643 it was commanded by Andres de Haro. At the same period the Cavalry of the Order was reformed and organised in a trozo of 12 troops. In 1641, from the province of Franche-Comté, a trozo of the Cavalry of Burgundy was formed under the command of the Baron of Bouthier. Later on, during this period others trozos were formed; trozo of the Cavalry of Flanders, trozo of the Cavalry of Castille and a trozo of the Cavalry of Naples. In the muster of 29 April 1644 before the campaign against Lérida, the Spanish Cavalry was organised in five *trozos* and one cavalry regiment with 40 troops, 378 officers, 3,356 mounted horsemen and 602 dismounted horsemen, giving an average of 98 horsemen (15 dismounted) per troop, excluding officers. If we take into account the dismounted men, those numbers are in accordance with the official ones.

In Flanders the poor performance of the Spanish cavalry on the battlefield at the Battle of Rocroi in 1643, the Battle of Lens in 1648 and in numerous small encounters against the French cavalry regiments was a great concern for the Spanish high command. After some delays Archduke Leopold of Austria, governor of Flanders took the decision to recruit as much as possible German cavalry disbanded after

2.12 Spanish harquebusier and lancer, siege of Ostend (1601–1604). Sebastiaen Vrancx. (Michał Paradowski's archive)

---

105 In Spain the three main religious orders were Calatrava (founded in 1146), Santiago (founded in 1170) and Alcantara (founded in 1154). They were created to fight against the Muslim states and support the Christian kingdoms. In the seventeenth century the orders were more of a prestige association than a military force. The Count-Duke Olivares tried to engage the Spanish nobility in the peninsular fighting, but by 1642, of the 1,400 horse from the cavalry of the orders, only one third were actually knights from one of the three orders. In the following years, some knights served as officers but most of the troopers did not belong to the orders.

1648[106] and to reform totally the cavalry units of the Army of Flanders. In 1649, the cavalry of the Army of Flanders was organised in tercios of cavalry for the Spanish, Italian, Burgundian and Walloon troops and in regiments for the foreign cavalry (Table 2.10). A tercio was formed by a *prima plana* of seven men[107] and six cavalry troops of 96 men[108] for a total of 53 officers and 528 horsemen (Clonard, volume 4, 1851). A muster from December 1649, provided by Juan Luis Sanchez,[109] gives a total numbers of 30 tercios and regiments (28 units in Table 2.10), four guard troops, two regiments of dragoons and one regiment of Croats with 188 troops, 1,847 officers, 9,397 mounted horsemen and 2,216 dismounted horsemen, 13,440 men. Following Table 2.10 and excluding officers, the average Spanish troop had 66 horsemen, the average Walloon troop 61 horsemen and the average German troop 59 horsemen. In Catalonia and Flanders we can assume that the officers of the troop's *prima plana* were eight men. Considering the army of Extremadura in 1662, the average troop had 48 men, including officers and in 1663 the 10 trozos had from five to 13 troops and the average troop had 53 horsemen, excluding officers. For the officers if we take into account seven men for the *prima plana* of each trozo we arrive to an average of 4.8 officers per troop, a number much lower than that found for the troops in Flanders.

The organisation in trozos / tercios gradually enhanced the efficiency of the Spanish cavalry in Flanders and in the Iberian Peninsula. In Lombardy, it is difficult to understand why any reorganisation of the cavalry of the State of Milan was carried out.

To finish our study we must add that the first companies of dragoons were formed in 1632 in Lombardy, even if we find others in the armies of Catalonia and Extremadura. In Extremadura, some companies were formed in 1641 but they had very bad press (White 2003), and they were disbanded probably in 1643. In Catalonia a tercio of dragoons for formed in 1643 commanded by Antonio Pellicer but it was disbanded the next year. In Lombardy, the first companies were formed by Pedro de Santacecilia y Pax and in 1634 in the army of the Cardinal Infante, we could find the five companies of Pedro de Santacecilia y Pax with 500 dragoons (Engerisser & Hrncirik 2009). In the Army of Lombardy, from 1640 to 1648, we find five companies with 408 to 560 dragoons and in 1647, the five companies had 44 officers and 503 soldiers (Ribot Garcia, 1990). In Flanders we do not find any indication of a company of dragoons.

---

106 From September 1649 to June 1651 up to 5,550 German veteran horsemen were hired by the Archduke to strengthen the cavalry force of the Army of Flanders (D. Maffi 2006). "Il potere delle armi. La monarchia spagnola e i suoi eserciti (1635–1700): una rivisitazione del mito della decadenza", *Rivista storica italiana*, 118(2), pp. 394–445.

107 *Maestro de Campo* (captain of the first company), *Sargento Mayor* (captain of the second company) and five men: secretary, account auditor, major surgeon, *capitan barrachel* and major cleric.

108 A captain, a lieutenant, an *alférez*, two trumpets, one blacksmith, a furrier, a cleric, five cabos and 83 soldiers.

109 Available at <http://caballipedia.es/Plantillas_de_Felipe_IV>, consulted May 2018, originally at <www.tercios.org>.

2.5. The Artillery of the Spanish Army

The infantry and cavalry could have thousands of men and a strict organisation; for the artillery we have nothing of that. Artillerymen were rare, musters of the seventeenth century in the Army of Lombardy or in the Army of Flanders rarely give more than 400 men (Maffi 2014). At that time, artillery had a static component and a mobile one. The static component was made of all the guns available in the Castles and fortresses of the province. In the State of Milan, the 18 fortresses had up to 400 guns in 1674.[110] In 1647 the artillery available to defend Lérida was 41 guns, but most of them were light guns.[111] For the mobile part, the artillery of the Spanish army did not have any organisation like the tercios of infantry or the companies in the cavalry. The military structure was a captain general of the artillery of Spain followed by a captain general of the artillery (*Capitán General de la Artillería*) in each territory, and the lieutenants of the captain general of the artillery (*Teniente de Capitán General de la Artillería*). After these officers came directly the men in charge of the guns, and the members of the artillery train. In 1609, with the publication of a royal decree, the Spanish artillery was officially standardised to four calibres:[112] full-cannon of 40 pounds, half-cannon of 24 pounds, quarter-cannon of 10 to 12 pounds[113] and light guns called quarter-culverin or saker of four to seven pounds. The first two guns were heavy guns (7,500 pounds for the full-cannon and 4,500 pounds for the half-cannon) and designed to breach walls during a siege operation. The quarter-cannon and lighter guns could be used in the battlefield but they were heavy. With the Thirty Years' War running, all belligerents tried to lighten their guns[114] in order to give them more mobility on the battlefield. In 1630, the Army of Lombardy was using an even lighter gun of four pounds (Maffi 2014). In 1638 the Spanish designed a new light gun called Mansfelts[115] or *Mansfelte* firing normally iron balls of five to six pounds or canister shot. With the heavier sakers, quarter-culverins and quarter-cannon they formed the field artillery.

Even with the attempt to standardise artillery guns most of the older weapons were still in use and foundries were still making guns with different calibres, such as the five half-cannon of 20 pounds made in Seville in 1622. In Spain guns were made in bronze or iron in the foundries or arsenals of

---

110 *Relación de todas las municiones y pertrechos de Guerra que faltan en todas plazas y castillos deste estado comprendidos en ellos el de Mila* ... Archivo General de Simancas E Leg. 3385 doc. 209, 1674.
111 Following Gonzalo et al. (1991) the artillery of the city of Lérida had of one full-cannon of 45 pounds (with 88 cannonballs), three half-cannons of 20 pounds (with 1,337 cannonballs), 10 quarter-cannons of 10 and 12 pounds (with 4,002 cannonballs), the rest being 18 lighter guns (sakers, mansfelts and falconets) of one and half to six pounds. In the Castle of Gardenny, near Lérida, the Spanish had nine guns, one half-cannon, five quarter-cannons, two sakers of four pounds and one falconet of one and a half pounds.
112 In Spanish sources of the seventeenth and eighteenth century the calibre corresponds to the calibre of the cannonball.
113 In reality you could find quarter-cannons from 10 to 16 pounds.
114 In Swedish service light 3-pounder bronze guns, called regimental cannons, appear in 1629 and were used extensively in 1631 at the Battle of Breitenfeld (Brzezinski & Hook, 1993).
115 Verdera Franco, "La evolución de la artillería", in *Los ingenieros militares de la Monarquía Hispánica en los siglos XVII y XVIII*, Spanish Ministry of Defence, 2005.

THE STRUCTURE OF THE SPANISH ARMY

2.13 (top): Artillery of Spanish garrison leaving Maastricht in 1632. Jan van de Velde (II), after Jan Martszen the Younger, 1632. (Rijksmuseum)

2.14: Spanish garrison leaving Maastricht in 1632. Jan van de Velde (II), after Jan Martszen the Younger, 1632. (Rijksmuseum)

Malaga, Seville, Burgos, Guipúzcoa, Lieganes, Lisbon, Barcelona, Naples, Milan or Mechelen in Flanders. At the beginning of the seventeenth century most of those factories were in private hands but due to the poor quality of their production some of them were later bought by the state.

On the Catalan front, the Spanish artillery trains had 12 to 30 guns. For example for the siege of Leucate in 1637, the Spanish army had an artillery train of 14 guns of 36 to 40 pounds and 23 lighter ones from two to 12 pounds. In 1640, for the first attack on Barcelona, the army of Marques of Le Velez had an artillery train of 24 guns (probably half of them were light guns and the others being half-cannons and quarter-cannons) with 250 gunners. Later on during the war, artillery trains used to have eight to 12 light guns for the field army and probably up to 30 guns for the army engaged in siege operations. In August 1651, the initial siege train of 20 guns for the operation against Barcelona was made of two half-cannons, six quarter-cannons, six sakers and six Mansfelts.

The artillery train was the artillery "unit" of the armies integrated by the men and the animals to move the guns and to transport the ammunition and all the tools needed to maintain such weapons. In all armies an artillery train could be formed for the campaign. The accepted rule was to have one or three guns for 1,000 men. for the siege of Leucate in 1637, the Spanish army had an artillery train of 14 guns of 36 to 40 pounds and 23 lighter ones from two to 12 pounds, 37 guns for an army of 13,300 men giving a ratio of 2.78 guns for 1,000 men. In 1640 the governor of Flanders had 112 field guns distributed in the different corps of his field armies,[116] a ratio of three guns for 1,000 men (Maffi 2014). In 1642, the main Spanish army of de Melo had up to 30 heavy and medium guns to bombard La Bassée. In 1645, the Duke of Amalfi[117] made a distribution of the available 32 guns with the main army of 16,000 men facing the French, 14 guns with the 12,000 strong army facing the Dutch and 12 guns for the small army of 6,000 men defending the Duchy of Luxembourg; in total 58 guns for 34,000 men giving a ratio of 1.71 guns for 1,000 men.[118] In August 1651, as we have seen, the siege artillery train for the operation against Barcelona had 20 guns for an army of 12,000 men giving a ratio of 1.67 guns for 1,000 men.

2.6 Weapons and Equipment

2.6.1 Pikeman, Harquebusier and Musketeer

The Spanish had been the first to combine efficiently the use of pikes and firearms in the sixteenth century in order to fight successfully against the heavy cavalry. In the seventeenth century the infantry was still the main element of the Spanish forces, the one with more prestige and reputation. Each infantryman had a speciality and was armed either with a pike or with a firearm, harquebus or musket but all of them had swords and most of them a dagger. For most of the people of that time, the sword was the distinction between soldiers and old soldiers from a common civilian. Of course noblemen had also a sword but the function and the type of sword was somehow different. The recommendation for a military sword of the middle of the seventeenth century for the infantry was a blade of 73 cm long, a shorter version than the ones used in the previous century (Rodríguez Hernández, 2015). Generally, for most of the raw recruits the sword was provided by the state, later on a veteran after several years in the army would buy or steal a better weapon. Spanish and Italian soldiers tended to be better trained than the others due to the fact that fencing was popular in those countries and that a lot of manuals were available.

---

116 Twelve guns with the corps defending the province of Flanders, 26 guns with the army facing the Dutch, eight with the troops in the province of Güeldres, 24 in Luxembourg and 48 with the main army.

117 Archivo Historico Nacional, E Lib. 978, el duque de Amalfi a don Miguel de Salamanca 2-01-1645.

118 By comparison at the battle of Jankow 1645, the Swedish had a ratio of 3.75 guns for 1,000 men and the Imperials 1.73. At the Second Battle of Nördlingen, the French had a ratio of 1.59 and the Bavarians 1.75 (Bonney, 2002).

2.15 Details of polearms of Spanish troops. Diego Velázquez's Surrender of Breda in 1625 (Michał Paradowski's archive)

The main weapon of the pikeman was a pike 5.0 to 5.4 m long (24 to 25 palmos[119]), rarely 4.8 m with an average diameter of 3.5 cm at the thickest part and a weight between three and four kilogrammes. The pike was made with robust wood such as ash with a steel head on the top. The head could be of the broad leaf shape, of square or a triangular section spike. The socket head was attached to the wooden shaft by 30–50 cm steel strips. Normally the pike had a steel ring at its base. Other pole weapons could be used such as halberd, partisan and chuzos,[120] when the fight occurred during a siege, or to take/defend a fortification, or to protect a detachment of harquebusiers. Pikemen were supposed to wear half-armour, consisting of back- and breastplates, gorget, pauldrons at the shoulder, tassets at the belly and groin and a helmet. In the sixteenth and seventeenth centuries, *morion* was the Spanish word for helmet, some of them could have a high-raised comb on a skull of clamshell shape and others a flat brim with an almond-shaped skull and narrow horizontal brim called a *capacete* (Lopez, 2012). The cost

---

119 A *palmo* was a unit from Castile equivalent to 20.873 cm.
120 The chuzo was a short version of the pike. It existed in two versions, the most common of which was 3.5 to 3.7 m and a shorter version of 2.3–2.5 m. typically this weapon was used aboard the ships and galleys of the armada. The weapon was also provided to new recruits when there was a shortage of pike (*Breve historia de los tercios*).

Table 2.11: Distribution of the soldiers by speciality following ordinance and from musters. Data from Parker (1990), de Mesa (2014) and the *Relación Verdadera de Todo lo Sucedido en los condado de Rosellon y Cerdaña*, University of Seville, A 111/008(24).

Year	Location	Pikemen	Harquebusiers	Musketeers	Ratio F/P
1617	Ordinance (Flanders)	43.0%	45.8%	11.2%	1.3
1632	Ordinance (Spain)	37.7%	37.2%	25.1%	1.7
1636	Ordinance (Flanders)	31.6%	11.3%	57.1%	2.2
1601	Flanders	37.4%	39.5%	23.1%	1.7
1639	Catalonia[26]	34.5%	33.3%	32.2%	1.9
1644	Extremadura	28.0%	41.4%	30.6%	2.6
1685	Flanders	33.0%	34.0%	33.0%	2.0

* For the two provincial tercios of Catalonia, we have 31.2 percent of pikemen, 44.6 percent of harquebusiers and 24.2 percent of musketeers. In the five tercios extracted from the militia, numbers were 27.8 percent of pikemen, 66.0 percent of harquebusiers and 6.1 percent of musketeers.

of a pike was six *reales de a plata*, and the salary of the pikeman was only four escudos/month (64 *reales de a plata*). In fact only veteran soldiers from the tercios or from German regiments were correctly armed, the other pikemen had probably only a helmet, and a back- and breastplate at best. Also, starting in the 1640s and 1650s, pikemen tended to drastically reduce their armour to the strict minimum or to have none at all. The reason was not only the weight of armour,[121] which was an inconvenience for soldiers, but the efficiency of such steel plate against a musket ball was limited or nil at close range. In reality armour was effective against the steel pike head but fighting between two pike formations was rare in the seventeenth century in comparison with combats of the previous century. The same tendency was observed in other armies in Europe: by 1640 armoured pikemen were rare in the Swedish infantry in Germany (Brzezinski & Hook, 1991).

The other category of soldiers, harquebusiers and musketeers were taking more and more a protagonist role over the years. The harquebus[122] was a weapon created at the beginning of the sixteenth century and in the seventeenth it was still in use even if the weapon of the seventeenth century was probably very different from that of the sixteenth. The musket, deployed in 1567 on the battlefield, was a heavier and more powerful weapon. The equipment of the harquebusier was of course a smoothbore matchlock

---

[121] For a suit of armour from Augsburg (1620), the estimated weight of helmet, gorget, breastplate, backplate and tassets is 7.3 kg and the full set with pauldrons and gauntlets rises to 12.4 kg (Spring 2017). A recreation of a sixteenth and seventeenth century armour set gives for helmet, gorget, breastplate and tassets a weight of 8.0–8.2 kg. The full half-armour (1570–1620) is given at 16.5 kg. (<https://lacasadelrecreador.com>, consulted in September 2018). Finally full pikeman's armour from the Graz armoury weighed between eight and 16 kg (Brnadic & Pavlovic, 2009).

[122] "Caliver" was the name for an harquebus in England, *rohr* or *schützenrohr* in Germany, *roer* in Holland and *rör* in Sweden (Schürger 2015).

harquebus, two powder flasks,[123] one or two match cords wrapped around the belt, a bag full of spherical lead bullets[124] and tools[125] to make the bullet. For protection the harquebusier had of course a sword and daggers and most of the time a helmet. The musketeer had exactly the same equipment but with a heavier weapon that might required the use of a rest.[126] In both case the soldiers could use a *bandolier of charges* with 12 small capped wood "bottles" or leather tubes of coarse gunpowder to deliver 12 shots. Later on, paper cartridge with the bullet and the correct amount of powder were delivered. Normally the musketeer did not have a helmet but more commonly a broad-brimmed hat.[127] In 1615 the full equipment, weapon included, had a cost of 35 *reales de plata* for a harquebusier and 50 *reales de plata* for a musketeer.

For both weapons the way to use them was to pour into the muzzle 50 to 70 percent of the weight of the bullet of gunpowder, load the bullet and push it into place using a ramrod. On the other side of the weapon the flash pan was primed with the finer-ground gunpowder from the *frasquillo*. The harquebusier then lit the matchcord and placed it in the serpentine. When the harquebusier or musketeer pressed the trigger the serpentine made a rotation to bring the burning matchcord to the flash pan, creating an intense flame that would pass through a touchhole to ignite the main gunpowder in the barrel. The explosion in the gun barrel would send the lead bullet at a velocity of 200–300 g m/s.

2.6.2 Harquebus and Musket

Following different ancient and modern sources (Lechuga 1611, Albi de la Cuesta 1999), in the first half of the seventeenth century the Spanish harquebus was typically firing a spherical lead bullet of 3/4 to 1 oz[128] (so, 21.6 g to 28.8 g if we use the ounce of Castile and 22.9 g to 30.5 g if we use the ounce of Viscaya). The gun barrel was between 95–105 cm giving a total length from 120 and 130 cm and a weight from four to five kilogrammes, so no musket rest was needed. In the instructions given to the arsenal of Placencia (Viscaya in the Basque Country) in 1652, the gun barrel should have at least a length of 102 cm to fire a bullet of one ounce (Rodríguez Hernández, 2015). The range of the weapon

---

123 The first was a small container (*frasquillo* in Spanish) with a fine-ground gunpowder of small grain size to be used in the flash pan. The second was a bigger flask (*frasco* in Spanish) containing some 690 g of powder with less refined grains. The powder from the second flask was used with the bullet in a proportion of 50 to 60 percent (depending of the powder quality) of the weight of the bullet (Lechuga, 1611).
124 It was recommended for a harquebusier to carry 50 bullets, while the musketeer had 25.
125 Normally each soldier received a "pasta" of lead and a pincer mould called a *turquesa* to make their bullets. Because each soldier was making his bullets, they were small variations between bullets and the shape of the bullet was not a perfect sphere. Due to differences in the making of weapons, the mould was provided with the firearm.
126 The rest or fork was used, as a normal musket had a weight from 7.5 to 10 kg. The rest was a staff with a rowlock-like fork at the upper end in which the barrel of the musket could rest. In Spanish service the size of the rest was 146 cm.
127 Wise musketeers continued to wear metal skullcap called a *secrete* under their hat (Brnadic, Pavlovic, 2009).
128 The ounce in Castile was 28.75 g, in Milan 27.38 g, in Valencia 22.19 g, in Viscaya 30.50 g and in Zaragoza 21.88 g.

was 200–220 m but after 75 m it was imprecise and it was recommended to fire at 50 m or less. The musket was a bigger weapon, able to fire lead bullet with a weight of 1.5 to 2 oz (43 to 57.5 g if we use the Castilian ounce). The instruction given to the arsenal of Placencia (Viscaya in the Basque Country) in 1656 indicates that the minimum barrel length was 118 cm.

A typical Spanish musket (Picouet 2014) weighed between 7.5 and 9 kg and maybe more (> 10 kg) in some cases. So with a gun barrel of more or less 120±5 cm, we can expect a total length of 140–150 cm. So while the harquebus could be used like that, a rest of 146 cm (7 palmos) was required to fire a musket.

Soldiers of the Spanish king were also using weapons made all over Europe, so let us see what was used elsewhere in the seventeenth century. By the 1640s the French army was using only muskets, and harquebus or caliver[129] were removed from service.

The ordinary musket, probably similar to the one introduced in 1600 by the Dutch, fired a bullet of 38–40 g (12 to the pound) weighing 7.0 to 7.5 kg and using a rest. Rapidly a lighter musket was used and following Louis de Gaya (1678), it had a length of 151.7 cm, a gun barrel of 119.2 mm, a weight of 6.2 kg or less (no rests) and fired a bullet of some 38 g.

Other muskets made in Germany were probably used, and from 1630 a new generation of light German musket (Engerisser 2009) with a length of 140 cm, a gun barrel of 102 cm (bore calibre of 19.7 mm), a weight of 4.5–4.7 kg, firing, in theory, 12 bullets to the pound (18.5 to 18.8 mm giving a weight of some 35 g). Following the same source, lighter muskets were also produced with a bore calibre of 17.4 to 18 mm firing a bullet with a calibre of 16.8 mm (28–29 g). In Swedish service (Brzezinski & Hook 1991), the "light musket" had a normal barrel length of 118.5 cm or shorter, 114 cm a weight of 6.4 kg and a bore calibre of 19.6 mm.

Nonetheless, for all belligerents, the weight of the lead bullet is probably overestimated and new information is available thanks to different authors (Foard 2009 and Schürger 2015). Archaeological evidence from the Rakovnik (1620), Edgehill (1642) or Lützen (1632) battlefields reveals interesting data. At Rakovnik, where tercios from the Spanish army participated (the Walloon tercio of Bucquoy and Neapolitan tercio of Spinelli), the average weight for a musket bullet was 23 g (average diameter 16.1 mm) and for a harquebus 19 g (average diameter 14.7 mm). At Lützen the largest bullets had a diameter of 18.9–19.9 mm (bullet calibre 20 mm) and came from a 7.5 kg musket (Schürger 2015). The most common bullet had a diameter from 15.9 mm to 17.2 mm with a peak at 16.4 mm. For Schürger (2015), those bullets were fired mainly by muskets made in Suhl (Germany) and Amsterdam (Holland) with a respective bullet calibre of 16.8 and 17 mm. In this case the original bullet at a maximum weight of 28.2 to 29.2 g. From Edgehill battlefield (Foard 2009) musket bullets had a weight from 27 to 40 g and caliver/harquebus bullets a weight from 21 g to 26 g (diameter 15.2 to 16.4 mm).

---

[129] "Caliver" was the name used in England and Holland for harquebus at the end of the sixteenth century and the beginning of the seventeenth.

Table 2.12: Estimate of the number of men in a squadron/battalion deployed during battles fought in the seventeenth century.

Year	Battle	Army	Infantry Squadron	Cavalry Squadron	Ref.
1622	Fleurus	Flanders	1,300	250	Du Cornet[a]
1635	Les Avins	Flanders	1,100	-	Sanchez (2003)
1635	Morbegno	Lombardy	1,300		Engerisser & Hrncirik 2009
1636	Tornavento	Lombardy	900	-	Maffi (2014b)[b]
1638	Saint-Omer	Flanders	1,000	-	Ceballos y Arce[c]
1639	Salses	Catalonia	880[d]	-	Arcon & Martinez (1998)
1641	Montjuich	Catalonia	1,000	-	Esteban Ribas, 2016[e]
1642	Honnecourt	Flanders	750	150	Picouet (2008)
1643	Rocroi	Flanders	820	190	Picouet (2008)
1644	Montijo	Extremadura	610	< 120	Estébanez Calderón (1885)
1644	Lérida I	Catalonia	730	< 100	Picouet (2014)
1645	Proh	Lombardy	500	110	Picouet (2010)
1646	Lérida II	Catalonia	540	150	Picouet (2014)
1648	Lens	Flanders	500	<150	Fuensaldaña[f]
1650	Tortosa	Catalonia	400	-	Mortara[g]
1656	Valenciennes	Flanders	460	<120	*Relación…*[h]
1658	Les Dunes	Flanders	500	120	Picouet 2010
1663	Ameixial	Extremadura	700–750[i]	110	de Menezes 1751

a. Seigneur du Cornet, *Histoire générale des guerres de Savoie de bohème du palatinat & des Pays-Bas*, volume second, A.L.P. de Roubaulx de Soumoy. *Collection des Mémoire à l'Histoire de Belgique*, Brussels 1869.

b. Maffi (2014b), "La victoria inútil: Tornavento (22 de junio de 1636)" in *Desperta Ferro, Richelieu contra Olivares, Francia en la Guerra de los Treinta Años*.

c. Lorenzo Ceballos y Arce, *Sucessos de Flandes en los años 37, 38, 29 y 40*, Colección de Libros Españoles Raros ó Curiosos, volume 14, Madrid 1880.

d. The number is given for the 7,000 infantry (eight *bataillons*) involved in the fighting to repulse a French attack in November 1639.

e. A.R. Estiban Ribas (2016), "La batalla de Montjuic", in *Desperta Ferro* <https://www.despertaferro-ediciones.com>.

f. We have 5,000 Spanish in 10 battalions. *Carta original del condé de Fuensaldaña à SM con relación de la batalla que se tuvo junto a Lens…* pp. 491–495, Estudios del reinado de Felipe IV, in *Obras de A. Canovas del Castillos* volume 2, Madrid, 1888.

g. Marques de Olías y de Mortara, *Conquista de Cataluña*, 1655.

h. For the infantry, the data is without officers. *Relación de la campaña del año 1656 en los estado de Flandes*, BNE H86, folios 344–349.

i. If we take into account 9,000 infantry deployed in 12–13 battalions.

So a Spanish harquebus was probably firing bullets of 16 to 23 g, and a Spanish musket bullet from 28 to 47 g. Those data indicates that in the seventeenth century the harquebus was still a useful weapon and that the Spanish musket was heavier than its counterpart and could fire a heavier bullet at a longer range. In Spanish service, such weapons were used by the Spanish and Italian tercios but the other nationalities used a musket similar to the ones in service in the Dutch army.[130]

2.6.3 Cavalry Equipment

Caballos Corazas and *Arcabuceros a Caballos* were the main type of horsemen in Spanish service. In relation with the trends followed by European armies, the Spanish cavalry progressively abandoned the three-quarter armour in favour of lighter protection. Therefore, in the forties the *Caballos Corazas* lost armour and became equipped with only front and back plates and a burgonet helmet, sometimes replaced by a wide brimmed hat.[131] Their main weapon was a pair of wheellock pistols carried in holsters located each side on the saddle and a straight sword designed for piercing and slashing.[132] For the *Arcabuceros a Caballos* the principal weapon was a wheellock harquebus[133] or a carbine supplemented by a straight sword and a one or two wheellock pistols.[134] They had less or no protection and relied instead on a buff coat or just a shirt to protect the thorax. For the head, the *Arcabuceros a Caballos* had a burgonet helmet, which was most of the time replaced by the felt hat. Their equipment was complemented by the necessary accessories for their harquebus: bullet pouch, priming flasks, powder flasks and wheellock spanner. In Spanish service sometimes the task of the *Arcabuceros a Caballos* was closer to that of dragoons in other armies, even if they normally had better horses. Sometimes the differentiation between the *Caballos Corazas* and *Arcabuceros a Caballos* was marginal and more related to the quality of the horses, the best ones being for the *Caballos Corazas* and the worst *for Arcabuceros a Caballos*. The distribution between them was probably 20–30 percent *Arcabuceros a Caballos* and 70–80 percent *Caballos Corazas*. For Walloon cavalry or German horsemen, most of them were cuirassiers, similar to the *Caballo Coraza*. From 1621 to maybe 1640, the typical Caballo Lanza[135] was equipped with lance, a pistol, a straight sword and for his

---

130 A. Rodrigues Hernández, "Evolución o Innovación, Los cambios técnico-tácticos en el armamento del ejército español durante el relevo dinástico: nueva consideración", *Cuaderno Historia Moderna* vol.41, pp. 273–294, 2016.
131 With the hot weather in Catalonia and Extremadura, most of the horsemen tended to have wide hats with a steel cap under their hat and not a full closed helmet. In Flanders and northern Italy, a helmet was more common.
132 The typical cavalry sword was a broadsword such as the Walloons' basket-hilted sword, weighing 0.95 kg for a length of 99 cm.
133 The wheellock harquebus was smaller than the common matchlock ones used by the infantry. (Brnardic & Pavlovic, 2010).
134 Pistols were a wheellock-fired weapon that could be used with one hand, while for the use of the carbine and small harquebus of the cavalry two hands were required. Pistol bullets tended to have a diameter from 11.2 to 11.7 mm, giving a weight of nine to 10 g (Schürger 2015).
135 For example the companies from the *Guardias de Castilla* started to introduce wheellock pistols with the ordinance of 1633.

protection he normally had three-quarter armour and a closed helmet. Such riders were only maintained in the guards companies, but after 1640 it is unclear if the Spanish still had horsemen equipped with a lance.

2.7 Tactics

Most of the time Spanish tercios were deployed in regions (Low Countries and Lombardy) where the famous trace *Italienne* fortification existed (Parker 2003). In such an area, common pitched battles were rare or irrelevant because a defeated army could quickly be reorganised, protected by a network of fortresses. So for the Spanish army the main task was to keep such a network of fortresses in place and to disrupt the one of their enemies. Battles were considered a very risky business when crucial veteran troops could be destroyed and were avoided most of the time. Generals, and particularly Spanish generals, would tend to adopt a more cautious attitude and would risk a pitched battle when they had no other option or when the pride and the prestige of the monarchy were at risk. So for the common soldiers, the main military activities were garrison duties and sieges, coupled with skirmishes and raiding parties in enemy territories.[136] Pitched battle were rare but all soldiers had to be prepared for it.

2.7.1 Weapons Distribution Between Soldiers

In the tercio, the *Sargento Mayor* had the task of drawing the battle formation, called a squadron. The first task of *Sargento Mayor* was to count the number of men and specially the number of pikemen available in the tercio. Following Table 2.11 regarding the ordinances of 1617, 1632, and 1636, the percentage of pikemen was respectively 36.7 percent, 37.7 percent and 31.6 percent and the ratio of shooters and pikemen 1.3, 1.7 and 2.2. For some musters we have the data with the distribution of specialities of the soldiers and they are not too far away from the ordinance. In the 1600s, the distribution between specialities in the four Spanish tercios of the Army of Flanders was 37.4 percent pikes, 39.5 percent harquebusiers and 23.1 percent musketeers, those values are close to the ordinance of 1632 for the tercios raised in Spain. For the other years, in 1639 the regular and provincial Spanish[137] tercios of the Army of Catalonia had 34.5 percent of pikemen (the data gives from 22.5 percent to 38.9 percent), 33.3 percent harquebusiers, and 32.2 percent musketeers.

In 1644, the number of pikemen goes down to 28.0 percent, with 41.4 percent harquebusiers and 30.6 percent musketeers. In the last case the ratio of shooters / pikemen is 2.6. Following Rodríguez Hernández (2015), after a decrease, the proportion of pikemen was maintained at more or less 30–33

---

136 In a sense, low intensity warfare as defined by Paul Azan (*Un Tacticien du XII siècle*, Librairie Militaire Chapelot et C°, Paris 1904).
137 In the same musters we have also data from the Irish Tercio of Tyrconnell with 30 percent pikemen and 70 percent musketeers and the Neapolitan Tercio of Tuttavilla with 27.4 percent pikemen, 28.3 percent harquebusiers and 44.2 percent musketeers.

percent in the half of the second seventeenth century due to the need to protect the harquebusiers and musketeers from the French cavalry. In 1685, we find those proportions of 33 percent pikemen, 34 percent harquebusiers and 33 percent musketeers. So for most of the period we will have between 28 to 35 percent of pikemen and for the shooters, probably more musketeers in the Army of Flanders and in the Army of Lombardy and more harquebusiers in the armies of the Iberian peninsula.

2.7.2 Tactical Squadron Formation in Use in the Spanish Army

When the *Sargento Mayor* decided to form the tactical "squadron" he would adopt a formation according to the terrain, the number of men, the mission accorded to his unit and the type of enemy. Since the sixteenth century, the Spanish had different formations, such as the *cuadro de terreno* (field square), *cuadro de gente* (square of men), *cuadro prolongado* (extended square) and *cuadro de gran frente* (wide-fronted square). To all of them we should add also the squadron *vacio* (empty squadron). In order to form the squadron the basic rules were that a soldier in the pike formation should occupy an area of 0.32 x 0.32 m with a space of 0.32 cm of each side, 0.96 cm in front of him and 0.96 behind him. So the distance between two pikemen was 0.64 cm, for the harquebusiers and musketeers the distance was wider (0.96 to 1.24 cm) in order to avoid accidents when handling the powder and burning match.

To form a squadron the Spanish designed a simple equation based on a square root (sqrt) calculation (Quatrefage 1988) to determine the number of ranks and files. The number of files could be estimated as $F = \sqrt{N \times P}$ and the number of ranks $R = N/F$, Where N is the number of pikemen and P a parameter designing the type of squadron, 1/1 for the *cuadro de gente*, 2/1 for *cuadro de terreno* (twice as many files as ranks), 7/3 for the *cuadro prolongado* (seven files to three ranks), and 3/1 for the *cuadro de gran frente* (three times as many files as ranks). To help in his task, the *Sargento Major* could use tables to calculate the square root, like the ones published in 1643 by Josep Doms (1643) or by Gerat Barry in 1634. Other authors such as Davila Orejón Gastón (1669) indicated that the calculation of the square root was a waste of time and suggested that in most cases the depth of the pike blocks was between five to nine ranks.

The block of pikes was therefore created with the pikemen of the first company forming the first files to the required depth and the rest formed with men from the other companies. The best-equipped men were always at the front, facing the enemy, and the worst and raw recruits at the back. When the pike block was done, it was common practice (Quatrefage, 1983) to split the block in two to leave a space of one to two ranks for the *banderas*.

Flanking the central core of pikes there would always be two linear detachments of harquebusiers called *guarnision*, with a frontage of three to five men to give fire support in all circumstances. The pike and the two *guarnision* was the basic brick of the tactical squadron.

As suggested by Gerat Barry (1634), it is possible that the pike block might also be protected by detachments of musketeers and harquebusiers in front and in the rearguard deployed in three to five ranks.[138] The rest of the shooters were grouped in strong detachments of 100 to 400 men called *mangas* ("sleeves" in English). In the seventeenth century, *mangas* were normally deployed in six to nine ranks, Davila Orejón Gastón (1669) gives an average number of seven ranks. *Mangas* could fight alongside the core tactical squadron or detached from it. In this last case, they were normally accompanied by halberdiers to provide support against troopers in case of sudden attack. Depending on the number of musketeers available, *mangas* could be made only by musketeers or harquebusiers or with a mix of them. In this case in seems (J. Doms, 1643) that the musketeers and harquebusiers were grouped in detachment with a frontage of five men and a depth of three to nine ranks.[139] Concerning the officers on the battlefield (captains, *alférez*, sergeants, drummers and *abanderados*), most of the *alférez* and *abanderados* were in the middle of the block of pike with the *banderas*, or in the first front ranks of the block of pikes.[140] The drummers were placed behind the pike block, some of the sergeants were around the pike block to maintain discipline and the rest with the *mangas* of shooters. The majority of the captains were with the *mangas* and the rest in the front line of the pike block. In comparison with the pike block, the *mangas* were detachments with a more open order that required tied discipline to resist the enemy fire, so the majority of the captains and sergeants were with them. Finally, to reinforce discipline in combat and to conduct detachments of shooters, the Spanish tercios could use the *reformados* as non-commissioned officers.

The Spanish system emphasised cooperation between the pikes and the shooters; against infantry, the shooters would fire regularly on the enemy to weaken their formation and the block of pike would advance at a slow pace (1 m/s) while pikemen would lift their weapons horizontally to come "point to point" in a movement called the push of pike. In the following great melee and hand-to-hand struggle, harquebusiers and musketeers would draw their swords or use their weapons like a club to support the pikemen.

Normally such combat would last some minutes before one of the two squadrons would withdraw, or the two sides would separate to reorganise the squadrons (Hanlon 2016). In a fight between two infantry formations, the first men to retire would be those in the rear followed by the rest when they knew that they could not hold the lines (Chalines 1999). Against the cavalry, shooters had little chance if their fire proved to be useless; they had to find cover behind or in the block of pike. In this case the pikemen would present a dense array of steel points, with the pike held diagonally, the butt end in the earth and the steel point facing the horse or the rider. Horses were not trained to impale themselves on a pike and normally refused to go further. We have seen before that the tercio of 3,000 men did not exist in practice in the seventeenth century and when they were deployed in battle

---

138 They could also be called garrison-like (Gerat Barry, 1634).
139 In his book, Melchor de Alcazar y Zuñiga (1703) presents diagrams of small blocks of pike surrounded by small detachments of musketeers or harquebusiers.
140 When not all the colours were deployed, the remaining *alférez* were with the front rank of the block of pikes.

in a tactical squadron. In Table 2.12 we present a compilation of the tactical squadron battle strength for the main battles fought by the Spanish army between 1621 and 1665. The table shows that from 1622 to 1640, battle formation could have between 1,000 to 1,300 men (officers and soldiers) later on; the tendency was a decrease of the size of the squadron to a minimum of 600–850 men in the period 1642–1644 and 400–600 men until the end of the reign. At Rocroi in 1643, we had already tactical squadrons of 820 men,[141] and in Montijo in 1644, the average tactical squadron had only 610 men deployed in six ranks.[142] In 1658, the Spanish had infantry squadrons of 500 men deployed for the Second Battle of the Dunes. Coming back to Davila Orejón Gastón (1669), the norm of 600 to 800 men per infantry squadron seems to be common in the Army of Flanders after 1635.[143] An important fact regarding the Spanish army, was the tendency to form ad hoc battle squadrons[144] or special detachments[145] of 400 to 1,000 men for a special task. In Spanish they were called *escuadrón volante* ("Flying Squadrons") and to form these, detachments of shot and pikes could be extracted from different tercios or regiments. Such units were particularly adapted to warfare in the Low Countries and to attack dykes or fortified positions (Albi de la Cuesta 2015). It seems also that the purpose of the Spanish high command of such ad hoc units was also to share losses and glory for tercios and regiments present in the army.

2.7.3 Firing Tactics

In Spanish service, firepower was delivered on the one hand by the two *garrisons*, flanking the block of pikes, and on the other hand by the *mangas*, detachments of 100 to 400 men, that could support the block of pikes or fight alone. From the *mangas*, smaller detachments of 15 to 45 men could be extracted to skirmish with their enemies. The idea of the Spanish firing system was to maintain a constant fire on their enemy, and with the weapons of the seventeenth century musketeers or harquebusiers had to spend some time reloading and could not fire more than four or five times before being obliged to cool down their weapon. Therefore to keep firing for hours, the Spanish would use their *mangas* to regularly reinforce a block of pikes by a constant rotation of detachments of shooters. In battles such as Nördlingen in 1634, Tornavento in 1636, or Rho in 1645, the Spanish used such a rotation of *mangas* of shooters to maintain a constant fire on their enemy.

---

141 For the battle of Rocroi, in the last stand of the Spanish tercios, the size of the squadron was judged to be too small to resist the attack of the French, therefore, in order to stiffen their resistance the Spanish decided to join all their troops in two big squadrons (Picouet 2008).
142 Albi de la Cuesta (2015).
143 We could add that it must be the norm in most Spanish armies of the mid-seventeenth century.
144 For example, during the Battle of Santa Cecilia in November 1646, Pablo de Parada had in hand 1,000 men, and formed a strong squadron of pike from four tercios to defend the access of Fort Rébé and placed the *mangas* of shot on the flanks.
145 During the battle of Montjuich in January 1641, the Spanish formed two flying squadrons of 1,000 musketeers/harquebusiers, one under the Duke of Tyrone and the second under Fernando de Ribera to attack the fort of Montjuich (A.R. Esteban Ribas, "La batalla de Montjuich", *Magazine Desperta Ferro*, Numero Especial 2011).

The Spanish used various firing systems, which can be summarised as follows:[146]

    a. In the first, called the "static", the first rank would fire and kneel to reload their weapon. The others ranks would perform the same procedure, fire and kneel to reload and when the last rank had fired the first one could fire again. This system had the advantage that the men would stay in place, but to reload a musket kneeling was not an easy task.

    b. In the second, shooters would use a "caracole" manoeuvre system. The first rank would fire and then moved to the rear to reload, passing between the files. Meantime the second rank would advance to fire. The system could also be called "fire by rank".

    c. A third system was called "fire by file", in this case the selected file advanced and deployed in front of the formation facing the enemy. After firing the file returned to its position. At the same time another file would begin to move.

    d. The fourth system can be called "open order", in this case each shooter would fire and reload at will. Such a system was normally used during skirmishes and when the shooter could find a cover behind an obstacle (a trench, tree, bush, wall etc.) when he was reloading. This firing system required certain training because the shooter was more or less alone and not completely integrated in a formation.

    e. The fifth system was more a tight order. The *manga* could be divided into sub-units or sections of 5 x 5 men. When the first five men had fired, the whole rank would move to the rear in the space available between the sub-units. It was similar to the Dutch system called "fire by ranks of divisions".

    f. Finally the triple rank volley fire, used firstly by the Swedish,[147] was achieved by advancing the rear ranks upon the front ranks, while echeloning to the right. Triple rank volley fire was performed with the first rank kneeling, second rank stooping, and third rank standing. By 1640 most of the best troops used this firing tactic.

To have the maximum efficiency, in his military precepts Miguel Perez de Xea (1632) recommended that a *manga* was commanded by a minimum of two captains and to have one sergeant or *cabo* for every 25 men. They would command the fire and from which position shooters should fire. Whatever the system used by the Spanish infantry, the firepower of the Spanish unit was well recognised by their enemies and most of the time it was superior (Maffi 2014).

---

146 Some of them are described in the military precepts of Miguel Perez Xea (1632).
147 It was popularised by the Swedish infantry in the Thirty Years' War, but other nations were probably using a similar firing system.

2.7.4 Tactics of the Cavalry

Cavalry was not the best arm of the Spanish army of Philip IV and was not considered as important as the infantry in the war fought in the Low Countries and Lombardy. As we have seen at the beginning of the King's reign, the ratio of cavalry to infantry was inferior in the Spanish and Dutch armies compared to the armies fighting in Germany. With the fight for hegemony against the French monarchy, the cavalry gained importance in the Spanish armies but it took time to create an efficient force, and German mercenaries were well appreciated for their experience and were hired in great numbers.

As we have seen, most of the cavalry were cuirassiers or *Caballo Coraza*, all of them with the same weapons and a different degree of protection from 1621 to 1668. Considering the tactics, Spanish cavalry squadrons[148] tended to follow those used in Imperial service. In Spanish service, cavalry squadrons of 250 horsemen were common in 1621–1630, later reduced to 150–200 horsemen or even fewer. Cavalry troopers were normally trained to commence their advance with a walk, increased the speed to a trot, firing their pistols at close range and then spurring their horse to a gallop,[149] sword in hand, for the final phase of the attack (Brnardic & Pavlovic, 2010). That was the theory and probably as suggested by the same author, only the best-trained troopers could do so. Cavalry officers did not trust their troopers to charge at gallop and preferred to maintain a smaller speed at trot to maintain cohesion and to oblige the troopers to charge (Chauviré 2007). In fact in most cases the two squadrons of cavalry would stop at 20 to 30 m distance from each other and exchange fire with carbine, harquebus and pistols. One side would advance to mix with their opponent or turn back to the rear. Therefore as stated by Hanlon (2016), cavalry engagements were brief and frantic and when the two bodies of horse came in contact, riders tended to find gaps to advance, firing their pistols or slashing with their sword any opponent within range. Such a frenetic melee would last for some minutes before trumpets and buglers would sound to disengage and reform. So one of the most important facts seemed to be the possibility of having a safe position, behind infantry squadrons for example, to reorganise the cavalry squadrons and send them back to the battle. At that game the French army had a better inter-arm cooperation than the Spanish and could explain partially the defeats of Rocroi 1643 and Lens 1648. But as we said before, pitched battle was not the main military operation and for the cavalry the main operation was to protect supply convoys, or to attack them, or to conduct raiding parties in enemy territory with small cavalry detachments.

2.7.5 Tactics During a Siege

Battles were an extraordinary event during the life of a soldier. Most of the time the fighting experience was more related to skirmishes, ambushes

---

148 In most of the Spanish original sources, cavalry squadrons are called *batallones* ("battalion" in English).

149 An evaluation of a walk gives a speed of 5.8 to 7.7 km/h; a trot 7.8 to 14 km/h; and a gallop 13.3 to 19 km/h (Chauviré 2007).

THE STRUCTURE OF THE SPANISH ARMY

between garrisons of opposite sides, or the defence of small outpost on a dyke, protection duties, or attacking supply convoys. Siege was a more common operation and in the seventeenth century most of the towns in Europe (especially in the Low Countries and northern Italy) had modern fortifications following the "Italian trace" with bastions, ditches, hornwork, half-moon, and so on.

Some towns had also citadels, such as the powerful five star citadel of Casale Montferrat or that of Torino. Such powerful fortifications were normally disconnected from the city and were difficult to take. But the control of a territory implied that the cities of the area had to be taken or controlled, so most of the campaigns of the seventeenth century had the goal of besieging a strategic town. Before Vauban, the science of besieging a city was well known and numerous manuals, such as that of Marolois (1638) or that of Pietro Sardi Romano,[150] would explain the art of fortification and the way to take a fortress.

Basically an invasion army would firstly surround the city and secondly start the construction of fortified camps to accommodate troops, supplies and ammunition and of two fortified lines, the line of contravallation facing the city, out of the range of their guns, and the line of circumvallation against the exterior. Each line was normally made by parapet ditches and earthwork defensive fortifications comprising bastions and revelins. Batteries of artillery would be erected to bombard the city defences and to reinforce the fortification's line of circumvallation. In the first case, the artillery siege (cannons, half-cannons and mortar) would be used; in the second one lighter artillery (quarter-cannons, mansfelts) could be used. Following Marolois (1638) a typical siege battery, formed by four cannons, covered a width of up to 18.5 m. The guns were placed on a wooden platform and the battery was normally protected from musket fire, by gabions[151] and parapets. At a short distance a cellar was dug in order to store gunpowder, match and shot until they were required. When the weakest spots of the city's fortification were detected, the besieging force would start its approaches. In Spanish service it was normal to have an approach for each nationality in order to have an emulation effect between the attacking forces. The digging work would start during the night with small trenches with depth and width of three feet protected by a small parapet, fagot brush and gabions. Later on, the depth and a width of the trenches would be expanded to between eight and 12 feet. It was dangerous work[152] because the defenders would do all they could to disrupt the approaches. At musket distance from the enemy fortification, fire steps would be cut to establish firing positions for the musketeers and for the engineers the information that they were digging in the correct direction. At some point, if the ground was suitable, the engineer could decide to dig

---

150 Pietro Sardi Romano, *Il capo de bombardieri: esaminato, & approvato del generale dell'artiglieria, opera nuova, utile e necessarissima à tutti que che fi vogliono essercitare* ... Venice, 1641.
151 Following Marolois (1638), three types of gabions were used: a standard one six feet high and three feet wide, a wider one seven feet high and seven feet wide, and a double gabion 10 feet high and seven feet wide. All of them were made by the soldiers and filled with earth.
152 Normally the men doing the digging would receive extra pay due to the danger of such a task.

a tunnel below the enemy fortification to install a mine. Once the mine had reached the walls, barrels of gunpowder would be placed at the end of the gallery and the entrance of the tunnel would be blocked to create a more powerful explosion. If the defenders suspected the besiegers were digging a mine, they would start a countermine in an effort to stop them. In such narrow tunnels, bitter and nasty fights could occur with daggers and pistols when the two parties met underground.

Another possibility was to launch an assault to take a fortification of the town. In this case (Davila 1668) the assault party, half of them with half-pikes, consisted of a vanguard of two groups of one sergeant and 25 men, mainly *reformados* or veterans, acting as grenadiers, supported by a detachment of 100 men commanded by two captains. Multiple waves of 150 men could be launched to achieve the objective or to secure the position if taken. As we can imagine, an attack on a fortification could be a bloody affair and was normally conducted on a small exterior fortification. In fact when a mine was in place or a breach was made with artillery fire on the main city fortification or before an attack, the garrison would be called upon to surrender. However, before answering, the governor of the garrison had to be careful: if he surrendered too soon he might be accused of treason by his own side,[153] but if he refused to surrender and held out beyond what was seen as honourable and with no hope of relief, then the city could be stormed, the garrison slaughtered,[154] and its inhabitants plundered for three days. On the contrary, if a town had been defended for an honourable amount of time, the garrison could surrender or capitulate and march out with the full honours of war. Therefore, depending on how the defence had been conducted, survivors could march with colours flying in the wind, drums beating, musketeers with lighted match and musket balls in the mouth, carrying light guns, and promised safe passage to a friendly position and so on. Each article of the capitulation would be negotiated and signed by the two parties in order that honour would be secured for both sides.

---

153 In 1635 the governor of La Capelle, Marcos de Lima, made a poor defence, was accused of cowardice and beheaded for the failure (Ceballos y Arce, op. cit.).

154 At the siege of Fontenoy le Chateaux in 1635, the French estimated that the defence had been too long in comparison with the size of the fortress, therefore the wounded governor and most of the survivors were slaughtered (Montglat volume 2, 1826).

3

Men, Logistics, and Finance

3.1 High Command

In the sixteenth century, the Duke of Alba had established rules to command and maintain the authority of Spanish kings on the armed forces in the Low Countries. As stated by Gonzales de Léon (2009), the Duke of Alba had a chain of command for his officers, a strict code of discipline and a system to correctly train his soldiers and officers, particularly the Spanish ones. Concerning training of officers, the basic idea was to start from the lower ranks as a soldier and to move on to sergeant, *alférez* and captain after a minimum of 10 years of service. At a higher level, officers with the rank of *Sargento Mayor* of a tercio could demonstrate their ability to manage several companies during the long journeys from northern Italy to Flanders or during a campaign. If they performed well they could be on the next list to be nominated *Maestro de Campo*.[1] Service in the staff of the captain general of the Army of Flanders or the Army of Lombardy was also a way to gain experience to be tested in order to reach higher ranks. With luck and professionalism a soldier could, in some cases, expect to reach the rank of *Maestro de Campo* or obtain governorship of a castle after a minimum of 18 years of service. Another point to be taken into account was that officers should lead their men in combat, thus casualties amongst them could be significant, offering the possibility for promotion to junior officers if they fulfilled the requirements mentioned previously. In a sense the Spanish army of the Duke of Alba was more guided by meritocracy than nobility and commoners had some possibility to reach the rank of captain or even higher. In the seventeenth century, we could find the example of Baltasar Mercader starting as a soldier and reaching the rank of *Maestro de Campo General* of the Army of Lombardy in 1657, and governor of the Castle of Milan in 1662 (Massi 2007). Fernando Solis y Vargas started as a soldier, progressed to captain, and became *Maestro de Campo* in 1646, then *Sargento*

---

[1] For a professional soldier in the seventeenth century, the most common course was soldier > *cabo* > sergeant > *alférez* > assistant to *Sargento Mayor* > xaptain > *Sargento Mayor* and *Maestro de Campo*. In the sixteenth century, the same course was soldier > *cabo* > sergeant > *alférez* > captain > *Sargento Mayor* and *Maestro de Campo* (Albi de la Cuesta 2015).

General de Batalla, to finish his career as captain general of the artillery of the Army of Flanders. Another professional soldier was Francisco de Meneses, nominated *Sargento general de Batalla* after 35 years of service (Maffi 2014). Finally a humble man like Bernabé Vargas was nominated *Sargento General de Batalla* and later governor of the castle of Ostend after 35 years of service.[2]

In 1621, the rules established by the Duke of Alba were still working in the two main armies of the Spanish monarchy, but already at the end of the sixteenth century and the beginning of the seventeenth system had presented some flaws (Gonzales de Léon, 2009). One of the flaws was the fact that for officers from other nations, particularly Italians in the Army of Flanders, native Spanish officers had advantages due to their nationality and did not need from their experience or years of service. Another flaw was that the system was not necessarily followed when a noble of the high Castilian nobility wanted to be involved in military service.

The meritocracy system was promoted by King Philip IV and his *valido* but at the same time they wanted to see more officers from the Spanish nobility and they wanted to ensure the pre-eminence of the Spanish nation over the others. Another wish of the Count-Duke Olivares was to recover the interest of the Spanish high nobility[3] (*Grande de España*) to send their relatives for the profession of the arms. To do so, one of the measures written in the ordinance of 1632 was to reduce constraints of the meritocracy system for noblemen reducing for example the years of service to four for a captain or to eight for a *Maestro de Campo* (Maffi 2014). With such measure Spanish gentlemen[4] came back and took over commands such as *Maestro de Campo*, such as the close servants of the Cardinal Infante,[5] and a lot of them had little or no military experience. One such officer was Juan de Borja y Aragon, nominated in 1643 cavalry general and chief of the cavalry on the Dutch front because he was the son of the Duke of Villahermosa, a high-ranking Spanish nobleman.[6] Pedro Gonzalez del Valle, a member of an important Spanish family, was nominated firstly general of the artillery of Milan in 1656 and then *Maestro de Campo General* in 1657 and was considered as

---

2 Archivo General de Simancas E Legado 2819 s.f., Consulta del Consejo de Estado, 4 February 1655.
3 To have an overview of interactions of royal favour with the high Spanish nobility please see A. Malcolm, *Royal Favouritism and the Governing Elite of the Spanish Monarchy 1640–1665* (Oxford: Oxford University Press, 2017).
4 An analysis of 379 services papers provides information of the career officers serving in the Spanish armies between 1640 and 1660. A figure of 18.5 percent came from the high Castilian aristocracy (Maffi, *Al di là del mito: Il corpo ufficiali spagnolo durante il regno di Filippo IV (1640–1660)*, in *Hacer historia desde Simancas homenaje a José Rodriguez de Diego / coord*, A. Marcos Martín (Valladolid: Junta de Castilla y León, Consejería de Cultura y Turismo, 2011), p. 515.
5 One of the first measures of Francisco de Melo when he took command was to nominate as *Maestro de Campo* a young Spanish noblemen, the Count of Villalba or Fernando de Quesada, Count of Garciez, from the Cardinal Infante's retinue (i.e. *entretenidos*).
6 Juan de Borja nominated Francisco de Melo, while another candidate, Pedro de Villamor, was a career officer with an outstanding service record. Juan de Borja performed badly, was captured in an ambush in 1643, and when liberated two years later he was again routed. In the opinion of the Marques of Leganés, Juan de Borja had few talents for command but to please his father he finished his career as captain general of the cavalry of Milan (1656–1661) and governor of the castle of Milan in 1657 (Gonzáles de León 2009 and Maffi 2007).

inefficient (Maffi 2014). Another example was Francisco de la Cueva, Duke of Albuquerque, *Maestro de Campo* in 1641 and general of the cavalry of Flanders in 1643 at the age of 24. The consequence of such policy was also that professional soldiers from low extraction had more problems reaching high command than before.

At that point, one question is how the mix of professionals and noblemen officers would perform on the battlefield. In the Army of Flanders, four of the nine captains general of the province had little or no military experience,[7] and they held such positions for political reasons. In the first period of the war, Archduchess Isabel of Austria could have the support of a great general such as Ambrogio Spinola[8] to command the army but later she had to rely on other soldiers with less prestige[9] and authority such as Hendrik van den Bergh or Alvaro de Bazán, Marquis of Santa Cruz. Cardinal Infante Fernando of Austria is one of them, but the fact that he was of royal blood was much more important than his military experience and he was well supported by professional soldiers.[10] The Marquis of Castel Rodrigo was normally supported by professional soldiers like Ottavio Piccolomini but the alchemy between high-ranking officers of the period did not work properly. Archduke Leopold of Austria was also a nobleman from royal blood but he already had experience in the Imperial army when he accepted the command of the Army of Flanders in 1647. In the Army of Lombardy four to five out of 17 governors (see Appendix XI) had little experience, the others had years of service in the Spanish army. Men like Juan de Velasco de La Cueva, Count of Siruela performed badly during their command while others such as Alfonso Peréz de Vivero, Count of Fuensaldaña had decades of service and managed to resist and to keep the Duchy of Lombardy in Spanish hands during the 1656–1659 period. In the armies deployed in the Iberian Peninsula, the need for troops was so significant that local nobility had to be mobilised to raise tercios and companies of cavalry. The counterpart was that local authorities would negotiate to have some benefit such as free patent of captain for their relative or other "rewards".[11] In Catalonia, despite some failures in 1640, 1641 and 1642, officers such as the Marquis of Léganes[12] or the Marquis of Oliás and Mortara managed to have some successes against French generals.

---

7   Archduchess Isabel of Austria (1621–1633), Cardinal Infante Fernando de Áustria (1634–1641), Francisco de Melo, Marquis of TorLaguna (1641–1644), Manuel de Moura y Cortereal, second Marquis of Castel Rodrigo (1644–1647).
8   Ambrogio Spinola was *Maestro de Campo General* of the Army of Flanders.
9   From 1631 to 1633, the Marquis of Santa Cruz was governor of arms, Hendrik van den Bergh was *Maestro de Campo General* (1631–1632) as well as Carlos Colonna (1631–1633) and the Marquis of Montesilvano (1631–1633), a lot of commnders for the Army of Flanders.
10 For example men such as the Marquis of Velada, Andrea Cantelmo, Jean de Beck or Claude de Lannoy Count of la Motterie.
11 With such a system local noblemen could nominate officials among their relatives, even if they had little or no military experience and therefore increase their control over their territories.
12 Diego Mexía Felípez de Guzman, Marquis of Leganés, was a cousin of the Count-Duke of Olivares. He was born in 1580 and he started his military career in 1600. In 1621, at the death of Archduke Albert he returned to Madrid. From 1622 to 1631 he was nominated general of the artillery and general of the cavalry of the Army of Flanders. Later he was nominated governor of the State of Milan and viceroy of Catalonia. He performed well in his role, winning important

After Ambrogio Spinola, it seems that the Spanish did not provide outstanding and dominant leaders but one must remember that the king and the council of war in Madrid had a certain control over the strategy of the different armies. Spanish commanders were probably less free than some of their enemy counterparts to command their respective armies. The Marquis of Leganés, who fought the inconclusive battle of Tornavento in 1636, was defeated in Lérida in 1642 with an army full of raw recruits but won also an outstanding victory in the same place in 1646 against the Count of Harcourt. Francisco de Melo won the battle of Honnecourt in 1642, before the defeat of Rocroi[13] the next year. Finally another point to be considered was that the Spanish strategy was more to keep all Spanish territories and not to gain new ones. In this case battle had to be avoided as much as possible and Spanish commanders were probably more cautious about engaging their troops in such operation than their French counterparts. One must be aware that even a commander like the Prince of Condé had problems adapting to the Spanish defensive strategy.

To summarise, commands were sometime given to *cortesanos* loyal to the Conde-Duke and not all of them had military experience but the old meritocracy system was still working and old soldiers could still reach high command by their merits. It can be noted (Maffi, 2014; Albi de la Cuesta, 2015) that the Dutch and French army had similar problems among their officers, not all of them were as good as Turenne or Condé.

In fact for all Spanish commanders, the main concern was the slow erosion of human and financial resources over the years and the fact that they had to keep an operational army at all costs, to survive.

3.2. Erosion and Recruitment

3.2.1 Erosion of the Spanish Army

In a sense, the art of war in the seventeenth century was to keep the army alive, and as we have seen in the previous chapter, the oscillation in the number of Spanish infantry in the main armies of the monarchy was important. The death and wounded in combat, the numerous epidemics of different illnesses (bubonic plague, typhus, dysentery and others) present in most military encampments where thousands of men were massed together rapidly decimated the military units of the monarchy. The poor state of medical knowledge and the poor consideration of the high command meant that hundreds of men could die without any proper care. In 1633 the Duke of

---

battles such as that of Lérida in 1646 (F. Arroyo Martín, 2002, "El marqués de Leganés: apuntes biográficos", *Espacio, tiempo y Forma, Serie IV, Histora Moderna*, volume 15, pp 145–185).

13 Rocroi was the typical example of how to poorly handle an army. Both commanders, Alvaro de Melo, general of the artillery, and the Duke of Albuquerque, general of cavalry, had little military experience and the Count of Fontaine, *Maestro de Campo General*, was an old man and sick. During the battle, professional soldiers such as Pedro de Villamor, Juan Pérez de Vivero, Baltasar Mercader or Jacinto de Vera were present but most of them subordinate to inexperienced noblemen. Others such as Andrea Cantelmo, Jean de Beck and the Count of Bucquoy were not present (Gonzáles de León, 2009).

Feria conducted an exhausting campaign in southern Germany, securing the Rhine valley from Konstanz to Brisach in Alsace, to end in Bavaria. From the end of August when Spanish and Italian Tercios (respectively those of Juan Díaz Zamorano; and the Marques of Torrecusa and Giovanni Panigarola) moved out from Lombardy at the end of December, the Spanish infantry lost 25.9 percent of their initial strength (2,564 men) and the Italians 57.6 percent for an initial strength of 3,771 men (de la Rocha et al., 2010). The majority of the losses were taken during the initial crossing of the Alps when hundreds of Italians deserted, and also during the withdrawal towards Bavaria when men were lost due to hunger, sickness (a typhoid epidemic) and desertion.

As stated by Maffi (2014), desertion was probably the main cause of losses, especially in newly raised units. In a new unit, with little experience and a lack of veterans, new recruits could not stand the hardships and discomfort of military life. For example in 1654, the tercio of Pedro Hurtado de Mendoza was sent from Spain to Milan, and in the process, of the original 522 new recruits, only 291 men (56 percent) arrived in Milan. For the others some 100 men were ill, left in the harbours of Malaga and Finale and the rest (25 percent) had deserted during the journey to Lombardy (Picouet 2010). Considering the provincial tercio, in 1658 the region of Grenada recruited a tercio of 1,800 men to reinforce the Army of Extremadura. During the journey of 440 km between Granada and Badajoz, up to 44 percent of men escaped (Estébanez Calderón 1885). We can give multiple examples, but such behaviour was common in all armies and as stated by Parrot (2001), to bring 1,200 men to the army, the French had to raise 2,000. Once immersed in the army of the monarchy, desertion was still a significant problem, especially when life was difficult. In the siege of Bergen op Zoom, probably up to 2,000 men deserted due to the hardship of the operation and in 1622 a lot of them deserted to the city. A similar situation occured during the siege of Gravelines in 1652, where of the 2,000 losses, 600 were a consequence of combat (dead and wounded) the others were mostly deserters (Maffi 2014). Poor hygiene conditions dictated that at any time an average of 10 percent of the men were ill and not fit for service (Storrs, 2006). In the armies of the Spanish Peninsula, the daily pay for a soldier was most of time inferior to the pay of a common labourer (Pazzis di Corales 2006). In those armies, where provincial tercios and militia were important, the number of deserters was always a factor during the months when farming activities were underway.

Of course losses in combat could be also significant: during the battle of Montijo in 1644, 15 percent of the troops were killed or wounded in a few hours. The Zubiburu muster in October 1637,[14] after a campaign in the French Basque country, indicates that 8.7 percent of soldiers died and 13.5 percent were wounded or ill, a casualty rate of 22.2 percent (White 2009). During July and August 1645, at least 2,500 men were killed or wounded in the Army of Flanders[15] due to skirmishes against the French. In the same army, from 1641 to 1647, only 2,200 men (Maffi 2014) were sent to the army;

---

14 Zubiburu is actually in the area of the city of Bilbao in the Spanish Basque region.
15 Archivo General de Simancas E. Leg. 2064 s.f., Letter of el duque de Amalfy al rey, 30 August 1645.

in the meantime the Spaniards decreased from 17,260 to 9,680 men, a loss of 9,580 in seven years giving an average of 1,400 men/year. Also in the Army of Flanders, in March 1631 the three Italian tercios had 3,430 men in 49 companies, but 18 years later the Italian contingent was reduced to only 1,750 men, a total loss of up to 10,360 men,[16] giving 575 men/year for a much smaller contingent. In the Army of Lombardy, the Spanish in 1640 had some 12,280 Spanish and 18 years later only 2,380, meanwhile up to 8,060 Spanish (Maffi 2007) were sent from Spain and Naples. Such numbers indicate that some 18,060 men were lost for different reasons or discharged from service, an average of 1,000 men/year.

Total losses of Spanish soldiers for the period are always difficult to assess, but if we follow Dominguez Ortiz[17] the number of Spanish soldiers killed in the war against France from 1635 to 1659 was 288,000 men[18], 12,000 men per year. If we consider the other troops of the Spanish monarchy we can easily double that number. Following White, one can easily understand that without a constant flow of men it was impossible to maintain the tercios in battle condition.

3.2.2 Recruitment

It is generally accepted that at the beginning of seventeenth century the need for men was 6,000 to 8,000 Spaniards per year. From 1630, these needs increased and with the war with France the number of soldiers increased again. From 1635 to 1640, a total of 28,510 Spaniards[19] were sent or recruited for the infantry of the Army of Lombardy and another batch of up to 20,000 men to Flanders (Esteban Ribas 2014). In total more than 60,000 men were recruited in Spain from 1635 to 1638 (Picouet 2010). Later on, with the war in Catalonia and Portugal, an average of 12,000 men per year were recruited in Castile. There were different systems to recruit these large numbers of men, explained as follows.

At the beginning of the seventeenth century, the main recruitment system was administrative recruitment *or recrutamiento por commission*. The decision to recruit new troops was taken by the town, and to do so captains and others aspiring for promotion had to submit their claim[20] to the council of war. If they were chosen, the captains received a licence, or *conducta* in Spanish, and instructions indicating the area of recruitment, the age of the volunteers to be enlisted, the expected number of men, the port to embark his company for Italy, North Africa, Flanders and so on. The first task of the captain was to select the company staff and the design of his *bandera*.

---

16 J.L. Sánchez, 2003, "La infantería italiana del ejercito de Flandes 1630–1648", *Researching & Dragona* n° 20.

17 A. Dominguez Ortiz, *La sociedad española en el siglo XVII*, vol. 1: *El estamento nobiliar* (Granada: Consejo Superior de Investigaciones Científicas: Universidad de Granada, 1992).

18 For France, the number of dead, for the same period 1635–1659, is estimated at 600,000 men (A. Corvisier, *La France de Louis XIV 1643–1715: ordre intérieur et place en Europe* (Paris: Sedes, 1990)).

19 The total for the infantry is 127,000 men (Maffi, 2007).

20 In their claim they had to furnish documents from their superior officers that certified their merit (López, 2012).

Then he would travel to the recruitment area,[21] contact local authorities, raised his *bandera* in a prominent place and beat the drums to summon attention. The captain and his staff, in their best clothes, would use all tricks avilable to attract volunteers. In theory, men under 20 years old could not be recruited, but in the seventeenth century the need of volunteers was so huge that teenagers[22] were also accepted. When enough volunteers had been collected[23] in four to five weeks, a muster was carried out by the *veedor*, to certify that the men were fit for service[24] and by the *pagador* to advance a sum of travel money that would be deducted from their first payment.[25] The acceptance of that first payment transformed a subject of the Spanish crown in a soldier of the King of Spain, no document was signed.

Those men were normally recruited for services outside Spain, and from their area of recruitment they would gather at one of the Spanish harbours (such as Barcelona, Almeria, Bilbao, A Coruña, Malaga) to embark to Italy (Genoa, Finale or Naples) or Flanders (Ostend or Dunkirk). On their arrival at their final destination the new soldiers, called *bisoño*,[26] tended to be placed in a garrison to learn how to master their weapons. It was expected that veterans would teach the proper use of the weapon and later the recruits would train with the rest of the company in battle formation. For the Spanish, instruction was important and it was a basic principle in Italy or Flanders not to send on campaign a soldier without proper training. Even when companies were sent directly to Flanders, during the first month they would be sent to garrison a quiet fortress to have time to train. Also on the arrival of new recruits, some of the companies were disbanded and their soldiers[27] distributed in the existing companies. When a new tercio was sent to Flanders or Lombardy, another practice was to exchange companies between the new tercio and the old ones, so that all the tercios had enough veteran soldiers to be useful on the field.

Such practices and the volunteers recruited by the administrative recruitment system were applied to the Spanish tercios deployed in the Low Countries, in Italy and in the Armada. For the regular or provincial tercios of the armies deployed in Spain, few companies or volunteers were used, most

---

21 Most of the time the recruitment area was an urban one, where an important pool of unemployed young men could exist. The countryside was not the proper territory for such recruitment because a captain did not want to travel from village to village to find two or three men. For him, while the mustering continued he had to pay the accommodation and food of his soldiers, so cities were a much better place to recruit enough volunteers in a short time.
22 Younger boys were accepted to work as porters or servants, and if they survived they would normally enlist as soldiers at 17–18 years old.
23 Already at the end of the sixteenth century and the beginning of the seventeenth a captain would be satisfied if he managed to recruit 100 to 150 men (Jiménez Estrella 2011).
24 Various characteristics of the volunteers were registered: age, name, dental condition, hair colour, absence of presence of scars and so on.
25 As in other armies, some swindlers (*tornillazo* in Spanish) would enlist, take the money and desert as soon as possible and repeat the trick elsewhere. If they were caught the sentence was normally despatch to the galleys.
26 The word *bisoño* is a deformation of the Italian *ho bisogno* that can be translated as "I need".
27 Some of the captains could serve in the tercio or army staff to perform various tasks (for example special tasks such as espionage) and the others would serve as officer *reformados* in the existing companies.

of the new men came from the companies raised by noblemen or particulars or were extracted from the militia by compulsory recruitment. Therefore the fighting quality and spirit of the tercios deployed abroad was normally much higher than those in the Iberian Peninsula. We can add also that Spanish veterans, especially from the Tercio of Naples and the Tercio of Sicily were regularly sent to Catalonia to boost the efficiency of the Spanish army. As we have seen, with time some of the provincial tercios began to became more permanent, enhancing their combat capability. By the end of Philip IV's reign most of the provincial tercios were as good as their counterparts deployed in Flanders and Lombardy.

For numerous reasons related to the economic and demographic crisis in Spain and mostly in Castile, the old recruitment system was not enough to support the tercios of Philip IV. In 1630 the war council was well aware that a new recruitment system should be used to address all compromises of the monarchy. It is symptomatic that in 1632, when the Crown wanted to recruit 8,000 men in Spain to be part of the army of the Cardinal Infante, fewer than half of them were actually sent to Italy (Negrerro del Cerro, 2016).

A new recruitment system, called *recruitamiento a costa*, was gaining more and more importance. In the new system a determinate person, normally a nobleman, sent an offer to the Crown to recruit, feed, arm a quantity of men at his own expense and send them to a destination determined by the Crown. For such service this person would ask for a patent of captain, even if he had no military experience or other administrative benefits.[28] The system was in contradiction with the Spanish military ordinances that indicated that a captain needed to prove 10 years of military service. Using a similar system, the Spanish Crown tried to oblige the high nobility to raise and maintain infantry and cavalry units, but for various reasons – lack of interest, privileges of the nobility, the high costs involved – the initiative did not work well,[29] in fact a significant proportion of the Spanish nobility did not want any military obligation. Local authorities and city councils had much more successe at recruiting and maintaining soldiers and it was the basis of recruitment for the provincial tercios in Castile and elsewhere. But it was not enough, and compulsory recruitment was applied to fill the ranks. For such a recruitment system, a quota of new recruits was defined by the council of war and the local authorities such as the Cortes of Castile, the Cortes of Aragon, or Valencia. In such negotiations a quota between the number of soldiers needed and the number of inhabitants was defined in each area of recruitment. Typically there was a proportion of one soldier for 50, 75 or 100 inhabitants.[30] For example in 1634 (Rodriguez Hernández, 2017), in order to prepare the defence of the Iberian Peninsula against France, Castile was

---

28 Some of the benefits could be, to be member of a selected religious order such as the order of Santiago or that of Alcantàra, or, for example, to have access to a employment as clerk in a local administration.
29 The only units with some prestige where the Spanish nobility would and should enlist were the cavalry units called the *Ordenes*. Even here, by 1643–1645, the tendency of the noblemen was to pay a substitute to fight for them.
30 In 1643, 7,950 soldiers were requested from Castile to reinforce the tercios of the army of Catalonia (Contreras Gay 1993–1994).

supposed to raise 12,000 men to complete garrisons and *presidios*. In April 1635 effectively only 7,533 men had been raised and sent to their destination, and up to 1,543 had already deserted.

To fill the quota of new recruits, local authorities such as the *Corregidor* ("shire" in English) and city council enlisted all the men considered as useless for the community even if it was against their will. The quota could also be filled by men from the militia, but in this case they would serve only for two or four months to defend their province and would be useless for more offensive actions.[31] Most of the time the quotas were not filled, and it was possible to convert the number of men into a sum of money. For example in 1632, of the 18,000 men asked by the Crown, 12,000 men were recruited and the other 6,000 converted into a sum of money. Such a system permitted the fast recruitment of a critical number of men, but the new recruits were quick to desert as soon as possible and most of them made poor soldiers because they came from the lowest strata of society. An advantage for local authorities was that with such a compulsory system they could nominate officers within local elites and that no other recruitment could be done in the same area the same year. Therefore the monarchy would have the men but would partially lose the possibility of controlling the troops.[32] Most of time this compulsory recruitment had to be repeated year after year in the 1640s–1650s, and it was unpopular in Spanish society, giving a very poor image of soldiers in particular and of military service in general.

3.2.3 Movement of Troops

Since the sixteenth century, logistics and movement of troops through the different territories of the Spanish monarchy was an important asset of the Spanish military structure. From 1621 to 1634, the main fighting forces were the Army of Flanders and the Army of Lombardy, but numerous outposts in North Africa and south Italy, not to mention the Atlantic area, which is out of our scope, also needed troops. At the same time soldiers of the Spanish monarchy were recruited in different regions and countries of Europe, and the logistics to transport them, feed them, clothe them, or give them weapons and horses had to be set up. It was the constant work of the Spanish administration and the men who served it to fulfil those important tasks to operationally maintain the armies of the monarchy.

So what was the main route to reinforcing the main armies of the monarchy? For the Spaniards we have seen that when recruitment was carried out, the troops were sent to one of the Spanish harbours.

In 1621 most of the native Spanish new recruits would embark in Barcelona or Malaga and would be shipped to Genoa and Finale to reinforce the Army of Lombardy, or to Naples and Palermo to reinforce the garrisons

---

31 In 1659, militia from Castile was an important contingent of the army of Luis de Haro to lift the siege of Badajoz, attacked by the Portuguese. When the Spanish decided to take the war inside Portugal and besiege Elvas, most of the troops from the militia of Castile and Extremadura deserted.
32 A. Rodriguez Hernández (2015), "El reclutamiento en el siglo XVII", *Desperta Ferro Numero Especial VII*, pp. 30–36.

Table 3.1.: Estimate of the troops sent to the Army of Lombardy from 1635 to 1659. Adapted from Maffi (2007)

Nation	Infantry	Cavalry
Spaniards	36,570 men	-
Neapolitans	28,920 men	6,390 men
Burgundians	7,700 men	-
Germans	74,980 men	18,610 men
Swiss	26,100 men	-
Others	12,850 men	3,090 men

of southern Italy. For the Low Countries the Spanish had two options, the Spanish Road or the maritime road. When contingents of troops were sent to Flanders, normally companies were extracted from the tercios based in Italy and/or from tercios raised in Spain. All troops were assembled in Milan to start the long road of 1,200–1,300 km across Europe. One of the alternatives was to cross the Alps via the Swiss cantons (Lugano, Bellizona, Schwytz and Baden), take the Rhine valley to enter Alsace and then go to Luxembourg, crossing the Duchy of Lorraine. Another route was to go through the lago di Como, the Valtellina valley, Lindau in the Tyrol, follow the Rhine valley (Alsace, North Rhine-Westphalia) and turn west to Luxembourg and the Low Countries.

The maritime road would start in one of the harbours of the Atlantic coast; the troops would embark in transport ships or galleons in small convoys and sail to the harbours of Ostend or Dunkirk via the Gulf of Gascony, the Celtic Sea and the Channel. Normally the maritime road took less time, but it was more traumatic for raw recruits and a lot of them arrived in the Low Countries in very bad shape. From 1635 to 1639, up to 21,941 Spaniards (Parker 1991) arrived in the Low Countries and from 1640 to 1658 a further 8,500–9,000 men were sent by the maritime road (Maffi 2014). On the way back Irish and Walloon troops were sent to the Iberian Peninsula after 1640.

Concerning the reinforcement of the Army of Lombardy, Table 3.1 shows the provenance of 215,210 men recruited between 1635 and 1659. Seventeen percent of them were Spaniards shipped directly from Spain or were extracted from companies of the tercios based in Naples and Sicily. But the movement of troops did not affect only the Spaniards, but also other nationalities, Neapolitans (16.4 percent), Germans (43.5 percent) or Swiss (12.1 percent). To such numbers we should add the local recruitment of 73, 700 men (86.1 percent for the infantry and 13.9 percent for the cavalry) for the regular units, and 34,850 militia.

3.3 Clothing and Logistics

3.3.1 Clothing

For most of the period covered by the book, Spanish infantry clothing was similar to that worn by civilians. Uniforms did not exist in the Spanish tercios but most of the soldiers wore the same type of clothing: basically a white shirt,[33] baggy half-trousers (breeches), knee socks and simple leather shoes or boots.[34] On top of the shirt, soldiers could have a jerkin called a *coleto*, or a doublet called a *jubón*. Jerkins and doublets could consist of the same cloth, but probably the jerkin was sleeveless and doublets had sleeves that could be opened with buttons. At least in Spanish service, for most of the seventeenth century the *jubón* had buttoned sleeves. The Spanish also tended to use a substitute of the leather *gambeson* (padded jacket) called a *cuera*, a sort of doublet with full sleeves. Jackets or *casaca* were also used, normally made of wool. Soldiers had also a large hat and a cape or cloak for protection against cold and humidity. A kerchief (*pañuelo*), normally with a red colour, was worn by Spanish troops below their hat or helmet. Finally there was a field sign, generally red lace, or ribbons could be attached on the sleeves to indicate a Spanish unit.

The quality of the cloth was directly connected to the status of the soldier and his fortune. Of course officers and noblemen tended to have to use materials of high quality in accordance with the fashion of the time. Ribbon and lace were also use to maintain knee socks. The main colours were easy to obtain, such as black, white, brown, blue and green. Red was connected to the Hapsburg monarchy and the Spanish wore a red Burgundian cross, but also red ribbons or laces and for the officers a red sash.

Normally soldiers were supposed to pay for their clothes, but at the end of the reign of Philip III it was common for the Spanish administration to supply clothes to the soldiers and to deduct the price from their wages. In, Spain, Italy and Flanders, contracts (*assientos*) could be signed with merchantmen for the supply of full cloth, called also ammunition cloth or *vestido de munición*. In 1633 a contract was signed in Naples with the merchant Pompeo Nigro to provide shoes, knee socks, hats, jerkins, doublets, breeches and shirts with collars[35] to the Neapolitan tercios of Gaspare Toralto and Lucio Boccapionola.[36] In 1643, another contract was signed in Naples to provide 5,760 full sets of clothes consisting of a jacket, a pair of breeches, a jerkin, a doublet, two shirts with collars, a pair of knee socks, a pair of shoes, a hat and a sword.[37]

---

33 Shirts could be of different shapes, especially where hte famous Walloon collar was concerned.
34 For the late sixteenth century, Quatrefages (1983) gives a pair of shoes, trousers and knee socks, two white shirts, jerkin and doublets.
35 In Spanish: *zapatos, medias, sombrero, jubones, ropillas, calzones, camisas y coletos*.
36 G. Boeri & G. Peirce (1992), *Origini delle uniformi del regno di Napoli*, Uff. Storico S.M.E. Roma. The two Neapolitan tercios fought during the battle of Nördlingen on 6 September 1634.
37 G. Boeri & G. Peirce, op. cit.

3.3.2 Logistics

One mode of thought was to regularly bring new recruits and to field an army, other was to supply, feed and provide enough ammunition and weapon to keep the present army in battle condition. One of the main tasks of a Spanish governor, where a Spanish army was present, was to extract the troops from their winter quarters in order to prepare the army for a campaign from spring to autumn. To do so, he had to raise new recruits to complement the existing companies and if he had enough financial resources he could raise new tercios from the local population. In accordance with Madrid he had also to raise regiments of mercenaries to fill the ranks of the army. The governor was responsible for preparing a decent artillery train with heavy guns for a siege and light guns for use on the field, and to find and pay for the gunpower and the different ammunition for the army. Even then his task was not over, because he had to find horses[38] to remount the cavalry,[39] to find, buy and store enough cereals and other food products to prepare the ammunition bread (*pan de munición*) or the daily ration for the troops, and the barley for the horses and other animals. Finally he had to take into account the weather, to be sure that enough water and grass would be available in the theatre of operation, and so on.

In this chapter we will focus more on elements such as the *pan de munición*, and supply of ammunition and gunpowder for the field armies. In Flanders, according to Quatrefage (1980), in the sixteenth century a daily ration was made of 1.5 to 2 lbs[40] (690 to 920 g) of bread,[41] 1 lb of meat products or half pound of fish, a litre of wine, oil and vinegar.[42] Fresh fruits and vegetables or dairy products were not provided and had to be bought by the soldiers in villages, towns and above all from the victuallers following the troops. In 1643 in the Army of Catalonia (Martinez Ruiz, 2008), the daily ration was 700 g of bread, 900 g of animal-based proteins (meat, cheese, eggs and fish), two litres of beer or three litres of wine. For the 1649 campaign, the general quartermaster (*proveedor general*) of the army of Catalonia had to provide 2,955,895 rations for the men and 611,116 rations of barley for the horses. In 1654, following Maffi (2007), the daily food ration in the Army of Lombardy was estimated at 28 oz of bread (805 g), two jars of wine (1.5 l) and eight ounces (230 g) of animal-based proteins. Following the same author, in 1639

---

38 Horses were also a particular problem, especially after 1635 with the increase of mounted arms in all armies of the monarchy. In numerous musters we have the cavalry separated into mounted and dismounted men. For the Spanish high command, the only solution was to directly provide horses to the troopers on credit and deduct the cost from their wages (Parker, 1991).
39 In 1639 the Army of Flanders needed 2,300 new horses, in 1644 3,000 animals and 5,000 in 1651. In Lombardy the army needed between 1,000 and 1,200 horses each year (Maffi 2014).
40 Here we are talking of Castilian pounds, *Libra castellana* corresponding to 460 g.
41 In the seventeenth century the "military" bread normally contained two thirds wheat and one third rye. During a difficult campaign and due to numerous frauds the bread could be made of whatever cereal and products were available. Officers had to be particularly cautions of such matter because the bread was the basic food of the soldiers and a lack of it usually meant the end of the campaign.
42 Spring (2017) gives for the Bavarian army a daily ration for a soldier as 2 lb of bread, 1 lb of meat and eight pints of beer. High and low officers tended to have different rations, according to their rank and prestige.

the Army of Lombardy had to buy 2,500 sacos[43] (some 212.5 tons) of wheat, 466 rubbi (3,807 kg) of rice, 10,800 rubbi (88.2 tons) of bacon, 3,066 rubbi (25 tons) of oil, 6,380 rubbi (52,1 tons) of cheese, 249 brente (18.8 hectolitres) of vinegar, 25 rubbi (204.2 kg) of salt and 626 sacos (53.2 tons) of legumes (chickpeas, lentils etc.), all these quantities to have been enough food for the 40,000 men. If we include the food supply for the horses we have, for example in the Army of Catalonia (Maffi 2014) during the 1649 campaign, 2,955,895 rations to feed the men and 611,116 rations for the horses were needed. In Extremadura in 1663, for an army of some 20,000 men, John of Austria started the campaign with 416.90 tons of biscuit and 240.9 tons of wheat, with 36 iron ovens to cook the bread and 661.3 tons of barley for the horses.

But a campaign would require not only food for men and feed for animals but also a huge amount of war ammunition. For example for the campaign of 1647, the Army of Flanders received 33 new guns, 290,000 pounds of gunpowder, 185,000 pounds of muskets and harquebus lead bullets, 41,300 cannonballs, 8,000 new muskets, 2,000 harquebus and 3,000 pikes (Maffi 2014).

In the sixteenth century soldiers had to pay for their ammunition and food with their pay, but due to lack of pay and numerous frauds, the Spanish high command tended to give the soldier pay in goods. The idea was that soldiers needed to be certain of having ammunition and food before starting a campaign. In fact the Spanish administration did not have the potential to provide the enormous quantity of supply required by the armies and by the end of the sixteenth century the system of using private suppliers or *asentistas* was established for the Army of Flanders. The system was later introduced in Lombardy and in all territories of the Spanish monarchy where Spanish troops were deployed. The management of supply of bread, whose quantity was one of the most significant expenses[44] of the army, was in private hands. The system was as follows: the local military authorities would sign a contract (*assiento*) with a victualler[45] to deliver "ammunition bread" to all the personnel of the army. In the contract, the bread quality and the price by pounds was established, and regularly the military authorities would inform the victualler of the number of loaves to be delivered and where.[46] Therefore, for the victualler, his profit was related to the price of the bread because the number of products to be delivered was always fluctuating. To provide ammunition of war and particularly gunpowder, Spanish authorities

---

43 Typically a saco was 85 kg, a rubbo 8.17 kg, and a brento 75.55 litres.
44 In 1663, for the troops operating against Portugal (Army of Extremadura and Army of Galicia), 35.5 percent of the expenses of 6.09 million Escudos was for bread and barley (Rodríguez Hernández, 2013).
45 For example to provide bread for the Army of Flanders, in 1621 and 1622, the contract was given to Giovan Battista Lazagna, a trader from Genoa, but in 1623 and 1624 the winner was Christophe Van Etten. The business was attractive and other traders like Marco Gentile or Amand de Hornes participated in the competition to provide the bread in the following years. Normally the traders did not make the bread or biscuit themselves but tended to subcontract bakers (Esteban Estringana, 2004).
46 All the costs of making the bread and transporting it were due to the victualler, even if sometimes raw material could be provided by the military authorities. Once the bread had been distributed, the paymaster would register the quantity of bread delivered and pay for it every month (Esteban Estringana, 2004).

also made contracts of three to five years with different traders in Spain,[47] but also in their different territories.

For a campaign most of the products and ammunitions had to be transported by two-wheeled carts, four-wheeled wagons or by animals such as horses, mules and donkeys. In Flanders a two-wheeled cart could transport 500 kg of material and needed only a horse to pull it, while a four-wheeled wagon could transport up to 2,500 kg but needed three to four horses or oxen to pull it (Swart 2016). During the siege of Breda in 1624–1625, the Spanish used 3,000 to 4,000 vehicles in big convoys of 300 to 650 vehicles protected by cavalry. In 1632, for transportation, the Spanish army needed 1,000 vehicles and 3,000 horses and oxen to pull them. Considering only the artillery train, the movement of the 40 guns required 1,030 horses and 257 men to conduct them (Maffi 2014). During the 1663 campaign in Extremadura, the army of John of Austria needed 2,000 two-wheeled wagons pulled by oxen, 350 four-wheeled wagons pulled by mules or horses, 500 donkeys and mules as well as numerous minor and private wagons[48] to transport supplies as well as the gunpowder and ammunition.

The effort required to supply an army in movement indicates that a general could not easily move his army from one place to another. For a Spanish general of the Army of Flanders, his bases were in the Low Countries and most of the time did not want to go far away from them.[49] The same could be said for the Army of Lombardy where density of population and number of cities was important as well as rivers and canals to transport supplies. But for the armies operating in the Iberian Peninsula, the long distance between cities, the poor population density in Catalonia, Portugal and Extremadura, and the arid climate, indicated that it was difficult to organise large armies and to maintain them for a long time. In Portugal, which had a long and hot summer, no significant military operations could be carried out in July and August, thus reducing the impact of an offensive movement of the Spanish army inside the country.

Another advantage of the war in the Low Countries and northern Italy was the presence and capacity of the two provinces to supply the Spanish army not only with food and feed but also with weapons and ammunition. The main drawbacks of the two territories were the lack of pastures for horse breeding. Therefore horses had to be imported from elsewhere,[50] mainly Germany and northern Europe. In the Iberian Peninsula horse breeding was possible, even if to get new horses for the army was always a challenge.

---

47 The Spanish monarchy signed contracts in the region of Murcia, Aragon, Navarre and Castile to provide 9,002 quintals (414.4 tons) of gunpowder (A.J. Rodríguez Hernández, 2013).

48 J.I. Ruiz Rodríguez, *Don Juan José de Austria en la Monarquía Hispánica entre la política, el poder y la intriga*. (Madrid: Dykinson, 2007).

49 During the campaign of 1636, after reaching the River Somme and besieging Corbie, Spanish officers were more concerned about securing supplies in the north of France, not too far away from their main base.

50 In 1651 the Spanish bought 5,000 new horses in Germany for the Army of Flanders. In Lombardy a minimum of 1,000 to 1 200 new horses were necessary each year to remount the cavalry (Maffi 2014).

3.4 Discipline and Life in the Tercio

3.4.1 Honour and Reputation

Centuries of war against Spanish Muslims of Al Andalus during the *reconquista* period have shaped the image of soldiers acquiring honour and wealth by the sword. In the mentality of the society of the sixteenth and seventeenth century, honour was an important concept that could transform somebody into an important person for his peers. The Spanish society of the period was obsessed by honour, reputation and glory (*la honra, la fama* in Spanish) much more than money. Honour is difficult to define but in a society governed by the appearance, good "reputation", earning honour fighting the enemies of the king could be more of a powerful motor to improve a social status than trading or working in the field (Giménez Martin, 1999). Honour could also be earned by a community of soldiers, for example around a standard.[51] The combination of individual and collective honour would have particular effects to motivate Spanish soldiers to fulfil their duties, sometime to unexpected extremes. Defence of honour would be particularly important in the military world and all dishonoured action would have to be washed away with blood. Officers would have to learn how to use to good effect such motivation (López, 2012). In effect the seeking of glory and honour could lead Spaniards to high profile military actions,[52] though it could also induce disasters. The concept means that Spaniards from the tercios of the Army of Flanders or from the Army of Lombardy saw themselves as superior to the other nations.[53] With regards to the other components of the Spanish army, Spanish tercios had precedence over all other units and would have all the places of honour, such as the right of line, the vanguards or rearguards depending on the actions and so on. In the sixteenth century nobody would much criticise such decisions, but in the middle of the seventeenth century other nations, particularly Italian tercios,[54] made similar demands to have the place of honour in the Army of Flanders: for example in 1626 for the succour of Groenlo, or in 1640 during the attack of the French lines in Arras leading to bitter contest between the two nations. In the Iberian Peninsula, where Spanish tercios were most of the time not the best troops available, the precedence of the Spaniards was challenged often and high-ranking Spanish officers and even the king had to deal with it, to remember the respective position of each nation and in the army.

---

51 In Spanish service, the standard or *bandera* of a company was a sacred symbol which all soldiers of the company should defend with honour.
52 For example during the Battle of Kaloo in 1638 or the Battle of Rocroi 1643. At Rocroi, the Italians stayed on the battlefield until their honour was safe and then retired, they did not stand with the Spanish. Maybe because they did not have the place of honour, on the right of the battlefield (Gonzáles de León, 2009).
53 For most of the sixteenth century, these high opinions of themselves were continuously exalted by Spanish officers and the monarchy (Lopez 2012).
54 In the hierarchy of the nations, in Flanders and in the Iberian Peninsula Italians were second to the Spaniards. In Lombardy the situation was different, Italians, particularly the Neapolitans, were not well appreciated for the fact that they had a strong tendency to desert.

THE ARMIES OF PHILIP IV OF SPAIN 1621–1665

3.1 The harsh reality of military discipline. Jacques Callot, 1628. (Rijksmuseum)

In time of the King Philip IV, the aristocratisation of the high command in the tercios and armies of the monarchy was a wish of the Count-Duke to attract Spanish and Italian noblemen to be officers in the Spanish army. The inconvenience of the system was that the question of reputation and prestige took even more importance at high level than before. Spanish, Italian or Walloon officers from high nobility sometimes had problems taking orders from battle-hardened officers with years of experience (Spanish, Italian, Walloon, Irish or German) but from a lower social status.[55]

3.4.2 Military Privilege

When the professional tercios were created, a particular legal framework was designed to deal with such men. The legal framework had to be severe but also fair, taking into account their reputation and honour (Albi de la Cuesta 1999). The military legal framework was called "military privilege", indicating that a soldier could only be judged by a military tribunal. In a sense civil legal framework could not be applied wherever the crimes occurred in the different territories of the Iberian Peninsula, Italy or Flanders. Military justice was supposed to be fair and rapid and depend on two juridical instances. At high level the *Maestro de Campo General* was supported by the auditor general to

---

55 Jean de Beck was the son of Paul Beck, a courier of the Luxembourg council. In 1601 he enlisted in the Army of Flanders for the siege of Ostend at 13 years old. He served in different units and with the start of the Thirty Years' War he was a lieutenant colonel in the Imperial army by 1627. In 1634 he was ennobled by Emperor Ferdinand II and in 1637 he returned to the Low Countries. There he rose to the governorship of the province of Luxembourg in 1642, and *Maestro de Campo General* in 1643 (Rahlenbeck, *Notice sur Jean Beck*, in *Le Messager des Sciences historiques de Belgique* (Gand, 1865, pp. 193–203).

deliver justice, his area was more concerned with different crimes against the army but also with all affairs between soldiers of different units. At a lower level, military justice was applied by the *Maestro de Campo* of the tercio. The exception was when officers, captains, *alférez* or particular noblemen were involved; in this case, military justice was given at higher level. For the case when civilians and soldiers were involved, it was a compromise between the two legal jurisdictions but sentences against soldiers could only be decided by the military ones.

The list of crimes was significant. If we follow Albi de la Cuesta (1999) we have treachery, desertion to the enemy, leaving the unit, insubordination, no respect for the standard, no respect for the guards, murder, sodomy (*pecado nefanto*), violence against women, robberies, sacrilege, looting, ambiguous firing, selling of weapons, as well as more minor offences or frauds. For the sentences, in the Spanish and Italian units the idea was to respect the reputation and honour of the soldier. To do so, some sentences were done with the "iron", indicating that the weapons of the executioner should be the sword or some pole weapons. If the sentence was death it was better to behead the soldier or kill him with an "iron" weapon than to hang him like a thief.

On the field justice could be fast, particularly when the objective of the commander-in-chief was to keep a good relationship with the civilians. In this case, sentences for murders and violence against civilians were most of the time to be hanged. On the other hand, if payment and supplies were scarce and men were on the edge of desertion and mutiny, commanders had the tendency to have a blind eye to violence against civilians, particularly in enemy territories.

3.5 The Life of the Spanish Soldier in the Seventeenth Century

3.5.1 Soldiers in Garrison

In the seventeenth century Spanish professional soldiers were deployed in different territories with different laws and habits. As we have seen, the main Spanish armies were in the Low Countries and Lombardy but we must not forget the numerous Spaniards deployed in southern Italy or in the *presidios* of North Africa. In the Low Countries and Italy the presence of Spanish soldiers was normally well accepted by the population,[56] but it was a different mater in North Africa. With the war spreading in the Iberian Peninsula, relations with the local population would become a significant problem, particularly in Catalonia, regarding sending troops into winter quarters. The relations of the soldiers with civil society were mainly related to the months of inactivity in winter when soldiers were billeted on the citizens. Following the ordinance of

---

56 In the Low Countries and Italy Spaniards were normally well accepted by the population; it was different for the German mercenaries or the auxiliary army of the Duke of Lorraine.

1605[57] edited by the Count of Fuentes, governor of Lombardy,[58] when civilians had to accept a soldier in their house they must provide a bed made of wood with good hay, feather or wool mattresses, a good blanket, two sheets and pillows. In winter the bed sheet had to be cleaned two days a month and in summer every eight days. Basic food[59] had to be provided by the civilian but fresh vegetables and fruit as well as fresh meat had to be bought by the soldiers on the market. The housekeeper also had a table, benches and a wine or beer jar and finally for hygiene a basin to wash up. For such service the soldier should normally pay one escudo/month,[60] but one must be aware that in some cases soldiers were not alone and civilians had also to attend their relatives. Such a burden on civilian society could be absorbed in some territories, living with continuous wars and where the elite benefited from it, but in the Iberian territories where the threats of war had been scarce in the sixteenth and beginning of the seventeenth centuries, such contribution was unacceptable.

---

57 Archives Générales de Simancas Vis.Leg. 187/17, ordenes para la infantería española y de otras naciones, Milano 1605.

58 In Lombardy Milan was a city with the privilege of not being obliged to accommodate soldiers (A. Buono 2009, Amministrazione militare e gestione dell'esercito in uno Stato 'pre-amministrativo'. Il caso dell lombardia spagnola (sec XVII). Archivio Storico Italiano, CLXVII, 620, pp. 521–551.

59 The daily ration of the soldier was 1.5 to 2 pounds of bread or biscuit, a pint of wine or beer, some meat or fish, oil and vinegar (Quatrefage, 1980).

60 Because soldiers had little money due to the lack of pay, normally civilians had their taxes reduced according to the number of soldiers billeted in their house.

3.2 Spanish camp followers during the siege of Jülich in 1621/1622. Pieter Snayers, 1622–1650. (Rijksmuseum)

Even in Lombardy, in the first decade of the seventeenth century, the civil population had asked their elites to find a solution to reduce the impact of maintaining the soldiers during the winter period; the solution was to separate the military personnel from the civilians.[61] At first, castles and citadels were used for such a purpose, but in Lombardy Spanish authorities created *casa berne*, a sort of barracks, and local authorities preferred to use specific houses to accommodate soldiers. In the Low Countries, the fact that Archduke Albert was captain general of the Army of Flanders but also a sovereign prince of Flanders meant that he had to balance the needs of the army and the interest of his subjects. In 1610–1620, the solution was to commute the obligation to lodge troops to a money payment and to construct more durable shelters in castles or citadels of the province. Following Parker (1991), such standard shelters contained accommodation for four to eight soldiers (two to four beds) but civilians still had to provide the beds, furniture and other commodities. Such solutions were not totally satisfactory, because not all soldiers[62] could be accommodated in such "pre-barracks", but also because such constructions were not very good and most

---

61 A. Buono, op. cit.
62 In the city of Nieuwport in 1631, up to 727 soldiers and their 278 wives needed accommodation, 194 men were lodged in the shelters of the king, but the rest (73 percent) with the wives had to be lodged in 269 houses of the city by the civilians. In total the city had some 580 houses (Parker 1991).

3.3 A scene from the Spanish military camp, siege of Breda 1624–1625. Jacques Callot, 1628. (Rijksmuseum)

of the time were cold and humid in winter time and soldiers preferred to be billeted in normal houses. Also, the lack of financial resources meant that they were difficult to maintain, especially after 1640 when the governors of the Low Countries and Lombardy had to spend their few funds elsewhere. Another innovation in the Low Countries was the creation of the first military hospital in Mechelen in 1585. Closed in 1609, the Hospital was re-opened in 1617 and was supported by smaller medical centres in Antwerp, Ghent and Cambrai. The Hospital of Mechelen had a staff of 48 men with seven doctors and eight surgeons and had 330 beds to attend patients (Parker 1991).

Further to the south in Naples and Sicily, we have a contingent of Spanish soldiers from the *Tercio Fijo de Napoles* and *Tercio Fijo de Sicilia*. In Naples soldiers could be accommodated in the three castles of the capital (Castel Nuovo, del Ovo and de Sant'Elmo) or in particular districts such as the *quartieri spagnoli*, and in the castle of the main city[63] of the kingdom. In comparison with Lombardy and the Low countries, for the 3,000–3,500 Spanish, life in Naples was close to being a paradise,[64] even if soldiers had to defend the kingdom against the actions of the corsairs of North Africa. In Sicily, the situation was mostly similar even if the climate was drier and the population more miserable. But for most of the Spanish soldiers, Naples and Sicily were just a stopover, as after some years they were generally sent to reinforce the tercios in the Low Countries, Lombardy and Spain.

In the Mediterranean area, North Africa was also a place where numerous Spanish garrisons were maintained. They did not fight a glorious war against the Protestants or against France but were important to keep the Ottomans

---

63 Brindisi, Crotone, Gaeta, Otranto and Tarento.
64 There was good wine, good food and a lot of women. Most of the Spanish veterans would finish their lives in southern Italy. Spanish literature of the sixteenth and seventeenth centuries, like that of Lope de Vega or Calderón de la Barca is full of stories of the good life in Naples.

THE ARMIES OF PHILIP IV OF SPAIN 1621–1665

3.4 Spanish field fortifications during the siege of Jülich in 1621/1622. Pieter Snayers, 1622–1650. (Rijksmuseum)

of Algiers at bay. The North African *presidios* could garrison from 50 men on the *Peñón de Vélez de la Gomera* to 3,000 men for the complex Oran-Mers el Kebir. Stuck in a fortress of stone or in a city surrounded by a hostile population, life in the *presidios* was hard and was considered a punishment by most soldiers and officers. As in other places, wages were still late and most of the supplies had to come from the Spanish mainland.[65] Trading with the local population was always complicated and in some cases *razzia* had to be done to find more supplies or to oblige Moorish tribes to deliver goods. In Oran the situation was a little bit better because the Spanish controlled a larger territory where orchards could be cultivated. The difficulties of life in the *presidios* due to malnutrition, illness and lack of prospects converted such places into a real jail. Numerous Spanish soldiers would desert to the Moorish and Ottomans, and become a "renegade" if they converted to Islam.

3.5.2 Soldiers on Campaign and The Wandering City

When the army was on campaign the ideal solution was to find a town or villages to accommodate soldiers. In this case, the quartermaster major and quartermasters of the companies would go in advance to negotiate with the local authorities the accommodation of the tercio.[66] Houses would be found to shelter the troops in groups of five to eight men from the same *camaradas*. In friendly territories arrangements were made with local authorities, but in hostile environments houses were simply occupied and owners had to suffer the occupation with the risk of seeing their houses reduced to ashes at the end.

On campaign most of the time troops had to be accommodated in an open field, normally near a wood and a stream. When the location has been designed by the high command, the space was divided into the *plaza de armas*, a central square where the troops could be joined in formation in case of necessity, the area for infantry quarters[67] (tercio or regiments), an area for horses and artillery and an area for sutlers and their wagons (O'Donnell 2006). When the tercio was in its assigned position, the squadron was organised, musters could be carried out to count the number of men; the *Mayor* drummer would give the orders and instructions of the commander of the army, and would remember the attitudes to have with civilians of the area and the possible punishments if crimes were detected. The *Sargento Mayor* would indicate the companies with night guard[68] duty and later soldiers would receive instructions from the quartermaster mayor of the tercio and the quartermasters of the companies to organise the camp. The space allocated

---

65 Supply came from harbours in Andalucia and Murcia by the Spanish galley squadron, and was dependent on the weather.
66 Arriving in the encampment area, the tercio would form squadrons and the quartermaster would give out a billet or *boletas* indicating where a soldier should be accommodated.
67 When troops from different nations were present they were separated to avoid problems and brawls.
68 To guard their camp the Spanish had normally three types of sentries. First the ordinary sentries located in groups of two soldiers and placed 30 feet from the camp, or from the hut of the guards; the second type were the security sentries placed at 30 feet from the first group; finally the "lost sentries" with the mission of advancing towards hostile forces to listen and observe without being seen (Picouet 2010).

to a tercio would depend of the number of men and companies in the field, but the organisation would follow more or less the same rules. The space was defined with a vanguard and a rearguard (Dávila Orejón Gastón 1669). The first element was the hut of the guards of the vanguard and followed by the chapel for the cleric and the gaming table (*Juego de mesa*) where soldiers could play dice, cards and other games being controlled by the guards and clerics. Behind there would be as many columns as companies with first a hut/shack/tent[69] for the standards (*banderas*) followed by a wooden structure called *Horcones de armas* to keep the long pikes and firearms (most of the time soldiers preferred to keep their weapon with them). After three feet would be the stove of the company, to cook the food. Normally the fire was surrounded by a small wall of earth, bricks, sod or ashes to reduce the risk of fire in the camps. Although close to their weapons, for the Spanish the idea was to have quick access to fire to light their matches in case of alarm or attack; in Dutch service (O'Donnell 2006) the stove tended to be close to the rearguard far away from the powder and weapons. Next in the column would be the hut/shack/tent of the *alférez* in order to survey the standard. Next was a space called the soldier's street to facilitate the movement of the troops towards the vanguard. Next the huts/shacks/tents or other facilities for sleeping were positioned in the column. Normally such elements could give shelter to five to eight men but in some cases only two or three men could be under cover of improvised construction. The column was ended by the huts of the sergeant and of the captain of the company. In Spanish service the distance between two columns was normally 1.28 m (close to four feet). On the rear of all the columns / companies of the tercios would be the tent of the *Sargento Mayor* and the tents of the *Maestro de Campo* and his staff. Civilian huts, and tents belonging to members of the tercio were placed at the rear and the last construction was the hut of the guard of the rearguard. Normally a tercio would cover a frontage of 40–50 m.

    The space allocated to horse companies was bigger than the one for a infantry company, the objective was not only to have more space for the animal but also that each horseman could have a clear view of his horse.

    For the artillerymen, they were located in a specific place inside the camp and with all their wagons to form a kind of wall with two or three entrances. Inside such a "wall", ammunition and gunpowder could be controlled and kept safe from the rest of the troops.

    It is not clear where latrines were installed. In the description of the creation of camps little reference could be found regarding such an important aspect of the hygiene of a camp (Hanlon 2016). Neither are latrines reported in the sketch provided by Davila Orejon (1669). A Spanish military manual from 1684 recommended constructing latrines at 100 paces from the parapet and to position guards to prevent soldiers relieving themselves too close to the camp (O'Donnell 2006). In fact, hygiene in the seventeenth was not a priority and it seems that men were used to the smell of human

---

69 On campaign soldiers were supposed to have "simple tents" but rarely they were available for all (Parker 1991), most of them tend to sleep below improvised shelters or a hut known in Spanish as a *barraca*, constructed from materials taken in the neighbourhood from houses and sheds.

MEN, LOGISTICS, AND FINANCE

3.5 Spanish garrison leaving Maastricht in 1632. Jan van de Velde (II), after Jan Martszen the Younger, 1632. (Rijksmuseum)

and animal excrement and waste, not to mention the smell of illness and death. The consequence was that after some days a camp could be converted into a biological hazard, especially in hot weather, and when the air became corrupted it was time to move the camp (Montecuccoli 1752).

When all the components of the army had been placed in the camp, drainage would will be constructed with a minimum of two accesses or doors (vanguard and rearguard). Such a construction was more or less complicated depending on whether the army would stay a night or several days in the same location and if they were in friendly or hostile territory. When the army was moving on, most of the time the temporary constructions were simply destroyed and burnt. The captain of the rearguard company would have the task of looking in the abandoned huts, houses and other accommodation looking for latecomers or deserters and to register the complaints of the villagers.

Regarding movement, a tercio of 13 companies of pikes and two companies of harquebusiers was formed as follows. The vanguard was always given to one of the companies of harquebusiers, supported behind them by a *mangas* of musketeers. Following this group of soldiers there would be a detachment of harquebusiers and musketeers from the companies of pikes followed by half of the pikes and the standards. Behind the standards would be the other half of the pikes and another detachment of harquebusiers and musketeers from the companies of pikes. Behind them, the non-combatants and civilians with the baggage and wagons were placed and in the rearguard the second company of harquebusiers. Depending on whether the operation was in friendly or hostile territory, and on tactical necessities, baggage, wagons, non-combatants, civilians and the sick could be left in a safe place protected by some harquebusiers. In peacetime, civilians and the baggage could go faster in front of the column to prepare the camp. There was a type of young civilian in the Spanish tercio called *mochileros*: teenagers below 15 years old who were more or less servants for some soldiers. Not all of them were Spanish; in fact most of them were from the country where the tercios were deployed (Albi de la Cuesta 1999).

If a tercio had to stay longer time in the same place, for example during a siege, stronger fortifications were made with lines of circumvallation and contravallation. The fortifications for the camps would be protected by deep ditches and palisades and earthwork bastions. In camps or in garrison, soldiers tend to waste their time playing cards or dice or playing a game called *taba*.[70] We have seen that in camps a special location near the hut of the guards was reserved, but most of the time soldiers would go to the civilian area to play theirs games unmolested. In such places, games and consumption of alcohol could rapidly degenerate into a brawl between the soldiers. Therefore officers were encouraged to fight idleness through regular military exercises.

---

70   *Taba* was an old gambling game, in English we could call it knucklebones. In such a game a small sheep bone (*taba*) would be thrown in the air, and upon falling, the people made bets to guess if it would fall upward (*suerte*) or backward (*culo*).

Table 3.2: Ordinary wages for a Spanish company after 1632 (Maffi 2007 & Clonard volume 4)

	Escudos / month		Escudos/ month
Captain + page	40+4	Drummers & Fifer	6
Alférez	15	*Cabos d'escuadra*	7
Abanderado	3 or 4	Musketeers	3+3
Sergeant	8	Harquebusier	3+1
Cleric	12	Pikeman	3+1
Barber	3	*Reformado* (*alférez*)	8
Fourier	3 or 4	*Reformado* (sergeant)	6

3.6 War and the Finances of the Spanish Army

In the seventeenth century the efforts of the Spanish monarchy and all states fighting for supremacy or just to survive, were to define the military structure to be able to maintain a reasonable fighting army and navy for some of them. In the sixteenth century the Spanish had already constructed a military system centred in Lombardy and in the Low Countries, supported by their dominions in southern Italy and America. Such a military structure had a significant cost and would represent the main spending for a monarchy. It is difficult to have a full overview of the cost (Storrs, 2006) due to the use of a variety of coins and unit accounts such as ducado, escudos,[71] maravedis, *reales de a ocho*, *reales de vellon*, florin, Scudi, Imperial lira and so on. The basis cost of the professional soldier (Table 3.2) was the wages and officially since the ordinance of 1632 the basic wage for a soldier was three escudos/month. By comparison the staff of the company had a cost of 107 escudos/month even if four of the 11 men had a wage of just three or four escudos. In fact on the basic wage, harquebusiers and pikemen had an extra of one escudo/month and musketeer three escudos/month due to the importance of their speciality. Soldiers with 12 years of service could have an extra pay of four escudos/month.

Cabo de escuadras, veterans, adventurers, and *reformados* also had higher wages than common soldiers. Using data from Table 3.2, a company of 70 soldiers including three *cabos de escuadra*, eight veterans with more than 12 years of service and four reformados (two *alférez* and two seargents), and a staff of 11 men would have a cost of some 505 escudos/month. According to Maffy (2007), the staff of an infantry tercio could have a cost of 381 escudos/month and if we had 15 companies the total cost for a tercio of 1,220 men would be some 7,060 escudos/month. By comparison a company of 60 cavalry (*Caballos Corazas*) could have a cost of 588 escudos/month[72] and one of 60 mounted harquebusiers at a cost of 527 escudos/month.

---
71 When data were not given in escudos, in our calculation data from Maffi (2014) were used and the following exchange rates were used: 1 scudi = 0.68 escudos; 1 ducado = 0.85 escudos.
72 Maffi (2007) gives a wage of 70.5 escudos/month for the captain, 34 escudos/month for the lieutenant, 27.3 escudos/month for the *alférez*, 7 escudos/month for the trumpet, the

But the cost of the army was also related to the ammunition bread,[73] artillery train, weapons and gunpowder, raising of new soldiers, new horses for the cavalry and also other costs such as clothing, new saddles, and so on. If we take into account data from Rodríguez Hernández (2013), the original budget of the royal finance (*Real hacienda*) for the Spanish armed force in 1663 was close to 15.29 million escudos[74] and 7.16 million escudos was for the army of Extremadura.

The spending was divided in 46.1 percent for the wages for the soldiers, 25.8 percent for the ammunition bread, 4.0 percent for the weapons and gunpowder, 3.7 percent for new horses, 11.0 percent for the wagons, 7.9 percent to raise new troops and pay the militia and 1.5 percent for other items. In fact, in 1663 the Spanish monarchy could not afford to pay such an amount of money and from the initial 7.16 million the army of Extremadura received only 5.73 million escudos, a reduction of 31 percent.

To sustain the war of the monarchy, most of the incomes[75] came mainly from Castile with 9.02 million escudos in 1623, 12.36 million escudos in 1633, 10.63 million escudos in 1655 and 14.67 million escudos in 1666.[76] Data comes from Andres Ucendo & Lanza Garcia (2008), and following them the average annual income from 1641 to 1664 was 12.31 million escudos. Surely, other territories of the monarchy were maintaining operational armies in the Low Countries and in Lombardy and the kingdoms of Naples and Sicily were regularly sending huge sums of money to finance the armies in northern Italy, Spain and Germany. For the Low Countries, the province had maintained part of the Army of Flanders since the beginning of the seventeenth century (Parker 1991), and with the war with France, this share increased over the years. In 1640, an income of 2.22 million escudos from the Low Countries came from local administration of the province[77] and the same year Spain sent 3.28 million escudos for the Army of Flanders. In the last decade of the

---

quartermaster, the blacksmith and 7.5 escudos/month for the troopers. In the companies of mounted harquebusies, we have the following numbers: 48.64 escudos/month, for the captain, 28.4 escudos/month for the lieutenant, 20.5 escudos/month for the *alférez*, 7 escudos/month for the trumpet, the quartermaster, the blacksmith and for the troopers.

73 In 1648, the Army of Flanders spent 603,808 escudos on ammunition bread, 45 percent of the total spending (Maffi 2014).

74 The budget was divided into 3.19 million escudos for the armies in Flanders and Italy, 3.16 million escudos for the army in Galicia and troops in the rest of Spain and the *presidios* of North Africa and 1.75 million escudos for the Armada. The budget for the armed forces was complemented by 3.60 million escudos for the normal spending of the monarchy (Rodríguez Hernández, 2013).

75 Another point to be taken into consideration was the relationship between the Spanish monarchy and European bankers. Bankers would advance and transfer the monies to pay the different armies and would impose conditions for such financial operations. It is not the purpose of the book to discuss these issues, but one should be aware that to military operations, the arrival of the treasure fleet was an important parameter in such an equation.

76 By comparison France spent an average of 13.80 million escudos each year for their war effort between 1635 and 1648 (Parker 2003).

77 With the governorship of Archduke Albert (1599-1621), the Low Countries had a certain autonomy from Madrid and it has been established that the province would pay annually some 3.6 million florins (1.44 million escudos) to maintain 12,000 men, sustain fortifications and provide part of the wagons for the artillery train. It was called in Spanish payment *via finanza* (Maffi 2014).

war, the contribution of the Low Countries was between 2.0 and 2.4 million escudos each year while the contribution from Spain was probably from 2.6 to 3.0 million escudos (Maffi 2014). In Lombardy, the general income during the reign of Philip IV could be estimated at an average of 1.20–1.26 millions escudos a year,[78] not enough money to maintain the Army of Lombardy, and subsidies from Spain, Naples and Sicily were necessary. Before 1645, the State of Milan's contribution to the defence of the Duchy was 15–20 percent. Later the state had to increase its share to 40–53 percent.[79]

The Kingdom of Naples was a rich and populous province of the Spanish monarchy and during the reign of Philip IV it provided not only thousands of troops for the army and sailors and rowers for the armada but also an important financial contribution to support the armies of the monarchy in Lombardy, Germany and Spain. From 1631 to 1636, an average of 0.50 million escudos were sent abroad. In 1639, 1.70 million escudos were sent abroad but the effort was too much for Neapolitan finances. Already in 1640, 1.10 million escudos could be sent to Milan (Maffi 2007). Even before the revolt of 1646-1648, the economic situation of the kingdom was in poor shape,[80] and the contribution of the kingdom to the armies of the monarchy had to be reduced to an average of 0.50 million escudos from 1650 to 1658.[81] Money came also from the Kingdom of Sicily, and from 1620 to 1650 up to 10 million escudos were sent to support Spanish armies in Lombardy and Spain, maintain the garrison in the island and the galley squadron of Sicily.[82]

As we have seen, money was found everywhere and most of the time at the cost of social disruption, revolts or open rebellion such as in Portugal and Catalonia. It was never enough, and spending had also to be reduced while maintaining as operational the armies of the monarchy. In fact the easiest way to save money was to "forget" to pay soldiers. If we go back to the example of the army of Extremadura in 1663: the reduction of 31 percent was mostly due to a reduction of the wages due to soldiers from an initial number of 3.30 million escudos, reduced to 1.45 million escudos, but at the same time costs such as ammunition bread, new horses or rising of new troops and payment of militia were left mostly untouched (Rodríguez Hernández, 2013). Such reductions of 56 percent could be made, to pay full wages only several times a year. That was already done in the Spanish armies of Flanders and Lombardy where an average of only three to five full wages was normally paid to the soldiers. An official report written in 1645 said that a soldier

---

[78] During the years 1628–1630, the economic crisis and the terrible plague epidemic made it difficult to reach such sums of money.

[79] From 1654 to 1660 (69 months), total spending for the army could be estimated at 12.30 million escudos with 48 percent provided by the State of Milan (Maffi 2007).

[80] The maximum income of the Kingdom of Naples was in 1646 9.98 million escudos and a debt of 127.8 million escudos. By comparison the total income in 1626 was 3.75 million escudos, in 1646 6.82 million escudos and in 1648 4.22 million escudos (Maffi 2014).

[81] For example, in 1652 426,000 escudos were sent to support the Army of Catalonia during the siege of Barcelona (Letter of the Count of Oñate to the King, 1 April 1652, Archivo General de Simancas E. Leg. 3275 doc.33).

[82] M. Aymard (1972), "il Bilancio d'una lunga crisi finanziaria", in *Rivista Storica Italiana*, LXXXIV, IV, pp. 988–1021.

3.6 A war veteran begging for support. Jacques Callot, 1628. (Rijksmuseum)

needed a minimum of six wages a year and the ammunition bread to survive (Rodríguez Hernández, 2015). But even such minimum was not often given to the soldier. The idea was to give one wage at the beginning of the campaign, one at the end, one or two during the campaign, and one in winter quarters. In the seventeenth century the payment was directly given to the soldiers to reduce fraud and the existence of "morte pay" or non-existent soldiers. The lack of pay indicates that soldier had to be partially financed and maintained by the civilian by the payment of money or goods in exchange for protection. The system, called "economic contribution", was directly organised between soldiers and local authorities, especially when resources for the army were scarce. Another system, for local authorities, was the possibility to give daily succour[83] corresponding to two thirds of the ordinary wage during winter quarters to complement their diet. Succour could also be given by the Spanish financial officer of the province.

The system of succour was sometime the only money received by the soldiers and was beneficial for the local authorities, because soldiers used the money to buy goods in the merchants of the city, but it also reduced problems created by starving soldiers.

---

83 Succours or *socorros* were established in the middle of the sixteenth century. During the reign of Philip IV, succours were sometime given to soldiers when full wages could not be paid, in order to give them a minimum of cash to buy food and clothes in order to survive.

4

Campaigns of the Spanish Armies

4.1 The Low Countries

4.1.1 The Campaign of 1622: the Battle of Fleurus, 29 August

In July 1622 the core of the Army of Flanders, commanded by Ambrogio Spinola, was starting the campaign against Bergen op Zoom, while the smaller Army of the Palatinate,[1] commanded by Gonzales de Cordoba, was in Lampertheim in Alsace with most of his troops after a difficult spring campaign against the Catholic forces. The Spanish high command received news that the Protestant troops of Ernst von Mansfeld and Christian of Brunswick had been officially disbanded by their patron Frederick V of Bohemia on 13 July and that they were looking for a new employer.[2] The Protestant commanders decided to move to a friendly place, the principality of Sedan, harassing villages in north of the Duchy of Lorraine in the process. At the same time, Gonzalo de Cordoba received the order from Brussels to join all his troops to deal with the Protestant army in case of necessity. In Sedan, Mansfeld tried without success to offer his service to the French king, but on the contrary the French sent an army commanded by Charles of Gonzague-Nevers to defend the Champagne area and the Duke of Lorraine raised an army to protect his duchy. Of all the possible candidates,[3] the two *condottieri* decided to go for the Dutch Republic and by mid August they were

---

1 At the beginning of 1622, the army of the Palatinate had 84 infantry companies (Spanish tercio of Cordoba), the Walloon tercio of Gulzin, the Burgundian tercio of Balanzon, the Italian tercio of Campolattaro and three German regiments: Isenburg, Baur and Emden), and 40 cavalry companies. The army was reinforced by the army of Bohemia with 95 companies of infantry (Walloon tercios of Bucquoy and Verdugo, Italian tercios of Spinelli and Caraccioli, German regiment of Fugger and 10 free companies) and 15 companies of cavalry (Reitzenstein, *Der Feldzung des Jahres 1622* … Zipperer`s Buchhandlung, Munich 1891).
2 Letter of Mansfeld to Gonzalo of Cordoba, 12 July 1622. CODOIN vol. 54, 1869, pp. 282–283.
3 French Protestant, King of Denmark, the Dutch Stadholder Maurice of Nassau or the French King Louis XIII (Esteban Rivas, 2013).

THE ARMIES OF PHILIP IV OF SPAIN 1621–1665

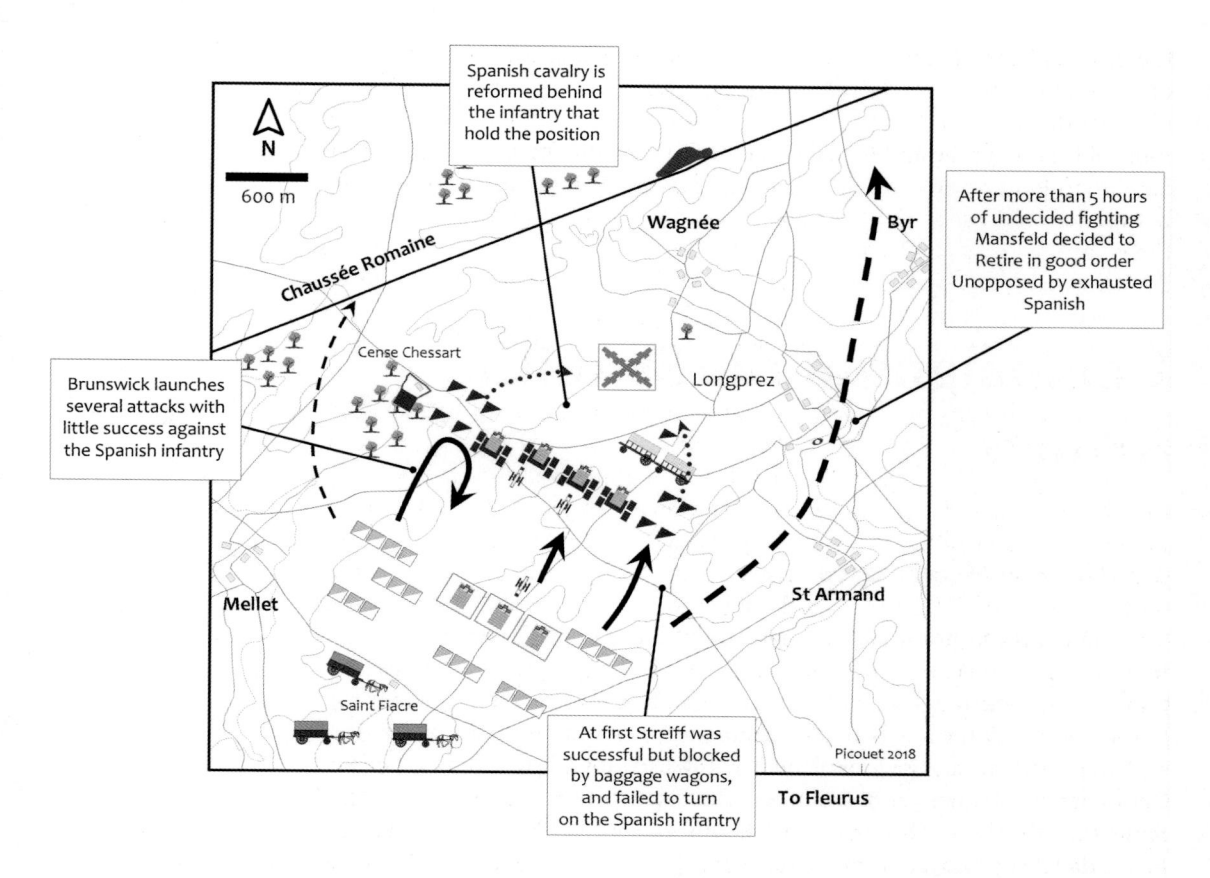

Spanish cavalry is reformed behind the infantry that hold the position

Brunswick launches several attacks with little success against the Spanish infantry

After more than 5 hours of undecided fighting Mansfeld decided to Retire in good order Unopposed by exhausted Spanish

At first Streiff was successful but blocked by baggage wagons, and failed to turn on the Spanish infantry

Map 4.1 The Battle of Fleurus (County of Hainaut), fought on 29 August 1622, between an invading Protestant army and the Spanish Army of Alsace. A tactical Spanish victory, won at heavy cost but a portion of the Protestant force managed to escape and join the Dutch territory.

preparing their army[4] to join Maurice of Nassau in north Brabant. Meantime, Gonzalo de Cordoba had departed from Lampertheim and was moving to protect the Duchy of Luxembourg. On 9 August, the Spanish army was in Thionville and later marched towards Yvoy (Carignan[5]) where they arrived on 12 August.[6] On 24 August, the Protestants were near Charleville-Mezieres, where houses and farms were sacked and burned and next day they moved towards Rumigny and Hirson. The initial goal was to take Chimay but the small city was well defended by the local militia.[7] Knowing that a Spanish army was in Luxembourg, Mansfeld decided to move more to the west in order to cross Brabant, and on 26 August was moving through La Capelle and Avesnes, bypassing Maubeuge, and the next day he was near Binche. On

---

4 In Sedan the Protestant army had probably 20,000 men. (*Count of Villermont, Ernest de Mansfeld*, volume 2, Brussels, 1866).

5 In the seventeenth century the city of Yvois was the capital of the *prévôté* of Yvois. In 1659, the territory was ceded to the Kingdom of France and the *prévôté* of Yvois was renamed the Duchy of Carignan and city of Carignan although the inhabitants were still called Yvoisiens.

6 The same day 2,000 Protestant horsemen were ambushed in a series of skirmishes by the Spanish losing hundreds of men. In Yvois the Spanish army had some 2,500 cavalry and 6,000–7,000 infantry (Cornet, 1868, p.58).

7 By order of the Archduchess Isabella of Austria, the governor of the province of Henau had mobilised 12,000 militia to reinforce the main cities of the country (Mariembourg, Philippeville and Charlemont), Esteban Rivas 2013.

CAMPAIGNS OF THE SPANISH ARMIES

the other side, the Spanish commander decided to cross the Ardennes and on 26 August crossed the River Meuse in Givet, sending cavalry parties to discover the movement of the Protestant army. The next day the Spanish left most of their baggage and the heaviest guns in Dinant and crossed the River Sambre in Pont de Loup. On 28 August the Spanish army arrived in a plain between a road called the Chaussée Romaine or Chaussée Brunehaut and the village of St Armand some kilometres north-west of the burg of Fleurus. Sentries were positioned in the village of Mellet while cavalry detachments observed the enemy. At dawn the first Protestant troops appeared near Mellet and the Spanish commander quickly deployed his troops between the Censes Cassard and the Village of St Armand (see Map 4.1).

The Spanish army[8] was deployed with their right anchorage on Chaussard Farm where 600–800 Walloon[9] musketeers commanded by Jacques de Haynin were positioned, followed to their left by the 1,200 cavalry commanded by the Baron of Gauchier deployed in five squadrons. In the centre the Spanish infantry (5,200–5,400 men) was deployed with, from right to left, 1st infantry squadron commanded by Francisco de Ibarra[10] (companies from the Spanish Tercio of Ibarra,[11] the Walloon tercios of Verdugo and Bucquoy and two companies from the Burgundian tercio of the Baron of Balanzon); 2nd infantry squadron commanded by Lieutenant Colonel Camargo (regiment of Othon Hendricks Fugger); 3rd infantry squadron commanded by Isenburg (regiment of Isenburg, one or two companies from the regiment of Emden and four free companies); and the 4th infantry squadron commanded by Campolataro (Italian tercios of the Marquis of Campolataro and Carlos Spinelli). On the left the Spanish had up to 800 cavalry commanded by Felipe da Silva deployed in four squadrons. Just behind the men of Felipe de Silva, the Spanish commander placed his wagons protected by three small companies of cavalry. The Spanish had also four light guns placed in front of the infantry. In total we could find a total of 8,000–8,200 men (6,000 infantry and 2,000–2,200 cavalry). For the Protestant side the army was deployed as follows: on the right, facing the cavalry of Felipe da Silva, the Protestant had a force of 1,000–1,500 cavalry commanded by Colonel Streiff. In the centre, commanded by Mansfeld, we have the Protestant infantry[12] probably deployed in three infantry "brigades" on a single line. On the left a strong body of cavalry of up to 3,000 horses[13] commanded by the Duke of Brunswick and lastly a second line with some cavalry squadrons. In total on

---

8   The Spanish order of battle was created using information from different sources: Cornet, 1868; Count of Villermont op. cit.; Canovas del Castillo, 1888; Esteban Rivas, 2013.
9   From the Tercio of Guillermo Verdugo and Tercio of the Count of Bucquoy.
10 Following Canovas Castillo (1898), Francisco de Ibarra decided to advance his squadrons of 50–60 feet to cover a gap with the cavalry.
11 The Spanish tercio of Ibarra was probably raised in 1619 and previously commanded by Gonzalo de Cordoba.
12 Most of the engravings of the battle show three infantry squadrons, one was probably commanded by Knyphausen. They could be arranged in the Dutch style with three to four *hopen* or battalions of 600–800 men.
13 Letter from the Baron of Gauchier (*Papiers d'Etat et de l'Audience n° 1983/2*; Archives générales du Royaume, Brussels).

THE ARMIES OF PHILIP IV OF SPAIN 1621–1665

4.1 Spanish infantry at the Battle of Fleurus in 1622 (painting often attributed as the Battle of Wimpfen, which seems to be incorrect). Pieter Snayers, 1615–1650. (Rijksmuseum)

the day of the battle, the Protestants had probably 5,000 cavalry,[14] up to 5,000 infantry,[15] and two guns.

The battle started in the morning[16] with a short cannonade between the artillery of the two sides. Soon after, the Protestants initiated a general advance towards the Spanish position. On the Protestant right the squadrons of Colonel Streiff attacked the weak Spanish cavalry of Felipe Silva. The Spanish cavalry squadrons were put in disorder and withdrawn to the rear to the wagons' position.[17] The Protestant cavalry was stopped by the intense flanking fire of the Italian musketeers and harquebusiers and the resistance of the cavalry protecting the baggage. Meantime on the Spanish right, the Duke of Brunswick attacked the cavalry of Gauchier and managed to disperse the first line. But the Spanish commander was able to use the squadrons of the second line to counter-attack, supported by the *mangas* of the infantry squadron of Ibarra. At last Brunswick reordered his squadrons and finally

---

14 It is possible that some horsemen refused to fight this day, so the number could rise to 6,000 men.
15 In Cornet (1868) we find numbers from 4,000 to 6,000 infantry, the reality could be close to 5,000 men.
16 Early in the morning the Protestant forces were deployed on the battlefield, and the battle started probably around 9:00 a.m.
17 Most of the baggage and wagons had been left behind in Dinant, but they still had some to transport powder and ammunition.

CAMPAIGNS OF THE SPANISH ARMIES

repulsed the Spanish cavalry. In the process the Protestant cavalry was continuously harassed by the Walloon musketeers deployed at Chaussard Farm. In the centre and right, Streiff, with the support of the Protestant infantry tried to turn the Spanish left but was blocked by the resistance of the Italian infantry and the remnants of the cavalry of da Silva protected by wagons.[18] During most of the battle the Protestant infantry made a poor action, exchanging only musket fire with the infantry squadrons of Fugger and Isenburg but was unable to fight closely. The main action was taking place on the Spanish right where Brunswick wanted to break the resistance of the Squadron of Ibarra and to turn on the rear of the Spanish army. The Protestants launched several charges against the Spanish, each time they had to suffer enfilade fire from Walloon musketeers of Chaussard Farm to be met by the stubborn resistance of the Spanish infantry. Losses were significant on both sides and Córdoba, seeing that the situation was stabilised on his left, sent musketeers and harquebusiers from the German regiments and Italian tercio to reinforce the squadron of Ibarra. At last in a desperate charge Brunswick was wounded even if some of the cavalry managed to escape to the Chaussé Romaine, bypassing Chaussard Farm. After more than five hours of intense

---

18 During the fighting some baggage was taken by the Protestant cavalry including money belonging to Gonzalo de Cordoba (Letter of Gonzalo de Cordoba to his brother Fernando, Berg op Zoom 26 September 1622, CODOIN vol. 54, 1869, pp. 311–315).

fighting both sides were exhausted, but the Spanish army was still holding its position and Mansfeld was unable to break it. The Protestant leader was able to leave the battlefield in an organised way undisturbed by the Spanish, taking the small roads towards Byr and the Chaussé Romaine to continue in his plan to reach the Dutch Republic. Gonzalo de Cordoba maintained his army in the same position for four hours in order to reorganise the cavalry and infantry, and during the night moved to Gembloux to find supplies. There, the Spanish high command decided to send the Spanish cavalry to follow the Protestant army. In the early morning of 30 August, the troops of Gauchier found the retreating Protestant army and their baggage between the villages of Landen and Saint Trond. Seeing their enemy, most of the Protestant cavalry ran away leaving the infantry unsupported. The Spanish cavalry had taken the Protestants by surprise and the infantry, unable to take a defensive position, was seriously damaged losing up to 2,000 men, the artillery and the baggage.

On 29 August, the battle had ended indecisively, both sides having suffered heavy casualties, some 1,200 dead (including the *Maestro de Campo* Francisco de Ibarra) and wounded for the Spanish and probably up to 1,500–2,000 men for the Protestants, and if we add the losses of the next morning total Protestant losses increase to 3,500–4,000 men. Mansfeld was able to cross the Bishopric of Liège and to reach Breda in Dutch territory on 10 September. During the long retreat, the Protestant troops were continuously harassed by militia and Spanish garrisons like that of Maastricht, losing more men. On Dutch territory, the two *condottieri* found fewer than 6,000 men[19] indicating that since 28 August, half of the army had disappeared. On the Spanish side, the small army of Cordoba[20] was recalled to Brussels by the Archduchess and later sent to reinforce the Spanish troops besieging Bergen op Zoom. There, such reinforcement was useless to break the resistance of the city and on 3 October 1622, on the arrival of the Dutch army, the siege was raised.

4.1.2 The Campaign of 1642: the Battle of Honnecourt, 26 May

Following orders from Madrid, the Spanish governor Francisco de Melo[21] decided, in a council of war, to attack some fortresses in French hands in an attempt to distract French troops from Catalonia.[22] The campaign started at the beginning of April and on 19 April the small town of Lens was taken; on 13 May it was the turn of the better-fortified city of La Bassée after a conventional siege of 22 days. On the other side, the combined French armies of Picardy (commanded by Harcourt) and of Champagne (commanded by Guise), with probably 28,000–29,000 men[23] in total, had

---

19 4,000 cavalry and 2,000 infantry (Count of Villermont op. cit.).
20 On 4 September the Spanish force had 5,000 infantry and 1 500 cavalry (Cornet, 1868).
21 In April the Spanish could field against the French an army of 20,000 infantry and 8,000 cavalry thanks to the reinforcements of a small Imperial contingent commanded by the Baron of Es (Canovas del Castillo 1888 volume 2).
22 We must not forget that at the same time the core of the French army, with the King of France and Richelieu, was in the County of Roussillon, besieging Perpignan.
23 The Count of Harcourt had the strongest one with 18,000 men and de Guiche had 10,000 to 11,000 men (Puysegur volume 2).

failed to relieve and save La Bassée and had adopted a defensive position. After the siege, Francisco de Melo had a significant army with him but he was still inferior to the combined French armies and would not risk a battle for it. But, the two French field marshals would give him an opportunity when they decided to split in order to cover from one side, the region of Boulogne and Montreuil with the army of Picardy and on the other side to cover the region of the Vermandois and Saint Quentin with the army of Champagne. The Spanish were quick to react and Francisco de Melo sent the core of the Spanish army against Field Marshal de Guiche leaving just a covering force in front of Harcourt's troops. The isolated army of de Guiche was in a fortified camp near Honnecourt-sur-Escaut,[24] and when French scouts reported that the Spanish force was only one day's marching distance from his camp, de Guiche refused to abandon his position by crossing the River Escaut.[25] On 26 May, Francisco de Melo was happy to find the French force entrenched behind their fortification and with his officers started to deploy the Spanish army[26] (see Map 4.2). On the extreme right wing were two squadrons of light cavalry/Croats (Colonel Sitnan), followed on the left by 12 squadrons from the ordinary cavalry of Flanders (Marquis of Velada and Juan de Vivaro), seven squadrons from the ordinary cavalry of Flanders (Francisco Pardo), three squadrons of mounted harquebusiers and a strong *manga* of 1,000 musketeers (Balthazar Mercader). All those troops were commanded by the Marquis of Velada. In the centre (Jean de Beck) were the infantry with a first line of five Spanish infantry squadrons[27] and two Italian ones.[28] The second line covered the hill on the left (behind the Italians) and was composed of three infantry squadrons of Walloons (tercios of Prince de Ligne, Count of Grobendonck and Lord of la Grange) and one of Irish (Tercio of Owen O'Neil), further to the right was a third line of four infantry squadrons of German regiments[29] and one of Walloons (tercio of the Lord of Conteville). The left wing (Bucquoy) was made of some 15–16 cavalry squadrons, three or four formed by Walloon companies of men-at-arms

---

24 It has been difficult to locate the battlefield from written sources, but using illustrations (Petrus Rucholle, *Planta de la batalla de Chastelet*… on the Gallica website; Anonymous seventeenth century battle plan from the battle of Honnecourt, Madrid Archivo Historico Nacional; Peeter Snayers, wrongly named *sitio de Bar le Duc*, Madrid Museo del Prado catalogue number P01741) and old maps of the area, the presence of the Abbey of Honnecourt and the old castle of Honnecourt is always mentioned. From our knowledge and after a personal correspondence with Pavel Hrncirik, the location of Honnecourt-sur-Escaut seems to be the more probable for both of us.

25 Field Marshal Rantzau insisted on retreating in the face of superior force but de Guiche argued that the position was strong and that they would wait for the enemy (Puysegur volume 2). Another possibility was that a retreat in the face of a superior enemy could be a disaster and it was better to face him (*Mémoire du Maréchal de Gramont*, volume 1, 1826).

26 The order of battle was created following the Spanish written sources (Sanchez-Martin, 2000; Canovas del Castillo 1888 volume 2; Vincart, *Relacion campaña de 1642*) and illustrations (Petrus Rucholle op. cit.; Anonymous seventeenth century, op. cit.).

27 Infantry squadrons from the Spanish Tercios of Alonso de Avila, Duke of Alburquerque (*Tercio Viejo de Hollanda*), Jorge Castelvi, Count of Villalba (*Tercio Viejo de Brabante*) and Antonio Velandia.

28 Tercios of Alonso Strozzi and Giovanni Delli Ponti.

29 First infantry squadron German regiments of Beck and Frangipani, second infantry squadron German regiments of Van der Bar and de Rouvroy, third and fourth infantry squadrons from respectively the German regiments of von Metternich and Baron of Verwoert.

THE ARMIES OF PHILIP IV OF SPAIN 1621–1665

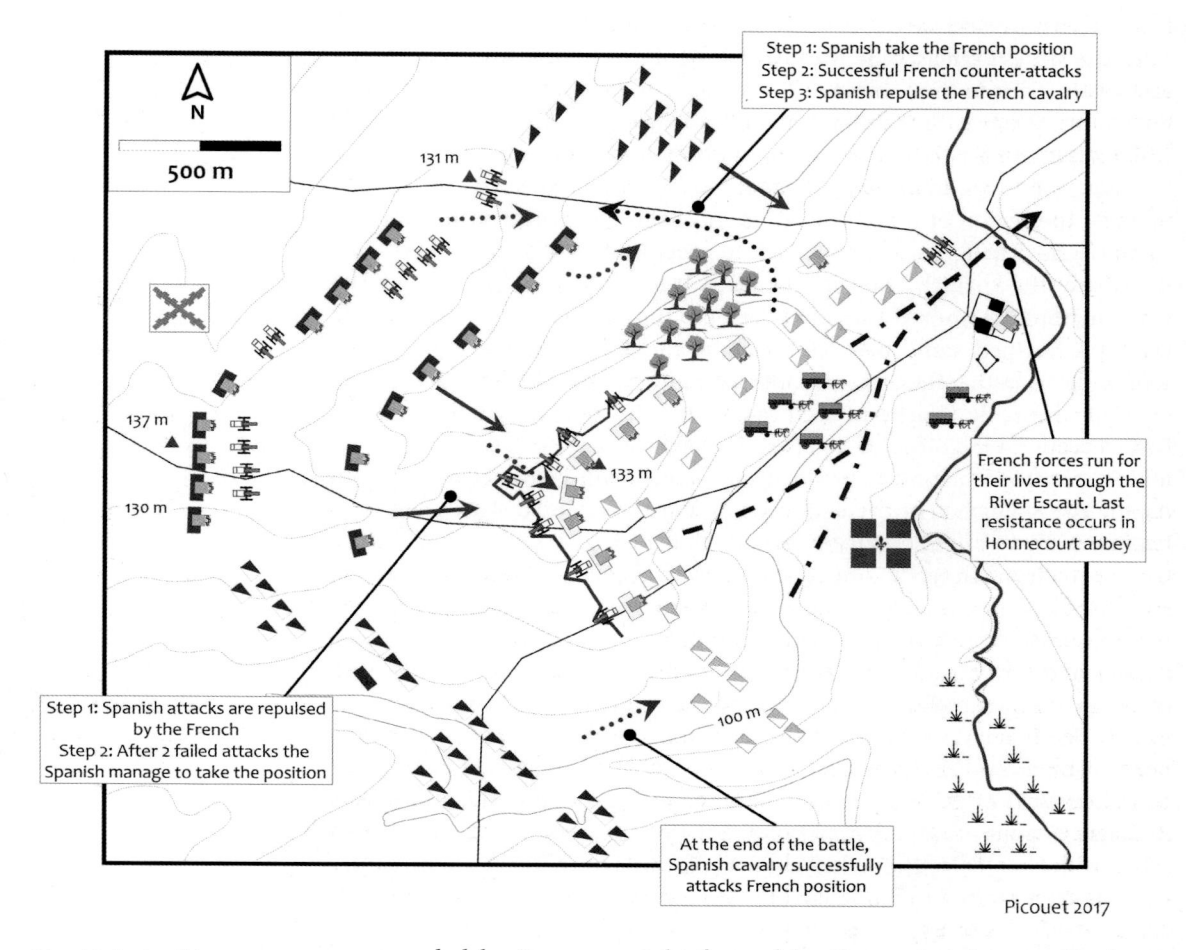

Map labels:
- Step 1: Spanish take the French position
- Step 2: Successful French counter-attacks
- Step 3: Spanish repulse the French cavalry
- French forces run for their lives through the River Escaut. Last resistance occurs in Honnecourt abbey
- Step 1: Spanish attacks are repulsed by the French
- Step 2: After 2 failed attacks the Spanish manage to take the position
- At the end of the battle, Spanish cavalry successfully attacks French position

Picouet 2017

Map 4.2 Battle of Honnecourt fought on 26 May 1642, In the semi-independent fiefdom of Cambrèsis between the Spanish Army of Flanders and the French Army of Champagne. A Spanish tactical victory with the destruction of the Army of Champagne but the Spanish commander could not press on due to the presence of the French Army of Picardy and enemy force in the Rhine valley threatening Catholic positions.

commanded by Bucquoy, eight formed by German regiments (Regiment of Padilla and Regiment of Castro) and four squadrons from the Imperial contingent.[30] The artillery had 14 to 20 guns and was placed on the small hill protected by the infantry of the second and third lines. In total Francisco de Melo had 13,000–14,000 infantry divided into 16 infantry squadrons, and one *manga* and some 6,000–6,500 cavalry in 41–42 squadrons.

On the opposite side de Guiche had entrenched his army, with on the right, commanded by the Baron of Courcelles, an infantry battalion (Vervins) and probably seven cavalry squadrons.[31] In the centre,[32] commanded by de Guiche, was a first line of infantry behind the fortification and a second and third line with seven to nine squadrons of cavalry. The left was commanded

---

30 After the defeat of Kempen in January 1642, some Imperial cavalry, commanded by the Baron of Enquefort, rejoined the troop of Luxembourg and the Army of Flanders (Negredo del Cerro, 2016).
31 Carabins of Arnault (one squadron), regiment of Bouchavannes (three squadrons), Gendarmes of Longueville (one squadron), and two other squadrons (Petrus Rucholle op. cit.).
32 Probably six French infantry *bataillons* (Piedmont, Rambures, Bussy-Lameth, Aubeterre, Courcelles and Saint Mégrin) and one Scottish/Irish amalgamated *bataillon*. The cavalry squdrons came from the regiment of Lenouncourt (three squadrons), the companies of gendarmes (one to three squadrons) and the regiment of Guiche.

by the Count of Rantzau with probably seven cavalry squadrons.[33] At last 500 musketeers from the German regiment of Batilly were deployed in the abbey and castle of Honnecourt and all the artillery was deployed along the right and centre position. In total we might have close to 10,000 men divided in 7,000 infantry and 3,000 cavalry supported by 10 guns.

During most of the morning all the Spanish contingent arrived on the battle ield and in the first hours of the afternoon, the battle started when the well-placed Spanish artillery opened fire on the French position with great effect. In the centre the Spanish tercio launched an attack on the French position, they were met by heavy musket and artillery fire. On the left wings the Spanish cavalry of Bucquoy had a first successful beating back of the force of Courcelle. Seeing the defeat of his right, de Guiche regrouped the cavalry of the centre and launched a furious counter-attack on the flank of the Walloon cavalry with success. The Spanish left retired in disorder and the French cavalry was able to disrupt and stop the advancing Italian tercios. De Guiche followed his movement to attack the artillery on the hill, but he was met by the Walloon tercios of the second line, particularly that of the Prince de Ligne. While de Guiche was fighting against the Walloons and Italians, the Spanish infantry of the centre renewed the attack but were repulsed a second time by the French infantry from the regiments of Rambure and Piémont. On the left, the Spanish cavalry and infantry had the upper hand and were beating back the French force. In the centre the Spanish infantry renewed their efforts and finally entered the French fortification. On the Spanish right, the French cavalry had been manhandled by the artillery and could not resist the general advance of the cavalry of the Marquis of Velada, supported by Spanish musketeers. Resistance collapsed and French soldiers became a giant stampede without order, with their only goal to cross the River Escaut to find a safe place. Despite a strong resistance of Rambure and Piémont in the abbey, most of the troops surrendered. The army of Champagne was totally destroyed, it is said that de Guiche found only 1,600 men, mostly troopers, in Saint Quentin.[34] Up to 80 or 85 percent of the army had been lost with some 3,200 dead, 3,400 prisoners, including 400 officers,[35] the others being deserters, while on the opposite side the Spanish army had lost only 400 to 500 men (Cánovas del Castillo volume 2, 1888). Francisco de Melo could not use his victory to harass the north of France or to take a French stronghold, as the movement of the Franco-German army of Guébriant on the Rhine valley threatened Brabant, and Harcourt with the army of Picardy had still 17,000 men in hand.

4.1.3 The Campaign of 1648: the Battle of Lens, 20 August

With the final peace treaty with the United Provinces in hand and the instruction from Madrid to take the offensive to distract the French forces away from Catalonia, the governor of Flanders, Archduke Leopold of Austria, decided to conduct several military operations to retake positions lost during

---

33 Regiment of the Baron of Leschelles (three squadrons), Regiment of Rocquelaure (three squadrons) Regiment of Bouillon (82 squadrons) (Petrus Rucholle op. cit.), and Périni volume 3.
34 *Mémoire du Maréchal de Gramont*, op. cit.
35 Puységur op. cit.

the previous years. The campaign started with a failed attack of the Spanish army against Courtrai in February. The campaign was followed by a French invasion against the city of Ypres on 12 May. The objective of the French, commanded by the Prince of Condé, was to have a better connection between Dunkirk and Courtrai. After a siege of two weeks the Spanish garrison of Ypres had to capitulate, but meanwhile Archduke Leopold of Austria was able to storm Courtrai[36] and retake the city and the citadel on 23 May after two days of fighting. On 16 June the French suffered a disaster when the troops of Field Marshal Rantzau were destroyed trying to take by surprise the city of Ostend. During the following weeks, while raiding parties of Spanish cavalry were conducting several operations in the north of France, the main Spanish and French armies were still manoeuvring, avoiding a pitched battle. Finally on 24 July a detachment of the Spanish army commanded by the Marquis of Sfondrati laid siege to the city of Furnes. The operation against the city was rapidly conducted, on 31 July the counterscarp was taken, and on 3 August the French garrison capitulated. On 11 August all the Spanish field army was located near Warneton, 24 km south-west of Courtrai while the main French force was at Hinges, five kilometres north of Béthune and 34 km from the Spanish position. The Prince of Condé was waiting for a detachment of 4,000–5,000 men from the army of Germany commanded by Colonel Erlach and decided to leave the initiative to the Spanish. On the other side, Archduke Leopold of Austria left a force to cover maritime Flanders from the garrison of Dunkirk and Ypres, and with the rest he moved to the south on 12 August taking the same day the castle of Estaires, a French position covering Béthune. On 14 August a strong skirmish took place when the Spanish vanguard tried unsuccessfully to cross the River La Lawe at La Gorgue. Seeing that the French army was correctly protecting Béthune, the Archduke continued his movement to the south in order to cut the communication between Arras and Béthune. The Spanish army passed a few kilometres from La Bassée, crossing the River Deule near the burg of Don on 16 August. The same river was crossed again at Pont à Vendin and on 17 August the Spanish were surrounding Lens. On the other side, the Prince of Condé had finally been reinforced by Erlach[37] on 16 August and decided to follow the Spanish army. The next day he was at La Bassée, preparing the French army in battle order. The Prince of Condé wanted to fight and restore his pride, badly affected by the failure of Lérida the previous year, but also by the losses of Courtrai and Furnes. The Spanish cavalry had detected the approach of the French and the Archduke decided to take position on a hill between the villages of Saint Lauren and Liévin. In two days the small garrison of Lens capitulated and on 19 August the French army moved in battle order and stopped 2,000 m from a line crossing the villages of Grenay and Loos (Aumale volume 5, 1889).

---

36 At that time the garrison of Courtrai had 1,500 to 2,000 infantry and 150–200 cavalry. The Spanish field army was estimated at 20,000 to 25,000 men including the auxiliary Army of Lorraine (Aumale volume 5, 1889).
37 Following Aumale (volume 5, 1889), of the original 4,000 men, Erlach could only present 3,000 men to Condé on 16 August, the rest had been left on the road or had deserted.

On 20 August the Spanish Army was in battle order (see Map 4.3), it was a composite army[38] with units from the multicultural Army of Flanders and the auxiliary Army of Lorraine. The total force is given as 18,000 men[39] with 38 artillery guns. The Spanish were deployed with a right wing of cavalry[40] commanded by the Count of Bucquoy and the Prince de Ligne. In the centre or *bataille*, in the first line, was a mixture of 10 infantry squadrons and seven cavalry squadrons.[41] Still in the centre, the second line had only six infantry battalions[42] with two cavalry squadrons (guards of the Archduke and guards of Fuensaldaña) between the lines. It is probable that the right of the *bataille* was commanded by the Count of Fuensaldaña, the left by the Baron of Beck and the Archduke was in the middle. The left wing[43] was under the command of the Prince de Salms and the Count of Ligneville and was made of a first line of 12 cavalry squadrons and a second line of nine squadrons. Finally we have up to 38 artillery guns located on the hill near Lens, defended by a reserve of four to seven cavalry squadrons as well as light cavalry squadrons of Croats and free companies of dragoons.

Seeing a well-ordinanced force on a hill, the Prince of Condé decided to avoid a futile blind attack and fall back to find supplies in La Bassée. The French began to move in six columns. On the other side the French movement was seen with surprise and the Archduke sent the cavalry of the Count of Ligneville supported by *mangas* of musketeers or dragoons to harass the French rearguard. The French rearguard was badly defeated and Condé tried to answer with his heavy cavalry but he was also bitten and was obliged to run away behind the French infantry. This first success was encouraging for some Spanish officers,

---

38   The order of battle is given following the illustration of Beaulieu (*La bataille de Lens en Flandre gaignée par l'armée du très chres[tien] Louis XIII ... le 20e d'aoust 1648: [estampe] / par le Sr de Beaulieu*, Cochin, Noël et Frosne, Jean. http/gallica.bnf.fr) with a list of Spanish prisoners and dead, Spanish sources indicating the Spanish units in 1647 (Vincart, *Historia de la Campaña de 1647*) and 1649 (Vincart, *Relacion de la Campaña de 1649*) as well as Galeazo Gualdo (1651).

39   For the Army of Flanders we could have 5,500 infantry and 7,500 cavalry and for the Army of Lorraine 3,000 infantry and 2,000 cavalry. In total we have 8,500 infantry in 16 battalions and up to 9,500 cavalry and dragoons in 54–57 squadrons.

40   The cavalry (22 squadrons) was deployed on two lines with eight squadrons from the cavalry of the state (Walloons) and four German squadrons (regiments of Brouck, Savary and Bucquoy), while the second line should have 10 squadrons from the cavalry of the state commanded by the Prince de Ligne.

41   From right to left we should have two Spanish battalions (Tercio of Fernando Solis and Tercio of Boniface reinforced by Irish companies from the Tercio of Murphy), one amalgamated German battalion (Regiment of Mouroy and Regiment of Beck), two amalgamated Walloon battalions (first, Tercio de la Motterie and Tercio of Grobendonck; second, Tercio of Bruay and Tercio of Crevecoeur), four cavalry squadrons, one Italian amalgamated battalion (Tercio of Bentivoglio and Tercio of Guasco), one amalgamated Lorraine battalion (Regiment of Touvenin and Regiment of Silly), three cavalry squadrons from Lorraine (Ligneville), two amalgamated Lorraine/Irish battalions (regiments of Clinchamps and des Marais, Tercio of Synot/Murphy and Regiment of Plunket) and one amalgamated Lorraine battalion (regiments of Remyon and Huillier).

42   From right to left we should have two Spanish battalions (Tercio of Toledo and Tercio of Vargas), one German battalion (Regiment of Berlau), two amalgamated Lorraine/German battalions (first, regiments of Housse and Chastelain; second, regiments of Mitry and Wanghen) and one amalgamated Lorraine battalion (regiments of Verduisan and Gondrecourt).

43   In the first line we have, a regiment of dragoons (Colonel Mormal), 10 squadrons from the free companies of ordinary cavalry of Flanders and a squadron from the guards of the Duke of Lorraine. The second line was made by nine squadrons from regiments of the cavalry of Lorraine.

THE ARMIES OF PHILIP IV OF SPAIN 1621–1665

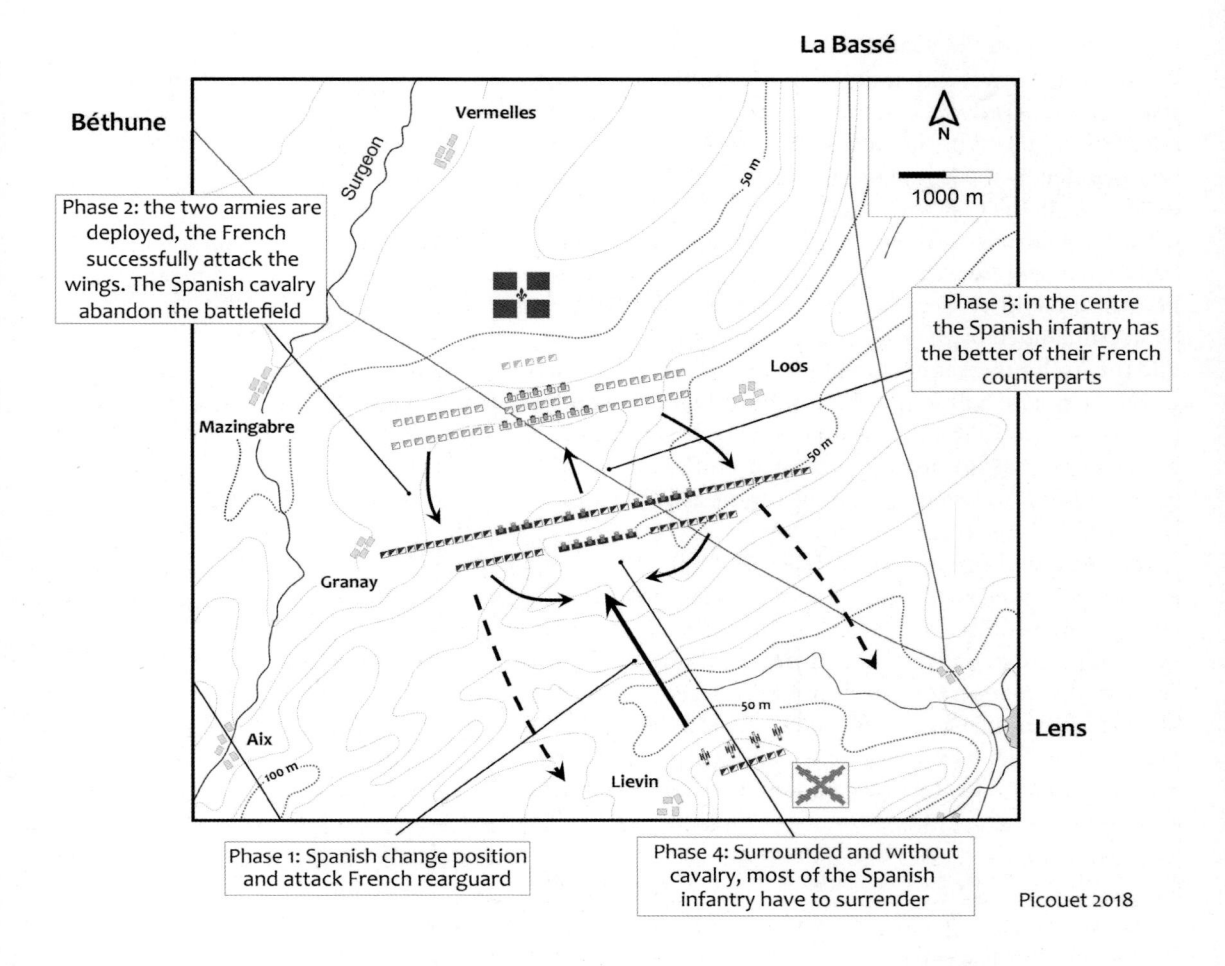

Map 4.3 The Battle of Lens, fought on 20 August 1648 in the County of Hainaut between the Spanish Army of Flanders and the French Army of Picardy. A clear Spanish tactical defeat but the French could not press on, mainly due to the political instability in Paris and lack of men.

and the Archduke was quickly convinced to move all the army to the previous French position. On the other side, the Prince of Condé understood that a retreat in such conditions could lead to a disaster and decided to stop and face the incoming Spanish. Thus, the Count of Ligneville halted his attacks and as quickly as possible the French commander reorganised his army[44] with 17 cavalry squadrons[45] on the right under his command, the infantry in the

---

44 The French order of battle has been constructed using the illustration of Beaulieu (Cochin, *La bataille de Lens en Flandres … le 20e d'aoust 1648*), French written sources (Aumale, 1889, Montglat volume 2 1826, and Périni volume 4, 1893); and Issac de La Peyrère, *La bataille de Lents*, Paris 1649. Gallica.

45 The right wing was commanded by the Price of Condé himself and had nine squadrons (1x Gardes du Prince, 2x Chappes, 1x Coudray-Montpensier, 1x Salbrick, 1x Vidame d'Amiens, 2x La Villette and 1x Ravenel) in the first line commanded by Aumont-Villequier and the eight squadrons (1x Royal, 1x Orléans, 1x La Meilleraye, 1x Streef, 1x Saint-Simon, 1x Bussy-Almoru, 1x Harcourt le Viel, 1x Beaujeu) for the second line commanded by the Lord of Noirmoutier.

4.2. Map of the Battle of Lens in 1648.

centre[46] commanded by the Gaspard of Coligny on the left, 16 squadrons[47] of cavalry under the command of Field Marshal Gramont and a reserve of five squadrons commanded by Colonel Erlach.[48]

With such arrangements, the French moved forward to retake their previous positions. Following Cánovas del Castillo (Volume 2, 1888), when the first fighting started on the Spanish left the Spanish army had not finished its deployment, the cavalry was in place but some of the infantry was just arriving on the battle field and the reserve squadrons were still on the hill in their original position.

On the French right, Condé was able to disperse the Spanish cavalry of the first line with ease[49] but he was successfully counter-attacked by the cavalry of Lorraine of the second line. During sometime the French and Lorraine cavalry fought bravely but like at Rocroi, the cavalry of the French

---

46 The first line had seven battalions (from right to left 1x Picardy, 1x Erlach/Perwol, 1x *Gardes Suisses*, 2x *Gardes Françaisess*, 1x *Gardes Ecossaises* and 1x Persan). The second line five battalions (Royne/La Bassée, Erlack/Bassigny, Mazarin-Italien, Conti and Condé) and between them six cavalry squadrons of heavy cavalry (companies of gendarmes and *chevaux-légers*).

47 First line nine squadrons (2x Bains, 2x La Ferté-Senneterre, 2x Gramont, 1x Mazarin, 1x Carabin d'Arnault, 1x Gardes de Gramont and Gardes la Ferté) commanded by la Ferté-Senneterre; and second line seven squadrons (1x Chemeraut, 1x Meille, 2x Norlieu, 1x Lillebonne, 1x Gesvres and 1x Rocquelaure) commanded by Plessis-Bellière.

48 The reserve consisted of German regiments (2x Erlach, 2x Sirot and 2x Ruvigny) from the Armée d'Allemagne.

49 On the Spanish left, few Spanish horsemen fought correctly this day. It seems that some of them ran away without firing their guns or taking out their sword (Canovas del Castillo, volume 2, 1888).

reserve managed to outflank their opponents. Attacked on the flank by Erlach and from the front by Condé the cavalry of Ligneville started to give ground step by step and in the end they ran away from the battlefield. On the other cavalry wing, the men commanded by the Count of Bucquoy clashed with their enemies, holding their position while exchanging pistol fire and sword thrusts with the French cavalry of Gramont. Finally, the superior organisation of the French cavalry took the upper hand and the Spanish cavalry started to step back and to abandon the battlefield. Meantime in the centre the French infantry led by the battalions of the *Gardes Françaises* and *Gardes Suisse* launched a massive assault on the Spanish infantry (Bonifaz and Mouroy/Beck). Successful at first, they were soon isolated from their comrades suffering terrible losses after a counter-attack by the Spanish tercios (Toledo and Vargas) and the cavalry of the centre. The French guards had to withdraw as quickly as possible to the French second line and the whole of the Spanish infantry advanced towards them, capturing the French artillery. The Spanish were halted by the strong resistance of French infantry of Picardy, Persan and *Gardes Ecossaises*, the attack of the squadrons of gendarmes and by the support of the French second line. Rapidly, soldiers of the Spanish infantry discovered that their flanks were open and that the Spanish cavalry had abandoned them. Panic started to spread in the Spanish centre and some of the infantry withdrew with the last cavalry squadrons present on the battlefield. On the other side, the two French wings managed to trap a good proportion of Spanish infantry and to overcome the last resistance of the reserve cavalry. In the following hours the French captured hundreds of Spanish including a wounded Baron of Beck. As at Rocroi, the better organisation of the French cavalry coupled with a better coordination between the different French units had won the day for Condé. As usual Spanish losses are difficult to establish, but following Spanish sources, losses could be estimated at 3,500 men (infantry only), while French accounts elevated the number to 8,800 men or 10,000 men. To our knowledge, the estimate[50] of Galeazo Gualdo (1651), should be close to the truth and if we take into accounts some deserters Spanish losses could be estimated at up to 6,000 men, most of them infantry, 38 guns and the majority of the baggage. On the other side, French losses were estimated at 600 men excluding officers (Galeazo Gualdo,1651).

4.1.4 The Campaign of 1656: the Battle of Valenciennes, 16 July

On 9 May John of Austria entered Brussels after a chaotic journey from Barcelona, to replace Archduke Leopold Wilhelm of Austria in the position of governor of Spanish Flanders. Accompanying him was the previous governor of the State of Milan, Luis de Benavides Carillo de Toledo, Marquis of Caracena. The first task of the new governor was not to prepare the Army of Flanders for the new campaign but above all to re-establish a relationship with Louis de Bourbon II Prince of Condé, one of the best generals available in the

---

50 Galeazzo Gualdo (1651) gives the numbers as 2,000 dead, 3,000 prisoners, 38 guns, 120 infantry and cavalry standards. He says also that 600 men were taken in Lens and 300 men in the neighbourhood.

CAMPAIGNS OF THE SPANISH ARMIES

Spanish army. Since the 1654 campaign, a general mistrust between Condé and members of the Spanish high command had undermined the efficiency of the Army of Flanders. John of Austria also had other problems: the lack of resources, the high debt of the army and the difficult relationship with the bankers of Antwerp. On paper, the Army of Flanders had 60,000–66,000 men, if we take into account all the troops including those in garrison in the Duchy of Luxembourg and the auxiliary army of Condé. The field force was reduced much further and for the 1656 campaign the goal was to have an army of some 26,000 men.[51] In 1656, the years of the *Fronde* were over and as usual the French army was able to start the campaign with two armies, one commanded by Field Marshal Turenne with 17,000 men[52] and the other by Field Marshal La Ferté-Senneterre with 10,000 men,[53] for a total of 27,000 men.[54] The objective of the French generals was to use the previous conquests of 1654–1655 (Le Quesnoy, Landrecies, Condé-sur-l'Escaut and Saint-Ghislain) and to bring the war ot the heart of the County of Hainault and the city of Tournay. The core of the French force initiated the campaign from Landrecies and on 12 June the cavalry of Turenne, commanded by the Marquis of Uxelles, moved fast, passing Le Quesnoy and Condé-sur-l'Escaut to arrive at the village of Pipaix just eight kilometres from Tournay. Although the Army of Flanders was not ready to be on campaign, the Prince of Condé, with a select force of 3,000–4,000 men anticipated the French movement and when the Marquis of Uxelles wanted to surround Tournay he found Condé and the Spanish waiting for him, deployed on the counterscarp of the city. With no wish to fight an alerted enemy, Turenne decided to find another target and on 15 June he was near Valenciennes on the River Escaut. The next day he was rejoined by the army of La Ferté-Senneterre. Immediately a line of circumvallation was made, with the army of Turenne on the east bank[55] of the River Escaut and that of La Ferté-Senneterre on the west with his headquarters on the small hill of Azin. The two armies were connected by several boat bridges on the north and south. On the other side, John of Austria and the Prince of Condé were reinforcing the garrisons of Douai, Cambrai and Bouchain and regrouping as many soldiers as possible so as to have a decent field army in hand. On 19 June the Spanish

---

51   Numbers given by the relation are 14,500 infantry and 10,900 cavalry (*Relación de la Campaña del año 1656 del Estado de Flandes*; BNE. H.86, folios 344–349. Colección de Libros españoles raros o curiosos volume 14).
52   The Army of Turenne had probably 9,000–9,500 infantry coming from 14 French regiments (*Gardes Françaises*, *Gardes Suisses*, Bussy-Rabutin, Vervins, Dumbarton, Vandy, La Couronne, Montausier, Rambures, Bretagne, Vendôme, La Marine, Turenne and Picardy) and five regiments from Lorraine (Tornielles, Marasque, Konos, Kusac and de Cascar), 7,500–8,000 cavalry and up to 40 guns. (Susane, 1853, and A. Calmet. *Histoire de Lorraine*. volume 6, 1737).
53   Even if it is difficult to estimate, the army of Field Marshal de la Ferté had probably some 6,000–6,500 infantry from 12 regiments (*Gardes Françaises*, *Gardes Suisses*, Piemont, Espagny, Lignières, La Ferté, Belzunce, Gardes Suisse, La Marine, Manchini), 3,500–4,000 cavalry and 15 guns.
54   Following the sources we have different numbers, from 24,000 men (Aumale volume 6) to 30,000 (*Récit du Siege de Valenciennes en 1656, publié d'après le manuscrit original de Simon le Boucq par Maurice Hénault*, Valenciennes, 1889).
55   On the north we have the quarter of the Turenne with up to 9,500 men, followed by the quarter of the auxiliary army of the Duke of Lorraine with 4,000 men, and in the south on Mont Houy, the quarter of the King's horse and infantry, 3,500 men commanded by the Duke of Navailles (*Mémoire du Duc de Navailles par M. Moreau*, Paris 1861).

THE ARMIES OF PHILIP IV OF SPAIN 1621–1665

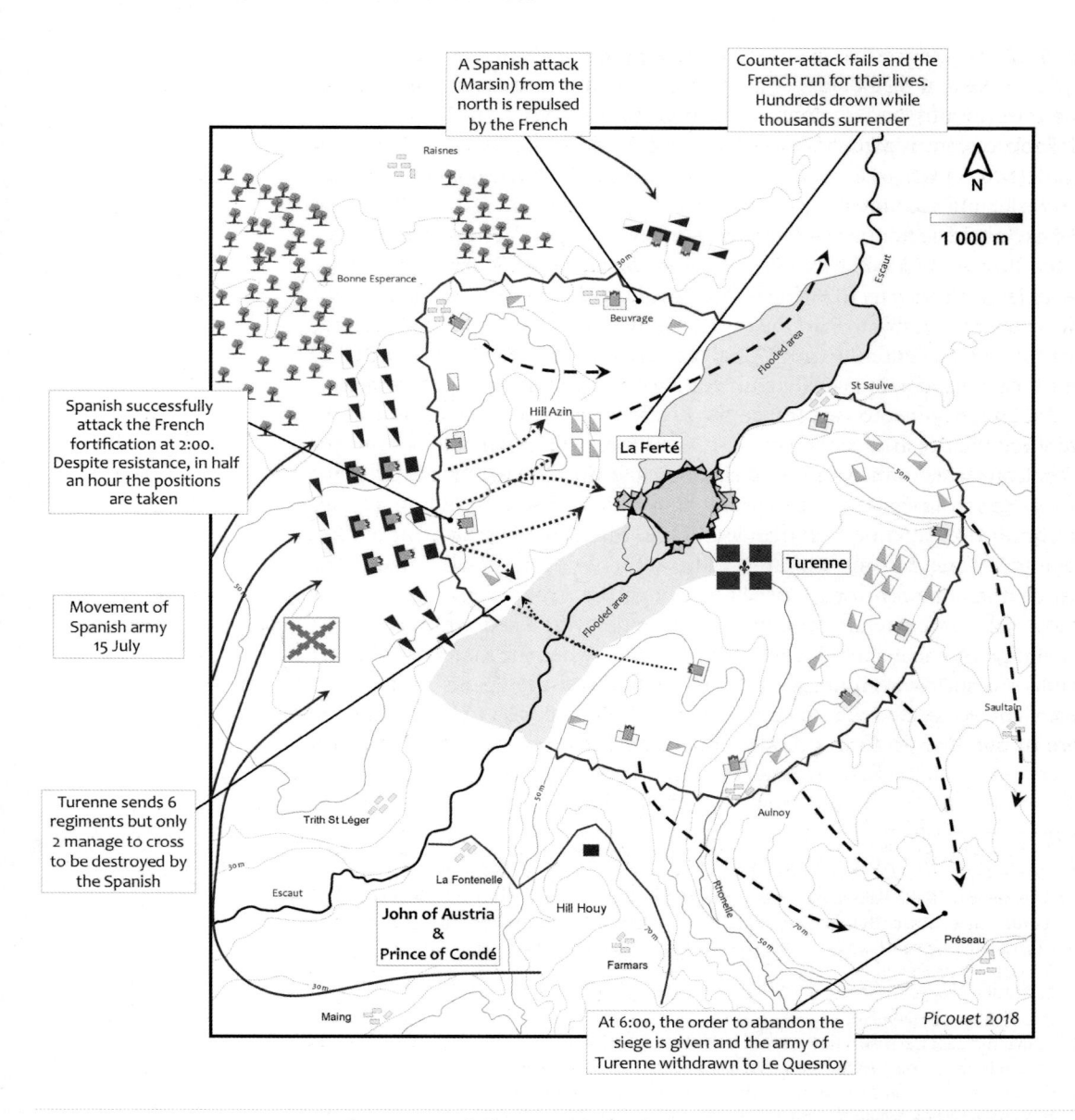

Map annotations:

- A Spanish attack (Marsin) from the north is repulsed by the French
- Counter-attack fails and the French run for their lives. Hundreds drown while thousands surrender
- Spanish successfully attack the French fortification at 2:00. Despite resistance, in half an hour the positions are taken
- Movement of Spanish army 15 July
- Turenne sends 6 regiments but only 2 manage to cross to be destroyed by the Spanish
- John of Austria & Prince of Condé
- At 6:00, the order to abandon the siege is given and the army of Turenne withdrawn to Le Quesnoy

Picouet 2018

Map 4.4 The Battle of Valenciennes (County of Hainaut) fought on 16 July 1656 between the French forces besieging the city and a succouring Spanish army. The battle was a strategic Spanish victory, the Spaniards managed to pierce the French lines, destroy half of the French army and save the city.

tried unsuccessfully to reinforce the garrison with 700–800 men and the same day the governor of Bouchain received the order to open the locks of the River Escaut in order to flood the area around Valenciennes. On the French side, despite the flooding, Turenne was satisfied, the line of circumvallation was finished and the two armies were now connected with bridges made of faggots and boats. The line of circumvallation was made by a first ditch and a wooden fence, a second ditch and two wooden fences. At regular intervals a redoubt was constructed and filled with infantry while cavalry detachments kept an eye on the fortification between two redoubts. On 25 June the French started the digging two approaches from the west and east to attack the city. In Valenciennes, the Marquis of Bournonville had only 1,000–1,200 infantry, 200–300 cavalry of the regular army and thousands of men from the town militia. Despite the low number of men, the governor of Valenciennes mounted several small successful attacks to disrupt the French approaches, this gave John of Austria time to assemble up to 21,800 men in Douai. The available force was probably close to 22,000 men with 5,000 to 5,500 cavalry and 10,500–11,000 infantry divided in 21 units, four to five Spanish tercios,[56] two to three Italian tercios, probably five walloon tercios,[57] two or three Irish tercios,[58] and five to eight German regiments[59] as well as the 5,800 strong army of the Prince of Condé.[60] On 27 June most of the Spanish army[61] moved to Valenciennes and established a fortified camp on Mont Houy, a hill between Famars, Maing, Trith Saint Léger with the River Escaut on the left and the small river Rhonelle on the right (see Map 4.4). Another detachment of 4,000 men,[62] commanded by the Count of Marsin, was in Saint Armand les Eaux.

On 29 June, the French managed to establish three batteries of six guns to bombard the city and on 8 July some French troops had managed to advance to the counterscarp. On the other side the Spanish were now installed south of the French line and started to skirmish with the French along their lines of circumvallation, looking for weak positions. The Spanish installed a battery of three heavy guns in a redoubt on Mont Houy to bombard the French position of the quarter of Lorraine, and that of the Duke of Navailles. On 14 July John of Austria organised a council of war to decide what to do, he had some news from the governor of Valenciennes saying that he would not hold for very long. The decision to force the French position was taken, the baggage was sent to the rear at Bouchain, and the next day the core of the Spanish force crossed[63] the River Escaut near Denain to attack

---

56 For the Spanish the *Tercio Viejo de los Estados de Flandes* (MdC Diego Goñi de Peralta), *Tercio Viejo de los Estados de Holanda* (MdC Juan Antonio Pacheco Osorio), *Tercio Viejo de los Estados de Brabantes* (MdC Antonio Furtado de Mendonça), the tercio of Gabriel de Toledo and maybe that of Gaspar Bonifaz. Most of the Tercio of Francisco de Menesses was in garrison in Valenciennes. (Picouet 2010, and *Récit du Siege de Valenciennes en 1656*, op. cit.).

57 A rough estimate gives two to three Italian tercios (Garaffa, Campi and Bentivoglio) and up to five Walloon tercios (possibly the Prince of Steenhuize, Count of Megen, Lord of Richebourg, Count of Noyelle and Verkest).

58 At that moment the Irish tercios in Flanders were the Tercio of the Count of Tyrone, the Tercio of Sean Murphy and possibly the Tercio of Thomas Nelson (Sánchez Martin 1999).

59 The only names I found were the regiments of Wolfgang of Bournonville, Count of Nassau, Baron of Lesbeguen, Count Hornes and Count de Archot & Aremberg (*Suite de la relation du siège mis devant Valenciennes le 15 juin 1656 para les français et levé le 16 juillet, avec leur entiére défaite*. Guillaume Scheybels, Brussels 4 August 1656).

60 For the army of the Prince of Condé we have perhaps 2,000 infantry (the French regiments of Persan, Guitaut and Condé, Irish regiments of Dempsey and O'Meagler), 3,500 cavalry and 300 dragoons (*Relación de la Campaña del año 1656*, op. cit.)

61 From the painting of David Teniers the Younger ("View of the city. Valenciennes 1656", oil on canvas, 177 x 205 cm. Koninklijk Museum voor Schone Kunsten, Antwerpen), we could count 21 infantry squadrons and 68 cavalry squadrons. That would give a force of some 10,000 infantry, 7,500 cavalry and 300 dragoons.

62 The relation of the campaign (*Relación de la Campaña del año 1656* op. cit.) gives a total of 27 infantry squadrons and 81 cavalry squadrons. Using the information from the painting of David Teniers the Younger, the Count of Marsin had probably some 2,500 infantry (six units) and 1,500 cavalry (13 units).

63 The movement of the Spanish army was undetected by the French due to the topographic configuration. Mont Houy managed to mask the Spanish movement.

the quarter of the Army of La Ferté-Senneterre. After dusk on 15 July, the Spanish army was deployed as follows: a small detachment 1,000 men with cavalry, dragoons and musketeers stayed on Mont Houy with the battery of heavy guns to continue to bombard the French; the Count of Marsin was on the north to attack the French line in front of Beuvrage; the core of the Spanish force was divided in three storming detachments with on the right (south) the Marquis of Caracena with six to seven infantry battalions formed by the Spanish and Irish tercios, in the centre, the Prince de Ligne with seven infantry battalions from the Italian and Walloon tercios and in the north, the Prince of Condé with seven infantry battalions from German regiments and the Regiment of Persan. The cavalry was deployed on the two wings with respectively 18 cavalry squadrons in the south and 31 in the north. Finally the Spanish had a reserve of 14 cavalry squadrons. In total the main Spanish attacking force against the position of la Ferté-Senneterre had some 20 infantry battalions and 63 cavalry squadrons and was ready to attack at 11:00 p.m. Facing them, the French had placed all their infantry[64] and half of their cavalry in the different redoubts or between them while La Ferté-Senneterre kept a reserve of 18 cavalry squadrons to counter-attack. In the city, locks and dykes were opened to reinforce the flooding and a force of regular infantry and militia was prepared to storm the French trenches on the west bank of the river. At 2:00 a.m. on 16 July, the heavy guns of Mont Houy started to fire giving the signal to attack. The men of Count Marsin courageously attacked the lines of circumvallation of La Ferté-Senneterre, but were met by a strong resistance of the *Gardes Suisses* and were obliged to withdraw. Meantime the three attacking columns started to move with in each case a vanguard of musketeers armed with grenades followed by two lines of infantry and pioneers. Rapidly they managed to cross the first ditch and fence but on the arrival at the second ditch they were met by heavy musket fire from the French. On the north and south the Spanish, Irish and Germans managed to take the second fences despite the fierce resistance of the French infantry, but in the centre the Italians and Walloons had to face the *Gardes Françaises* and their attacks were halted. The Spanish in the south and Germans in the north had taken their respective objectives and hundreds of pioneers worked to fill the ditches and to open a road for the cavalry. In the centre the Italians and Walloons launched three more attacks and finally managed to take the French position. On the other side, Turenne realised quickly that the main attack was against La Ferté-Senneterre and sent urgently six French regiments to support his colleagues. Masters of a large proportion of the French fortifications, the Spanish started to move to the city, while the garrison of Valenciennes also exited their position to meet the succour. With his reserve La Ferté-Senneterre tried to counter-attack but his forces were stopped by the Spanish infantry and the first Spanish cavalry squadrons. The French resistance crumbled and the French soldiers wavered,

---

64 After one month of siege the army of La Ferté-Senneterre was probably down to 8,000–9,000 men.

running for their lives trying to cross the River Escaut in the north.[65] In the south the Spanish tercios destroyed two of the regiments sent by Turenne that had just crossed the River Escaut and established a position to block the other four. After less than two hours, the first Spanish cavalry squadrons entered Valenciennes and it became clear for Turenne that the battle was lost and it was time to urgently withdraw. The French infantry of the army of Turenne was extracted as fast as possible from their trenches and at 6:00 a.m. the French army abandoned the siege, most of their guns and baggage. The French forces regrouped near the village of Perseau and started to retreat to the south-east. The movement was covered efficiently by the troops of the King's horse and by evening Turenne could regroup his force[66] at le Quesnoy. The Spanish had managed to destroy most of the army of La Ferté-Senneterre even if up to 2,500 men managed to escape to Condé-sur-l'Escaut or with Turenne.[67]

Taking into account the losses during the siege, total French losses could be estimated at 7,000 to 8,000 men including 2,500–3,000 prisoners[68] and 46 guns. By contrast Spanish losses could be estimated at 500 men during the battle and 200 to 300 men during the siege. The last episode was the siege of Condé-sur-l'Escaut, where some of the survivors of the army of La Ferté-Senneterre had found shelter. Despite being an important garrison the French surrendered the city on 18 August after a formal siege of 25 days.

4.2 Northern Italy and Germany

4.2.1 The Campaign of 1634: The Battle of Nördlingen, 6 September

In 1634, the second step to send reinforcements and to regain the initiative in southern Germany was launched when Cardinal Infante Fernando of Austria started to move his army of 14,650 men[69] from Milan to Bavaria on 30 June. On 3 July the army was in Como and on 11 July the Cardinal Infante was in Tirano, the capital of the Valtellina valley. The expedition finally arrived at the Inn valley by the end of July and on 25 July troops were accommodated between Kufstein and Rattenberg. There Spanish troops[70] arriving from Milan

---

65 Hundreds of men were drowned trying to cross the River Escaut and the flooded area (Aumale volume 6).
66 The next day at Le Quesnoy Turenne received a reinforcement of 1,500 infantry and could deploy a sizeable force of 17,000 men (Lettres de la marquise de Sévigné et du Conte de Bussy-Rabutin).
67 The army of Turenne was mostly intact, but he had lost a significant proportion of his artillery.
68 *Récit du Siege de Valenciennes en 1656*, op. cit.
69 12,480 Infantry divided into 2,220 Spanish (Tercio of Fuenclara), 10,120 Italians (Neapolitan Tercios of Gaspar de Torralto and Pedro de Cardenas, regiments from the Principe of San Severo, tercios from Lombardy of the Marquis of Lunato and Carlos Guasco) and 150 Swiss; 2,170 cavalry (two guards companies, four companies from the Cavalry of Lombardy, 10 companies from the Cavalry of Napoles and the regiment of the Count de la Tour). Ribot Garcia 1990, and Aedo, 1635.
70 The crossing of the Alps had been difficult, and when the army arrived in the Tirol only 9,530 infantry (1,910 Spanish, 7,510 Italians and 120 others) and 2,040 cavalry could be found. The rest (some 3,070 men) had been lost through desertion and illness (Ribot Garcia 1990).

THE ARMIES OF PHILIP IV OF SPAIN 1621–1665

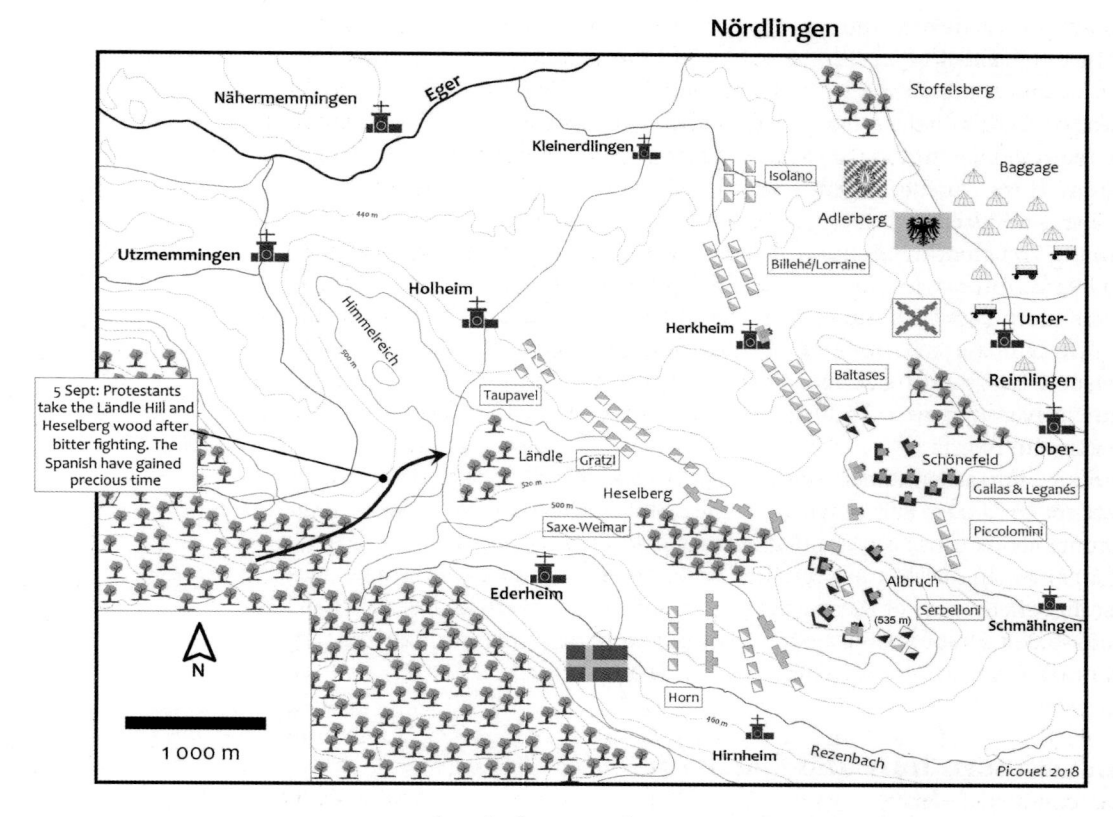

Map 4.5 The Battle of Nördlingen (southern Germany) fought on 6 September 1634, between a coalition of Catholic armies (Imperial, Spanish and League) and the main German Protestant field armies. The military operation was an attempt to save the city of Nördlingen, besieged by the Catholics. It ended in a strategic Catholic victory and the total destruction of the Protestant force.

were merged with the Spanish contingent[71] of the old army of the Duke of Feria,[72] now commanded by the Count of Serbelloni. While the troops were resting and the latecomers were arriving, the Cardinal Infante went to Munich to discuss with the Duke of Bavaria the follow-up of the campaign. The news of the next arrival of the Spanish contingent had boosted the morale of the Catholics and Imperial Commanders after the defeats of the previous years. At the start of the campaign, in May 1634, the main Imperial army[73] was located in Pilsen (Plzen, in the Czech Republic) and had the support of Aldringer's Imperial corps, the Bavarian army and the remnants of the Spanish force commanded by Serbelloni (Guthrie 2002). For the Imperial army the campaign started on the wrong foot when the Silesian corps commanded by

---

71 Concerning the Spanish tercios; the former tercio of Juan Diaz Zamorano was given to Martin de Idiaquez and reinforced with seven companies from Milan and with the rest the Count of Fuensaldaña reorganised his proper tercio. Therefore by mid August the Cardinal Infante had two Spanish tercios, namely the tercios of Idiaquez with 1,800 men in 27 companies and the Tercio of Fuelsaldaña with 1,450 men in 17 companies (Aedo, 1635)

72 In August 1634, the units of the previous Army of Alsace had still some 6,160 infantry, divided between the Tercio of Zamorano (Spanish), Tercio of Torrecuso (Italian), Italian Tercio of Paniguerola (Italian), Tercio of the Count of Arberg (Burgundy), Tercio of Jean Jacques de la Tour-Moncley (Burgundy), Regiment of the Count of Salm and Regiment of Wurmser. Also 1,870 cavalry from the Cavalry of Naples (Gambacorta), the Regiment of de la Tour (Burgundy) and the regiment of the Baron of Seebach (German). Engerisser & Hrncirik, 2009.

73 15,000 infantry, 9,000 cavalry, 1,500 dragoons and 3,000 croats commanded by Ferdinand of Hungary and Mathias Gallas (Guthrie, 2002).

CAMPAIGNS OF THE SPANISH ARMIES

Colloredo was defeated during the battle of Liegnitz on 13 May. While some units were sent to protect the province of Bohemia, the core of the Catholic force took on the offensive, re-capturing Regensburg (defended by 3,840 men) on 27 July after a siege of 42 days and Donauwörth on the River Danube was stormed on 16 August. On the other side, the main Protestant armies of Gustav Horn and Bernhard of Saxe-Weimar had joined in Augsburg on 12 July and decided to advance towards the south-east of Germany, taking the town of Landshut on 22 July as a diversionary attack to save Regensburg. By mid August, the Protestant force of Saxe-Weimar was located on the left bank of the River Danube, while Horn was near Ulm and both of them were unable to save Donauwörth. The next day the Imperial high command decided to pursue the offensive and moved towards the city of Nördlingen. On 17 August the Protestant city was surrounded by 18,000–21,000 men (Guthie, 2002). The garrison of Nördlingen had probably 1,100–1,200 men despite the arrival of reinforcements, but the situation was gloomy and it was only a matter of weeks until the city capitulates, if nothing was done. Unfortunately for the Protestant commanders their combined armies now located in Bopfingen had only 16,000 men (Engerisser & Hrncirik, 2009), too few to expect to lift the siege. Reinforcements from other Protestant corps were requested, and on 29 August 6,000–7,000 troops arrived from nearby garrisosn and from the Württemberg *Landvolk* (militia). Other troops commanded by Field Marshal Gratz and the Rhinegrave Otto were en route.

Further to the south, on 24 August the Spanish army of Cardinal Infante Fernando of Austria moved closer to Munich where a general muster was conducted, giving some 15,040 infantry (two Spanish tercios, seven Italian tercios and two German regiments), 3,100 cavalry (50 companies) and 10 guns other 2,350 men[74] (two Burgundian tercios and one German cavalry regiment) were with the Bavarian army in Nördlingen (Engerisser & P. Hrncirik, 2009). On 26 August, the Spanish army left Munich, four days later the river Lech was crossed at Rain and on 31 August the army was at Donauwörth.[75] There the army was organised for a possible battle, and contact was made with the Imperial high command to discuss the deployment of the Spanish army around Nördlingen. The Cardinal Infante also received news from the Protestant armies, estimated at 22,000 men with 4,000 more close by (Aedo, 1635). On 3 September the Spanish army was in Nördlingen and on the other side the Protestants were expecting the arrival of Gratz for 5 September. On the 4th, the garrison of Nördlingen managed to repulse an attack of the Imperial troops but on the night of the 4th/5th the Protestant high command received the news that the city could not resist much more. During an agitated council of war, the Protestant

---

74 1560 infantry, 712 mounted cavalry and 83 dismounted. Following Aedo (1635) the infantry German regiment of Walter Leslie was also in Spanish service. The regiment had incorporated in April/May the regiment of Schaumburg from the army of Feria, paid originally by the Spanish. In September 1634 it was probably on the Imperial payroll with 650 to 1,600 men (Engerisser & P. Hrncirik, 2009).

75 E. de Mesa (2003), *Nördlingen 1634, Victoria Decisiva de los tercios*. Guerreros y Batallas n° 9, Edition Almena, 63 pages.

THE ARMIES OF PHILIP IV OF SPAIN 1621–1665

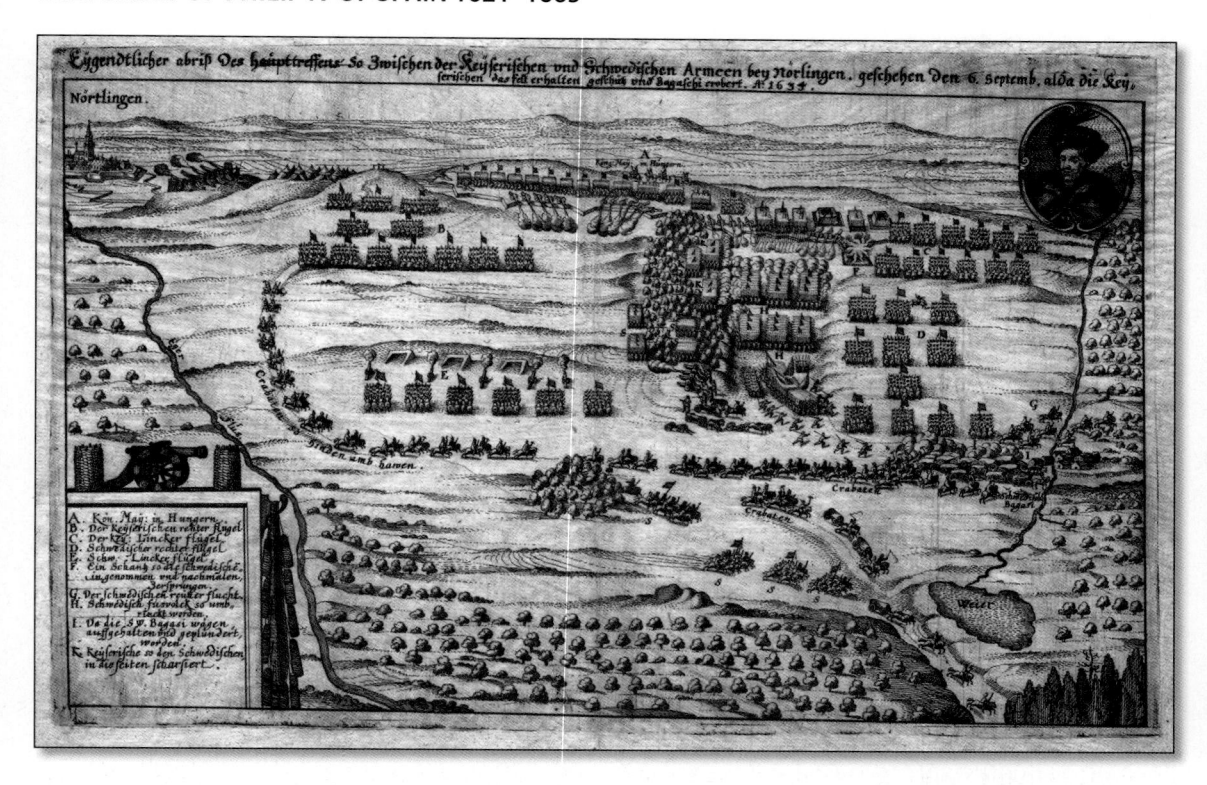

4.3 (above and right): Maps of the Battle of Nördlingen in 1634. (Riksarkivet, Stockholm)

leaders voted to attack the Catholic positions despite the arrival of the Spanish army;[76] they were overconfident and for most of them another town could not be lost to the enemy. On the 5th, the Protestant army started to move, the plan was to cross the River Rezenbach and to occupy the hills south of the Catholic camps in order to cut their line of communication with the Danube and Donauwörth. Surprisingly, little reconnaissance had been done so the Protestant commanders had no clear view of the topography of the area. The movement of the Protestant army was detected by Croat patrols, but when Gallas learned that they were moving from Bopfingen to Neresheim, he thought that they were withdrawing to Ulm.[77] At 11:00 a.m. in Neresheim, the Protestant leaders were joined by the corps of Gratz, there they left the baggage protected by 2,000–2,500 men from the Landvolk of Württemberg and they turned to the east. Saxe-Weimar with the cavalry and some musketeers took a north-easterly direction towards Holheim while Horn, with the infantry and the artillery, took the direction of Ederheim via the villages of Kösingen and Schweindorf. At 3:00 p.m. the outpost of Spanish dragoons as well as parties of Croats and parties of mounted harquebusiers detected the movement of the Protestant vanguard led by

---

76 Intelligence was deficient in the Protestant camps, Saxe-Weimar and other commanders were convinced that the Spanish army had only 7,000 men, and that the total of Imperial/Bavarian/Spanish force was 25,000 men. Gustav Horn was more cautious and wanted to wait for the arrival of the 6,000 men of the Rhinegrave (Guthrie 2002).

77 In fact Gallas was expecting a more direct approach following the south bank of the River Eger (Engerisser & P. Hrncirik, 2009).

Saxe-Weimar. Seeing that they were totally outnumbered, the Catholics urgently sent information to their headquarters[78] and decided to concede the Hummelreich and Arnsberg hills in order to concentrate their defence on the Ländle hill.

During more than three hours, the Protestants had to fight against tenacious Spanish dragoons to take the hill. Meantime the first reinforcement was sent with 3,000 cuirassiers and mounted harquebusiers commanded by Rudolf von Morzin to skirmish with the Protestant cavalry. After some bitter fighting, the cavalry of Saxe-Weimar managed first to hold the Imperial cavalry and later, with the help of commanded musketeers, to repulse them to their former position. Unfortunately for Saxe-Weimar, precious time had been lost and when the exhausted Protestant force arrived at 6:00 p.m. at their next objective, the Heselberg wood, they were stopped by a detachment of 800 Spanish musketeers, harquebusiers and dragoons commanded by Sergeant-Major Francisco Escobar. Saxe-Weimar had to wait for the infantry conducted by Gustav Horn,[79] but the infantry could not move at

---

78 News arrived at 4:00 p.m. at the headquarters, and it was rapidly decided to send a detachment of 500 musketeers and harquebusiers commanded by Sergeant Mayor Francisco Escobar from the Tercio of Fuenclara to reinforce the dragoons. The infantry was extracted from the Spanish Tercio of Fuenclara, the Italian Tercio of Torralto and from the Burgundian Tercio of La Tour (Aedo, 1635).

79 Horn's movement was through Kösingen, Schweindorf and Ederheim.

the same speed as cavalry and was delayed by drizzle and damp. At 10:00 p.m., the infantry of the Swedish general was ready to attack, but during that four hours the Spanish managed to gain more time, and on 6 September at 2:00 a.m. they finally received the order to retreat towards the Albuch hill where friendly troops were now positioned. With the time gained by the Spanish, the Catholic high command reorganised the deployment of his troops, sending eight tercios and regiments to occupy and fortify the Albuch hill. At 5:00 a.m. the Catholics were deployed as follows (see Map 4.5).

On the Albuch hill, three defensive earthworks had been constructed during the night and the position[80] was under the command of the Count of Serbelloni. On the right, facing the Heselberg wood, the first earthwork was defended by the Italian Tercio of Toralto, in the centre the earthwork was defended by the brigade of Salm (Regiments of Salm and Regiment of Wurmser) and on the left, the last earthwork was occupied by the brigade of Leslie (Regiment of Leslie and the Regiment of Fugger[81]). A first group of cavalry squadrons (Cavalry of Naples and Imperial cavalry of Piccolomini), commanded by Morzin was positioned between the Italians and Germans and a second (Cavalry of Naples, Regiment of La tour and Imperial cavalry of Piccolomini) commanded by Gambacorta was placed to cover the left of the Leslie position. Behind the centre, the Spanish positioned the Spanish Tercio of Idiaqués and on the right to support the Italians the Imperial brigade of Teutschvoll made of 1,000 musketeers. The defence of the hill was completed by two Italian tercios (Tercio of Panigorola and Tercio of Guasco) in reserve. The defensive earthworks were reinforced by the presence of 14 light guns.

The centre of the Catholic position was located on the Schönefeld hill with artillery and on one side the Spanish infantry[82] commanded by Brancaccio and from the other side Imperial infantry[83] commanded by Matthias Gallas. Between the two hills the Catholics had also 2,000–2,500 infantry from the Imperial brigade of Webel and the Bavarian infantry brigade of Hartenberg.[84] The cavalry was in front of the Schönefeld hill divided into a detachment of 4,000 Imperial cavalry commanded by the Marquis of Balbases and 1,800 Spanish cavalry commanded by Paolo Dentici. On the space between the two hills the rest of the Imperial cavalry of Ottavio Piccolomini[85] was deployed.

---

80 In total some 7,000–7,500 infantry, probably 2,500–3,000 cavalry and artillery.
81 Leslie's was an Imperial regiment, while Fugger's was a Bavarian one, it is probable that the brigade was formed with only some of the companies from the two regiments. The brigade had probably 1,500 men (Guthrie 2002).
82 Spanish Tercio of Fuenclara, Regiment of San Severo, Tercio of Torrecusa, Tercio of Cardenas, Tercio of Alberg and Tercio of Lunato, probably 7,000 to 7,500 men.
83 The Infantry regiments were those of Tieffembach, Alt-Adringen, Neu-Aldringen, de Suys, Jung-Breuner, Pallant-Moriamez, Diodati and Keraus. Not all the troops were on the hill, some of them were in the trenches facing Nördlingen, if we consider a total infantry of 5,000–5,500 men an estimate would give a maximum of 2,500 men on the hill and the rest in the trenches.
84 The Webel brigade was formed with the Regiment of Webel and the Regiment of Alt-Saschsen and the Hartenberg brigade was formed by the Regiment of Hartenberg and the Regiment of Ruepp.
85 Ottavio Piccolomini commanded a group of six regiments of cuirassiers (Guards of Gallas, Alt-Piccolomini, Pietro Piccolomini, Aldobrandini, Nicola de Noyrel, Alt-Saschen) and two regiments of harquebusiers on horse (Alt-Rietberg and Tornetta). Up to 1,000 horsemen were positioned on the Albuch Hill, the other 1,700 in the valley between the two hills.

CAMPAIGNS OF THE SPANISH ARMIES

On the right covering the space between Herkheim and Kleinerdlingen, was the Bavarian/league infantry,[86] and on their right 11 cavalry regiments[87] of Bavarian/league commanded by Maximillian de Billehé. On the extreme right just behind Kleinerdlingen were up to 2,500 Croats[88] commanded by Isolano. All the troops of the right flank were commanded by the Duke of Lorraine. More Imperial and Bavarian troops were facing the city of Nördlingen, while most of the dragoons were protecting the baggage and the camp where thousands of followers were packed west of Reimlingen waiting for the results of the journey. Depending on the sources, the total number of available troops during the battle moved from 33,000 men to 39,000 men (Engerisser & Hrncirik, 2009). From our calculation we have some 9,000 to 10,000 men on the Albuch Hill, 19,000 to 20,000 men in the centre and up to 8,500 men between Herkheim and Kleinerdlingen including the Croats, giving a total of 36,500 to 38,500 men (15,500–16,000 for the Spanish, 14,000–14,500 for the Imperials and 7,000 for the Bavarian) supported by probably 50–60 guns. To command such a numerous and diverse army, Fernando of Austria and Ferdinand of Hungary had established a common headquarters on the Adlerberg hill, they were supported by the Marquis of Leganés as *Maestro de Campo General* and Mathias Gallas as lieutenant general of the Imperial army.

On the other side, the Protestant commanders had divided their troops into basically two main corps. On the right with the objective to take the Albuch hill, were the corps of Gustav Horn, with up to 4,000 cavalry[89] and 800 dragoons on the right followed by 8,800 infantry divided in five brigades.[90] In the centre, from the Heselberg wood, the Ländle hill and the village of Holheim we find from right to left 4,800 infantry divided into four infantry brigades[91] and 400 cavalry from Bernhard's Liebregiment, followed by 2,700 cavalry deployed in two lines.[92] On the extreme right we have

---

86 Regiments of Alt-Pappenheim and of Johann Puck, such as the Imperial infantry (Regiment of Reisach) some of the men were in the trenches so 1,000 to 1,500 were defending Herkheim.
87 Regiments of cuirassiers of Billehé, Fürstenberg, Keller, Neu-Werth, Busch, Hasland, Bracciolini and Meven and regiments of mounted harquebusiers of Werth, Binder and Espaigne, in total a maximum of 3,700 men.
88 Regiments of Isolano, Marsinay, Corpes, de Gymes, Perwast, Revay and Prichowsky.
89 The cavalry was commanded by Friedrich von Rostein and had 13 regiments (regiments of Horn, commanded by Witzleben, Oxenstierna, Wittenberg, Wachtmeister, Wrangel, Schaffalitzky, Platow, Rostein, Cratzenstein, Hofkirchen, Godlstein, Ruthven an Brincken) deployed in 19–20 squadrons.
90 The infantry was made of 19 regiments of infantry deployed in the Scottish Brigade (regiments of Gunn, Spens, Mackay, Ramsay, Ruthvens and Cunningan), the Vitzhum Brigade (regiments of Vitzhum and Pfalzgraf von Blikenfeld and Limbach), the Horn brigade (regiments of Horn, Pfuels, Forbus and Schneidewindt), the Rantzau Brigade (regiments of Rantzau, Wurmbrandt, Houwald and Schaffalitzky) and the Württemberg's *landvolk* brigade commanded by Philip von Liebenstein. Commanded musketeers were provided by the Regiment of Banérs to support the cavalry.
91 The infantry comprised regiments of infantry deployed from right left, the Thurn brigade (regiments of Thurn and Gelbes), the Cratz/Tiesenhausen Brigade (regiments of Tiesenhausen, Cratz and James King), the Rosen Brigade (regiments of Rosen, Mitzlaff and Zerotin or Red Regiment) and the Green Brigade (regiments of Bernhard's Green Liebregiment and Ludovic Leslie).
92 The cavalry was commanded by Field Marshal Gratz and had seven regiments (regiments of Ehm/Ohm, Markgraf von Brandenburg, Karberg, Landgraf von Hessen-Braubach, Pfalzgraf von Blikenfeld, Duke of Saxe-Weimar and Courvil) in the first line and nine regiments (regiments

THE ARMIES OF PHILIP IV OF SPAIN 1621–1665

4.4 Spanish and Imperial forces at the battle of Nördlingen in 1634. Pieter Snayers. (Nationalmuseum, Stockholm)

500 cavalry[93] and 800 dragoons commanded by Christoph von Taupadell. Each infantry brigade had five to six infantry regimental light guns, while 20 medium and heavy guns[94] were deployed in several batteries along the front of Bernhard Saxe-Weimar. To summarise, the Protestants seem to have had on the battlefield some 13,600 infantry in nine brigades, 7,600 cavalry in 40 squadrons, 1,600 dragoons, and with the 2,500 men left to protect the baggage we arrive at a total of 25,300 men. Therefore the Protestants were badly outnumbered even if in the Albuch Hill sector they had a local temporary superiority of 13,600 against 10,000.

The battle started at dawn with the first light of the day, when the troops of Horn moved to attack the Albuch hill in four echelons. The first echelon was made by the Scottish and Vitzhum brigades and three cavalry squadrons commanded by Witzleben, the second by seven cavalry squadrons, the third with the other three brigades and one cavalry squadron on the right and the fourth with eight cavalry squadrons. Moving faster than the infantry, Witzleben soon discovered that the field on the extreme right was not suitable for cavalry due to the presence of a ravine running from the hill to the River Resenbach. They rapidly came closely in range of the muskets of the Leslie Brigade and when they were attacking the entrenchment they were counter-attacked on the flank by the Spanish cavalry of Gambacorta and had to retire. Further to the left the Protestant infantry attacked the central position and despite the resistance of their officers the German raw recruits of Salms and Wurmser gave ground and abandoned their position. This time the Spanish cavalry on the right counter-attacked successfully the Protestants and the troops of Salm's and Wurmser's regiments were rallied and reoccupied their previous position. Horn reorganised his troops and this time the Infantry supported by the cavalry of the second echelon attacked again the central position. With the death of Erhart Wurmser and the wounds of the Count of Salm, the German infantry broke away and this time the Catholic cavalry was fighting against their Protestant counterparts and could not support their infantry. The Count of Serbelloni ordered the Spanish to retake the position immediately. Preceded by a *manga* of harquebusiers and supported by cavalry squadrons, the Spanish infantry squadron of Idiaqués moved towards the central entrenchment. After brief fighting the disorganised Protestant infantry was beaten and had to withdraw. It was 6:00 a.m., the Italians of Toralto, the Spanish of Idiaqués and Germans of Leslie were holding their position while the Protestants were preparing a new attachment. While reorganising the Scottish and Vitzhum, Horn sent the Horn and Rantzau brigade with cavalry to attack again the central position. This time the Protestants were met by the Spanish and could not approach the enemy position, taking heavy losses

---

of Beckermann, Bransensteim, Kurland, Livonia, Cratz, Wettberg, Hohenlohe and Karpf) in the second line, in total 16 squadrons.

93 Three squadrons from the following regiments: Taupadel, Sattler, Rosen and the company of Rittmeister Adolf.

94 Württemberg's *landvolk* Brigade had no regimental guns. Therefore the total of artillery was probably close to 40–48 2.5 and 3-pdr light guns and 20-, 6-, 12-, and 24-pdr guns.

from the Spanish musket fire.[95] On the other part of the front the Catholic batteries of the Stönefeld hill and the Protestant guns of Saxe-Weimar were exchanging fire but no troop movement was going on. In the Catholic headquarters, seeing the main effort was on the Albuch hill, Leganés began to send three *mangas* of musketeers and harquebusiers (from the tercios of Cardenas and Torrecusa) to support the Spanish position, at the same time Gallas ordered Piccolomini to send 1,000 cavalry to the hill. A fourth attack was launched on the Spanish and Italian positions with the Scottish, Vitzhum and Württemberg brigades. Like the previous one, the Protestant infantry and cavalry were met by heavy musket fire, blocks of pikes and cavalry squadrons. This fourth assault failed and while reorganising his force, at 7:30 a.m., Horn knew he needed reinforcements and sent a messenger asking for support to Saxe-Weimar. The Protestant commander decided to send the Thurn brigade on the Albuch hill and to carry out a diversion on the central front. For the next hour, Gustav Horn continued to launch several assaults on the Spanish position, especially with the Scots and Horn brigades, but despite their suicidal attacks, the Catholics were holding their positions. To hold their position, the Spanish and Italians were regularly receiving *mangas* of musketeers and harquebusiers from the Stönefeld hill.[96] At 8:00 a.m., the Thurn brigade supported by the last cavalry reserve of Horn moved towards the hill and ran directly onto the Italian position of Toralto. Thurn was unable to take the position and was suffering from the enfilade fire of the musketeers of Teutschvoll. Thurn received reinforcements from the Rosen brigade renewed his attacks with little success, being blocked by the Italian tercio and the Imperial musketeers after bitter fighting. The final check occurred when Serbelloni moved his reserve[97] (Guasco and Panigarola) to support the cavalry of Morzin and the troops of Toralto.

On the Protestants' extreme left wing, the dragoons of Taupadel managed to block a party of Croats trying to outflank their flank near Kleinerdlingen. Further to the right, Saxe-Weimar had moved the first line of his cavalry, pushing ahead the Catholic skirmishers to their main line. With no wish to attack the Imperial cavalry, they ended up trotting near Herkheim, where they were met by an intense musket fire from the Bavarian infantry. Disordered, they were counter-attacked by the Catholic cavalry supported by Spanish musketeers from the Tercio of Fuenclara and had to run back to their previous position and Saxe-Weimar had to send five cavalry squadrons to restore the situation.

At 9:30 a.m., Gustav Horn was tired, his troops were exhausted and unable to take a foot on the Albuch hill, and even if fighting had been heavy with significant losses on both sides, the Protestant force had taken the worst. The troops of Thurn (Thurn and the Green Brigade) took refuge in the Heselberg

---

95 To counter the famous Swedish salvo, the soldiers of Idiaqués were ordered to crouch down when the Protestants were firing and return fire at close range with great efficiency (Aedo, 1635).
96 This time seven *mangas* from the tercios of San Severo, Cardenas, Lunato and Alberg (Aedo, 1635).
97 In the fighting the Count of Panigorola was killed and Carlos Guasco was wounded. The two tercios were merged into one infantry squadron commanded by Sergeant Mayor Juan de Orozco (de Mesa 2003).

wood while Horn's troops were dispersed between the River Retzenbach and the slope of the Albuch hill, exchanging musket fire with their enemy. After a last attack before 10:00 a.m., the position of Albuch hill was out of reach and in a short meeting the Protestant commanders decided to stop the offensive and hold their positions to wait for the night and withdraw safely to Ulm (Guthrie 2002). The idea seemed to be to hold the right flank between the Heselberg wood and the Ländle hill, while Horn's corps pulled back into a safer position between Elderhiem and the Heselberg wood.

On the Catholic side, the brigade of Webel had been committed to the Albuch hill and noting that the Protestants were pulling back, Serbelloni ordered a cautious advance. Further to the right, the Imperial and Bavarian cavalry advanced towards the Protestant line. After a short melee, and despite the commitment of his reserve, the Protestant cavalry of Gratz was soon defeated, retiring to the Ländle hill. Soon the withdrawing of the Protestant horses and dragoons degenerated into a rout; Gratz was captured trying to rally his troops. At the same time another detachment of Imperial, Bavarian and Spanish cavalry led by the Duke of Lorraine and the Marquis of Balbases attacked the troops[98] defending the north approach of the Heselberg. Supported by Bavarian infantry and the musketeers of the Tercio of Fuenclara, the Catholics drove into the wood, destroying the Protestant force in the process. On the Protestant right, Horn was unaware of the collapse of the left of the army, but soon he realised that fighting was occurring in the Heselberg wood. At the same time, the Italians of Orozco and the Imperials of Webel were advancing also towards the Heselberg chasing the troops of Thurn. The Spanish and the cavalry of the Albuch hill did not remain inactive and Serbelloni could order a general advance against the troops of the Swedish general. Suddenly squadrons of Bavarian or Imperial cuirassiers emerged from the wood cutting the orderly retreat of Horn. In a matter of minutes the Protestant force dissolved, with the cavalry running away as fast as they could, chased by the Croats and the Catholic cavalry. A portion of the infantry (Rantzau, Württemberg and Horn) and the artillery was attacked from all sides and all were killed or made prisoners including the proper general Gustav Horn. The last troops (Scottish and Vitzhum) were partially destroyed and chased down through the woods after crossing the Retzenbach.

The Catholic cavalry, particularly the Croats, continued the pursuit of the Protestant soldiers well into the night. The Croats and some cavalry squadrons reached Neresheim, attacked by surprise the baggage of the Protestant army and in less than one hour the other half of the Württemberg *landvolk* was partially massacred or was running away. The last Protestant survivors run away towards the city of Ulm, 66 km from Elderhiem, where some of them found a temporary refuge.

---

98 Probably the infantry Cratz/Tiesenhausen, and Green Brigade with some cavalry squadrons including Bernhard's Liebregiment.

Coming back to the battlefield, on the afternoon of 6 September Fernando of Austria and Ferdinand of Hungary went to the Albuch hill where they could contemplate the magnitude of the Catholic victory.

As always losses are difficult to estimate correctly, the Catholic losses are estimated at 1,600 men (dead and wounded), 600 for the Spanish army and 1,000 for the Imperial and Bavarian forces (Aedo, 1635). In the Spanish army, several high-ranking officers[99] had been killed or wounded, most of them during the battle for the Albuch hill. On the Protestant side, numbers are difficult to establish but we have from 7,500 dead and 3,000 prisoners given by Engerisser & Hrncirik (2009) and the 8,000 dead during the battle, 4,000 prisoners and 9,000 dead during the pursuit given by Aedo (1635). Real numbers of dead, wounded, prisoners and deserters from 5–7 September are probably close to 12,000 to 14000 men,[100] the great majority being infantry. For the materiel, the Protestant losses amounted to 42 to 54 guns, hundreds of standards and cornets and most of the baggage.

This astonishing victory meant on the one hand that the defence of Nördlingen was useless and on 8 September the garrison capitulated with honourable terms; on the other hand the Spanish army could continue safely its journey to the Low Countries.[101] On 9 and 10 September, the Spanish cavalry started the movement, taking and sacking some castles in Protestant hands. On 11 September the Spanish army moved towards Giengen-am-der-Brenz, while the Imperial were moving towards Ulm in order to conquer the Duchy of Württemberg. On 18 September they were in Esslingen am Neckar, there the Catholic commanders decided to send 6,000 men[102] to succour Brisach and to recover other cities on the Rhine valley. On 19 September the Spanish with an Imperial contingent crossed the River Neckar and following the river they passed near Heilbronn four days later. On 27 September Catholic forces were at Bad Freidrichshall (before it was called Kockendorf), where the two armies split.[103] On 30 September the Spanish crossed the River Main with 16,200 men[104] and 2,000 Imperial cavalry, and three days later were near Aschaffenburg. The army resumed its march, chasing out all Protestant garrisons, and on 15 October they finally arrived on the River Rhine. Crossing the river was not an easy task but it was done in three days

---

99 Killed or mortally wounded: Count of Panigorola (*Maestro de Campo*), Count of Salm (colonel), Wurms (colonel) and Diego Bustos (*Sargento Mayor*). Wounded Carlo Guasco (*Maestro de Campo*), Tiberio Brancacio (lieutenant of the *Maestro de Campo General*), Alvaro de Quiñones (general of the cavalry of Naples) and Gerardo Gambacorta (general of the cavalry of the army of Serbelloni). Aedo, 1635.
100 In *Theatrum Europaeum* (Bd III, p.335), we have 12,000 dead and 6,000 prisoners. In Frankfurt the muster of the survivors of the Protestant army was 12,200 men excluding Württemberg's *landvolk* (Engerisser & Hrncirik, 2009), but it is probable that some garrisons were collected during the retreat.
101 The other mission of the Cardinal Infante was also to succour the city of Brisach (de Mesa, 2003).
102 The 1,000 cavalry and 5,000 infantry were extracted from the garrison of Landau and Konstanz and from the Spanish and Imperial army (Aedo, 1635).
103 Heilbronn, with a regular garrison of 1,200 men. was besieged by the Imperial force, and surrendered on 29 September.
104 Originally the Spanish had 12,000 infantry and 2,900 cavalry, but the Spanish cavalry was sent back to find 1,300 latecomers, so in total we have 16,200 men in the Spanish army.

using pontoons provided by the Elector of Cologne. On 25 October the army was in Julich, there it met the League army of Count Philip of Mansfeld. The Cardinal Infante transferred the German regiments of infantry and most of his cavalry to Mansfeld[105] and with the rest he crossed the river Meuse at Stevensweert (between Maastricht and Nijmegen) on 28 October. The triumphal arrival in Brussels was carried out on 4 November.

4.2.2. The Campaign of 1636: the Battle of Tornavento, 22 June

After the event of February against the Duke of Modena, the Spanish governor had to leave the initiative to the alliance of France (Field Marshal Créquy), Savoy (Victor Amadeus, Duke of Savoy) and Parma (Francisco Duke of Parma). On 19 May a combined army of 17,500 and 3,300 cavalry[106] had been joined in Monferrato while another force of 4,500 men commanded by the Duke of Rohan was in the Valtellina Valley to threaten the region of Lecco. On the Spanish side, the Marquis of Leganés had distributed his field force in different detachments and corps. To protect the north, the Count of Serbelloni had 3,000 men supported by the militia of Como and Lecco. The access to the important harbour of Finale was protected by a detachment located on the River Bormida. The south of the duchy and particularly the River Scrivia between Tortona and Alessandria was protected by 7,000 to 8,000 men, commanded by Gherardo Gambacorta deployed behind entrenchments (Hanlon 2016). The core of the Spanish army was with Leganés in Pavia while a detachment, commanded by Martin de Aragon, was further to the north to cover Novara.

The first movement of the combined army was to march towards the River Scrivia, maybe to attack Tortona, but the Spanish position along the river was considered to be to strong by the Allied commander and they decided to withdraw to Casale Monferrato and Breme on the river Pô. At that time the movement of the army was delayed by bad weather and muddy roads. Another movement was made on 6 June towards Valenza de Pô, but a successful attack of the garrison against a detachment of the cavalry of Savoy indicated that the city was well protected.[107] For the Allies the only benefit was that their movements had attracted Leganés to Castel Nuovo. The Allies decided to carry out a new manoeuvre, this time, while the main Spanish army was in the south, they would move to the north in order to meet the small army of Rohan and to attack Milan. On 8 June, the French and Savoyard armies[108] started their march towards the small town of Oleggio, while the

---

105 With such reinforcements, the new League army now had 9,000 infantry and 4,000 cavalry.
106 Savoy: 7,500–8,000 infantry (11 regiments) and 1,500 cavalry; France: 6,000 infantry (nine regiments), and 1,200 cavalry; Parma 3,500 infantry and 600 cavalry. Totalling some 20,300–20,800 men divided into 17,500 infantry and 3,300 cavalry (Hanlon 2016). An older source gives 18,000 infantry and 5,000 cavalry (*Mémoire du Comte de Souvigny lieutenant General des Armées du Roi*, volume 1, edited by Ludovic de Contenson, Librairie Renouard, Paris 1906).
107 It seems that Valenza de Pô had a garrison of 5,000 men including companies of the militia (Hanlon 2016).
108 Probably 9,500 infantry and 1,500 cavalry for the Duke of Savoy and up to 6,000 infantry and 1,200 cavalry for the French army of Créquy (Hanlon 2016).

Duke of Parma was left in Nizza Monferrato with 3,600–4,000 men.[109] On 13 June, the two allied armies moved in different paths, the Duke of Savoy decided to clear out the surrounding castles of Romagnano, Fontano and Borgomanerop, while Créquy was going directly to Oleggio. On 14 June, Oleggio was taken with little resistance and French scouts managed to cross the River Ticino the same day. The French general saw the opportunity and as fast as possible he established a bridgehead of 500 men in a place called Casa della Camera close to a hamlet (*Cascina*) called Tornavento.[110] The garrison of Fontano made a gallant resistance, killing the Marquis of Toiras in the process, but had to surrender on 15 June on honourable terms.

The Spanish detachment commanded by Martin de Aragon had withdrawn behind the Ticino, at Buffarola, leaving a strong garrison in Novara. When it was clear for the Marquis of Leganés that the Allies were moving to the north, he marched towards Pavia on 15 June sending a message to Gambarcorta to join him in Abbiategrasso.[111] Créquy did not remain inactive after the construction of a boat bridge, on 16 June all his army was on the other side of the River Ticino. There, while the infantry was building an entrenchment 500 m east of Tornavento using the Fossa della Cerca (an irrigation canal) and Panperduto canal, the cavalry started to raid the countryside taking Lonate Pozzolo. During the next three days, parties of French cavalry and infantry raided the surrounding area, sacking and devastating crops, villages and monasteries. On 20 June the two allied commanders agreed to move to the north in order to rejoin the Duke of Rohan. Therefore, Créquy left Tornavento and moved towards Somma Lombardo and the Duke of Savoy towards Borgo Ticino. In the following days, spies in the Spanish camp informed the Duke of Savoy that the Spanish were ready to move towards them, the Allies wanted to join their armies to face Leganés, but the Ticino north-west of Case Nuove had too much current and it was impossible to create a bridge there. Urgently, the French sent back their troops to reoccupy their previous fortified position in Tornavento.

Meantime, Leganés had managed to join a sizeable army of professional soldiers and thousands of militia in Boffarola Sopra Ticino and on the 20th orders were given to move towards Castano Primo and Vanzaghello. The next day while the Spanish vanguard[112] was arriving in Vanzaghello, a small skirmish with French cavalry parties indicated that the army of Créquy was concentrated just six kilometres away around the hamlet of Tornavento. During the night of 21 June, in a council of war, the Spanish high command decided to attack the French in their position before they could receive the reinforcements of the troops of the Duke of Savoy. Leganés was not totally

---

109 3,000–3,500 infantry (six regiments: Puy-Saint-Martin, Castreville, Urfé, Vernatel and Féron) and 500–600 cavalry (eight companies of *chevaux-légers*). Brussoni 1661, and *Mémoires du Cardinal Richelieu*, volume IX.
110 The crossing of the French was only slightly disputed by the action of the militia of the area (*Mémoires du Cardinal Richelieu*, volume IX).
111 Oltrona Visconti, 1970, *La battaglia di Tornavento nelle fonti spagnola*, Gallaratte pp. 31–49.
112 *Tercio de la Mar de Naples*, Regiment of Borgo d'Este and companies of dragoons (*Relación de la batalla de Tornavento*, in a letter from the governor of Milan, the Marquis of Leganés to the King of Spain, Archivio General de Simancas, Secretaria de Estado, legajo 3344).

THE ARMIES OF PHILIP IV OF SPAIN 1621–1665

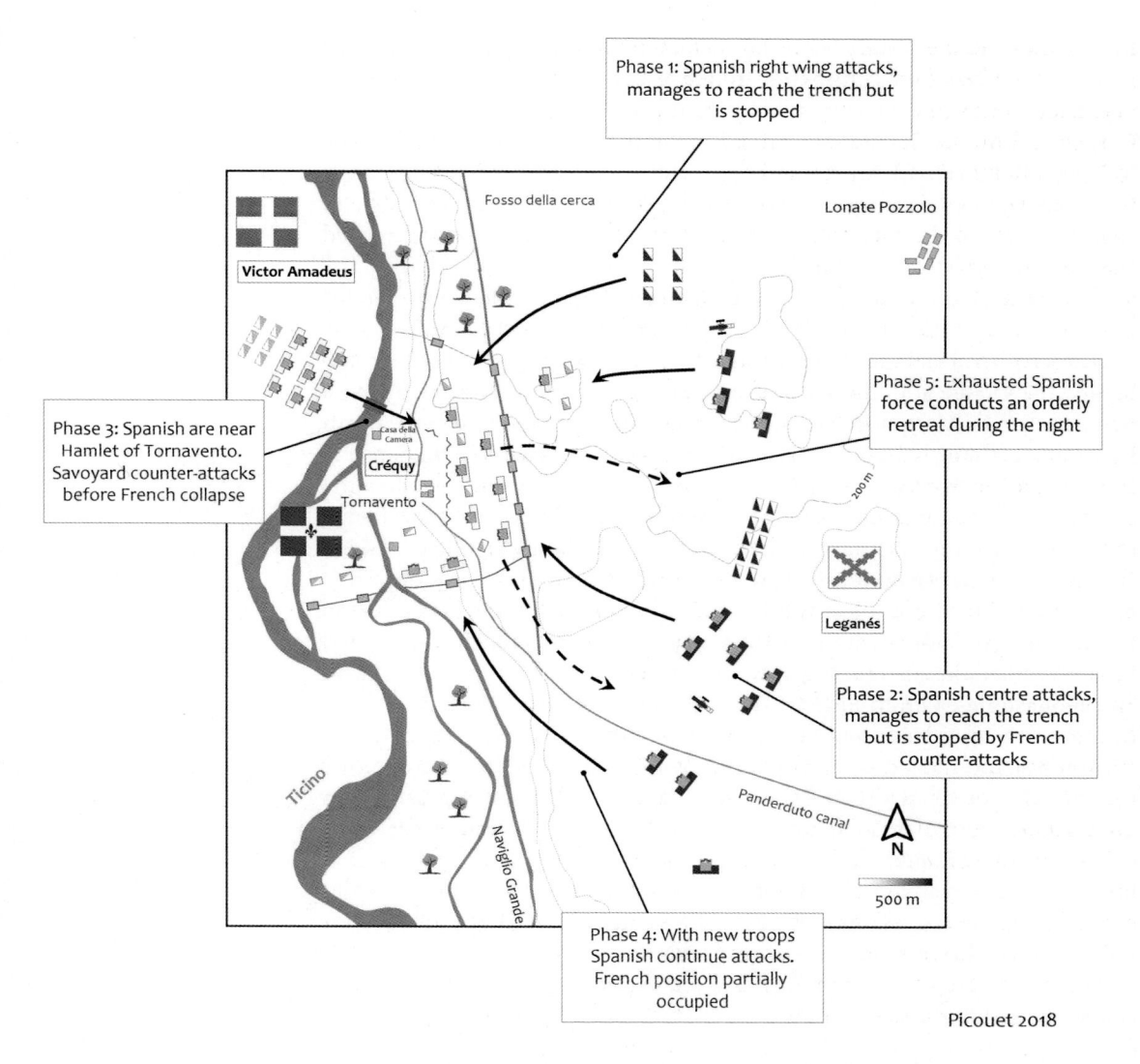

[Map with annotations:]

- Phase 1: Spanish right wing attacks, manages to reach the trench but is stopped
- Phase 2: Spanish centre attacks, manages to reach the trench but is stopped by French counter-attacks
- Phase 3: Spanish are near Hamlet of Tornavento. Savoyard counter-attacks before French collapse
- Phase 4: With new troops Spanish continue attacks. French position partially occupied
- Phase 5: Exhausted Spanish force conducts an orderly retreat during the night

Labels on map: Fosso della cerca, Lonate Pozzolo, Victor Amadeus, Casa della Camera, Créquy, Tornavento, Leganés, Ticino, Naviglio Grande, Panderduto canal, N, 500 m

Picouet 2018

Map 4.6 Battle of Tornavento fought on 22 June 1636 on the River Ticino, between an invading French-Savoyard force and the Spanish Army of Lombardy. The battle was a tactical French victory, but the invasion was halted and in the long term it was a Spanish strategic victory.

convinced about starting a full battle, but he could not wait for the arrival of all the troops of Gambacorta from Tortona,[113] the elite and the population of Milan wanted an action to punish the devastation of the allied army.

Early in the morning the Spanish army was probably deployed as follows (see Map 4.6), on the right the vanguard of 3,500–4,000 men,[114] commanded by Antonio Sotelo, with two strong infantry squadrons (Tercio de la Mar de Naples and the Regiment of Borso d'Este) supported by the Cavalry of Naples (Gherardo Gambacorta) and perhaps companies of dragoons (Colonel Juan Lope de Gijón). In the centre, Leganés had six infantry squadrons[115] deployed

---

113 The cavalry of Gambacorta joined the army at the end of 21 June, some of the infantry arrived in the morning but most of them were still on the road.
114 The vanguards had probably 2,000–2,500 infantry, 1,000 cavalry and 500 dragoons.
115 On the right two small squadrons from the Spanish tercios (Tercio of Marquis of Mortara and companies from the Tercio of Saboya and tercio of Juan de Garay), followed by two Italian tercios

in two lines and the cavalry[116] behind them. On the left they had probably an infantry squadron from the Spanish Tercio of Lombardia (Martin of Aragon) and later during the journey the regiment of Modena[117] (commanded by Camillo del Monte) joined the battle. In total the centre had probably 7,000 to 7,500 infantry, 3,000 cavalry and five guns[118] deployed on the Pamperduto Canal taking in enfilade some of the French positions. The Spanish had more men en route but also thousands of militia useless at fighting in an entrenched position and probably guarding the baggage.

The French army had built up a strong defensive position using the linear Fosso de la Cerca, an irrigation ditch 500–600 m west of the hamlet of Tornavento. The Fosso de la Cerca was connected to the Pamperduto Canal, a large irrigation ditch running just below the hill of Tornavento (on the east part and underneath the crest of the plateau) and joining the gentle plateau towards Castano (Hanlon 2016). It seems that the French entrenchment ran along the Fosso della Cerca and before joining the Pamperduto ran towards the River Ticino on the south flank. On the north one of the French entrenchments turned to the west to connect to the River Ticino. Following Hanlon (2016), the semi-circular French position was well made with the ditch and a parapet and presence of small forts at regular intervals. From right to left, the French had a contingent[119] to guard the slope and the narrow floodplain running from the river to the plateau. On the plateau, the French had positioned musketeers in the little forts and just behind the parapet a line of four infantry battalions, behind them a second line with two infantry battalions, a detachment of musketeers, and four squadrons of cavalry. In front of the fortified position, on the left, the French had also two squadrons of cavalry supported by commanded musketeers. In total the French must have had 5,500–6,000 infantry[120] and 1,200 cavalry[121] and dragoons. Early in the morning of 22 June, the Duke of Savoy was on the opposite bank of the River Ticino with a bridge mostly complete but with troops not prepared for battle. Allied commanders were surprised to see the Spanish army deployed in battle order ready to attack; recovering from their surprise they accelerated the preparation of their force for the coming fight, an easier task for Créquy than for the Duke of Savoy.

(Tercio of Boccapionola and Tercio of Spinola), two German regiments from Gilles de Haes and Edmund Lener, reinforced by German free companies and the Tercio of Tuscany in reserve.

116 The cavalry consisted of two company of guards (200–250 men), companies from the Cavalry of the State and the German regiment of Count of Schilk (900 men).

117 The troops from Modena and Tuscany presented only 1,120 men in a muster at the end of May (Maffi 2007).

118 It is possible that Leganés had more guns but they were not deployed during the first stage of the battle (Hanlon 2016).

119 Two small infantry regiments (Florainville and Peyregourde) supported by a cavalry squadron (Estang) and the company of Gendarmes of Alincourt and probably companies of dragoons or carabins (*Mémoires du Cardinal Richelieu*, op. cit.).

120 Taking out the regiment cited before, the right was for the regiment of Sault, the left for the regiment Lyonnais, between them and behind them were the regiments of Aiguebonne, Henrichemont, Roure, Roquefueil and de Bonne (*Mémoire du Comte de Souvigny*, op. cit., and Susane, *Infantry Française*, 1853). French battalions were weaker than the Spanish infantry squadrons, probably some 400 to 700 men.

121 At that time French cavalry was organised in squadrons of three companies and at Tornavento the plateau was defended by six squadrons of cavalry (Hanlon 2016).

The Spanish attack started, the vanguard moved towards the French position, with the *Tercio de la Mar de Naples* leading the attacks supported by the German of Borgo d'Este on the left and the cavalry on the right. To delay such a steamroller, the 300 cavalry commanded by de Boissac started to skirmish with the Spanish with the support of the regiment of Lyonnais. The French were rapidly outclassed by the Spanish musket fire and the cannonade of the Spanish artillery. Rapidly the French were obliged to run back to their entrenchments to find cover. The Spanish force continued its movement with *mangas* of musketeers ahead, followed by the two pike squadrons. Despite heavy musket fire from the French position and a fierce defence, the Spanish managed to take the parapet and started to pull it down with spades and pikes. Victory was for them, but the Spanish officers were also concerned to try to keep the cohesion or their formation. Unfortunately for them, when Créquy launched a counter-attack with the second line, the Spanish were disorganised and no support cavalry had been deployed in this closed space. The French were able to chase the Spanish before them and to retake their entrenchment. They did not persecute the Spanish infantry running away because it was just outside in battle formation. The infantry had to be reorganised and the Marquis of Leganés decided to continue the pressure, sending the Spanish cavalry of Gambacorta. Mounted harquebusiers dismounted, and when they were attacking the French position defended by the cavalry and some musketeers, Gambacorta was killed in front of his men. The Spanish attack collapsed and the Spanish had to retire out of range of the French musketeers. For the moment the Spanish had failed to pierce the French position and Leganés decided to engage his *bataille*. The infantry squadrons of the centre were led by the Tercio of Mortara and after fierce fighting they were able to take the French entrenchment. This time the French counter-attack was only able to stop the Spanish but not to repulse them and retake their previous position. On the Spanish right the vanguard renewed its attack and in combination with the attack in the centre, the French started to move back to the hamlet of Tornavento despite the numerous cavalry charges supported by the infantry. On the other side of the river the engineers of the Duke of Savoy had finished building the bridge,[122] and the first troops from the Regiment of Chamblay were crossing the Ticino. After three hours of fighting, with the arrival of fresh troops the French could hold their positions on the Pamperduto Canal but the Spanish refused to give away their conquest and intense fighting occurred along the hamlet and the canal. The Spanish commander had more troops in reserve on the left flank of the Pamperduto Canal, the Tercio of Lombardy, followed by the Tercio of Spinola, were engaged to attack the French south position. At first the Spanish drove away the French regiment of Florainville and Pierregourde but the tied space and the counter-attack of the French cavalry stopped the advance. The arrival of more and more infantry reinforcements[123] from the other side of the River Ticino converted the following hours into a desperate

---

122 Following Hanlon (2016) it seems that the bridge was finished at sunrise but infantry *bataillons* had not been formed and were not ready to be engaged.
123 Regiments of Bois David, Sénante, Marolles, Cevennes, Montchenu, La Tour and Ferté (*Mémoire de Souvigny*).

fight of rotating musket fire and hand-to-hand combat. The Spanish retired the troops to replace them by their reserve, including the Tercio of Tuscany and the newcomers from the regiment of Modena. In the middle of the afternoon and after a last attempt to break the French line with their infantry deployed on the right flank, it became clear for the Spanish high command that the situation was stalemated. The Spanish troops were exhausted and thirsty on this hot summer day, they were fighting for hours and losses were significant. Using the French old entrenchment the Spanish reinforced their position, but by late afternoon the decision was taken to continue the combat until the night and then to conduct an orderly retreat under the cover of darkness. Protected by dragoons, the Spanish army engaged in this perilous manoeuvre with success, going first to Castano, Boffarola and Abbiategrasso. On the other side of the hill, Créquy and the Duke of Savoy and their senior officers had a difficult meeting, losses had been significant and a lot of them wanted to retreat. In the end they decided to stay in their position, probably because the troops were exhausted and because no officers wanted to be accused of cowardice (Hanlon 2016). Their surprise came with the first light of 23 June, when the Allies discovered that the Spanish army had marched away during the night.

The Battle of Tornavento was exceptional in the way that there was 14 hours of continuous fighting. Losses were significant, and in a letter to the King, the Marquis of Leganés admitted up to 1,500 dead and 1,000 wounded; it is possible that more men had deserted during the retreat to Abbiategrasso. On the other side, even if Richelieu gave only 500–600 men for the French, the French ambassador in Torino admitted losses of up to 1,300 men. Finally we can give for certain the estimate of Hanlon (2016), giving losses (killed, wounded, prisoners and deserters) of 2,000 men for the French and 4,000 men for the Spanish.

The allied army had survived the Spanish attack and was still on the battlefield, but it was too exhausted, and remained immobile around Tornavento and their bridge on the River Ticino. In a place full of cadavers in decomposition, the usual poor hygiene conditions of seventeenth century camps, poor supplies, and the heat of summer forced the Allies[124] to move on 7 July towards Somma Lombardo and Sesto Calende. On the other side the Spanish were recovering and reinforcements were arriving. On 2 July, Leganés had 12,000 men ready for combat and by mid July he had 15,000 men in hand. The Spanish started to conduct raids in Piedmont.[125] To disturb their enemies' supply lines, using the position of the city of Novarra. Further to the north the small army of Rohan was blocked not only by the contingent of Servelloni but also by lack of pay and supplies, and at the beginning of August the French were back to the Valtellina valley. For Créquy and Victor Amadeus, their strategic campaign had failed and by the end of July their army[126] had returned to defend the territories of the Duke of Savoy and the army of Rohan.

---

124 Rapidly up to 3,000 to 4,000 men fell sick and the French ambassador said that the army had only 8,000 men fit for service (Hanlon 2016).
125 On 16 July Gattinara was attacked by a strong Spanish detachment and even if the attack was repulsed, the threat was clear (Saluces volume 4, 1818).
126 Despite reinforcements of some 2,000 to 3,000 men, the Allies had only 10,500 infantry and 2,500 men (Hanlon 2016).

4.2.3 The Campaign of 1653: the Battle of Rochetta Tanaro, 23 September

In spring 1653, the French government of Mazarin was winning the contest in Aquitaine against the supporters of the Prince of Condé. This victory enabled Mazarin to adopt a more aggressive attitude in northern Italy after the disillusion of the previous year with the losses of Trino and of the stronghold of Casale Monferrato on the River Pô. Despite such successes, the Spanish governor of the State of Milan, the Marquis of Caracena, had to face a difficult financial situation and the Army of Lombardy was reduced to just 20,000 men and with 50–60 percent of them involved in garrison duties. Therefore the Marquis of Caracena was unable to take the offensive. The campaign started in June, when the French commander, the Count of Quincé moved to Castello di Annone with a small army of 6,000 men (Saluces, volume 4, 1818) in order to harass and to extract contribution from villages of the province of Alessandria. The Spanish governor was slow to organise his field army but by the end of July Caracena was on the north bank of the River Pô with 8,000 men threatening Crescentino and harassing the province of Vercelli. The French were obliged to move to the north but the Spanish commander refused to commit his army in a pitched battle.[127] Unable to force a battle, Quincé decided to move back to the south, crossing the rivers Pô and Tanaro and passing Alessandria from the south in order to harass the province of Tortona. The Spanish commander did not follow the French army and decided to conduct a small war, raiding and harassing the territories of Piedmont in the province of Crescentino. The continuous raids from the French army against Serravalle, Scrivia and Orba and complaints of the local authorities forced Caracena to move down to the south. On the news of the arrival of Spanish army, the French, probably down to 5,000 men, withdrew to the west behind the River Tanaro between Alba and Asti followed by Caracena. By mid September the Spanish were west of Nizza Monferrato while the French forces were located north of Alba along the river. The situation changed when the Count of Grancey crossed the Alps with reinforcements[128] from the army of Guyenne. Meantime, Caracena decided to move back to the north-east towards the city of Felizzano in the province of Alessandria crossing the River Tanaro in Rocchetta Tanaro. On the news of the departure of the Spanish, the new French commander the Count of Grancey decided to catch the Spanish following the north bank of the River Tanaro. In the early morning of 23 September the Spanish were in Rocchetta Tanaro, and Spanish cavalry squadrons were already crossing the river via a ford to establish a defensive position and secure the construction of the bridge for the rest of the army. Meantime, the French vanguard commanded by Montpessat arrived on the hills north of Cerro

---

127 Spanish high command was well aware that the French cavalry tended to be superior to the Spanish one in northern Italy and were reluctant to engage their force in a hazardous battle (Hanlon 2016).

128 Between 1,200 and 2,000 men following the sources (Galeazzo Gualdo 1672, and *Relación de la insigne victoria que han tenido las armas de su majestad gobernadas del excelentísimo señor Marques de Caracena Gobernador del estado de Milan*.... J. Gomez de Blas, Seville 1653).

Tanaro, followed by the rest of the army, and Grancey saw an opportunity to catch the Spanish unbalanced while crossing the river. Both commanders urged their troops to deploy in battle formation for the French and to cross a solid bridgehead for Caracena.[129] The race was won by the Spanish, and a defensive position (see Map 4.7) was established in a loop of the River Tanaro between a farm of Cascina on the left and the hamlet of Cerro Tanaro on the right to protect the bridgehead.[130] The first line of the Spanish army[131] was commanded by Vincenzo Monsuri and was deployed as follows: on the right were companies from the Tercio of Lombardia (*Maestro de Campo* Luis de Benavidez), followed by three infantry battalions formed by the Spanish Tercio of Saboya (*Maestro de Campo* José de Velasco), the Burgundian Tercio of Beltin and the Spanish Tercio of Diego de Aragon, to finish on the left with companies from the *Tercio de la Mar de Naples* (*Maestro de Campo* Diego de Quintana) defending the Cascina. On the extreme left, probably 10–15 m ahead, a small church was occupied by two *mangas* of 100 Spanish and Italian musketeers.

Due to the lack of space, the cavalry was deployed[132] behind the first line of infantry and a reserve or third line was organised with the Italian tercios[133] crossing the river. It seems that to protect the deployment of the army three cavalry squadrons supported by two to three *mangas* of musketeers were placed in front of the trench on the right. In total the Marquis of Caracena had up to 5,000 infantry[134] and 3,000 cavalry.

On the other side the Count of Grancey divided his forces in two corps: the right one was commanded by Marquis of Montpezat and was deployed with a first line of four infantry battalions (regiments of Navarre, Baron de Perrault Marquis d'Aiguebonne and Gardes Suisses) flanked on the right by seven regiments/squadrons of cavalry and a second line of two infantry battalions (regiments of Sault and Carignan). On the left the French had a corps commanded by Marquis of Vardes with a first line with three infantry battalions (regiments of Quincé, Lyonnais and Orléans), two French cavalry regiments, the cavalry of Savoy[135] and two infantry battalions (regiments of Marquis de Ville and Montpezat); and a second line with one infantry

---

129 The Spanish had problems building the bridge and were delayed more than two hours (*Relación de la insigne vitoria…* op. cit.).
130 In the sources, the Spanish position it is not clear. It is possible that the hamlet of Cerro Tanaro had only a few houses in the seventeenth century but it is mentioned in seventeenth century maps. Between Cerro Tanaro and the big farm the Spanish had also established a small line with an unfinished parapet to protect their deployment.
131 The Spanish order of battle is given by the relation (*Relación de la insigne Vitoria*, op. cit.), Brussoni, 1661, and Saluces volume 4, 1818.
132 Cavalry commanded by Galeazo Trotti was made from the 2nd Company of Guards, companies of the State of Milan, Cavalry of Naples and regiments of German cavalry.
133 Tercio of the Count of Sartirana, Tercio of Daniele Ala, Tercio of Giuseppe Brancaccio, a tercio from the militia of Milan and the German regiment of Carlo Borso d'Este.
134 The *Relación* (*Relación de la insigne Vitoria*, op. cit.) gives only 4,000 infantry but I do not know if the militia of Milan was counted.
135 Cavalry of Savoy (two to three squadrons) was commanded by Alessandro Monti Marquis di Farigliano and was made by the regiment of Ville and free companies commanded by the Marquis de Monte Veronois (Galeazzo Gualdo 1672).

THE ARMIES OF PHILIP IV OF SPAIN 1621–1665

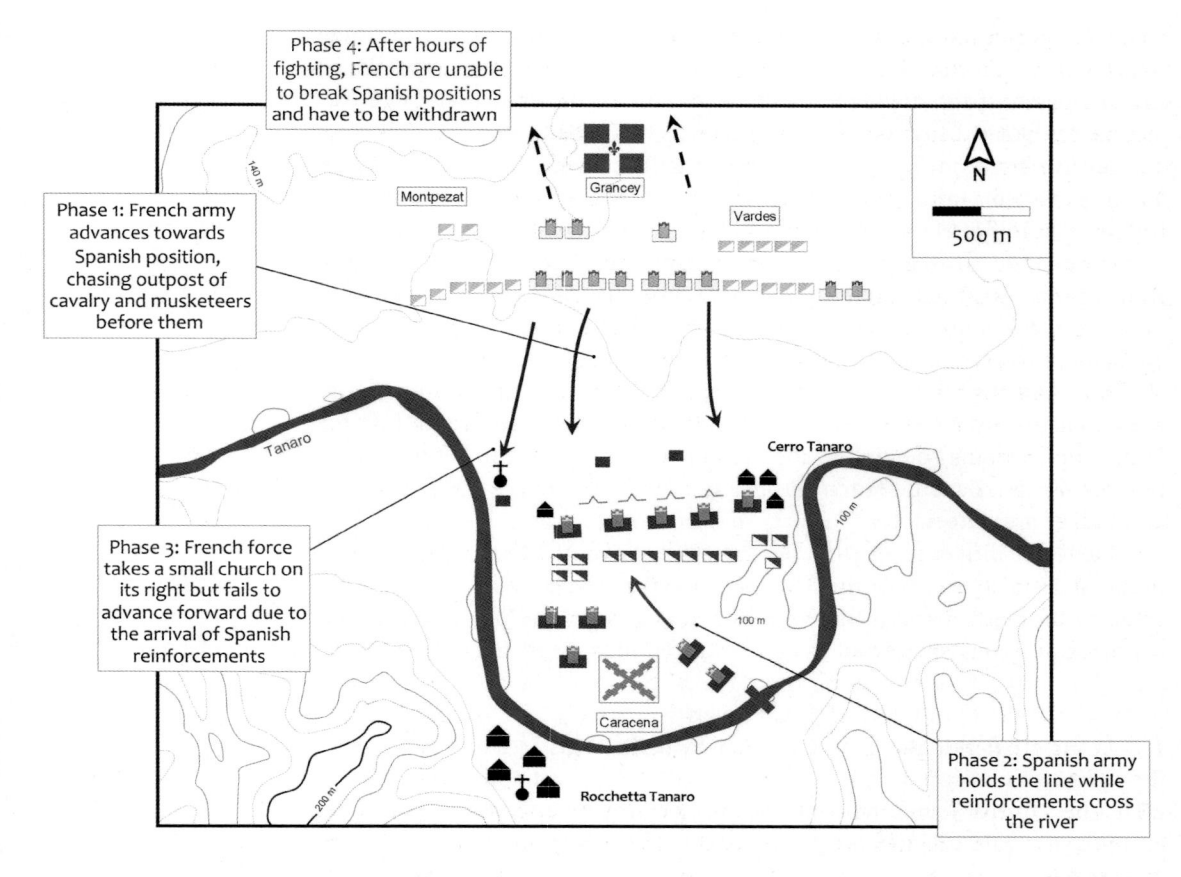

Phase 4: After hours of fighting, French are unable to break Spanish positions and have to be withdrawn

Phase 1: French army advances towards Spanish position, chasing outpost of cavalry and musketeers before them

Phase 3: French force takes a small church on its right but fails to advance forward due to the arrival of Spanish reinforcements

Phase 2: Spanish army holds the line while reinforcements cross the river

Picouet 2015

Map 4.7 The Battle of Rocchetta Tanaro, fought on 23 September 1653, on the River Tanaro between the Spanish Army of Lombardy and a French Savoyard force. The battle was a Spanish tactical victory but the strategic situation in northern Italy did not change at all.

battalion (Regiment of Grancey), companies of gendarmes, the Guards of Savoy and three cavalry regiments. In total,[136] Grancey seems to have up to 5,000 infantry and 2,000 cavalry.

The battle started at the beginning of the afternoon, when the French army moved towards the Spanish lines chasing the three squadrons of Spanish cavalry and the *mangas* of musketeers before them. The French right (Monpezat) was the first to engage the combat with the Spanish tercios of Mar de Naples and Saboya. While approaching the Spanish position the French regiments were harassed by the skirmishers and afterwards by the fire of the Spanish located in the Cascina or behind a small trench. At last the pikemen were engaged but the French attack was repulsed and Montpezat had to recall his troops. On the Spanish right, the attack was led by the troops from the Duchy of Savoy with infantry and cavalry. They were met by a heavy fire from the Spanish troops and failed to meet their objective of capturing the hamlet. On the Spanish left, Montpezat tried to outflank the Spanish position, taking first the small church after a short fight. Following orders[137] the Spanish withdrew to the

---

136 *Relación de la insigne Vitoria*, op. cit.
137 The *mangas* of musketeers had the order to delay the French attack and to fall back in front of a massive attack (Brussoni 1672).

rear. The French advanced towards a gully but quickly discovered that they were blocked by battalions from the Spanish reserve deployed in front of them. On the Spanish right, the fight had intensified, Grancey sent troops from the second line but the heavy musket fire coming from the Spanish troops and the engagement of some Spanish cavalry halted all the attacks. In the fighting Alessandro Monti was killed in front of his troops as well as numerous French and Savoyard officers. As in Tornavento 17 years earlier, step by step the fighting degenerated into a great skirmish[138] where ranks of musketeers were firing at each other but without engaging in hand-to-hand combat. After three hours, some French regiments[139] started to run out of ammunition and Grancey understood that the Spanish position could not be broken. With night coming, the French troops started to withdraw towards the hills in battle formation a few kilometres from Cerro Tanaro. They stayed in this position all night, and early in the morning of the next day they moved to Montemagno. The Spanish sent patrols to follow the French force and in the afternoon of 24 September they moved towards Felizzano. French losses exceeded Spanish ones (Brussoni, 1661) and could be estimated at 700–1,000 men[140] while the Spanish losses could be estimated at 300 men[141] with few officers killed or wounded. The Battle of Rocchetta Tanaro could be classified as a tactical victory for Caracena, but the strategic situation in northern Italy did not change at all.

4.3 Campaigns in the Iberian Peninsula

4.3.1 The Campaign of 1644: the Battle of Montijo, 26 May

In 1644, like the previous year, the Portuguese commander of the army of Alentejo, Matías Albuquerque, wanted to conduct military operation in Spanish territories while the fighting capacity of the so-called Spanish Army of Extremadura, was weak.[142] On 18 May, the Portuguese army regrouped near Campo Maior and initiated the campaign, moving north-east with the idea of taking the small town of Albuquerque, 44 km north of Badajoz, the main Spanish base. The initial operation failed because the Spanish *Maestro de Campo General*, the Marquis of Torrecusa, sent 600 men to reinforce the garrison of Albuquerque and because the Spanish were still controlling the main water well of the area. The Portuguese commander moved the army of Alentejo further to the south, pillaging all the crops and villages they encountered. On

---

138 The lack of artillery to support the infantry on both sides gave a lot of importance in musket fire and at that game the Spanish had the advantage (Saluces volume 4, 1818).
139 For example the Gardes Suisses had to use the buttons of their cloth to send some bullets against the Spanish (Brussoni 1672).
140 The Spanish give 600 dead and wounded and numerous prisoners (*Relación de la insigne Vitoria*, op. cit.]. Other Spanish sources give 1,000 men between dead wounded, prisoners and deserters (Letter from the Marquis of Caracena to the king, 18 December 1653, Archivo General de Simancas E Leg. 3371/4). The French admitted 200 dead and with the wounded we might arrive at a total of 400–500 men (Quincey).
141 Letter from the Marquis of Caracena, op. cit.
142 F.D. Costa (2005), "Interpreting the Portuguese War of Restoration (1641–1668) in a European Context", *Journal of Portuguese History*, vol. 3, pp. 1–14.

THE ARMIES OF PHILIP IV OF SPAIN 1621–1665

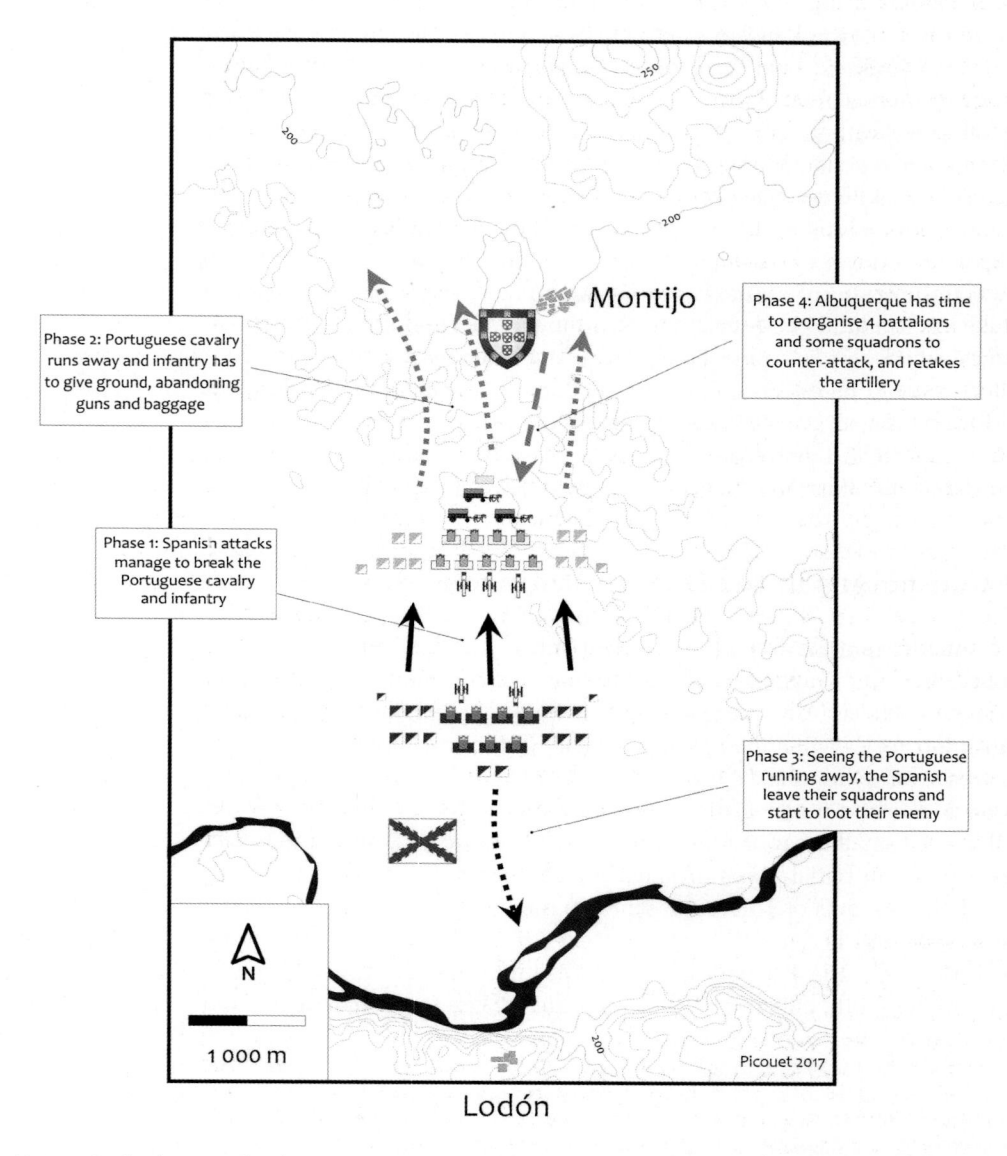

Map 4.8 Battle of Montijo, fought 26 May 1644, east of Badajoz in Spain, between the invading Portuguese Army of Alemtejo and the Spanish army of Extremadura. The battle was a draw for the two armies.

CAMPAIGNS OF THE SPANISH ARMIES

22 May, a fortified camp near the village of Montijo was established. On the opposite side, the Marquis of Torrecusa[143] was near Ouguella with the core of the Spanish army and on the news of the enemy movement to the south he called back some of the men sent to Albuquerque and asked for reinforcement from Badajoz. On the 23rd the Spanish joined all their forces[144] in Talavera la Real, on the south bank of the River Guadiana. On 24 May, the Spanish army was at the village of Lobón and sent small parties of cavalry to provoke the Portuguese, finally on 25 May, in the afternoon, the Spanish crossed the River Guadiana. Matías Albuquerque knew he could not stay much longer on the same spot and when he learned the movement of the Spanish army he decided to accept the challenge and organised his army for battle for the next day.

Let us have a look at the two armies (see Map 4.8); sources diverge. For the Spanish, numbers of troops go from 4,000 infantry and 1,700 cavalry[145] to 8,000 infantry and 3,000 cavalry (Estébanez Calderón Volume 1, 1885). If we take into account previous comments the army should have 4,300–4,500 infantry, 1,600–1,700 cavalry (12 squadrons and two companies) and four artillery guns. The Spanish right, commanded by the Baron of Molinghen, was formed by six cavalry squadrons from Spanish free companies or from the *Guardias de Castillas*, deployed in two lines, reinforced by two to three detachments of musketeers and one or two companies of mounted harquebusiers on the extreme right (Leonardo de Ferrari, 1655). The centre was formed by four infantry battalions[146] in the first line and three infantry battalions in the second line. On the left, commanded by Francisco Velasco, were three squadrons from the Italian cavalry of Extremadura, three squadrons from free Spanish companies, two to three detachments of musketeers and companies of harquebusiers of horse on the extreme left. The Spanish had a reserve of two cavalry squadrons and the artillery was deployed in front of the infantry.

For the Portuguese, a classical number gives 6,000 infantry, 1,100 cavalry and six guns (de Menezes Luis, volume II, 1751). A map of the battle[147] gives for the Portuguese army 7,000 infantry, 1,400 cavalry, 200 dragoons and

---

143 Some sources (C. Ziller Camenietzki, D. Magalháes Porto Saraiva & P.P. de Figueriredo Silva (2012), O'papel da batalha: a disputa pela viória de Monteji na public´sta do século XVII, Topi, 24, pp. 10–28) indicate that Torrecusa was not present on the day of the battle. Others (Palau Cuñat op. cit.) give the testimony of a cleric saying that the Marquis of Torrecusa was present.
144 Numbers of the Spanish force oscillate between authors, White (2003) gives 2,100 cavalry and 7,000 infantry for all the army of Extremadura and if we take into account the Garrison of Badajoz of 1,000 infantry and 200 cavalry (J. Palau Cuñat, 1994, "La batalla de Montijo", *Opinión*, *Revista Dragona* n° 5) and the small garrisons left in the region, it is difficult to have a Spanish army above 6,000–6,500 men.
145 See indication in an illustration of the Battle of Montijo (Leonardo de Ferrari, 1655).
146 First line from right to left, two Spanish battalions from respectively the Tercio of José del Pulgar and the Tercio of Francisco Xelder, one amalgamated battalion formed by the Irish tercio of James FitzGerald, reinforced by companies from the Tercio Viejo de Extremadura and one Italian battalion from the Tercio of Giovanni Battista Pignattili. Second line, three battalions from respectively the Tercio de Francisco de Agüero, the Tercio of Juan Rodriguezde Olivares and Tercio Viejo de Extremadura (*Maestro de Campo* Sancho de Monroy) (Estébanez Calderón volume 1, 1885; J. Palau Cuñat, op. cit.; de Mesa 2014).
147 Map from Leonardo de Ferrari, 1655.

six guns. The order of battle[148] gives, on the Portuguese right, six cavalry squadrons commanded by Francisco de Melo. In the centre were the infantry, commanded by Diogo Gomes de Figueyredo with nine battalions[149] deployed in two lines and the baggage behind them protected by 400 musketeers. On the left, commanded by Gaspar Pinto Pestanha, were five cavalry squadrons.[150] Companies of dragoons[151] were probably present on the cavalry wings. The artillery was deployed in front of the infantry.

The battle started at 9:00 a.m. with an inefficient bombardment which lasted one hour. On the Spanish right, the cavalry of Molhingen advanced towards their opponent and after a short exchange of fire and slashing of swords, the Portuguese cavalry ran away. The Spanish followed their movement to attack the exposed flanks of the Portuguese infantry. The Spanish battalions on the right (Agüero and Fitzgerald) were also advancing and soon the Portuguese were attacked by the flank and the front. The Spanish and Portuguese melted; exchanging musket fire combined with short thrusts with the pikes. On both sides troops from the second line were called to support the first, but after hard and bitter fighting the Portuguese troops were forced to give ground and to retire to the rear. On the left the same scenario was followed, with a clear victory of the Spanish cavalry against their Portuguese counterparts. The Portuguese infantry was again attacked by the Spanish infantry (mainly battalions of Pignattili and Extremadura) and the cavalry and had no choice but to run away. At that time most of the Portuguese cavalry had abandoned the battlefield; the infantry had lost hundreds of men and was withdrawing, leaving behind the artillery and baggage. Victory seemed to be on the Spanish side but thereafter the Spanish army lost its combat discipline. Men (infantry or cavalry) abandoned their positions to loot the enemy baggage and animals, returning back to the rear with their hands full of goods. In a short time, several Spanish battalions and squadrons were totally disorganised, unable to follow orders to pursue the Portuguese. On the other side, the poor discipline of the Spanish troops gave Albuquerque enough time to reorganise four infantry battalions and some cavalry squadrons and to decide to retake his artillery. The Portuguese attack surprised the Spanish commanders with few troops in hand. Albuquerque was able to defeat the small Spanish detachments and to recapture his guns. The next step of the battle is somewhat confused; following Spanish accounts, Torrecusa and Molhingen managed to restore enough discipline in their troops to stop the Portuguese. With little infantry, the Spanish

---

148 The map of Leonardo de Ferrari, (1655) shows 11 battalions of infantry, 10 cavalry squadrons and four small companies of cavalry.
149 First line, five battalions respectively from the Tercio of Saldanya, Tercio of Mascarenhas, Tercio of da Silva, Terço of de Soussa and Tercio of de Mel, second line four battalions respectively from the Tercio of Ferreira, Tercio of Pick, Tercio of Caley and Tercio of the Count of Prado (de Menezes volume II, 1751).
150 Including a squadron of 150 "Dutch" cavalry (de Menezes volume II, 1751).
151 In a muster at the end of June the company of dragoons of Castanho is presented (NTT, Conselho de Guerra, Consultas, 1644, mç. 4-A, nº 264, doc. anexo à consulta de 12 de Julho de 1644, "Rezumo das Companhias de Cauallo que neste Ex.to Seruem a SMgde Apresentado na mostra que se comesou em 29 de Junho 1644").

could not disrupt the ordered retreat of the Portuguese army with their guns. Portuguese sources indicated that Albuquerque remained master of the battlefield while the Spanish retreated towards the River Guadiana and Lodón. It was only during the night that the Portuguese finally withdrew towards Campo Maior.[152] Concerning losses, it seems that the Portuguese had lost[153] some 900 men[154] (dead and prisoners) as well as 300 deserters.[155] On the other side, the Spanish admitted the losses of 433 dead and 375 wounded.[156] As pointed out by recent authors[157] even in the twenty-first century it is difficult to give a clear winner, it looks that the battle was a bloody affair[158] and that the Portuguese army was forced to retire to Portugal. So we might have a tactical draw during the battle but a much more Spanish "victory" for the 1644 campaign in Extremadura.

4.3.2 The Campaign of 1644: the Second Battle of Lérida, 15 May

In 1644, the main effort of the Spanish monarchy was made on the Catalan front and most of the resources were sent there to organise a field army able to defeat the French and retake Lérida. On 6 February, King Philip IV left Madrid to Zaragoza in Aragon. The arrival of the court boosted the organisation and build up the army commanded by Felipe da Silva. On 2 May, the General Captain of the army of Catalonia[159] was able to present, in Berbejal seven kilomtres south-west of Barbastro, an army of 9,554 infantry[160], 4,336 cavalry[161] with an artillery train of six heavy guns, 10

---

152 See Ziller et al. (op. cit.) for a discussion on the controversy of the Battle of Montijo.
153 A Spanish source gives 4,300 men (600 prisoners) (*Aviso de 31 de Mayo de 1644, Semanario erudito que combrehende varias obras ineditas…* vol. 33, A. Valladares de Sotomayor, Madrid 1790).
154 Two *Maestros de Campo*, Nuno Mascarenhas and Ayres de Saldanha, were killed as well as 13 other *Sargento Mayors* and captains (infantry and cavalry: one *Maestro de Campo*, Eustaquio Pique, was captured as well as 8–9 captains (infantry and cavalry) (de Menezes volume II, 1751).
155 Ziller et al. (op. cit.).
156 *Relación de la batalla de Montijo* in Estébanez Calderón volume 1, 1885. Following the same source the *Maestro de Campo* José del Pulgar was killed as well as 16 captains (infantry and cavalry).
157 de Mesa (2014) and Ziller et al. (op. cit.).
158 In seems that a total of 1,700–1,800 men (13 percent of the total) were lost in five hours of fighting with a 50 percent death rate.
159 Felipe da Silva was captain general of the army of Catalonia, the Marques of Mortara was *Maestro de Campo General*, Don Juan de Vivaro was general of the cavalry and Francisco Tuttavila general of the artillery. Finally we have three lieutenants of *Maestro de Campo* Pedro de Valenzuela, Gaspar de Mesa and Alonso Garnica (Campaña de 1644, CODOIN, vol. 95, 1893).
160 Six Spanish units, the Regiment of the Guardia del Rey, commanded by Simón de Mascareña; Regiment of the Principe, commanded by Nuño Pardo de la Casta; Tercio of Martin de Mujica o Muxica; Tercio of Esteban de Ascárraga; Tercio of Alsonso de Villamayor and Tercio of Francisco Freire. Two Walloon units, Tercio of Charles Antoine de Calonne, Tercio of André Van der Sraeten. Three Neapolitan units, Tercio of the Baron of Amato, Tercio of Frey Tito Brancaccio; Tercio of the Duke of Laurenzana. Four German regiments forming two amalgamated battalions: Regiments of Galaso, Regiment of Glosflet or Grosfeit, Regiment of Ludwig Haumel and Regiment of the Baron of Seebach.
161 The cavalry had probably some 100 companies (40 squadrons) coming from six trozos/regiments: Trozo of Rousillon (commanded by Andres de Haro), the Trozo of the Ordenes (Commanded by Juan de Oto), Cavalry of Flandes (Commanded by Blas Janini), Cavalry of Naples (Commanded by Ferdinand Limonti), the regiment of Burgundy (Commanded by the Baron of Bouthier) and contingent of the Old Guards of Castilla (Commanded by Don Roque Matamoros).

quarter-cannons (10 pounders) and up to eight *mansfeltes* (five pounders) to the king. The campaign to retake Lérida started two days later when the army crossed the River Cinca. On 6 May, Felipe da Silva was in Tamarit. On the 8th, French detachments were detected near Castelló of Farfanya, taken without resistance. On the French side, the French commander Philippe de la Mothe-Houdancourt, following the Spanish preparations, had reinforced the garrison of Lérida[162] and was waiting for reinforcements from France to build up his field army.[163]

On 9 May, during the night a strong vanguard (3,000 cavalry and 500 musketeers) commanded by Juan de Vivaro was sent to find an unguarded ford to the south of Balaguer and to cross the River Segre. When it was done, Felipe da Silva sent a reinforcement of 3,200 infantry extracted from eight tercios and regiments (Tercio of Mujica, Tercio of Brancaccio, the two Walloon tercios and the four German regiments) and two light guns. The Spanish manoeuvre was detected by the French, and 800 men from the garrison of Lérida were urgently sent to Balaguer on 9 May. More were sent on the 10th and 11th from Cervera. On 11 May, when the small Spanish force of Juan de Vivaro arrived to block the bridge of Balaguer, they found a strong garrison[164] and the Spanish decided to abandon the operation against the city and to go back to the village of Térmens. On 12 May, Juan de Vivaro received the order to take position at Vilanoveta[165] in front of Lérida. The next day, the Spanish vanguard was in a fortified position around Vilanoveta waiting for the arrival of the main army. In fact the forces commanded by Felipe da Silva were still on the River Noguera, some kilometres south-east of Albesa, delayed by heavy rain. Meantime, the French had plenty of time to prepare a decent mobile force and on 13 May they were concentrated west of Bellpuig, at just 30–35 km from Lérida. The position of the Spanish army was dangerous, separated in two entities and with a French force of 8,500–11,000 men[166] in the neighbourhood with the objective of reinforcing Lérida and fighting the Spanish army if necessary.[167] The need to join the Spanish army was urgent and a detachment commanded by Simon of Mascareña was sent to control the ford of Corbins on the River Segre the night of the 13th and 14th of May. At dawn a French vanguard appeared and

---

162 Lérida had a garrison of 2,500 men (six regiments) reinforced by 600 militia from the city. J.L. Gonzales, A. Riber & O. Uceda (1999).
163 On 5 May a naval squadron of 20 warships (nine galleons, nine galleys and two smaller ships) escorting 40 merchants arrived in Barcelona with 5,000 infantry, supplies and ammunitions.
164 With the reinforcements the garrison had probably 3,000 men (Picouet 2014).
165 It is possible that some infantry, especially the German regiments of Haumel and Seebach went back to the main army.
166 Miguel de Parets (*Memorial Historico* vol. 24), La Mothe-Houdancourt had 7,000 foot and 1,500 horse. Gonzalo et al. (1997) gives 9,000 foot and 2,000 horse.
167 In French documents (Letters of Pierre de Marca and Letters of Mazarin) it is said that another batch of reinforcements (3,000 men including the regiment of La Marine) had to land in Barcelona by the 19–20 of May. The haste to challenge the Spanish army had probably different reasons, on one hand La Mothe-Houdancourt had been criticised for his inaction during the 1643 campaign and on other hand, even with this reinforcements, the total was 13,000 men and with this force it would have been difficult to force the Spanish line of circumvallation. Finally the fortification of Lleida was not completely finished, and the garrison was insufficient to resist a siege.

found the Spanish in a good defensive position and decided to retire. For the Spanish commander, time was running out and as soon as possible the construction of a boat bridge, 1.8 km north-east of Lleida, was undertaken to join the infantry with Vivaro's forces in order to unify a decent fighting force on the east bank of the Segre. On the morning of 15 May, Felipe da Silva could deploy an army of 9,000 men.[168] The 6,000 infantry, 3,000 cavalry and four Mansfeltes (5-pounder light guns) were deployed as follows (see Map 4.9). On the right flank we find Juan de Vivaro, with three trozos of cavalry (Flandres, Rosellón and Borgoña) an infantry battalion formed by the Regiment of the Guardia Real. In the centre, commanded by the Marques of Mortara, we find two Spanish infantry battalions from the Tercio of Nuño Pardo and Tercio of Mujica, one Walloon battalion (Tercio of Calonne and Tercio of Van der Straeten), one German battalion (Regiment of Galaso and Regiment of Glosflet) and one Italian battalion (Tercio of Brancaccio and half of the Tercio of Amato). On the left, commanded by the Marquis of Cerralvo, we have also three trozos of cavalry (Cavalry of the Ordenes, Naples and Old Guards of Castilla) an Italian infantry battalion (Tercio of Laurenzana and the other half of the Tercio of Amato) and the artillery. The reserve was formed by a Spanish battalion formed by the Tercio of Freire. Finally the Spanish army had a detachment under the command of Pablo Gil de Espinosa, with 300 musketeers from all nations and a company of cavalry in Vilanoveta guarding the access to the main bridge of Lérida. On the French side, the French commander La Mothe-Houdancourt deployed his army on a hill three kilometres east of Lérida. Contrary to the Spanish one, the French deployment is not well known and had to be reconstructed (Picouet 2014). The right was formed by seven to eight squadrons of cavalry[169] commanded by the Baron du Terrail. At first the infantry[170] in the centre was deployed in two lines, with six infantry battalions in the first lines and five infantry battalions in the second one. The left was also formed by seven to eight squadrons of cavalry commanded by the Lord of Boissac. The artillery of 10 or 12 guns was installed in front of the infantry in two batteries.

The battle started around midday when the Spanish initiated a movement following a parallel route to the French position one kilometre from the French batteries. The French artillery opened fire and were partially counter-attacked by the Spanish guns. The Spanish movement surprised the French officers, some of them were even thinking that the Spanish did not want to

---

168 Not all the troops crossed the River Segre. The Spanish rearguard was commanded by Francisco Tuttavila, with 300 horse, the Tercio of Villamayor, the Tercio of Ascárraga, German regiments of Haumel and Seebach, the main artillery, the baggage and all supplies, in total up to 2,500 men.
169 In total the cavalry came from the company of guards of La Mothe-Houdancourt, and from seven regiments, la Mothe-Cavalerie, Baron d'Alais, Bussy-de Vair, de Villeneuve, du Terrail, Count of Chateaubriant, Boissac and Balthasar, in total some 1,800–2,000 cavalry (Susane volume 3, 1883 and Picouet 2014).
170 The infantry was formed from the seven French regiments, namely the regiments of Lyonnais, La Mothe-Houdancourt, d'Albret, Mompouillan, Vandy, Rébé and Chastellier-Barlot, probably two Swiss regiments (Regiment of An-Buchel and probably the one of Jean Jacques Rhan) and two tactical Catalan battalions (one commanded by the Baron of Carpotella), in total some 7,000 infantry (Picouet 2014).

THE ARMIES OF PHILIP IV OF SPAIN 1621–1665

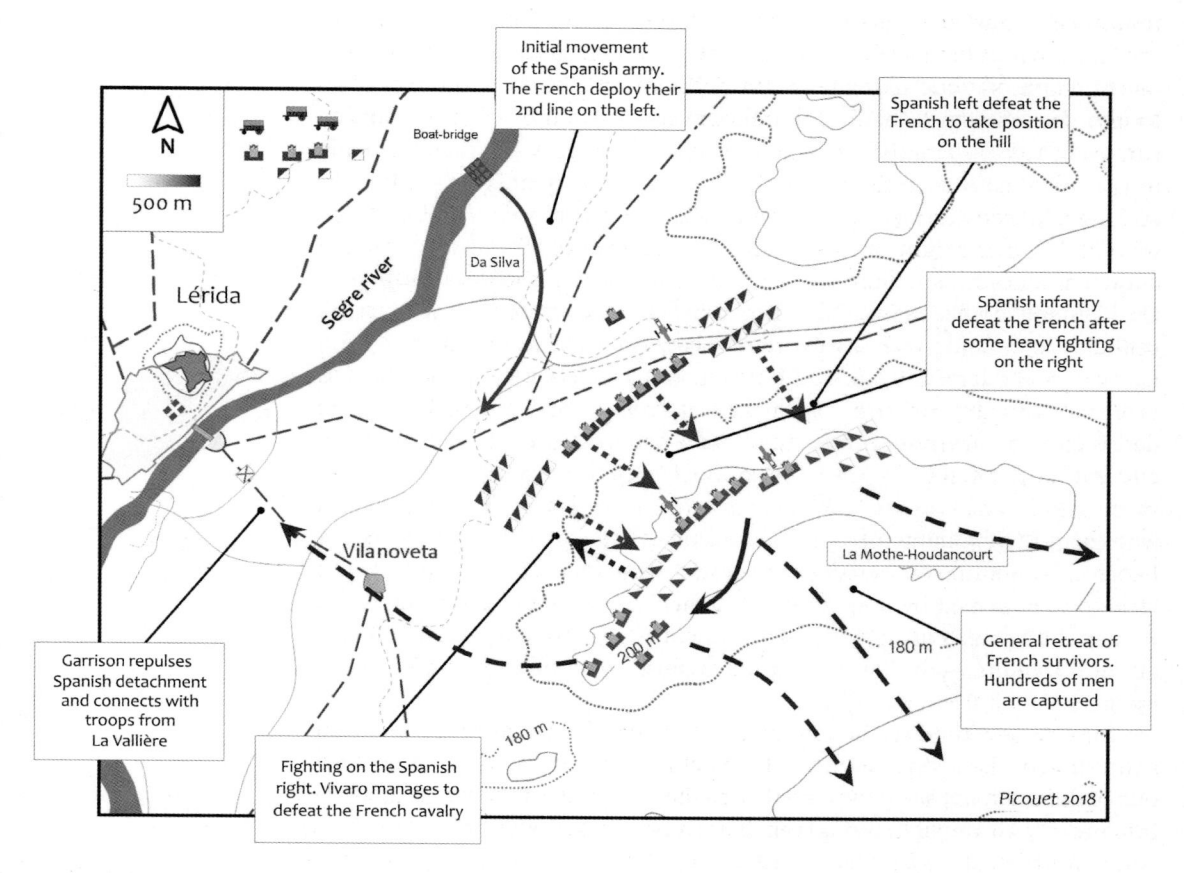

Map labels:
- Initial movement of the Spanish army. The French deploy their 2nd line on the left.
- Spanish left defeat the French to take position on the hill
- Spanish infantry defeat the French after some heavy fighting on the right
- General retreat of French survivors. Hundreds of men are captured
- Fighting on the Spanish right. Vivaro manages to defeat the French cavalry
- Garrison repulses Spanish detachment and connects with troops from La Vallière
- Boat-bridge
- Segre river
- Lérida
- Da Silva
- Vilanoveta
- La Mothe-Houdancourt
- Picouet 2018

Map 4.9 The Battle of Lérida, fought on 15 May between the Spanish Army of Catalonia and the French army, during the campaign to retake Lérida. The Spanish victory destroyed the main French force and allowed the siege of the city to be taken on 30 July 1644.

fight and retreated to Tarragona. La Mothe-Houdancourt had another idea, he was thinking that Felipe de Silva was trying to outflank his exposed right and he ordered to move the second infantry line (commanded by Marquis of la Valière) to the left. With the extension of their front, the French force could cover the entire hill. For an hour and half the Spanish battalion marched under artillery fire, taking casualties when full ranks of soldiers were killed by a "fortunate" cannonball. Finally the Spanish stopped, and turning to the left they faced the French position. They started to move directly towards the French crossing a small ditch full of water. With the advantage of the slope, the French squadrons of Boissac decided to move to challenge the Spanish cavalry of the right. At first the encounter was inconclusive, but when Juan de Vivaro launched the three squadrons of the second line in a flanking movement, they managed to repulse the French. In the centre, the Spanish infantry battalions were advancing step by step to meet their French counterparts. On the Spanish left, the cavalry of the Marquis of Cerralvo, was successful and after a poor resistance the cavalry of du Terrail ran away from the battlefield. The Spanish infantry on the right, lead by the Spanish battalion of the Guardias del Rey, engaged the regiment of La Mothe-Houdancourt. The two units fought fiercely during some time with musket fire and pike fighting but at last the Spanish prevailed and French started to give ground. More to the centre, the different French infantry regiments made a poor resistance against the incoming Spanish forces. They spoiled their musket fire and most of the time refused to fight with their pikes. With no second line to counter-attack and with the partial destruction of the regiment of La Mothe- Houdancourt, the French infantry first line started to vanish and to run away. On the Spanish left, the troops of Cerralvo were occupying the top of the hill; more to the centre the Spanish infantry finished off the last resistance of the regiment of La Mothe-Houdancourt, only the French left was still in battle condition. Meantime, the governor of Lérida had prepared a force of 600 men to attack the small detachment of Pablo Gil de Espinosa. The French infantry crossed the bridge by surprise, killing all the Spanish soldiers they encountered and therefore securing the access to the city. With the troops of his left, La Mothe-Houdancourt decided to send the Marquis of la Valière with a strong detachment of French troops,[171] including the debris of the regiment of Lyonnais, to make contact with the garrison of the city. Although pressed by the Spanish cavalry the French managed to enter safely into Lérida. On the hill, the exhausted Spanish force still had to deal with three French infantry battalions withdrawing slowly in direction of the Borgues Blanques. Juan de Vivaro was sent with some squadrons and with little hope of escape; the French lowered their weapons and surrendered.

French losses could be estimated to some 3,500–4,000 men,[172] all the artillery and the baggage while on the Spanish side losses were 500 to 600 men (Picouet 2014).

The first benefit from the victory was to boost the morale of the Spanish and Felipe de Silva sent a letter to the inhabitants of Lleida to surrender. But one of the consequences of the battle was the entrance of the French infantry into the city, meaning that the French governor had enough men[173] to resist, and a formal siege had to be carried out. The Spanish constructed a full line of circumvallation and five fortified camps.[174] The first important action took place on 22 May with the assault of the half-moon of the Cappont protecting the entrance of the stone bridge. After bitter fighting and a counter-attack from the garrison, the position was occupied by the Spanish and fortified. In June, while the French commander La Mothe-Houdancourt received more reinforcements from France to rebuild his army, the Spanish received

---

171 Sources diverge on the numbers but 2,000 men seems to be a good compromise. On these numbers not all men were fit for battle and an appreciable proportion had lost their weapons or were wounded, thus unfit for action. The next day, in Lleida, the regiment of Lyonnais had only 25 officers and 439 soldiers, half of the original number.
172 French sources such as the *Gazette de France 1644* give losses of 2,000 men.
173 Following a letter from Pierre de Marca dated from 25 of June 1644, the French garrison had 181 officers and 3,575 men inside the city (Picouet 2014).
174 The first one was located in the north-east of Lleida in a place called Secá de San Pere and was called the quarter of the King (*Cuartel del Rey*) with most of the troops and supplies. To the south of this fortification, the boat bridge on the River Segre was covered by a redoubt with infantry. On the other side of the River Segre was the second largest quarter located in Vilanoveta. The distance from Vilanoveta to the River Segre and the boat bridge was covered by the quarter of the Molino. To cover the approach from the north, the Spanish established the quarter of Villamayor. Trenches and palisades were constructed between the different quarters (Picouet 2014 and sketch from Biblioteca Nacional de España Bellas Arte n.Inv. 68186).

reinforcements[175] from Castile, Aragon, Navarre and Valencia to strengthen the siege.[176]

On 17 June the Spanish made important progress, taking the occupied fortress of the Gardeny's hill. With his new army, La Mothe-Houdancourt tried desperately to introduce men and supplies into the city, but each time the Spanish managed to frustrate his movement. On 26 July, the French withdrew their army to the south of Barcelona. The French governor of Lérida understood that the city could not resist any longer. Negotiations started the same day and on 30 July the city capitulated to Felipe da Silva with honourable terms. On 7 August the King of Spain could make a triumphal entrance into the city.

4.3.3 The Campaign of 1651–52: the Siege of Barcelona, August 1651 to 1652

In January 1651, the Spanish controlled three main cities of Catalonia, Lérida, Tortosa, and Tarragona, and the state council in Madrid could give the order to start the operation against the capital of Catalonia. It seems that the situation was favourable for such operations: engulfed in the *Fronde* movement, Mazarin was unable to reinforce the French army of Catalonia commanded by the Count of Marchin estimated at 3,000 infantry and 2,500 cavalry. The plague epidemic[177] of 1649–1654, coupled with 11 years of continuous war, had disrupted the social organisation and economy of the province killing up to 14 percent of the population and the poor harvest of 1650 contributed also to the weakness of the defence of Barcelona. Despite such constraints, Barcelona was still a populated city of 40,000–50,000 inhabitants[178] with strong fortification,[179] and a militia of 1,000–2,000 men.[180] The problem for the Franco-Catalans was that they had not enough men to defend Barcelona, central Catalonia and the coast of the Emporda. Nonetheless, the Spanish had to face serious difficulties when the Marquis of

---

175 From Castile 6,000 infantry and horses for the dismounted cavalrymen, 3,000 men from the militia of Aragon and 1,200 men from the Tercio of Valencia (only 600 arrived), commanded by Jéronimo Mansiuri and 1,000 men from the Tercio of Navarre, commanded by Baltasar de Rada (*Campaña de 1644* CODOIN vol. 95, 1893).

176 In the hot summer, poor hygiene conditions, lack of water, casualties and desertions were high. At the end of May, Spanish commanders estimated their available forces on active service around the city were only 5,000–5,500 infantry and 2,000 cavalry.

177 In Catalonia the epidemic started in 1649 in Tortosa, spreading to Tarragona in February 1650 and south of Catalonia (Baix Ebre, Ribera d'Ebre and Alt Camp). Following the trading route, the plague continues to advance to the north-east (Girona, Olot and Camprodon) and the Ampurdan. The coast and Barcelona was most affected at the end of 1650 and beginning of 1651. Officially the plague epidemic ended in 1654. The human cost was significant and can be estimated at 58,000–66,000 dead for Catalonia and 4,200 to 8,100 for Barcelona alone (J.L. Bertán Moya (1990), "Sociedad y peste en la Barcelona de 1651", *Manuscrits*, 8, pp. 225–282).

178 Due to the war and devastation on the countryside, the population had increased from 30,000 inhabitants to close to 50,000. Bertán Moya op. cit.

179 The medieval walls had been reinforced by 10 bastions, a hornwork and ravelins. Since 1641, the Fort of Montjuich had been heavily fortified and was connected to the city by a fortified path (iIllustration from *Mapa del setge de Barcelona de 1652*, And. Parisius, c.1652. Biblioteca de Catalunya, sig. XV.3 M R.E. 22374).

180 Meseguer and Bell, 2012.

CAMPAIGNS OF THE SPANISH ARMIES

Mortara marched out of Lérida on 5 July with only 5,700–5,800 infantry,[181] 2,500 cavalry[182] and 22 guns. On 25 July the army arrived in Tarragona, bypassing well-defended Cervera but taking the small town of Montblanc on the way. In Tarragona, John of Austria and the Marquis of Mortara decided to move towards the River Llobregat just 12–13 km from Barcelona. On 4 August the Spanish army was on the river and close to the sea, there they received reinforcements[183] and increased to 12,000 men[184] and 42 guns with the support of a fleet of 60 sails and 22 galleys.[185] Four days later they crossed the River Llobregat, took a small tower and moved towards Sanz, Cortes de Sarria and the convent of the Pedralbas while the fleet followed the coast to find a proper place to set up a fortified camp. Meantime, the Franco-Catalans had joined all their forces under the walls of Barcelona, but during the Spanish movement only skirmishes between the two cavalry took place. On 13 August the Spanish army[186] was on a plain north of Barcelona, near the village of San Marti and the small River Besos. There, the Spanish started the construction of a powerful fortified camp, connected with the fleet while the cavalry was raiding the villages and orchards of Barcelona. The Spanish extended there fortifications taking hills west of the city and on 21 August Mongat's Tower was stormed. The Franco-Catalans had not enough men to protect the city and attack the Spanish; they decided to use their force to protect supply convoys coming from Martorel, on 8 September a big convoy managed to enter the city despite some losses.[187] At the same time, John of Austria[188] was also exploiting dissensions between the French high command and the Catalans to his benefit. The French monarchy was engulfed in the

---

181 The Spanish army of Catalonia had some 8,200 infantry (100 Spanish companies, 60 Italian companies, 62 Walloon companies and 49 German companies). Sixty-three companies (some 2,500 men) were left behind for garrison duty, for the field army 5,700–5,800 men (208 companies) could be a reliable number (*Relación diaria de todo lo que ha sucedido desde que salio …desde el 22 de junio hasta primeros días de agosto deste año 1651*, Gómez de Blas, A 110/060(22) University of Seville).
182 The Spanish army of Catalonia had some 3,700 cavalry (80 companies), 935 were dismounted and 240 were left behind for garrison duty (*Relación diaria de todo lo que ha sucedido…* op. cit.).
183 By the end of July, 3,300 men from southern Italy (Spanish from Italy, Italian new recruits and two German regiments) were disembarked and hundreds of men from Catalonia and garrisons in Aragon (Marques de Olías y de Mortara, *Conquista de Cataluña*, 1655).
184 *Relación diaria de todo lo que ha sucedido…* op. cit.
185 17 warships, 22 galleys and other smaller ships (Meseguer and Bell, 2012).
186 19 Infantry units: four Spanish tercios (Regimiento Guardia del Rey, Tercio of Gaspar de la Cueva, Tercio of Lisbon commanded by Cristobal Caballero and Tercio of Luis Juan de la torre), two Provincial tercios of Aragon (Tercio of Pedro Esteban and Tercio of Francisco de Sada), three Italian tercios (Tercio of the Baron of Amato, tercio of Tiberio Garaffa and Tercio of di Gennaro), three Walloon tercios (Tercio of Calonne, Tercio of Clerch and Tercio of Franqué), two Irish Tercios (Tercio of Tyrone and Tercio of O'Cahan) and five German regiments (Baron of Seebach, Keingans, François Chappius, Careme and Ercole Visconti). The cavalry was made of the companies of guards, Trozo of Rosellon, Trozo of Flandes/Borgoña, Trozo of Ordenes Militares and an unknown unit).
187 Marques de Olías y de Mortara, op. cit.
188 John of Austria was also asking the Spanish court to send more men and resources to besiege Barcelona. Despite some disagreements in the Spanish Council, on 20 September the King finally gave authorisation to continue the siege while he ordered reinforcements sent to the army of Catalonia (Francisco Abrobre, *Historia de los hechos del serenisimo señor Juan de Austria en le principado de Cataluña…*, Madrid 1673).

Fronde episode and it was well known that the Count of Marchin was a supporter of the Prince of Condé. When the revolt of the princes started in France, the Spanish had the opportunity to negotiate a free passage of Marchin towards the Guyenne province in France. At the end of September Marchin managed to convince some French officers to desert with him, and with the complicity of the Spanish he escaped on 23 September towards the French border with 1,400–1,500 men.[189] The Catalans and the French authorities were totally taken by surprise and urgently Joseph de Margrit was nominated governor of the city with the task of reorganising its defence.

On the other side, with a clear opportunity in hand, the Spanish took the burgs of Sarria, Santz (3 October) to continue with l'Hospitalet on 11 October. With the last operation Barcelona was totally surrounded and the Spanish could install artillery to bombard the city (Maffi 2014).

On 14 October the Spanish tried to take the castle of Montjuich, but even if the attack failed they managed to occupy and fortify the Hermitage of San Ferriol and the convent of San Madrona.[190] By the end of October, the Spanish had created lines of circumvallation and contravallation with a series of fortifications (see Map 4.10) and three quarters.[191] Reinforcements[192] arrived in November and December to help to cover all the fortification in place. In Barcelona, the situation was critical with the desertion of Marchin, even if 300–400 men managed to enter the city by the south on 24 October. Three days later, French infantry managed to enter the city, avoiding the Spanish blockade in small boats. On 5 November, the Franco-Catalans launched an attack to take the Hermitage of San Ferriol, but they were repulsed by the counter-attack of troops from the quarter of Santz commanded by Giovanni Pallaveccino.[193] Finally, Philippe de la Mothe-Houdancourt was nominated viceroy of Catalonia on 24 October by the Queen Regent with the order to save Barcelona. The Spanish did not stop their purpose to occupy key positions around Barcelona, Tarrasa was taken on 7 November and San Boi de Llobregat on the 18th.[194] In Perpignan, Philippe de la Mothe-Houdancourt was assembling a relief army of 6,500 men[195] and on 12 December he was ready to move. At the end of

---

189 1,000 Infantry (regiment of Marchin, regiment of Monpouillan, Swiss regiment of Gesvres) and 400–500 cavalry.

190 A strong battery of six guns was installed in the convent to bombard the south of Barcelona (Mortara 1655, op. cit.).

191 Quarter of San Marti in the north connected to the sea, Quarter of Nuestra Señora de Gracia on the west and Quarter of Sanz in the south-west facing the hill of Montjuich (illustration from *Mapa del setge de Barcelona de 1652*, And. Parisius, c.1652. Biblioteca de Catalunya, sig. XV.3 M R.E. 22374).

192 October, November, 1,000 men from Castile, 1,200 from Valencia with more guns. In December up to 1,650 infantry (Meseguer and Bell, 2012), and Marques de Olías y de Mortara, *Conquista de Cataluña*, 1655.

193 Spanish losses were estimated at 100 men and the Franco-Catalan ones at 300 men (Marques Mortara, op. cit.).

194 Further to the south the castle of Ciurana was taken by the governor of Tortosa on 27 November.

195 4,000 infantry and 2,500 cavalry (M. Paret, "De los muchos sucesos dignos de memoria que han ocurido en Barcelona y otros lugares de Cataluña entre los años 1626 y 1660", volume V in *Memorial Histórico español, Colección de documentos opúsculos y Antigüedades*, volume 24, Madrid 1893.

CAMPAIGNS OF THE SPANISH ARMIES

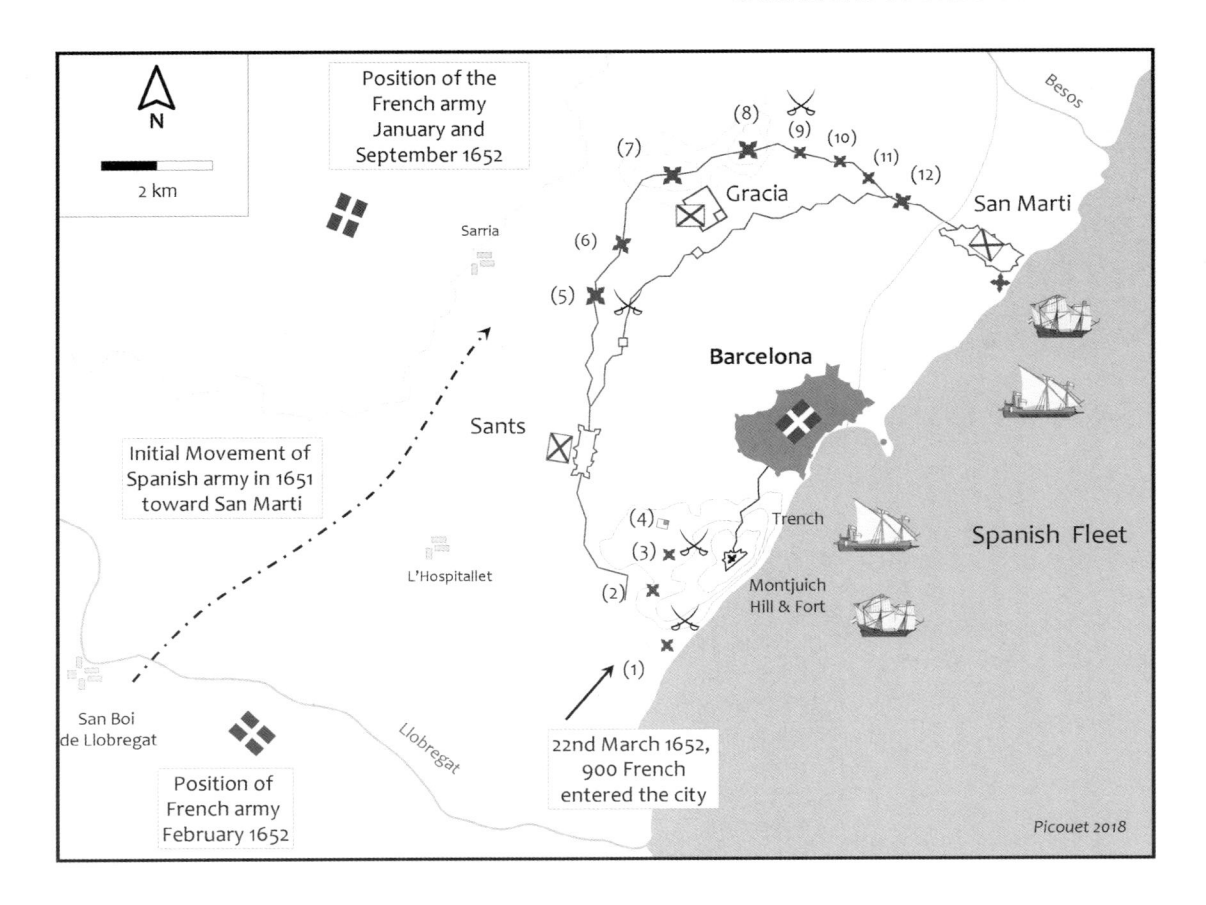

December, the Marquis of Mortara finally received reinforcements[196] and the Spanish fortifications on Monjuich were reinforced by the construction of the Fort of San Juan de los Reyes. During winter time, troops in the Spanish lines or in the city of Barcelona would suffer from hunger and plague, fighting small skirmishes in the large plain between the city walls and Spanish position or on the Monjuich hill. For the Spanish the main objective was to keep their line of circumvallation intact and a sizeable fleet to blockade Barcelona. On the opposite side the Catalans had to maintain enough defenders fit to fight, and bring reinforcements and above all supplies[197] for a big city waiting for a relief army. By mid January 1652, the French commander was in the hills (the district of west of el Valle de Hebron) joining armed Catalans from the *somatem*.[198] For some days the French unsuccessfully tested the Spanish

Map 4.10 The Siege of Barcelona 1651–1652. The situation by January 1652. Legends of main Spanish fortifications on the map are presented in Table 4.1. The operation involved the Spanish army of Catalonia against the garrison of Barcelona (French and Catalans) supported by a French succouring army. The 15-month siege ended in October 1652 by a full Spanish victory and the end of the Catalan revolt.

---

196 1,000–1,100 men from the Tercio of Martin de Alzor, 500 men from the Tercio of Diego Montargull and 200 men to reinforce the other Spanish tercios.
197 On 14 December a group of 14 boats full of supplies forced the blockade, nine managed to get through and five were captured by the Spanish (Marques Mortara, op. cit.).
198 The *somaten* was a local militia, organised in companies depending of each *vegueria* (shire) and could be called for the defence of an area of the Catalan territory. In 1646 a review of the French authorities gives between 2,400 and 3,400 men (Letter of Pierre de Marca to Le Tellier, 19 October 1646, BNF, Fond Baluze n°104, fol. 340).

Table 4.1: The names of the main Spanish forts presented in Map 4.10

Number	Name	Number	Name
(1)	Fortin de San Isabel	(7)	Fortin de Vizconde
(2)	Fortin de San Juan de los Reyes	(8)	Fortin de San Manuel
(3)	Hermitage of San Ferol	(9)	Fortin de San Bernado
(4)	Fortified Convento of San Madrona	(10)	Fortin de Montserrat
(5)	Fortin de San Buena Ventura	(11)	Fortin de la Trinidad
(6)	Fortin de san Miguel	(12)	Fortin de San Jorge

defences to find a weak point. On 28 January 2,000 infantry and 500 cavalry exited Barcelona in an attempt to coordinate an assault on the Spanish fortifications. Misunderstandings between the two Franco-Catalan forces made the attack impossible.[199] In a mountainous area with little supply, on 1 February La Mothe-Houdancourt decided to move to San Boi de Llobregat, retaking Sarria in the process. On 8 February the French army[200] advanced towards the quarter of Santz, but seeing the good Spanish fortifications they returned to San Boi, protected by the River Llobregat. While the Spanish were receiving reinforcements to hold their positions, the French commander decided to force the Spanish line near the sea, taking the Fort San Isabel. On 22 March, while troops were conducting diversionary attacks on Santz, San Ferriol and San Madrona, La Mothe-Houdancourt managed to take Fort San Isabel and to enter Barcelona with 900 men.[201] The success of the operation indicted that now La Mothe-Houdancourt was in charge of the operation in Barcelona. The military operation continued with bombardment and bloody skirmishes between the two enemies. On 27 April, the French general was wounded in a skirmish around the Alfonso Tower on the Montjuich hill. On 3 May, despite reinforcements arriving every month, the Spanish army was down to only 7,800 men[202] due to sickness (plague, typhus, dysentery), desertion and fighting, but still held the line. On 13 May the Franco-Catalans tried without success to take the hermitage of San Ferriol.[203] The next month, on 16 and 17 June, the Spanish conducted a successful amphibious attack on the small harbour of San Feliu de Guixol where the Catalans were amassing supplies for the city.[204] For the Franco-Catalans and the population of Barcelona, the siege was becoming a hell, and on 16 of July they mounted an impressive operation to take the fort of San Juan de Reyes. The operation was a success and the 100 defenders present that day were taken prisoner or killed. The Spanish decided to retake the position with 2,700 men from Santz and after bitter fighting against a similar

---

199 M. Paret, op. cit.
200 2,000 cavalry and 4,000–5,000 infantry, M. Paret, op. cit.
201 San Isabel was retaken later on by the Spanish (Marques Mortara, op. cit.)
202 6,000 infantry and 1,800 cavalry (Marques Mortara, op. cit.)
203 Poor coordination, and scaling that was too short, frustrated the assault (M. Paret, op. cit.).
204 The operation was made with a force of 1,000 infantry (half of them from the armada) and 30–50 cavalry transported by 14–16 galleys. In the operation 25–29 boats loaded with supplies were taken or destroyed and the village was sacked (M. Paret, op. cit.), and Marques Mortara, op. cit.

Franco-Catalan force, San Juan de Reyes was retaken on 19 July.[205] Despite the failure, morale of the defenders of Barcelona was high because a French fleet was on its way to break the Spanish blockade. On 2 August, the French fleet[206] of the Knight of La Ferrières arrived in San Feliu where 30 boats had been assembled full of supplies for Barcelona. The next day, while the French fleet was moving towards Barcelona protecting the convoy, the Spanish fleet[207] sailed to meet the incoming enemy, leaving only five galleys near Barcelona. La Ferrières was well aware that he was outnumbered; he decided to turn away attracting the Spanish fleet. The convoy managed to enter Barcelona, losing three or four boats in the process. When the two fleets were close enough a heavy wind started and obliged the boats to abandon the combat. On 5 August the Spanish fleet returned to Barcelona and on 9 August the French fleet appeared on the horizon but La Ferrières refused to risk his boats and returned to San Feliu. There in a council of war the mood of the French crew was not very good and La Ferrières decided to return to Toulon, abandoning Barcelona.[208] At the end of August the Catalans had raised a new relieve army of 5,700 men[209] and a coordinated attack was organised with the defenders of Barcelona. On 4 September, the attack was launched against the Fort of San Buena Ventura with the support of the garrison. During most of the day the Franco-Catalans fought desperately to break the Spanish lines, but they failed due to the inexperience of Catalan soldiers, the accurate fire of the Spanish artillery and counter-attack of the Spanish cavalry. While the Spanish losses were moderated, some 100 men, the Franco-Catalan losses were important some 1,000–1,500 men.[210] The Spanish decided to capture some cities along the coast and with a small force of 2,200 men,[211] Mortara was able to capture Mataró on 19 September and later on Blanes, San Feliu and Palamos. The possibility of saving the city had vanished, and on 6 October the Catalan opened negotiation to capitulate. On 11 October Barcelona capitulated after a siege of 14 months and the next day the French garrison evacuated the city. In a matter of weeks all Catalan cities returned to the obedience of the Spanish king except Rosas and the territories of the Roussillon.

---

205 During the fighting, Spanish losses were estimated at 450 men (140 dead, 250 wounded and 60 prisoners), while the Franco-Catalan losses could be estimated at 600–650 men (Marques Mortara, op. cit.).
206 The fleet had three ships of the line (*Le Brézé*, *Le Soleil* and *Le Chasseur*) with 132 guns and five smaller ones, and four fireships (Abrobre, *Historia de los hechos…* op. cit.)
207 Spanish fleet 14 vessels and 14 galleys (Abrobre, *Historia de los hechos…* op. cit.)
208 Abrobre, *Historia de los hechos…* op. cit.
209 5,100 infantry (1,100 French and 4,000 Catalans) and 600 cavalry (French) commanded by Josep de Pinos. De Pinos was the Catalan ambassador in Paris and in July he managed to leave Barcelona to raise this army. From Barcelona some 2,000–2,300 men were available (Marques Mortara, op. cit.).
210 Probably 400 dead, 530 prisoners as well as numerous wounded (Marques Mortara, op. cit.).
211 Probably 1,600 infantry coming from the Tercio of Lisbon, Tercio of Valencia, Tercio of Garaffa, Tercio of Farnese and the regiment of Visconti), 600 cavalry and nine guns (Marques Mortara, op. cit.). To these numbers we can probably add 400 infantry from the Armada (Abrobre, *Historia de los hechos*, op. cit.).

4.3.4 The Campaign of 1663: the Battle of Ameixial, 8 June

In 1663, John of Austria received the order to carry out a full scale invasion of Portugal and to attack an important Portuguese position like Elvas o Estremoz. The Spanish had sent thousands of veterans from Flanders, Italy and Germany and by the end of April the field army of Extremadura had some 22,200 men[212] divided into 15,000 infantry and 7,200 cavalry.[213] For the campaign, John of Austria was assisted by the *Maestro de Campo* Diego Caballero (also general of the cavalry), the governor of the arms the Duke of San German, three lieutenant generals (Gian Giacomo Mazzacani, Melchor Portocarro and Alejandro Moreda) and the general of the artillery Luis de Terrerio. On 6 May the Spanish army moved, crossing the River Guadiana near Juromenha and five days later they were getting around Extremoz in battle formation where the core of the Portuguese army[214] was located. Now the objective of John of Austria was clear, and on 15 May the Spanish were besieging Evora.[215] To speed up the siege operation, no lines of circumvallation were built and the next day a first battery was installed to bombard the fortification of the city. From the 18th to the 19th of May heavy fighting took place for the Convent of the Carmelitas. On 21 May the Spanish were building mines to destroy the fortification and the next day the governor of Evora asked for negotiation. The city capitulated on 23 May and even if the officers of the garrison[216] could exit free the city, the soldiers were all taken prisoner. While, the Spanish were repairing the fortification of Evora, John of Austria sent a detachment of 2,500–3,000 men to harass the countryside, taking Montenor o Novos on 26 May and sending cavalry parties towards Alcacer do Sal.[217] On the other side, the Portuguese army now had up to 16,000 men[218] commanded by the Count of Villa-Flor, and was located between Alandroal and Redondo. On 2 June the Portuguese moved towards Evora and the next day the two armies were in battle formation at five to six kilometres north-east of Evora. Seeing that the city was in Spanish hands the Portuguese decided to retire

---

212 Following Rodríguez Hernández & P. Rodríguez Rebollo (2007), the Spanish field army had 15,040 infantry (13 Spanish Tercios, five Tercios from Militia of Seville and Granada, one tercio of Portuguese, one tercio of Frenchmen, seven Italian tercios and five German regiments) and 8,090 cavalry. A muster (probably taken between April and may 1663) of the field army proposed by António Álvares da Cunha (Álvares da Cunha, 1663) gives the same number of infantry units (20 Spanish Tercios, seven Italian tercios and five German regiments) with 2,904 officers and 12,205 soldiers for the infantry and 756 officers and 7,260 troopers (including 887 dismounted).

213 If we consider that the dismounted horsemen did not participate in the campaign, we arrive at the number of 7,100–7,200 cavalry.

214 At that time the Portuguese had probably 5,000 infantry and 3,000 cavalry commanded by Count of Villa-Flor (de Menezes volume IV, 1759).

215 Evora was defended by Luiz Mezguita and had a strong garrison of 3,700 men reinforced by the militia of the town but fortifications were weak in comparison with other cities like Extremoz or Elva (Álvares da Cunha, 1663).

216 The garrison of 2,955 infantry and 573 cavalry capitulated on 23 May (Estébanez Calderón volume 2, 1885).

217 With the difficult political situation of the King Alfonso VI in Lisbon, the presence of Spanish cavalry detachments raiding the Portuguese hinterland and John of Austria in Evora lead to approaching movement of some Portuguese noblemen to evaluate to negotiate with the Spanish monarchy (White, 2003).

218 12,000 infantry and 4,000 cavalry (Álvares da Cunha, 1663).

CAMPAIGNS OF THE SPANISH ARMIES

in a fortified position behind the River Degebe.[219] They were followed by the full Spanish army but when the Spanish high command saw the good defensive position of the Portuguese army they just spent most of 4 June bombarding their enemy from the other side of the river. On 5 June, the army was near the Convento do Espinheiro (4.7 km north-east of Evora) and John of Austria had to take a crucial decision; the Portuguese army was between him and the Spanish bases, he could not stay much longer in Evora and he had to follow the orders of Madrid. Therefore he decided to leave a strong garrison in Evora as well as part of the baggage and artillery and with the rest to move back to Aronches,[220] where it was expected to receive infantry reinforcements from Galicia.[221] During the night of 5/6 June, up to 3,000 infantry and 600 cavalry were sent to reinforce the garrison of Evora[222] and with the rest he moved towards Vimieiro. They were followed the next day by the Portuguese army. On 8 June at dawn, Portuguese and Spanish scouts reported to their respective high command that the enemy was close. Even if a large proportion of the baggage had been left in Evora, the Spanish army was slower than its counterpart and John of Austria decided to adopt a defensive position north-west of Estremoz on hills around the actual village of Vittoria do Ameixial. The Spanish had left infantry in Evora and they had probably 9,000 to 10,000 infantry (12–13 battalions) ready to fight and up to 6,000 cavalry (53–55 squadrons) supported by eight field guns.[223]

At first the Monte dos Ruivinos was occupied by a detachment of cavalry and infantry of the Spanish army but the Portuguese sent a vanguard[224] commanded by Manoel Freire to take the position. At 11:00 a.m., the two armies were at just 500–1,000 m from each other.

The first line of the Spanish infantry was made of seven battalions[225] and was deployed between the Monte da Granja and the Monte Carapetalinho,

---

219 Probably at one or two kilometres north-west of the village of Nossa Senhora de Machede.
220 For the Spanish to arrive to Aronches they had to turn around north of Estremoz, probably via Vimieiro, Soussel, Veiros, Monforte and Aronches, some 106 km.
221 The decision to divide the Spanish army was against the wishes of some Spanish generals, such as the Duke of San German (Estébanez Calderón 1885 volume 2).
222 Probably 700 men were in Evora at that time and with the reinforcement the garrison commanded by the Count of Sartirana was expected to have some 4,200–4,400 men. The infantry came from five Spanish Tercios, those of Juan de Barbosa (Tercio of Armada), Ignacio Alatriva (Tercio of Aragon), Pedro de Fonseca, Juan de la Carrera, Joseph Piñoz, two Italian Tercios, the ones of the Count of Sartirana and Fabrizio Rosseo and two German regiments, François Franqué and Baron of Crandolet.
223 The order of battle of the Spanish army was constructed using mainly Portuguese sources (Álvares da Cunha, 1663, and de Menezes volume IV, 1759) completed by a Spanish source (Estébanez Calderón volume, 1885).
224 The vanguards consisted of 500 cavalry and 1,300 infantry (Tercio of de Mendoça and English regiment of Henry Pearson) (de Menezes volume IV, 1759).
225 From right to left: 1st Spanish battalion formed by the Tercios of Aniello Guzmán (Tercio de Madrid) and Luis Frias, 2nd Spanish battalion formed by the Tercios of the Count of Escalante and Gonzalo de Cordoba, 3rd Spanish battalion from the Tercio of Rodrigo Mujica (Tercio Viejo de Extremadura), 4th Spanish Battalion formed by the Tercios of Juan Enriquéz and Lope de Abreu (Tercio of Lisbon), 5th German Battalion formed by the Regiments of the Count of Chargni and of Lorestain, 6th Italian battalion from the Tercio of the Marquis of Casin and 7th Italian Battalion formed by the Tercios of Antonio Guindazo and Camillo de Dura.

THE ARMIES OF PHILIP IV OF SPAIN 1621–1665

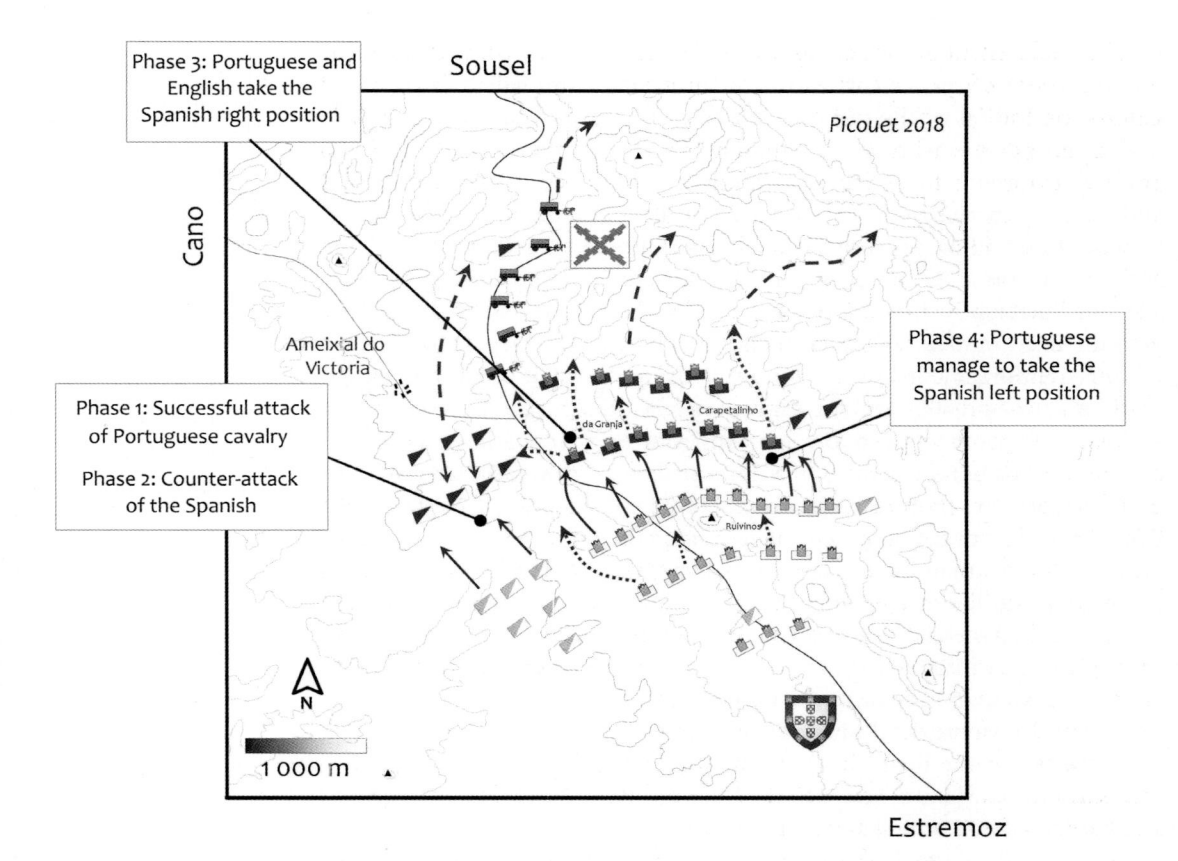

Map 4.11 The Battle of Ameixial was fought on 8 June 1663 in central Portugal, Provincia do Alemtejo, between the invading Spanish Army of Extremadura and the main Portuguese field army. The battle ended in a strategic victory for the Portuguese, the invading army was destroyed. It was a major blow for the Spanish monarchy.

behind them we had probably five to six battalions.[226] On the Spanish right, on the road of Estremoz–Cano, we find the cavalry commanded by Diego Correa with 35 squadrons[227] deployed in two lines. On the left, we might have 15 squadrons[228] deployed in two lines commanded Antonio Morera. Behind them with the baggage and prisoners was a reserve of 500 cavalry.[229] At last the Spanish had two batteries of four light guns deployed on the right on the Monte da Granja, and on the left on the Monte Carapetalinho (see Map 4.11).

---

226 No sources give the deployment of the second line but the three to four Spanish battalions were formed by the tercios of Diego Bracamonte (Tercio de Burgos), Rui Pérez de Vega, Diego de Vera (Tercio de Toledo), Francisco de Tello, Gill de Villalva (Tercio del Casco de Granada), Francisco de Araujo, Baltasar de Urbina, Jacques de Gomin. We have also a battalion formed by the German regiment of the Baron of Kaserstein and an Italian battalion formed by the Tercios of Marcello Orilla and Andres Copula.

227 The cavalry had 20 squadrons in the first line (Guards, Trozos of Catalunya, Flandes and Ordenes Militares) and a second line, commanded by Melchior Porticarrero, with 15 squadrons (Trozos of Milan, de Feria and Extremadura)

228 The cavalry on the left had probably nine to ten squadrons (Trozos of Milan and Francisco de Aguiar) in the first line and five to six squadrons (Trozo Guardias de Castilla) in the second one commanded by Giovanni Mazacabi.

229 The reserve was made with the trozo of Fregenal and from other cavalry units to reach the number of 500.

The deployment of the Portuguese force[230] is better known with probably a detachment of 300 cavalry (five squadrons commanded by Mathias da Cunha) on the right followed by a first line of infantry with 11 battalions[231] and a second line with seven battalions.[232] On the left were some 3,000 cavalry deployed in three lines[233] commanded by Diniz de Mello. The reserve was made by three battalions[234] and two cavalry squadrons. The Portuguese artillery was deployed on the Monte dos Ruivinos and could fire directly on the Spanish positions. During several hours the artillery of the two sides were bombarding their opponent and at that game it seems that the Portuguese were much better inflicting losses on the Spanish side. The goal of the Spanish commander was to hold the line and to wait for dusk to withdraw from the battlefield. The problem was the baggage and by mid afternoon the order was given to start to move the heavy wagons. On the Portuguese side the Count of Schomberg was feeling that Spanish morale was not as good as expected,[235] and managed to convince Villa-Flor to attack the Spanish position, and by 3:00 p.m. orders were given to initiate the combat.

Rapidly the English cavalry regiments supported by three French companies moved to attack the cavalry of the Spanish right. At first they were successful[236] and the Spanish first line turned back to the rear. Fortunately for the Spanish, the Portuguese cavalry was slow to take advantage and Porticarrero was able to counter-attack and to repulse the enemy. The Portuguese sent their second line and numerous cavalry engagements took place with no clear winner.

In the centre, a brigade of three Portuguese tercios and an English regiment attacked the Spanish position of the Monte da Granja. The English regiment was particularly successful and marching rapidly on the top of the hill in little time they fired a mortal discharge on the Spanish battalions. Attacked from all the sides, the Spanish infantry made a poor resistance and abandoned their positions in great disorder.[237] On the Spanish left the seven Portuguese battalions were also victorious and after bitter fighting the Italian and German infantry were obliged to abandon their positions and the artillery. On the right, some cavalry squadrons were transferred from the left to the right as well as Italian infantry from the second line (probably from the Tercios of Marcello Orilla and Andres Copula) and for a while it seemed that the Spanish could win

---

230 10,800 infantry (21 *battaillons*/regiments), 3,400–3,500 cavalry and two to four guns.
231 From right to left, Tercios of Pedro Mascarenhas, Roque Costa Barteo, Simao Vasconcellos, Miguel Barbosa de França (possibly a French officer), Diogo da Faro, Sebastião de Lorvela, Lourenço de Menezes, Tristão de Cunha, Francisco de Moura, João de Mendoça and Henry Pearson (English).
232 From right to left, tercios of Pedro de Menezes, Martin da Sà, Jacques Tolon (French?), Alexandre da Moura, Manoel Rebello, João de Brito and James Apsley (English).
233 The cavalry of the Portuguese left had 46 small "squadrons" deployed in three lines commanded respectively by Manoel Freire, Joao da Silva and Manoel de Ataíde.
234 Tercios of Paulo de Andrade, Lourenço Garcez and Luis da Silva.
235 Général Dumouriez op. cit.
236 It seems that the death in the early stages of the captain of the guards of John of Austria had a negative impact on the poor performance of the Spanish.
237 The poor actuation of the Spanish Infantry is noted in the Portuguese and Spanish sources. It is difficult to explain because the position looked strong, but perhaps the bombardment of the Portuguese artillery, the resolute attack of the English regiment combined with poor morale could explain such disgrace.

the engagement. The victorious Portuguese infantry held their position, and with the second line Schomberg could successfully engage the Spanish cavalry and reduce the last Spanish resistance. Attacked from all sides the Spanish started to give ground, and when in the rear the revolt of the Portuguese prisoners started, the Spanish army melted away. Before dusk the soldiers of the Spanish army were running away as fast as possible, abandoning their weapons, artillery and baggage. Spanish troops were partially saved because the Portuguese did not pursue their enemy during the night and retired to Estremoz.[238] John of Austria was saved by a detachment of Spanish cavalry sent by the Duke of San German, but thousands of Spanish lay dead or were prisoners. As usual it is difficult to establish losses of the defeated army, for the battle of Ameixial Spanish losses runs from 5,000 to 10,000 men.[239] For the Portuguese the fighting had been significant and losses were estimated at 1,300–1,400 dead.[240] The next day, the Portuguese finished to plunder the Spanish baggage and with the core of the army they moved straight to retake Evora. On 14 June, Evora was again under siege and the Spanish garrison, with no hope of succour, capitulated on 24 June. The great expectation of the Spanish to finish the war had been doomed by the defeat of Ameixial, on the other side the power of the young King Alfonso VI had been greatly strengthened.

5

Conclusion

Inefficient, using outdated tactics, having incompetent generals and an inability to adapt to the new military environment: so much has been said of the Spanish army of the seventeenth century and of the decadence of the Spanish monarchy of Philip IV of Spain.

Even today numerous publications stress the fact that military systems developed in the Netherlands, Sweden and France were ultimately superior to the Spanish military structure. It is true that they had their advantages but it is also true that all these states had weaknesses and drawbacks in the use and organisation of their armed forces. Speaking of the Dutch, they had a good army and navy, correctly paid but all through the war Dutch commanders were unable to breach the belt of Spanish fortress after the siege of Breda in 1637.[1] During the period studied here, the main Spanish enemy was the French monarchy, with a military structure most of the time inferior to the Spanish one even after Rocroi. As we have seen, the Spanish cavalry in Flanders was greatly improved after 1649, while the efficiency of the infantry remained intact.

The great advantages of the French were a geographical ones, they could regularly send armies to the main Spanish territories in northern Italy, Flanders in collaboration with the Dutch and in the Iberian Peninsula to support the revolt and rebellions of the Portuguese and Catalans. By contrast, as stated by Maffi (2014), the Spanish had only the Army of Flanders as a military tool to threaten Paris, the heart of the French monarchy. Unfortunately for them, the Army of Flanders had also to fight the Dutch and in most cases was outnumbered after 1635.

Another point was that Hapsburg hegemony on Europe was inherently unstable,[2] but that was the case of other Empires of the period. Spain was a multinational state with an imperfect structure and where local authorities had some power and would use it to restrain their effort towards a global military policy.

Also, the Spanish government of Philip IV was bound by honour and glory for their king and by the fact that most of the threats to their position

---

[1] Even if some victories were obtained, particularly with the capture of Hulst in 1645.
[2] J. Black, 2006, "The military revolution and early modern Europe: the case of Spain", in E. Garcia Hernán & D. Maffi (eds.), *Guerra y Sociedad en la monarquia hispanica*, vol. I, Madrid, pp. 17–30.

must be challenged. The necessity to maintain their position not only in Europe but also in North Africa, America, and Asia drained a lot of men and money that their enemies did not have to spend; or if they did spend them, it was to attack Spanish positions.

The Spanish military structure managed to adapt to the new challenge and its armies were able to respond with success, even in the 1650s with victory in Pavia (1655) or Valenciennes (1656).[3] Unfortunately, the Spanish monarchy could not deploy enough men, and did not have the finance resources to turn victories in political advantages.[4] At the end of the 1650s all the vital components of the monarchy, human, finance and material resources were exhausted. During the final campaign of 1658, for the first time the French were able to penetrate the heart of the Spanish Flanders, while in Italy some fortresses (Novara and Valenza di Po) were in French hands. Philip IV had no choice: he had to sign a peace and fortunately for him France was in not much of a better state.[5] After the treaty of the Pyrenees, the Spanish king thought he could regroup all his veteran units to deal with the Portuguese, forgetting that the Portuguese could do the same with some support from the French.

At the death of the king, the Spanish military structure could not compete again directly with the new French army of Louis XIV but during most of the second half of the seventeenth century, the Spanish army would prove to be an important ally for the different coalitions fighting against the Sun King (Storrs, 2006).

---

[3] It is strange that in modern military history, the siege of Pavia or the succour of Valenciennes are mostly forgotten.
[4] D. Parrott, 1987, "The cause of the Franco-Spanish war 1635–59", in Black (ed.), *The Origins of War in early Modern Europe*, pp. 72–111.
[5] In 1661, the French monarchy had huge debts and was obliged to suspend all debt repayments (Maffi, 2014).

Appendix I

The Main Fronts and Their Duration During the Reign of Philip IV of Spain

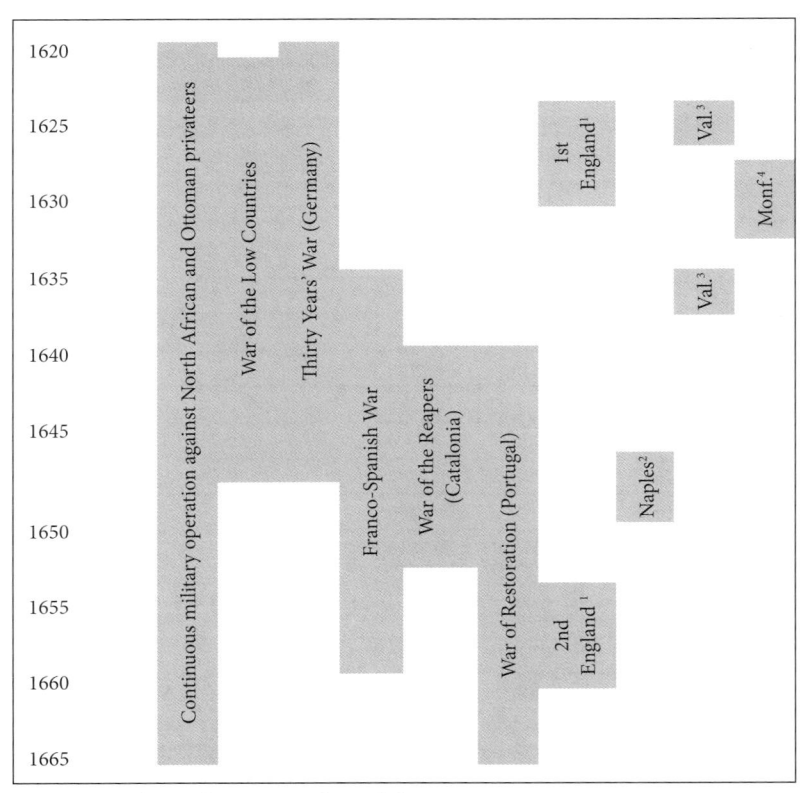

1620									
1625	Continuous military operation against North African and Ottoman privateers	War of the Low Countries	Thirty Years' War (Germany)				1st England[1]	Val.[3]	
1630									Monf.[4]
1635								Val.[3]	
1640				Franco-Spanish War	War of the Reapers (Catalonia)	War of Restoration (Portugal)			
1645							Naples[2]		
1650									
1655							2nd England[1]		
1660									
1665									

1 First War and second war against the English crown
2. Revolt of Naples
3. War in the Valtellina valley
4. Second War of Monferrato or War of Mantua

Appendix II

Summary of Troops of the Four Main Armies of King Philip IV

Data organised according to tables in Appendix III, Appendix IV, Appendix V and Appendix VI.

Years	Flanders	Lombardy	Extremadura	Catalonia
1621		20,150		
1622				
1623	62,610	9,120		
1624	85,290			
1625		33,600		
1627	69,340			
1631		11,310		
1632		15,000		
1633	62,720	28,840		
1635		13,250		6,450
1636	82,700	34,340		
1637	85,000	33,250		14,600
1638		40,460		
1639	88,072	42,810		30,760 [1]
1640	88,280	36,620		37,268 [2]
1641		24,450	12,000	30,000
1642		25,950	9,390 [3]	-
1643	77,620	25,800	9,680	23,400
1644	75,310	26,840	9,100 [4]	23,890
1645	84,600	21,450	15,000	24,000
1646	69,657	19,480	8,940	-
1647	65,460	19,850		22,600
1648		20,250		-
1649	71,840		8,080	-
1650	57,200		7,690	19,900
1651		21,090		10,500

APPENDIX II

Years	Flanders	Lombardy	Extremadura	Catalonia
1652				20,000
1653	63,400			9,600
1654			6,420	9,500
1655		22,910	13,020	
1656		23,960	6,750	
1657	74,540		17,240[5]	
1658		20,404	16,500	
1659	67,420 [6]		17,500	8,800
1660		17,230		
1661	33,010	7,040	21,710	
1662			22,030[7]	
1663			31,430	4,190
1665	11,000		22,660	

1. Some 12,000 to 13,000 men were Catalans from Provincial tercios or from the Militia.
2. Here we have the total of troops deployed in the Iberian Peninsula, maybe 15,000 were in Catalonia (in April 1640 we have 8,180 foot near Perpignan).
3. Following White (1998) the total number of troops on the Portuguese Border was close to 28,000 men.
4. If we add the army of Galicia used for the expedition of Salvatierra we have some 16,000 men.
5. Probably up to 46,100 men were fighting against Portugal in 1657. (Ribot Garcia, 2004, *Las naciones en el ejército de los Austrias,* pp. 661–663).
6. Included the armies of the Prince of Condé and of the Duke of York
7. If we add the army of Galicia we arrive to 41,030 men.

Appendix III

Estimate of the Effectives of the Spanish Army of Flanders Between 1621 and 1660

Data extracted from Parker (1991), Maffi (2014) and Saavedra (1986).

	Infantry	Cavalry	Finance[1]	Total
June 1620	37,200	7,000	-	44,200
June 16222	50,000	7,000		57,000
March 1623	55,210	7,400	-	62,610
April 1624	63,620	7,570	14,600[3]	85,790
January 1627	62,530	6,810	-	69,340
September 1633	45,070	7,650	(10,000)	52,720 (62,720)
February 1636	-	-	(13,000)	69,700 (82,700)
1637	65,000	7,000	(13,000)	72,000 (85,000)
January 1639	62,950	10,620	(14,500)	88,070
January 1640	62,230	11,350	(14,700)	88,280
December 1643	48,830	14,200	14,590	77,620
November 1644	50,160	13,320	11,830	75,310
April & May 1645	55,200	17,390	(12,000)	72,600 (84,600)
February 1646	42,540	16,650	10,470	69,660
February 1647	44,350	11,740	9,370	65,460
December 1649	46,180	14,660	(11,000)	60,840 (71,840)
May 1650	30,520[4]	14,660	(9,000)	(57,200)
March 1653	40,580	12,920	(10,000)	53,400 (63,400)
May 16565	27,400	19,600	(10,000)	47,000 (57,000)
March 1657	40,580	21,560	(11,500)	62,140[6] (73,640)
November 1659	35,910	18,930	-	54,840[7]
September 1661	25,030	7,980	-	33,010

278

APPENDIX III

1. Finance, where troops were directly paid by the finance administration of the Low Countries. They were recruited directly in the country and their numbers oscillated between 9,000 and 15,000 men, between infantry and cavalry to serve the numerous garrison of the country. In some cases we have the muster for these troops but when data is suggested Parker (1991) and Maffi (2014), a number in parenthesis corresponding to a 1/6 to 1/7 of the total number was added.
2. Letter from Gonzalo de Córdoba to his brother Don Fernando, 23rd of June 1622. CODOIN Vol. 54 , 1869, pp. 266–267.
3. 1,600 cavalry and 13,000 infantry (Letter from the Archduchess Isabella of Austria to Philip IV March 1634. Archive Générales du Royaume de Belgique, SEG, reg.190, ff.110 r.y.v.).
4. 10,280 men were in garrison in the Duchy of Luxembourg.
5. Numbers are extracted from *Relación de la Campaña del año 1656 del Estado de Flandes (*BNE. H.86, folio 344–349) but I do not think the garrison of the Duchy of Luxembourg is included, so some 10,000 infantry had to be added.
6. The army of the Prince of Condé was estimated at 14,290 men (Archivo General de Simancas, Estado, Leg. 2091, Letter from Garcia Osorio to Jeronimo Torres, 24th of June 1657).
7. To this number we should include the armies of the Prince of Condé (8,203 men) and of Charles II, future King of England (4,377 men).

Appendix IV

Estimate of the Effectives of the Spanish Army of Lombardy Between 1621 and 1660

	Infantry	Cavalry	*Presidios Fijos*	Total[1]
April 1621	16,560	1,890	≈ 1,700	20,150
November 1623	5,860	1,560	≈ 1,700	9,120
May 1625[2]	26,700	5,200	≈ 1,700	33,600
August 1631	8,430	1,080	≈ 1,700	11,310
1632	-	-	-	15,000
April 1633	17,780	1,360	≈ 1,700	28,840
May 1635	9,500	2,050	≈ 1,700	13,250
May 1636	27,900	5,740	≈ 1,700	35,340
March 1637	25,010	6,540	≈ 1,700	33,250
1638	31,590	7,170	≈ 1,700	40,460
1639	34,780	6,330	≈ 1,700	42,810
October 1640	30,340	4,580	≈ 1,700	36,620
June 1641	17,840	4,910	≈ 1,700	24,450
June 1642	18,430	5,820	≈ 1,700	25,950
August 1643	19,280	4,820	≈ 1,700	25,800
August 1644	19,000	6,140	≈ 1,700	26,840
June 1645	13,330	6,420	≈ 1,700	21,450
January 1646	12,300	5,160	2,020	19,480
April 1647	12,440	5,460	1,880	19,780
March 1648	12,420	5,980	1,850	20,250
July 1651	14,510	4,880	≈ 1,700	21,090
April 1655	15,890	5,320	≈ 1,700	22,910
February 1656	16,310	5,950	≈ 1,700	23,960
June 1658	13,720	6,690	1,710	22,210
May 1660	10,770	4,760	≈ 1,700	17,230
July 1661	3,320	2,020	≈ 1,700	7,040

APPENDIX IV

Data adapted from Ribot Garcia (1990), Maffi (2007) and Maffi (2014).

1. Garrisons from the *presidios fijos* are included in the total number, when we do not have data a value of 1,700 men is given. Following Maffi (2014), the number of troops should be between 1,400 and 2,000 men.
2. The Field army of the Duke of Feria had 27,000 men; if we had a minimum of 2,700 men in Genoa and the reinforcement of 2,000 foot and 200 horse sent in April we arrive at those numbers (Luca Assarini, *Delle Guerre e Successi d'Italia volume prim*, Torino 1665).

Appendix V

Estimate of the Effectives of the Spanish Army in Catalonia and Aragon between 1635 and 1663

In most cases the garrison numbers are estimated.

	Infantry	Cavalry	Garrison[1]	Total	Ref.
1635	4,000	1,200	1,250	6,450	(a)
August 1637	12,000	1,300	1,250	14,550	(a)
September 1639	21 700	3,060	6,000	30,760	(b)
January 1641	15,000	2,000	≈ 13,000[2]	≈ 30,000	(c)
October 1643[3]	8,500	3,900	≈ 11,000	≈ 23,400	(d)
April 1644	9,550	4,340	≈ 10,000	≈ 23,890	(e)
September 1644	9,000	2,600	-	12,000	(d)
June 1645	8,000	3,000	≈ 13,000	≈ 24,000	(d)
October 1646	12,000	3,500	≈ 10,000	≈ 25,500	(f)
September 1647	10,600	3,000	< 9,000	22,600	(f)
November 1649	7,000	3,000	7,160	17,160	(g)
November 1650	11,400	3,500	≈ 5,000	≈ 19,900	(g)
August 1651	8,500	2,500	≈ 7,000	≈18,000	(d)
September 1652	-	-	5,000	20,000	(g)
September 1653	5,300	1,800	≈ 4,500[4]	11,600	(g)
February 1654	4,300	1,200	≈ 4,000	≈ 9,500	(h)
February 1659	4,900	3,900	-	8,800	(h)
January 1663	3,690	500	-	4,190	(h)

(a) Zudaire Huarte (1960), *Empressa de Leucate, Lance fatal del Virrey Cardona*, Annals de l'Institut d'Estudis Gironins, vol. 14 .

(b) *Relacion Verdadera de Todo lo Sucedido en los Condados de Rosellon y Cerdaña, desde los primeros de Iunio, que entrò el enemigo por aquel principado, hasta diez y nueve de Setiembre, que se dio la batalla al Frâces, enla qual queò desbaratado*, A 111/008(24) University of Sevilla.

(c) Field army at the Battle of Montjuich 26 January 1641, initially the army had 26,100 men, the difference is explained by the garrisons left in Tortosa, Tarragona and Villafranca, losses and desertion. A.R. Estiban Ribas, *Desperta Ferro*, 2016.

(d) Picouet, 2014.

(e) Review of 29 April 1644, *Campaña de 1644*, CODOIN Vol. 95. For the cavalry, the total is 3,734 mounted and 602 dismounted cavalrymen

(f) J.L. Gonzalo, A. Riber & O. Uceda (1999).

(g) Maffi 2014

(h) Espino Lopez (2014)

1. The ordinary garrison in Catalonia was around 1,250–1,300 men for 13 fortresses and castles. Carrio Aruri 2000.
2. An estimation of the Garrison in the Roussillon give, 3,000 in Perpignan, 2 500 in Collioure, 500 in Salses and 2,000 in Rosas. Picouet (2014).
3. "The Aviso del 3 de Noviembre 1643", *Semanario erudito* volume 33. V. Balaguer (*Historia de Catalunya* volume 8) gives 13,000 men divided between 10,000 foot and 3,000 horse.
4. The garrison of Girona had 2,500 men, there were other troops in Hostarlic, Barcelona Puigcerda, Lérida, and Tarragona.

Appendix VI

Estimate of the Effectives of the Spanish Army of Extremadura Between 1641 and 1665

Data from Maffi (2014), White (2003), Estébanez Calderón (volumes 1 and 2, 1885), Rodríguez Hernández & P. Rodríguez Rebollo (2007) and Rodríguez Hernández (2017).

	Infantry	Cavalry[1]	Total	Galicia
October 1642	7,410	1,980	9,390	
February 1643	7,770	1,910	9,680	
May 1644	7,000	2,100	9,100	< 8,000[2]
October 1645	12,000	3,000	15,000	
September 1646	6,340	2,600	8,940	
October 1649	5,000	3,080	8,080	
December 1650	4,800	2,890	7,690	
1652				1,800
May 1654	3,480	2,940	6,420	
July 1656	4,520	2,230	6,750	
April 1657	13,090	4,150	17,240	4,100
September 1658	12,000	4,500	16,500	7,700[3]
January 1659	14,000	3,500	17,500	
May 1661	14,500	7,210	21,710	
October 1662	16,020	8,010	22,030	19,000[4]
April–May 1663	22,480	8,950	31,430[5]	
June 1665	15,000	7,660	22,660	

1. In these numbers an average of 16 percent of the cavalry is dismounted (minimum 5 percent, to 28 percent) and are useless for field operations (Rodríguez Hernández, 2017).
2. Following Calderón (1955), the Spanish army of Galicia raised to retake Salvatierra consisted of the militia of the province, cavalry from the nobility supported by regular troops, in total 8,000 infantry and 2,000 cavalry commanded by the Archbishop of Santiago. The numbers are probably exaggerated and with such troops desertion was always high.

3. Field army of Galicia with 4,000 infantry, 700 cavalry and 3,000 militia under the command of the Marquis of Viana (Emilio González López, *El águila caída: Galicia en los reinados de Felipe IV y Carlos II* (Vigo: Galaxia, 1973).
4. In 1662 in Galicia there were 9,000 regular infantry soldiers, 4,500 militia, 2,500 infantry from the Armada, 500 men for the artillery, 1,900 horsemen and 910 dismounted horsemen. A total of 19,000 men (J. Castilla Soto & A.M. Cuba Regueira, 1996, "Espacio, La aportación de Galicia a la Guerra de Secesión de Portugal (1640–1668)", *Tiempo y Forma* series IV, *Histora Moderna* volume 9, pp. 231–242.
5. The field army had a total of 23,180 men divided into 15,090 infantry and 8,090 cavalry (Rodríguez Hernández, 2017).

Appendix VII

Musters of Spanish Tercios Deployed in Flanders and Lombardy between 1622 and 1647

Where available, the officers of the *prima plana* of the tercio are indicated in parentheses.

Date	Location	Tercio	Coy.	Officers	Soldiers	Total	Ref.
1619	Flanders	Tercio Viejo de Holanda	17	180	1,270	1,350	(a)
1622	Palatinate	Tercio de Córdoba	16	168 (16)	1,175	1,343	(b)
1632	Flanders	Tercio Viejo de Holanda	21	220	1,380	1,600	(c)
1633	Flanders	Tercio Viejo de Holanda	15	163	1,320	1,646	(c)
1633	Lombardy	Tercio de Saboya	20	210	2,329	2,539	(c)
1634	Lombardy	Tercio de Idiáquez	18	182	1,906	2,088	(d)
1635	Flanders	Tercio de Guevara	15	166	946	1,112	(e)
1638	Flanders	Tercio Viejo de Brabante	20	190	2,103	2,293	(e)
1640	Flanders	Tercio de de la Torre	15	149	1,567	1716	(f)
1643	Flanders	Tercio de Avilla	18	192	1,515	1707	(g)
1643	Flanders	Tercio de Villagutiérrez*[1]	12	122	481	603	(f)
1647	Flanders	Tercio de Vargas	16	169	804	973	(f)
1647	Lombardy	Tercio de Lombardia	11	137 (25)	718	755	(d)
1647	Lombardy	Tercio de la Mar de Nápoles	15	175 (25)	876	1,051	(d)
1659	Flanders	6x Spanish Tercios[2]	122	1,243	2,520	3,763	(h)

(a) E. de Mesa Gallego (2015), *Los Tercios en Combate* (II), *Desperta Ferro especiales, Los Tercios* (II) 1600–1660, pp.16–21.

(b) *Muestra pasada a los tercios de infanteria española en 10 de enero 1622*, CODOIN 54 pp. 35–38.

(c) Website of Juan Luis Sanchez <www.tercio.org>, consulted January 2015.

(d) Ribot Garcia (1990).

(e) J.L. Sánchez (2003), "Cadena de mando del tercio de la sangre", *Researching & Dragona* nº 19.

(f) J.L. Sánchez & A. Laguna, (2000), "Un plano inédito de la batalla de Honnecourt en 1642", *Researching & Dragona* nº 12.
(g) J. L. Sánchez, 1993, "Las incógnitas de Rocroi", *Dragona* nº 3.
(h) Rodriguez Hernandez (2015).

1. Muster was taken in November 1643, after the Battle of Rocroi (J L. Sánchez, 1993).
2. Spanish tercios are those of Diego Goñi de Peralta y Fernandez, Juan Pacheco Osorio, Antonio Furtado de Mendonza, Gaspar Bonifaz de Escobedo, Francisco de Meneses and Antonio Pimentel de Prado.

Appendix VIII

Musters of Some Provincial Tercios During the 1640–1667 Period

Date	Location	Tercio	Coy	Officers	Soldiers	Total	Ref.
1642	Extremadura	Tercio de Falies	13	80 (5)	511	591	(a)
1642	Extremadura	Tercio de Xedler	11	81 (7)	752	833	(a)
1647	Catalonia	4x Spanish tercios1	64	-	-	1,601	(b)
1649	Aragon	Tercio de Sada	10	56	606	662	(c)
1649	Aragon	Tercio de Castellón	10	52	697	749	(c)
1657	Extremadura	Tercio de Rodrigo Gijón	8	52	508	560	(d)
1663	Extremadura	Tercio de Diego de Vera	5	38	206	244	(h)
1663	Extremadura	Tercio de Armada	16	110	469	579	(h)
1663	Extremadura	Tercio Viejo Extremadura	14	91	685	776	(h)
1664	Galicia	Tercio fijo de Asturias	7	53 (7)	492	102	(e)
1667	Castile	Tercio provinvial fijo de Toledo	21	143	493	636	(f)
1667	Castile	Tercio provinvial fijo de Burgos	17	116	523	639	(f)

(a) Archivo General de Simancas, Guerra y Marina, Legajo 1460, "Relación detallada del número de infantería y caballería que forma parte del denominado Real Ejército de Extremadura, acuartelado en la ciudad de Badajoz y villas circunvecinas. Julio de 1642".

(b) Catalán, Jimenéz, Don Gregorio de Brito, Revista de archivos, bibliotecas y museos tomo 38 & 39. Madrid 1919.

(c) Archivo Diputación de Zaragoza Ms.723, "Servicio del Reino a su Majestad. Ordenes al Pagador General de la Gente de Guerra del Reino" ff. 256–256v, Hecho en Zaragoza el 22 de marzo 1649.

(d) Consejo de guerra 15 y 16 de Febrero AGS Guerra Antigua Leg 1894, Junta de Guerra de España 16 avril 1657.

(e) J.L. Calvo Pérez, "El tercio fijo del principado de Asturias, 1663," *Researching & Dragona* nº 20, 2003.

(f) Clonard, volume 5.
(h) A. Álvares de Cunha, *Campanha de Portugal, pela província do Alemtejo na primavera do anno de 1663…* Lisbon 1663, p.89.

1. The garrison of Lérida consisted in; 352 men from the Tercio de la Guardia, 412 from the Tercio of Pedro Osteriz, 398 men from the Tercio of Galleon, 439 men from the Tercio of the Count of Aguilar.
2. Muster of 11 January 1664, eight to nine months before 482 soldiers, excluding officers, were sent to Galicia. In April 1664 a levy of 451 was made in Asturias to fill the tercio.

Appendix IX

Musters From the Italian and Walloon Tercios in the Spanish Armies Between 1622 and 1662

Date	Location	Tercio	Nation	Coy	Officers	Soldiers	Total	Ref.
1622	Palatinate	Tercio of Gulsin	Walloon	17	159 (14)	1,185	1,344	(a)
1622	Palatinate	Tercio of Balanzon	Burgund.	15	132 (16)	1,238	1,386	(a)
1631	Lombardy	6x Lombardy tercios[1]	Italian	68	670	5,566	6,236	(d)
1631	Lombardy	4x Neapolitan tercios	Italian	42	409	4,842	5,251	(d)
1633	Flanders	Tercio Vecchio de Cantelmo	Italian	16	165	1,411	1,576	(b)
1635	Flanders	Tercio of Sfondato	Italian	16	178	1,062	1,240	(b)
1639	Flanders	Tercio Vecchio of Toraldo	Italian	16	172	1,002	1,174	(b)
1643	Flanders	Tercio Vecchio of delli Ponti	Italian	15	168	737	905	(b)
1643	Flanders	Tercio of Frey Luigi Visconti	Italian	15	169	895	1,064	(b)
1643	Flanders	Tercio of Cesare Toraldo	Italian	15	161	828	989	(b)
1643	Flanders	Tercio of Beaumont	Walloon	20	215	560	775	(f)
1643	Flanders	Tercio of Gobbendoncq	Walloon	20	219	1,021	1,240	(f)
1643	Flanders	Tercio of Lamoterrie	Walloon	15	161	632	793	(f)
1643	Extrem.	Tercio of Carrafa	Italian	-	90	644	734	(c)
1647	Lombardy	Tercio of Frey Palavesino	Italian	15	175 (25)	1,086	1,261	(d)

APPENDIX IX

Date	Location	Tercio	Nation	Coy	Officers	Soldiers	Total	Ref.
1647	Lombardy	Tercio of Wateville	Burgund.	8	104 (24)	457	561	(d)
1647	Flanders	Tercio of Bruay	Walloons	17	179	702	881	(e)
1661	Gibraltar	Tercio of Carrafa	Italian	16	118	1,201	1,319	(g)
1662	Extrem.	Tercio of Torrecusa	Italian	-	-	-	548	(c)
1663	Exrem.	Tercio of Marcio Orella	Italian	14	95	430	525	(h)

(a) *Muestra pasada a los tercios de infantería española en 10 de enero 1622*, CODOIN 54 pp. 35–38.

(b) J.L. Sánchez, "La infantería italiana del ejercito de Flandes 1630–1648", *Researching & Dragona* nº 20, 2003

(c) Estébanez Calderón (1885), volume 1.

(d) Ribot Garcia (1990).

(e) J.L. Sánchez & A. Laguna, "Un plano inédito de la batalla de Honnecourt en 1642", *Researching & Dragona* nº 12, 2000.

(f) J.L. Sánchez (1999)

(g) *Relación de los oficiales y soldados de infantería italiana del Maestre de Campo don Manuel Carrafa*, Gibraltar, 1 August 1660, Archivo General de Simancas, GA Leg. 1955.

(h) A. Álvares de Cunha, *Campanha de Portugal, pela província do Alemtejo na primavera do anno de 1663…* Lisbon 1663, p.89.

1. Six tercios of Lombards (68 companies) and four tercios of Neapolitans (42 companies).

Appendix X

Musters of Irish Tercios and German Regiments in the Spanish Armies Between 1631 and 1665

Date	Location	Tercio or Regiment (Rgt.)	Nation	Coy.	Officers	Soldiers	Total	Ref.
1631	Lombardy	2 regiments	German	17	307	3,412	3,719	(a)
1633	Flanders	Tercio of Tyrone[1]	Irish	14	150	672	822	(b)
1633	Flanders	Tercio of Tyrconnel	Irish	18	159	1,103	1,262	(b)
1640	Flanders	Rgt. von Metternich	German	13	247	1,576	1,823	(c)
1640	Flanders	Rgt. of von Rittberg	German	13	392	1,247	1,639	(g)
1640	Flanders	Rgt. of Frangipani	German	10	167	972	1,139	(g)
1642	Extrem.	Tercio of Fitzgerald	Irish	7	64 (15)	347	411	(d)
1643	Flanders	Rgt. of Van der Laar	German	13	228	590	818	(c)
1643	Flanders	Rgt. of Rechlingen	German	13	226	720	946	(c)
1643	Flanders	Rgt. of Count of Isenburg	German	17	502	1,075	1,577	(g)
1643	Flanders	Rgt. of von Rittberg	German	14	233	371	604	(g)
1647	Lombardy	Rgt. of d'Este Borso	German	10	120	881	1,001	(a)
1647	Flanders	Rgt. of Jean de Beck	German	10	153	541	694	(c)
1647	Catalonia	5x regiments[2]	German	-	-	-	1,711	(e)
1650	Catalonia	4x regiments[3]	German	-	-	-	2,461	(e)
1653	Flanders	Tercio of Sean Murphy	Irish	14	136	410	546	(f)
1659	Flanders	Tercio of George Cusack	Irish	15	153	521	674	(f)
1659	Flanders	Tercio of Philip O'Reilly	Irish	14	143	792	935	(f)
1665	Extrem.	Tercio of O'Calahan	Irish	12	76	254	330	(h)

APPENDIX X

(a) Ribot Garcia (1990)

(b) E.de Mesa, *The Irish in the Spanish Armies in the Seventeenth Century* (Woodbridge: Boydell Press, 2014).

(c) J.L. Sánchez & A. Laguna, "Un plano inédito de la batalla de Honnecourt en 1642", *Researching & Dragona* nº 12, 2000.

(d) AGS, Guerra y Marina, Legajo 1460, "Relación detallada del número de infantería y caballería que forma parte del denominado Real Ejército de Extremadura, acuartelado en la ciudad de Badajoz y villas circunvecinas. Julio de 1642".

(e) D. Maffi, "Contribución militar del Sacro Imperio a la perviven¬cia de la Monarquía española en el siglo XVII", in *Presencia germánica en la milicia española*, edited by E. Garcia Hérman, CEHISMI Cuaderno de Histora Militar 3, pp. 63–98, 2015.

(f) J.L. Sánchez, Las Tropas Británicas de la casa de Austria 1582–1699, *Researching & Dragona* nº 8, 1999.

(g) J.L. Sánchez, Rocroi, el triunfo de la propaganda, *Researching & Dragona* nº 16, 2002.

(h) A.J. Rodríguez Hernández (2017).

1. One year later the two tercios were reduced to 15 companies each.
2. The five German regiments were those of Baron of Seebach, Count of Gronsfelt, Louis Duamel, Baron of Verlo, Jean de Coret and Kaspar Lützow.
3. The four German regiments were those of Baron of Seebach, Louis Duamel, Count of Visconti and François Chappuis.

Appendix XI

List of the Captains General of the Army of Flanders and the Army of Lombardy

Adapted from Parker 1991 and Maffi 2007.

Years	Flanders	Years	Lombardy
1621–1633	Archduchess Isabel of Austria[1]	1618–1626	Gomes IV Suárez de Figueroa y Córdoba, Duke of Feria
		1626–1629	Gonzalo Fernandez de Cordoba
		1629	Ambrogio Spinola, Marquis of Balbases
		1629–1631	Álvaro de Bazán, Marquis of Santa Cruz
		1631–1633	Gomes IV Suárez de Figueroa y Córdoba, Duke of Feria
1633–1634	Francisco de Moncada, Marquis of Aytona	1633–1634	Cardinal Infante Fernando de Áustria
1634–1641	Cardinal Infante Fernando de Áustria	1634–1635	Cardinal Gil de Albornoz
		1635–1636	Diego Felipe de Guzman, Marquis of Leganés
		1636	Felipe de Rivera y Enriquez, Duke of Alcalá[2]
		1636–1641	Diego Felipe de Guzman, Marquis of Leganés
1641–1644	Francisco de Melo, Marquis of Tor Laguna	1641–1643	Juan de Velasco de La Cueva, Count of Siruela
1644–1647	Manuel de Moura y Cortereal, II Marquis of Castel Rodrigo	1643–1646	Antonio Sancho Davila, Marquis of Velada
1647–1656	Leopold Wilhelm, Archduke of Austria	1646–1648	Bernardino Fernando de Velasco, Duke of Frias
		1648–1656	Luis de Benavides Carrillo, Marquis of Caracena

Years	Flanders	Years	Lombardy
		1656	Prince-Cardinal of Trivulzio
1656–1660	Juan José de Austria	1656–1660	Alfonso Peréz de Vivero, Count of Fuensaldaña
1660–1664	Luis de Benavides Carrillo, Marquis of Caracena	1660–1662	Francesco Gaetano, Duke of Sermoneta
1664–1668	Francisco de Moura y Cortereal, III Marquis of Castel Rodrigo	1662–1668	Luis de Guzmán Ponce de León, Count of Villaverde

1. The Archduchess was the Captain General of the Army of Flanders, but real command was in the hands of the *Maestro de Campo General* from 1621 to 1631 (Ambrogio Spinola, Marquis of Balbases, 1621–1627 and Hendrik van den Bergh 1628–1631), and the Gobernador de las armas Alvaro de Bazán, Marquis of Santa Cruz from 1631 to 1633.
2. Only for two months, nominated diplomats in Germany (Maffi 2007).

Appendix XII

List of Viceroys of Catalonia and Captains General of the Army of Extremadura

Adapted from Paret (volumes II, III, IV and V, 1889–1893), Picouet (2014) and A.M. Teodoro (2008), *Apuntes para la Historia Militar de Extremadura, Badajoz*, Editorial 4 Gatos, pp. 105–123.

Years	Catalonia	Years	Extremadura
1633–1638	Enrique de Aragón Folc de Cardona y Córdoba, duke of Cardona		
1638–1640	Dalmau de Queralt		
1640	Enrique de Aragón Folc de Cardona y Córdoba, Duke of Cardona		
1640–1641	Pedro Fajardo y Pimentel, Marquis of Los Vélez		
1641	Federico Colonna	1641–1643	Juan de Garay y Otañez, Marquis of Villarrubia
1641	Juan Ramírez de Arellano y Manrique de Lara	1643–1644	Diego de Benavides y de la Cueva, Count of Santisteban
1642–1644	Pedro Antonio de Aragón	1644–1645	Gerolamo Maria Caracciolo, Marquis of Torrecuso
1644–1645	Andrea Cantelmo	1645–1647	Diego Felipez de Guzman, Marquis of Leganés
1645–1647	Diego Felipez de Guzman, Marquis of Leganés	1647–1648	Enrique Pimentel, Marquis of Tavara
1647–1648	Guillén Ramón de Moncada, Marquis of Aitona	1648–1650	Diego Felipez de Guzman, Marquis of Leganés
1648–1650	Juan de Garay y Otañez, Marquis of Villarrubia		

APPENDIX XII

Years	Catalonia	Years	Extremadura
1650–1652	Francisco de Orozco, Marquis of Mortara	1650–1661	Francisco de Tutavila y del Tuffo, Duke of San Germán
1653–1656	Juan José de Austria		
1656–1663	Francisco de Orozco, Marquis of Mortara	1661–1664	Juan José de Austria
1663–1664	Francisco de Moura Corterreal, Marquis of Castel Rodrigo		
1664–1667	Vicente de Gonzaga y Doria	1664–1667	Luis de Benavides y Carrillo, Marquis of Caracena

Appendix XIII

List of the *Maestros de Campo* of the Main Spanish Tercios Serving in the Army of Flanders from 1621 to 1665

Information from Juan Luis Sanchez's website[1] consulted in 2009, 2010 and 2011, from Clonard (volumes 7, 8, and 9), and from Albi de la Cuesta (2015 and 2016). Information has been presented in Picouet 2010.

Name	Created	Disb.	Maestro de Campo	Nominated
Tercio Viejo de Flandes	1537	Active[2]	Simao Antunes	1601
			Diogo Luiz de Oliveira	1623
			Francisco de Medina Carranza	1625
			Jacinto de Velasco, Count of Salazar	1631
			Francisco Zapata Osorio	1632
			Enrique de Alagon y Pimentel, Count of Fuenclara	1636
			Jeronimo de Aragon y Tagliava	1640
			Juan de Velasco y Henin, Count of Salazar	1642
			Fernando de Quesada, Count of Garciez	1642
			Francisco d'Eça y As	1646
			Juan de Rocafull y Ladron de Guevara	1654
			Diego Goñi de Peralta y Fernandez	1655
			Francisco de Velasco, Count of Colmear	1659
			Juan de Toledo y Portugal	1661
Tercio Viejo de Hollanda	1581	1987	Iñigo de Borja y Velasco	1603
			Iñigo de Brizuela y Urbina	1622
			Juan de Guzman, Marques of Fuentes	1623
			Luis de Benavides y Colmenares	1627
			Baltasar de Santander	1630
			Alsonso de Córdoba, Marques de Celada	1632
			Antonio Sancho Davila, Marques of Velada	1636
			Jose de Saavedra, Marques of Rivas	1640
			Francisco de La Cueva, Duke of Albuquerque	1641
			Baltasar Mercader y Carroz	1643
			Juan de Quijada y Almaraz	1653
			Juan Pacheco Osorio, Marquis de Cerralbo	1654
			Pedro de Zavala y Laezeta	1660

APPENDIX XIII

Name	Created	Disb.	*Maestro de Campo*	Nominated
Tercio Viejo de Brabante	1591	Active	Diego Mejia de Guzman, Marquis de Leganés	1617
			Juan Niño de Tavora y Villena	1623
			Fernando de Guzmán	1625
			Alonso Ladrón de Guevara	1627
			Alonso Perez de Vivero, Count of Fuensaldaña	1636
			Pedro de Leon Villaroel	1640
			Bernardino de Ayala, Count of Villalba	1642
			Fernando de Noronha, Count of Linares	1643
			Fernando de Solis y Vargas	1646
			Antonio Furtado de Mendonça	1653
Tercio de Portugal	1619	1623	Diogo Luiz de Oliveira	1619
Tercio de Córdoba	1619	1623	Gonzalo de Córdoba	1619
			Francisco de Ibarra	1622
			Jerónimo Boquin y Pardo	1622
Tercio de Medina	1623	1625	Francisco de Medina Carranza	1623
Tercio de Ponce de Léon	1629	1632	Luis de Guzmán Ponce de León y Toledo	1629
Tercio de Rivera	1631	1632	Fernando de Rivera	1631
Tercio de Fuenclara	1634	1636	Enrique de Alagon, Count of Fuenclara	1634
Tercio de Saavedra	1637	1733	José de Saavedra	1637
			Juan de Velasco y Henin	1640
			Alonso de Ávila y Guzmán	1642
			Gaspar Bonifaz de Escobedo	1644
			José Manrique de Luyando	1661
Tercio de Aragón	1638	1660	Jerónimo de Aragón y Tagliava	1639
			Gabriel de la Torre y Aranda	1640
			Bernadino de Rebolledo	1641
			Pedro de la Cotera	1641
			Antonio de Velandia y Arellano	1642
			Pedro Rocco de Villagutierrez y Mercado	1644
			Bernabé de Vargas Machuca y Munoz	1646
			Francisco Gonzáles de Albelda	1654
			Francisco de Meneses	1656
Tercio de Gamarra	1639	1660	Esteban de Gamarra y Contreras	1639
			Gabriel de Toledo y Zuñiga	1646
			Antonio Pimentel de Prado	1658
Tercio de Castelvi	1639	1646	Jorge Castelvi y Hijar	1639
Tercio de Castrejón	1654	1656	Francisco Antonio Castrejon	1654
			Francisco Davila Orejon	1656

1. Website was shut down in 2012, pages had been downloaded previously.
2. Some of the actual regiments of the Spanish army were still active in 2018, such as the 64th Mountain Infantry Regiment "Galicia" (*Tercio Viejo de Flandes*), the 9th Infantry Regiment "Soria" (*Tercio Viej de Brabantes*), 6th Mechanised Infantry Regiment "Saboya" (*Tercio de Saboya*), 67th Infantry Regiment (*Tercio Viejo de Sicilia*) and 3rd Infantry Regiment "Príncipe" (*Tercio Viejo de Lombardia*). See the website of the Spanish army <http://www.ejercito.mde.es/unidades/>, consulted in September 2018.

Additionally 12 itinerant tercios, listed below, with a short life of three to six months, were sent to or created in Flanders. The most famous was that of Martin de Idiaquez y Camarena. It was created in July 1634 in Milan and placed in the army of the Cardinal Infante. It fought at the battle of Nördlingen 6 September 1634, arrived in Brussels, and disbanded in November 1634.

Tercio of Fuentes	1623
Tercio of Medina	1623
Tercio of Zapata	1631
Tercio of Cervellon	1632
Tercio of Idiaquez	1634
Tercio of Melo	1639
Tercio of Sarria	1639
Tercio of Correa da Franca	1639
Tércio of Bethencourrt	1639
Tercio of the Condestable de Castilla	1639
Tercio of Solis	1645
Tercio of Meneses	1654

Appendix XIV

List of the *Maestros de Campo* of the Main Spanish Tercios Serving in the Army of Lombardy from 1621 to 1665

Information from Juan Luis Sanchez's website consulted in 2009, 2010 and 2011, and Clonard volumes 7–9, 1851, 1854 and 1856.

Name	Created	Disbanded	*Maestro de Campo*	Nominated
Tercio Viejo de Lombardy	1568	Active	Manuel Pimentel, Count of Feira	1617
			Luis Fernandez de Cordoba	1621
			Jerônimo Agustín y Agustín	1627
			Martin de Aragón y Tafalla	1629
			Juan de Garay y Otañez	1636
			Luis de Guzman Ponce de Leon	1637
			Luiz de Alencastro	1639
			Rodrigo Mujica Butron y Valdes	1641
			Frey Iñigo de Velandia y Arce	1646
			Valdirio Godinio y Yunque	1648
			Luis de Benavides y Colmenares	1650
			Pedro de Cunha, Marques of Asentar	1659
			Gaspar de Tevês y Cordoba	1665
Tercio de Saboya	1610	Active	Juan de Bravo de Lagunas	1607
			Juan de Cardenas y Manrique Lara	1621
			Francisco Gomez Sandoval y Padilla	1629
			Rodrigo Lopez de Quiroga	1630
			Juan Diaz de Zamorano	1633
			Martin de Idiaquez y Camarena	1633
			Juan Vazquez de Coronado	1634
			Vicente Monsoriu	1642
			Frey Iñigo de Velandia y Arce	1646
			Jose de Velasco y Velasco	1648
			Diego de Aragón	1655
			Pedro de Cunha, Marques de Asentar	1656
			Gaspar de Teves y Córdoba	1665

THE ARMIES OF PHILIP IV OF SPAIN 1621–1665

Name	Created	Disbanded	*Maestro de Campo*	Nominated
Tercio Nuevo de la Mar de Napoles	1635	1898	Gaspar de Acevedo Bonal Antonio Arias Sotelo Pedro Gonzalez Del Valle Diego Quintano y Rosales, Marques de Matonte Fernando Garcia-Rabanal Agustín Sañudo Miguel Fernandez de Córdoba y Alagón,	1635 1636 1642 1646 1656 1657 1665
Tercio Viejo de Napoles	1548	1707	Pedrosa Sarmiento de Pastrana Count of Ayala Principe de Ascoli Cristobal Salgado y de Queiza Francisco Carnero de Santa Cruz	1613 1622 1628 1648 1649
Tercio Viejo de Sicilia	1568	Active	Manuel Ponce de Léon Manuel Carrillo de Toledo Manuel Franco de Andrade Francisco de Castilla Gabriel de Toledo y Dávalos Fernando Fernández Mazuelo y Nalda Vasco Colmenero de Andrade y Morais	1612 1622 1637 1639 1652 1657 1662

Colour Plate Commentaries

An introduction by the artist, Sergey Shamenkov

Reconstructions on this series of drawings are based on the works of Spanish painters of this period (1620–1660) such as Diego Velázquez (1599–1660), Félix Castello (1595–1651), Bartolomé Esteban Murillo (1617–1682), Vincenzo Carducci or Vicente Carducho (1576–1638), Vicent Mestre (1550? –1620?), and Francisco de Zurbarán (1589–1666), as well as Juan van der Hamen (1596–1634), Mattheus Melijn (1589–1653) and Pieter Snayers (1598–1664).

Front Cover
Our Spanish musketeer is ready to follow Ambrogio Spinola for the campaign against Breda in 1624–1625. Although the style is similar to the clothing of the officer, the clothes are of lesser quality and our man has decided to go for a red colour. He has his Basque-origin musket with a rest, as well as a bandolier strap attached with 12 individual wooden powder flasks, and a sword. He has no armour and wears a wide-brimmed hat.

Rear Cover
Spanish captain of the army of Flanders from the beginning of Philip IV's reign. He has elaborate clothing, a green doublet, a half-baggy green pair of breeches made of expensive material, white hose and leather shoes. For protection he has blackened half-armour and leather gloves. As a Spanish officer he also has a red scarf. Our captain wears a wide-brimmed plumed hat, if in combat with the squadron he will replace it with a more useful helmet such as an open-face burgonet type.

Plate A: 1620s
The man on the left is a sergeant; he is the third officer in a Spanish company. Our sergeant wears a halberd, the insignia of his rank, and a morion-style helmet. His clothes are typical of the period, with a blue coat with false sleeves. In combat the sergeants had to run to maintain order and discipline and most of them had no armour.

The man on the right is an *alférez*, the second officer of a Spanish company. He is well dressed for a ceremonial parade in front of the Archduchess Isabel, hence why he decided to wear smart boots. The *alférez* is responsible for the colours (*banderas* in Spanish) of the company and in our plate such an important element is placed on a short shaft. In combat the standard will be placed on a longer shaft and our officer will normally have half-armour and a helmet.

Plate B: 1630s
Spanish musketeer from the Tercio of Idiáquez, belonging to the Army of the Cardinal Infante, walking on a German road in 1634. He has the same weapon as his colleague on the front cover of this book, but the fashion of his clothes is more in accordance with the period. The bandolier is well protected from the weather by his cassock.

We are near Tornavento, northern Italy, in 1636 and this Spanish pikeman from the front ranks is prepared to fight against the French position. Our soldier is a veteran, he has a full set of upper body armour with short tassets, a long pike of 5.2 m (17 feet) and a sword. For our man, to fight in the hot summer of 1636 with such equipment will test his stamina to the limit.

Plate C: 1640s
In the image we have a Spanish sergeant of 1645 from the Army of Lombardy in northern Italy. At that period few Spanish reinforcements were arriving in Lombardy, indicating that our man is a veteran with years of service. He belongs to a Spanish company in garrison in one of the main cities of Lombardy such as Pavia, and like all Spanish officers he wears a red waist sash.

The Spanish musketeer belongs to a Spanish tercio of the army of Catalonia. Our man has been raised recently from a city of Castile and he is prepared to participate in the campaign of 1644 to retake Lérida. In comparison with the other musketeers, our man has a crude cartridge box attached to his waist. His clothes are common, from cheap material, and could have been provided by the Spanish administration.

Plate D: 1650s–60s
Our Spanish musketeer belongs to the Army of Flanders in 1656. He is going to participate in the expedition to rescue the city of Valenciennes, besieged by the French. He has a bandolier, a flask with fine powder, and a bag full of lead bullets as well as a musket with a rest. The Spanish tend to maintain the "heavy" musket because they can fire heavier bullets. To be more agile they had harquebusiers armed with a harquebus of 4–5 kg, firing a bullet of 0.75–1.0 Castillian ounces.

Our Spanish pikeman belongs to a tercio fighting in Portugal in 1663. In comparison with the pikeman of 1636 our man has only a breastplate on the top of a buff leather coat with small tassets. He probably fights in the front rank because other pikemen have even less armour, maybe only a thick woollen garment or the buff leather coat with a helmet, which in the hot weather of Portugal would probably be a better choice.

COLOUR PLATE COMMENTARIES

Flags

In the seventeenth century each company had a *bandera de guerra* (war flag) with different geometric design and colours, made of costly material such as taffeta by professional tailors. But the preeminent geometrical element was the red cross of Burgundy located in the middle.

Figure E.1: reconstruction of a *bandera* from 1606 from a Spanish Tercio, according to a painting from P. Snayers, *Le Siège de Groenlo 1606*. (Public domain)

Figure E.2: Reconstruction of a *bandera* from 1625, according to the painting of Velasquez, *Las Lanzas o la rendicion de Breda* (Museo del Pardo, Madrid, Spain).

Figures E.3 & E.4: Reconstruction of *banderas* from companies of Spanish tercios from the Army of Flanders showed during a ceremonial parade in 1615 in Brussels called the Ommengang parade (*L'Ommegang de 1615. Le Défilé des serments sur la Grand-Place de Bruxelles*, Painting of Denys van Alsloot, Musée Royaux des Beaux-Arts de Belgique).

Figure F.1: *Bandera* reconstructed from a damaged standard taken by the Swedish, probably in 1633 (Collection of the Armémuseum in Stockholm, Sweden).

Figures F.2 & F.3: Modern reconstructions of models from professional tailors of *bandera de guerra* dated respectively from 1618 and 1640. Reconstruction from the books by Francisco de la Rocha Burguen (*Geometria y trazas perteneciente al oficio de sastre…* Valencia, 1618) and Martin de Anduxar (*Geometria y trazas perteneciente al oficio de sastre*, Madrid 1640).

Figures G.1, G.2 & G.3: Reconstruction of three *banderas* taken between 1635 and 1643 by the French army in Flanders, according to an engraving from N. Cochin the elder (*Les Cornettes, Guidons et Drapeaux pris sur les ennemis en la bataille de Rocroy portés en cérémonie à nostre Dame par les cent Suisses*, BNF, Paris).

Figures H.1 & H.2: Reconstruction of two *banderas* of the Army of Flanders taken by the Dutch before 1648, according to a painting of Van Delen of the Ridderzaal of 1651 (*Great Assembly of the States-General in 1651*, Rijksmuseum Amsterdam).

Bibliography

Source note:
CODOIN = *Colección de Documentos Inéditos para la Historia de España*, edited by the Marques de la Fuensanta de Valle

Before 1930

Anonymous, "Campaña de Cataluña y Extremadura del año 1644", in CODOIN vol. 95 (Madrid, 1893), pp. 361–465

Aedo y Gallart, Diego de, *El Memorable Viaje del Infante Cardinal Don Fernando de Austria, desde el 12 de abril que salió de Madrid con su Magestad D. Felipe IV, su hermano para la ciudad de Barcelona, hasta 4 de Noviembre de 1634 que en entró en la de Bruselas* (Antwerp 1635)

Ademollo, Alfonso, *Assedio di Orbetello Dell'Anno 1646* (Grosseto: Tipografia di Enrico Cappelli, 1883)

Álvares da Cunha, António, *Campanha de Portugal pella provincia de Alemtejo, na Primavera do anno de 1663* (Lisbon: Officina de Henrique Valente de Oliveira, 1663)

Aumale, Henri d'Orléans, *Histoire des princes de Condé pendant les siècles sixteenth et seventeenth par le Duc d'Aumale*, vol. 5 (Paris 1889), and vol. 6 (Paris 1892)

Brancaccio, Lelio, *Cargos y preceptos militares: para salir con brevedad famoso y valiente soldado, assi en la infantería, caballería como artillería, y para saber guiar, alojar y hazer combatir en varias formas vn exercito, defender, sitiar y dar assalto a vna plaça / traduzidos en castellana por el P. don Ildefonso Scauino…* (1639). Biblioteca Virtual Miguel de Cervantes

Barry, Gerat, *A discourse of Military Discipline, devided in three boockes, declaringe, the partes and sufficiencie ordained in a private Souldier, and in each Officer; Servinge in the Infantery, till the election and office of the Captaine general and the last booke treating of fire ourckes of rare executiones by sea and lande as alsoe of fortifications* (Brussels, 1634)

Brusoni, Girolamo di, *Dell' Historia d'Italia, dall'ano 1625 sino al 1660* (Venice, 1661)

Cánovas del Castillo, Antonio, *Estudios del reinado de Felipe IV*, vols. 1, 2 (Madrid, 1888)

Clonard, Conde de, *Historia orgánica de las armas de infantería y caballería españolas desde la creación del ejército permanente hasta el día*, vols. 4, 5, 9 (Madrid 1851, 1854 and 1856)

Cornet, Louis de Haynin, seigneur du, *Histoire générale des guerres de Savoie, de Bohème, du Palatinat & des Pays-Bas, 1616–1627*, A.L.P. de Robaulx de Soumoy (ed.), vols. 28, 29 of *Collection de mémoires relatifs à l'histoire de Belgique* (Brussels : publication of the Société de l'histoire de Belgique, 1868)

Corresponding letters of fathers from the Companies of Jesus covering events of the years 1640 to 1648. *Memorial Histórico Español: Colección de Documentos Opúsculos y Antigüedades*, vols. 16, 17, 18, 19 (Madrid, 1864 and 1865; published by the Spanish Royal Academy)

Dávila Orejón Gastón, Francisco, *Política y Mecánica Militar para Sargento Mayor de Tercio*, Julian de Pared (ed.) (La Habana, 1669)

Doms, Josep, *Orde de batalla, o breu compendi militar de alguns advertisements que deven tenirse formant esquadrons…* (Barcelona, 1643)

BIBLIOGRAPHY

Estébanez Calderón, Serafín, *De la Conquista y Pérdida de Portugal*, vols. 1, 2, *Colección Escritores Castellanos, Historiadores* (Madrid, 1885)

Feliu de la Peña and Farell, Narcis, *Anales de Cataluña y epilogo breve de los progressos, y famosos hechos de la nación catalana… hasta el presente de 1709*, vol. 3 (Barcelona, 1709)

de Ferrari, Leonardo (1655), *Recuentro del Montijo. Digital Image from Imágenes de un imperio perdido. El atlas del marqés de Heliche, Plantas de diferentes plazas de España, Flandes, Italia y Indias.* I.Testón Núñez, R. Sánchez Rubi and, C.M. Sánchez Rubio (eds.). Edition 4Gatos, 2005, nº 5.

Fernández Duro, Cesáreo, *Historia de la Armada española desde la Unión de Castilla y Aragón*, vols. IV, V (Madrid, 1895 and 1898)

Firth, C.H., "Royalist and Cromwellian armies in Flanders 1657–1662", *Transactions of the Royal Historical Society*, 17, pp. 67–119 (London, 1902)

Gaya, Louis de, *Traité des armes, des machines de guerre … et des Instruments Militaires* (Paris, 1678)

Gramont, Antoine de, *Mémoires du maréchal de Gramont*. In *Collection des Mémoire relative à l'Histoire de France* (Paris: Petitot, 1826)

Galeazzo Gualdo, Conte de, *Dell Historie del Conte Galeazzo Gualdo, Parte Quarta, Nella quale fi contengono …dall Anno 1645 fino al Anno 1649* (Venice, 1651)

Galeazzo Gualdo, Conte de, *Histoire du Ministère du Cardinal Mazarin*, vol. 2 (Paris, 1672)

Henríquez de Villegas, Diego, *Levas de gente de guerra* (Madrid, 1647)

Informe del duque de Cardona sobre la empresa de Loecata Carpeta: Perpiñàn. A S. Md. (A su Majestad), 1637; Archivo General de Simancas, *Registro Guerra Antigua*, 1186

Histoire général des pays-bas, in *Histoire général des Province-Unies: dédiée a Monseigneur le duc d'Orleans, premier prince du sang*, vol. 7 (Paris : chez P.G. Simon, 1757–1770)

La Roncière, Charles de, *Histoire de la Marine Française*, vol. V, *La guerre de trente ans*, Colbert, (Paris : Plon Nourrit, 1920)

Lechuga, Cristóbal, *Discurso del capitan Cristoual Lechuga: en que trata de la artilleria, y de todo lo necessario à ella, con un tratado de fortificacion y otros aduertimentos* (Milan, 1611).

Letters from Philip IV related with the war of the reapers in 1647. CODOIN vol. 97 (Madrid, 1890), pp. 1–67

Luna y Mora, Diego, *Relación de la campaña del año 1635 que fue la primera que el serenisimo Cardinal infante don Fernando tuvo en Flandes*, CODOIN vol. 75 (Madrid, 1880), pp. 389–411

Marolois, Samuel, *The Art of fortification, or architecture militaire as well offensiue as defensiue, compiled & set forth, by Samuell Marolois reviewed, augmented and corrected by Albert Girard mathematician & translated out of French into English by Henry Hexham* (Amsterdam, 1638)

Mello, Francisco Manuel de, *Historia de los movimientos, separación y guerra de Cataluña en tiempo de Felipe IV* (Cadiz: University of Cadiz, 1842)

Mémoires de François de Paul de Clermont, Marquis de Monglat, *Contenant l'Histoire de la guerre entre la France et la maison d'Autriche…* vol. 1, 2 and 3. In *Nouvelle collection des mémoires pour servir à l'histoire de France depuis le XIIIe siècle jusqu'à la fin du seventeenthIe siècle*, J.-F. Michaud and J.-J.-F. Poujoulat (eds.), vol. 49, 50, 51 (Paris, 1826)

de Menezes, Luis Ericeira (Conde da), *Historia de Portugal Restaurado*, vols. II, III, IV. Biblioteca Pública de Nova Iorque, Lisbon 1751 to 1759

Montecuccoli, Raimondo, *Mémoire de Montecuccoli … divisez en trois livres* (Nouvelle édition): I. *de l'Art militaire*; II. *de la Guerre contre le Turc*; III. *Relation de la campagne de 1664*. Wetstein (ed.) (Amsterdam, 1752).

Novoa, Matías de, *Memorias de un ayudante de cámara de Felipe IV*, CODOIN vols. 61, 69, 77, 80, 86 (Madrid, 1875), and 1878, 1884, 1883, 1895.

Palafox y Mendoza, Juan de, *Sitio y Socorro de Fuenterrabía y sucesos del año de 1638* (Impresión Madrid 1793), fondo bibliográfico de la Biblioteca de la Facultad de Derecho de la Universidad de Sevilla

Paret, Miguel, *De los muchos sucesos dignos de memoria que han ocurido en Barcelona y otros lugares de Cataluña entre los años 1626 y 1660*, vols. II–V. In *Memorial Histórico Español: Colección de Documentos Opúsculos y Antigüedades*, vols. 21–25. Published by the Spanish Royal Academy in Madrid in 1889, 1891, and 1893

Périni, Hardy de, *Batailles Françaises*, vols. III, IV (Paris 1893)

Plessis-Besançons, *Mémoires de Du Plessis-Besançon, publiés pour la Société de l'histoire de France et accompagnés de correspondances et de documents inédits* (Paris, 1892)

Quincy, Marquis de, *Histoire Militaire du règne de Louis le Grand Roy de France, où l'on trouve un détail de toutes les batailles, sièges…* vol. 1 (Paris 1726)

Richelieu, *Mémoires du Cardinal Richelieu sur le règne de Louis XIII, depuis 1610 jusqu'à 1638, vol. IX* (Paris : M. Petitot, 1823)

Salas y Cortes, Ramon de, Memorial Histórico de la Artillería Española (Madrid, 1831)

Saluces, Alexandre de, Histoire Militaire du Piedmont, vols. III, IV (Turin, 1818)

Susane, Louis, *Histoire de la Cavalerie Française*, vol. 3, J. Hetzel (ed.) (Paris, 1874)

Susane, Louis, *Histoire de l'Ancienne Infanterie Française*, vols. 5, 8, J. Corréard (ed.) (Paris, 1853).

Turenne, Vicomte de, *Histoire du Vicomte de Turenne*, vol. 2 (Paris, 1735)

Ufano, Diego de, *Artillerie, c'est à dire Vraye instruction de l'artillerie et de toutes ses appartenances* (Zutphen, 1621)

Vincart, Juan Antonio, *Relación de la campaña del año 1636 y 1642*, CODOIN vol. 59 (Madrid, 1873), pp. 4–205

Vincart, Juan Antonio, *Relación de la campaña del año 1643*, CODOIN vol. 75 (Madrid, 1880), pp. 415–469

Vincart, Juan Antonio, *Relación de la campaña del año 1645, in Coleccion de Documentos Inéditos para la Historia de España*, CODOIN vol. 67 (Madrid, 1877), pp. 459–540.

Vincart, Juan Antonio, *Relations des campagnes de 1644 & 1646, in Collection de mémoires relatifs à lhistoire de Belgique*, vol. 67, P. Henrad (ed.) (Brussels : Gand & Leipzig, 1869)

Vincart, Juan Antonio, *Relación de la campaña de Flandre de 1649, Publiée d'après un manuscrit de la Bibliothèque royale, par E. Lameere. Compte rendu des séances de la commission royale d'histoire*, 2nd series, vol. 4 (1894), pp. 325–410

Vincart, Juan Antonio, *Relación de la campaña del año 1650*, CODOIN vol. 75 (Madrid, 1880), pp. 475–487

Valladares de Sotomayor, Antonio, *Semanario erudito que comprehende varias obras ineditas, criticas…* vols. 31–33 (Madrid, 1890).

Most of the references can be found in pdf form, from the portals of national libraries such as Biblioteca Nacional de España (<http://www.bne.es>), Bibliothèque nationale de France (<http://www.gallica.fr>), British Library (<http://www.bl.uk/>), Biblioteca Nacional de Portugal (<http://livrariaonline.bnportugal.pt>) or on the Internet Archive website (<http://archive.org/>).

After 1930

Amadei, F., *Cronaca universale della città di Mantova*, vol. III

Mantova, Citem, in *Biblioteca Teresiana, Comune de Mantova*, 1955, pp. 547–555.

Ancón, J.L. & Martínez, L.P., "En torno al mural del moli dels frares: los asedios de Salses en 1639", *Researching & Dragona* n° 5, p.104, 1998

Andujar Castillo, F., *Ejércitos y militares en la Europa moderna* (Madrid: Síntesis, 1999)

Bonney, R., *The Thirty Years' War 1618–1648. Essential Histories* (Oxford: Osprey Publishing, 2002)

BIBLIOGRAPHY

Borreguero Beltrán, C., *De la erosión a la extinción de los Tercios españoles. In guerra y Sociedad en la monarquia hispànica: política estrategia y cultura en la Europa moderna (1500–1700)*. Coordinated by E. García Hernán and D. Maffi, vol. 1, pp. 445–484

Brnardic, V. & Pavlovic, D., *Imperial Armies of the Thirty Years' War (1): Infantry and artillery*. Men-at-Arms 457 (Oxford: Osprey Publishing, 2009)

Brnardic, V. & Pavlovic, D., *Imperial Armies of the Thirty Years' War (2): Cavalry*. Men-at-Arms 457 (Oxford: Osprey Publishing, 2010)

Brzezinski, R. & Hook, R., *The Army of Gustavus Adolphus 1: Infantry*. Men-at-Arms 235 (Oxford: Osprey Publishing, 1991)

Brzezinski, R. & Hook, R., *The Army of Gustavus Adolphus 1: Cavalry*. Men-at-Arms 262 (Oxford: Osprey Publishing, 1993)

Carrió Arumí, J., *Catalunya en l'estructura militar de la monarquia hispànica (1556–1640). Tres aspectes: les fortificacions, els soldats i els allotjaments*. PhD, University of Barcelona, 2008

Celi, A., *Le Grandi battaglie del Piemonte sabaudo* (Rome: Newton Compton, 2006)

Chalines, O., *La Bataille de la Montagne Blanche: Un mystique chez les guerriers* (Paris : Noesis, 1999)

Chauviré, F., "Le problème de l'allure dans les charges de cavalerie du XVIe au XVIIIe siècle", *Revue historique des armées*, 249, pp. 16–27, 2007

Contreras Gay, A., "El servicio militar en España durante el siglo XVII", *Cronica Nova*, 21, pp. 99–122, 1993–1994.

De la Rocha, C., Cañete, H.A., and González Martín, J., *El ejercito de Alsacia, intervención española en el alto Rhin 1633/1634* (Zaragoza: Satrapa, 2010)

Dominguez Orti, A. *Estudios Americanistas* (Madrid: Real Academia de Historia, 1998)

Elliott, J.H., *The revolt of the Catalans: a study in the decline of Spain (1598–1640)* (Cambridge: Cambridge University Press, 1963)

Elliott, J.H., *El Conde-Duque de Olivares* (Barcelona: Grijalbo Mondadori, 1990)

Engerisser, P. & Hrncirik, P., *Nördlingen 1634: Die Schlacht bei Nördlingen – Wendepunkt des Dressigjährigen Krieges* (Weissenstadt: Verlag Heinz Späthling, 2009)

Espino Lopez, A., *Las Guerras de Cataluña, el Teatro de Marte (1652–1714)* (Madrid: Edaf, 2014)

Esteban Estringana A., (2004). "La ejecución del gasto militar y la gestión de los suministros: el abastecimiento de pan de munición en el ejército de Flandes durante la primera mitad del siglo XVII", in *Le forze del principe: recursos, instrumentos y límites en la práctica del poder soberano en los territorios de la monarquía hispánica*: actas from International Seminar, Pavia, 22–24 septiembre 2000. José Javier Ruiz Ibáñez, Mario Rizzo, Gaetano Sabatini (eds.), vol. 1, 2004.

Esteban Ribas, A.R., *La batalla de Tuttlingen 1643: Guerra de los Treinta años*, Guerra y Batallas series (Madrid: Almena, 2014)

Foard, G., "Guidance on Recording Lead Bullets from Early Modern Battlefields", <www.heritagescience.ac.uk>, 2009

Gonzáles de León, F., *The road to Rocroi: class, culture and command in the Spanish Army of Flanders, 1567–1659* (Leiden: Brill, 2009)

González López, E., *El aguila caida: Galicia en los reinados de Felipe IV y Carlos II* (Vigo: Galaxia, 1973)

Gonzalo, J.L., Riber, A., & Uceda, O., *Els setges de Lleida 1644–1647* (Lleida: Servei de Publicacions de la Regidoria de Cultura, Ajuntament de Lleida, 1999)

Güell, Manuel M., "Expugnare Oppidum: el setge de Condé (Lleida, 1647)", *A Carn!* nº 2, <http://blocs.tinet.cat/acarn/numeros/>, 2006

Guthrie, W.P., *Battles of the Thirty Years' War: From White Mountain to Nördlingen, 1618–1635* (Westport, Conn.: Greenwood Press, 2002)

Guthrie, W.P., *The Later Thirty Years' War: From the Battle of Wittstock to the Peace of Westphalia* (Westport, Conn.: Greenwood Press, 2003)

Hanlon, G., *The Twilight Of A Military Tradition: Italian Aristocrats And European Conflicts 1560–1800* (London: UCL Press, 1998)

Hanlon, G., *Italy 1636: Cemetery of Armies* (Oxford: Oxford University Press, 2016)

Hrncirik, P., *Spanier auf dem Albuch, Ein Beitrag zur Geschichte der Schlacht bei Nördlingen im Jahre 1634* (Aachen: Shaker, 2007)

Israel, J., *Conflicts of Empires: Spain, the Low Countries and the Struggle for World Supremacy 1585–1713* (London: The Hambledon Press, 1997)

La Cuesta, J. Albi de, *De Pavía a Rocroi, Los Tercios de infantería española* (Madrid: Balkan, 1999)

La Cuesta, J. Albi de, *Entre Nördlingen y Honnecourt (I): Los tercios españoles del Cardinal infante 1632–1636*, Guerra y Batallas series (Madrid: Almena, 2015)

La Cuesta, J. Albi de, *Entre Nördlingen y Honnecourt (II) : Los tercios españoles del Cardinal infante 1637–1641*. Guerra y Batallas series (Madrid: Almena, 2016)

López, I.J.N., *The Spanish Tercios 1536–1704*, Men-at-Arms 481 (Oxford: Osprey Publishing, 2012)

Maffi, D., *Il Valuardo della Corona. Guerre Esercito, Finanze e Societa' Nella Lombarda Seicentesa (1630–1660)* (Firenze: Le Monnier University, 2007)

Maffi, D., *En defensa del Imperio: Los ejércitos de Felipe IV y la guerra por la hegemonía europea (1653–1659)* (Madrid: Actas, 2014)

Maffi, D., "Contribución militar del Sacro Imperio a la pervivencia de la monarquía española en el siglo XVII", in *Revista Internacional de Historia Militar nº 93, Presencia germánica en la milicia española*, pp. 63–98, 2015

Maffi, D., "Fieles y leales vasallos del rey. Soldados Italianos en los ejércitos de los Austrias hispanos en el siglo XVII", in *Revista Internacional de Historia Militar* nº 94, Presencia Italiana en la milicia Española, pp. 39–47, 2016

Magnussen, D.O., *Cadiz expedition of 1625*, thesis, dissertation, professional paper, Paper 1729, University of Montana, 1964

MacKay, R., *The Limits of Royal Authority: Resistance and Obedience in Seventeenth-century Castile* (Cambridge: Cambridge University Press, 1999)

Martinez-Ruis, E., *Los Soldados del Rey: Los ejércitos de la Monarquía Hispánica (1480–1700)* (San Sebastian de los Reyes: Actas Editorial, 2008)

Martin Gomez, P., *El ejército español en la Guerra de los treinta años* (Madrid: Almena, 2006)

Martin Canales, F., *La guerra de sucesión de Mantua (1628–1631): Los tercios de Fernández de Córdoba y de Spinola en Italia*. Guerra y Batallas series (Madrid: Almena, 2017)

Mesa, E. de, *The Irish in the Spanish Armies in the Seventeenth Century. Irish Historical Monographs* (Woodbridge: Boydell Press, 2014)

Meseguer, P. & Bell, *El setge de Barcelona de 1651–1652, le Ciutat Contal entre dues Corones*. PhD Thesis from Universitat Autónoma de Barcelona, 2012

Mirecki Quintero, J.L., "La orgánica vigente en Rocroi: Ordenanzas de 1636", *Dragona* nº 3, pp. 43–47, 1993

Muñoz-Sebastià, J.H. & Querol-Coll, E., *La Guerra dels Segadors a Tortosa (1640–1651)* (Valls: Cossetània, 2004)

Nadal, J., *La población española (siglos XVI y XVII)* (Barcelona: Ariel, 1984)

Negredo del Cerro, F., *La Guerra de los treinta años* (Madrid: Síntesis, 2016)

Nimwegen, O. van, *The Dutch Army and the Military Revolutions, 1588–1688* (Woodbridge: Boydell Press, 2010)

O'Donnell, H., Duke of Estrada, *Estudio del campamento temporal dl tiempo de los austria. Guerra y sociedad en la monarquía hispánica: política, estrategia*…vol. 1, De Enrique García Hernán, Davide Maffi, pp. 381–400, 2006

Parker, G., *La Guerra de los treinta años* (Madrid: A. Machado Libros, 2003)

BIBLIOGRAPHY

Parker, G., *El Ejército de Flandes y el Camino Español 1567–1659* (Madrid: Alianza, 1992)

Parrot, D., *Richelieu's Army: War, Government and Society in France, 1624–1642* (Cambridge: Cambridge University Press), 2001

Picouet, P., "The Battle of Rocroi: new and old facts…", *Arquebusier*, vol. XXXI, pp. 2–20, 2008

Picouet, P., *Les Tercios Espagnols: 1600–1660* (Auzielle : LRT, 2010)

Picouet, P., *The Franco-Spanish war: the Sieges of Lleida from 1644 to 1647* (Farnham: Pike & Shot Society, 2014)

Quatrefages, R., *Los Tercios* (Madrid: Coleccion Ediciones Ejercito, 1983)

Ribot Garcia, L., *El ejercito de los Austrias. Aportaciones recientes y nuevas perspectivas* (Madrid: Temas de Historia Militar, t. I, 1983)

Ribot Garcia, "Milán Plaza de armas de la monarquía", *Investigaciones históricas: Época moderna y contemporánea*, nº 10 , pp. 203–238, 1990

Ribot Garcia, L., "Las Provincias Italianas y defensas de la monarquía", *Manuscrit* nº 13, pp. 97–122, 1993

Ribot Garcia, L., "Las naciones en el ejército de los Austrias", *La Monarquia de la Naciones*, A. Alvarez-Ossorio, & B.J. García García (eds.) (Madrid: Fundación Carlos Amberes, 2004)

Rodríguez Hernández, A.J. & Rodríguez Rebollo, P., "Entre la Guerra y la Paz: La Guerra de Restauración Portuguesa en Extremadura y las Negócianos de Paz en Portugal (1640–1668)", in *Iberismo. Las relaciones entre España y Portugal. Historia y Tiempo Actual*, pp. 141–154, 2007

Rodríguez Hernández, A.J., "Assientos y Asentistas Militares en el Siglo XVII: el Ejemplo del Pan y la Polvora", *Stud. hist., Hª mod.*, 35, pp. 61–98, 2013

Rodríguez Hernández, A.J., *Breve Historia de los Ejércitos: Los Tercios de Flandes* (Chicago: Nowtilus, 2015)

Rodríguez Hernández, A.J., "El primer modelo de reclutamiento forzoso en España", *Milliars Espai i historia*, vol. 43, pp. 151–167, 2017

Rodríguez Hernández, A.J., "La presencia militar irlandesa en el ejército de extremadura (1640–1668)", in *Irlanda y el Atlántico Ibérico, Igor Pérez Tostado & Enrique García Hernán* (eds.) (Valencia: Albatros, 2017), pp. 127–153.

Saavedra, D. de, *España y Europa en el siglo XVII: Correspondencia de Saavedra Fajardo*, vol. 1, Quintin Aldea Vaquero (ed.), CSIC centro de Estudio Historio, 1986

Sánchez Martin, J.L., "Las incógnitas de Rocroi", *Dragona* nº 3, 1993

Sánchez Martin, J.L., "Las Tropas Britanicas de la casa de Austria 1582–1699", *Researching & Dragona* nº 8, 1999

Sánchez Martin, J.L., & Laguna, A. "Un plano inédito de la batalla de Honnecourt en 1642", *Researching & Dragona* nº 12, 2000

Sánchez Martin, J.L., "Rocroi: El triunfo de la propaganda", *Researching & Dragona* nº 16, 21 (2002, 2003)

Sánchez Martin, J.L., "El Tercio de Lombardia 1536–1636", *Researching & Dragona* nº 17, 2002

Sánchez Martin, J.L., "Cadena de mando del tercio de la sangre", *Researching & Dragona*, nº 19 (2003)

Sanz-Camañes, P. (2001), " 'Alojamiento foral' y conflicto de jurisdicciones en la frontera catalano-aragonesa durante la guerra de Cataluña (1640–1652)", *Revista de Historia Militar* nº 22, 2004

Spring, L. (2017). *The Bavarian Army during the Thirty Years' War 1618–1648, the backbone of the Catholic League* (Solihull: Helion & Company Limited, 2017)

Storrs, C., *The resilience of the Spanish Monarchy 1665–1700* (Oxford: Oxford University Press, 2006)

Stradling, R.A., *The Armada of Flanders: Spanish Maritime Policy and European War, 1568–1668*. Cambridge Studies in Early Modern History (Cambridge: Cambridge University Press, 1992)

Swart, E., "El asedio de Breda, 1624–1625", *Desperta Ferro Especial VII*, pp. 46–54, 2016

Vázquez, L. Amigo, "Instituciones y gobirno extraordinario. Flandes en tiempos del Gran Condé (1651–1659)", in *Philostrato. Revista de Historia y Arte nº extraordinario*, pp. 111–148, 2018

White, L., "Guerra y Revolución Militar en la Iberia del Siglo XVII", *Manuscrits* nº 21, pp. 62–93, 2003
Xavier Hernandez Cardona, F., *Historia Militar de Cataluña, vol. III: Defensa de la Terra*, Rafael Dalmau (ed.) (Barcelona: Rafael Dalmau, 2003)
Zudaire Huarte, E., "Empresa de Leucata, lance fatal del virrey Cardona, 29 de agosto–29 de septiembre de 1637", Institut d'Estudis Gironins (Annals) vol. 14, pp. 85–116, 1960

Websites and Blogs

<http://www.tercio.org> website of Juan Luis Sanchez-Martin. Shut down in 2012
<http://guerrasegadors.blogspot.com.es/> blogs from Àlex Claramunt Soto
<http://guerradarestauracao.wordpress.com/>